Such Bright Hopes

To Ron Gainey   11·24·99

Bessy

& Walter Scragg

Such Bright Hopes

Walter R.L. Scragg

REVIEW AND HERALD PUBLISHING ASSOCIATION
Washington, DC 20039-0555
Hagerstown, MD 21740

Edited by Raymond H. Woolsey
Designed by Richard Steadham
Cover photo by Comstock

PRINTED IN U.S.A.

Library of Congress Cataloging in Publication Data

Scragg, Walter R. L., 1925-
   Such bright hopes.

   Includes index.
   1. Youth—Prayer-books and devotions—English.
2. Devotional calendars—Seventh-day Adventists.
3. Seventh-day Adventists—Prayer-books and devotions—
English.   4. Adventists—Prayer-books and devotions—
English.   I. Title.
BV4850.S36 1987   242'.2   87-12773

ISBN 0-8280-0389-0

About the Author

Walter R. L. Scragg, born in New Zealand, is a citizen of Australia. He attended Avondale College and graduated from the University of Adelaide. Currently president of the South Pacific Division of Seventh-day Adventists, he has also served the church as president of the Northern Europe-West Africa Division and before that, as director of communication of the General Conference, in Washington, D.C.

Elder Scragg was author of the Morning Watch book for juniors, *Run This Race*, and the aids to Sabbath school lesson study, *The God Who Says Yes*, and *The In-between God*, all published by the Review and Herald Publishing Association. In addition to writing, he enjoys gardening. He and his wife, Elizabeth Esther, are the parents of three children.

"May our Lord Jesus Christ himself and God our Father, who has shown us such love, and in his grace has given us such unfailing encouragement and such bright hopes, still encourage and fortify you in every good deed and word!"—2 Thess. 2:16, 17, NEB.

TO BETTY, my wife, whose unfailing encouragement and cheerfulness has made a reality of this book, and so much more besides.

SUCH BRIGHT HOPES

His grace has given us such unfailing encouragement and such bright hopes. 2 Thess. 2:16, NEB.

New Year's Day! A time to add new items to the menu of life, and hope for a better feast than last year's. Time to examine the printout of the past with its successes and failures, and punch into the computer new plans and desires.

January 1—a time, above all times, to hope for better things. God sends the earth around the sun and starts a new year every 365 days to give us a fresh opportunity to consider and begin anew. Summer and winter, seedtime and harvest, roll around by His decree. As He did ancient Israel, He invites us to go with Him into the new year that He has, in His grace, given us.

Then, what might you be hoping for this year? The list probably churns through your mind at the very asking of the question. Like every rational being on this earth, you have a future filled with hopes.

Hope focuses on spiritual as well as worldly objects. The Bible speaks of the hope that God gives or that man places in God. A little reading of the Word will soon show you that such hope isn't a way of raising a question mark over God's future deeds. Not at all. Rather, hope assures us that God waits for us in the future, ready to do for us all the good things that He has done in the past. It's a way of saying, "Jesus Christ, the same, yesterday, today, and forever."

So He gives us "bright hopes." They sparkle in the promises of God. They write a check onto which God invites us to write our name.

God-inspired hope tells us of the activity of grace. What God did for us in Jesus becomes our hope for today and every day of our future. Day by day He presents us faultless before the throne of His grace. Day by day we live in Him. Day by day He gives us victory.

Hope also brings the future into our today. In Christ we have eternal life. In Christ victory swallows up death. In Christ we walk in newness of life. Hope in God reaches across the unknowable tomorrow and gives us the blessings of God's new world today.

Such are God's bright hopes. Fill out your shopping list of promises and let God say yes to them in Christ Jesus. The price is paid, and they are all yours.

"All our hopes have their foundation in Christ" (Selected Messages, *book 1, p. 56).*

THE WAR IS OVER

And he said unto them, I beheld Satan as lightning fall from heaven. Luke 10:18.

It took hunger to drive Scots Guardsman Philip Williams out of his hiding place. Carefully he approached the little settlement at Bluff Cove in the Falkland Islands. To his delight, he heard English voices. Moments later he learned that the war with Argentina over control of the islands had ended six weeks before.

For those weeks he had sheltered in an abandoned hut, hiding when helicopters passed over, unsure whether they were British or Argentinean. His dwindling supplies finally ran out, and he wandered for three days before spotting the houses at Bluff Cove and making his cautious approach.

His record of six weeks seems nothing when compared to that of Japanese soldiers cut off from their commanders during World War II. In the Philippines, one soldier gave himself up after more than 30 years of hide-and-seek in the jungle.

In His comment to the 70 after their tour of missionary duty, Jesus assured them that their reason for success was the defeat of Satan. That adversary's meteoric descent from heaven had marked victory for Christ.

Jesus' defeat of Satan in the temptation of the wilderness opens marvelous prospects for us. "Today Satan presents the same temptations that he presented to Christ, offering us the kingdoms of the world in return for our allegiance. But upon him who looks to Jesus as the author and finisher of his faith, Satan's temptations have no power" (Selected Messages, *book 1, p. 224*).

The defeat of Satan carries its message of hope, not just to those who have accepted the victorious work of Christ, but also to those who pray and hope for others. When Colonel Dew brought the news of Philip Williams' return, his mother said, "We never thought we would see him again, although we had that little bit of hope."

Jesus' victory makes the star of hope shine over every life. Our prayers for loved ones and friends carry weight because in Him the enemy of souls lies eternally defeated. Though we carry on the struggle day by day, let there be no doubt. Satan knows his defeat. The war is over.

Satan "cannot cause to sin the one who will accept by faith the virtues of Him who was tempted in all points as we are, yet without sin" (Selected Messages, *book 1, p. 224*).

THROUGH THE WICKET GATE

Make every effort to enter through the narrow door, because many, I tell you, will try to enter and will not be able to. Luke 13:24, NIV.

Only a ruined shell remains of John Bunyan's House Beautiful. The Slough of Despond grows cabbages for the London market. A paved road curves from the lowlands up the Hill Difficulty.

Writing from prison, Bunyan remembered the landscape of his beloved Bedfordshire and wrote its hills and marshes into *Pilgrim's Progress*. From Houghton House, the model for House Beautiful, the land drops sharply away toward Ampthill, the boyhood home of the tinker-turned-preacher.

The pilgrim, Christian, plods across bogs and swamps toward distant hills, encountering various hardships and distractions. At length he arrives at the hilltop mansion where gracious ladies wait to care for his every need.

His story of the ardent pilgrim still delights us. After the Bible, *Pilgrim's Progress* ranks as the world's all-time number one bestseller. It still heads the list in Nigeria!

In the story, Evangelist points Christian to the little wicket-gate set in the fence that guards the approaches to the highlands. Through this gate he must enter if his pilgrimage is to succeed. As a tinker, Bunyan must have scrambled through many such gates set into a wall or into a larger gate. Most of them would barely permit the entry of a grown man. Anyone loaded down with pots and pans or any possessions would have to unpack before he could enter.

Just such a gate Jesus had in mind when He summoned us to enter through the narrow door. Not that the gate will not open, or is impossible to negotiate. Only when a sinner refuses to shuck off the things of the world does the narrowness deny entry.

Bunyan has Christian approaching the gate with fear. He says to himself: "May I now enter here? Will he within open to me, though I have been an undeserving rebel? Then shall I not fail to sing his lasting praise on high."

He had to pass through that gate. At no other point might he enter. To his joy, the gate opened quickly. He went through and onward to the Celestial City. And so it is for all who have that destination.

"Strength and grace have been provided through Christ to be brought by ministering angels to every believing soul" (Steps to Christ, *p. 53*).

PARENTING FROM DAY ONE

My little children, of whom I travail in birth again until Christ be formed in you. Gal. 4:19.

We were kept out of the labor room. We paced. We sweated. Whatever happened in that woman's world we would never know in full.

But that's another generation. Today my sons proudly display the photos *they* took moments after the birth of a son or daughter. They hold hands with their beloved, encourage her in her birth contractions, even attend classes where they go through the same exercises that prepare a mother for childbirth.

Just when the exclusion of fathers from the birth of their children began isn't clear. Certainly, middle- and upper-class practices in the Western world enforced it for more than 100 years until the revolution in thinking about 15 or 20 years ago.

But just what Paul had in mind in his text hardly seems to match what we know of childbirth. He felt, it seems, that at the moment of birth forces took control of the child that shaped its future. Therefore he could talk about the time of labor as the moment when Christ might be born in the Christian.

He seized on the marvelous moment of birth to make a most important point about Christian living. As evangelist he had preached to the Galatians, studied with them, watching and working for the moment when the light of Christ's salvation would bring new life. That was his travail, his birth pangs on their behalf.

How much the apostle wanted that new birth to be according to God's plan for His new creatures! It had seemed all had gone well. Healthy Christian babes formed the communities of faith in Galatia. Now things had gone wrong. Only a new beginning, another birth, could set them right.

What had seemed perfectly formed now showed deformities, malignant tendencies that were excluding his children from full life in Christ.

Could there be a new forming in Jesus Christ? Could Paul hope, could the Galatians hope, for another birth in Christ that would offer brighter prospects?

In writing as he does, Paul offers to us all the undying hope of a new beginning in Christ. Whatever the past, Christ may be formed in you. Yes, right now, today.

"We can do nothing of ourselves. We must come to Christ just as we are" (Steps to Christ, p. 31).

14

ROBBED OF JOY

I shall see you again, and then you will be joyful, and no one shall rob you of your joy. John 16:22, NEB.

How well I remember that windup motorcycle! It buzzed and scooted across the linoleum floor. Again and again its clockwork motor responded to my eager fingers.

With the fanaticism that only a child can know, I refused to heed the warnings of my father and mother. I had to have that toy. For half an hour the little machine responded to my gleeful promptings. Then it happened. *Poing!* went the spring. My father's head shook ruefully. My mother's hand reached out in sympathy. Tears flowed.

Learning to meet and overcome disappointments is one of the most important lessons of life. When life seems to rob us of joy, what will we do? Shake an angry fist at the world? Vent our frustration on others? Withdraw into sullen despair? Weep on another's shoulder?

Jesus could see it coming for His disciples. In a few days' time He would die on the cross. Could they stand the bitter despair of that time of loss? He offered them the most wonderful of promises: "I shall see you again." They would know the threat of assassination. They would suffer severely. But if they found their ultimate joy in His presence now, the time would come when they would see Him again. At that time no one would be able to steal away their joy.

Jesus was talking about the time after His death when they would all be together again. He was also looking forward to the day of His second coming when no more partings would happen. Yet He would be with them in another way. In the Spirit He would come and be with them. In the Spirit they would never part again.

Despair may turn off the lights in our lives. Today may turn out to be the very day when Satan murders joy in your life. The future that you thought held only brightness and delight may darken with disappointment and failure.

What will you do if the world robs you of your joy? Jesus says, "I shall see you again." He is waiting to go with you through that loss. You will see Him again. As the resurrection of Jesus healed the wounds of separation for the disciples, so in faith it will heal yours.

"Circumstances may separate us from every earthly friend; but no circumstance, no distance, can separate us from the heavenly Comforter" (The Desire of Ages, *p. 670).*

THE NEW BROOM

And Hezekiah rejoiced, and all the people, that God had pre-
pared the people: for the thing was done suddenly. 2 Chron. 29:36.

Next door to Hezekiah's palace stood Solomon's Temple. Though it glittered and gleamed at the arriving traveler, it offended the newly crowned king. Worship had ceased. The doors stood shut, trash and filth blown against them. Devotees of heathen idols paraded through the streets. Pagan shrines dotted the way to the Temple steps.

With the swiftness of a modern military coup the king acted. Soldiers leveled the shrines; parades of idols ceased. In the first year of his 29-year reign, in the first month of that reign, he ordered the doors of the Temple opened. Priests and Levites loaded the trash into baskets and dumped it into the brook Kidron outside the walls of the city. To the delight of the musicians, in the recesses of the Temple they found the musical instruments David had assembled for the worship of God. With the interior gleaming and clean, and the priests and Levites ready to carry out the ancient services, the celebration began.

Thus a young king gave his people a fresh start. Joy filled the courts of the Temple, and music filled the streets of Jerusalem. While the Levites "sang praises with gladness," the nation responded to the leadership of their king.

Under the surface of idolatry and pagan practices lived the hopes of the true Israelites. They believed that only the worship of the true God could bring prosperity to the nation and its people. The king found a people ready to respond. All the time Jotham, Hezekiah's grandfather, had been compromising with pagan influences for political reasons, the people had watched and waited. The Lord was waiting with His people for a leader to show the way.

We ask ourselves today, where will reformation and revival start? Yet we mistake the intentions of our God if we look to others. The preparation begins with each of us. God must rule individual lives before He can rule a people. Renewal and its joy begins with you. We sometimes say "the last movements will be rapid ones." God proved it thus in Hezekiah's revival. It will be just as true as God prepares His people in the end of time.

"We cannot take a step toward spiritual life save as Jesus draws
and strengthens the soul" (Selected Messages, *book 1, p. 391*).

GOD'S YES MAN

With him it was, and is, Yes. He is the Yes pronounced upon God's promises, every one of them. 2 Cor. 1:19, 20, NEB.

The incident began as a common enough event. The preacher had to change his travel plans. In fact, he had to cancel them. Nothing very serious in today's world, though it can prove embarrassing.

Before long the local tongues had the story going that one could not trust the preacher. If he could not keep his word on such a simple thing as a travel visit, could one believe anything he said? I wish that we could be sure that this sudden assault on the preacher's credibility meant that travel was more certain in those days. We know otherwise. Ships foundered, bandits lurked, sickness struck.

Well, the preacher defended himself, as might be expected. He did it with vigor. You can read about it in the first chapter of Paul's second letter to the church at Corinth.

Then, in one of those amazing side paths of thinking that delight the reader of Paul, he stops defending himself and starts talking about Christ. He, Paul, might break promises, but God—never.

What particular promises did Paul have in mind? Doubtless he thought of those that affected the church at Corinth. The promises about victorious living, about unity in Christ, about the timeliness of Christ's first advent, and the certainty of His second. All these passed through his mind.

Students of the Bible try to number the promises of God. One places them in the hundreds, another in the thousands. For years in our home we have cherished a little promise box. In it nestle hundreds of tightly rolled pieces of paper, each engraved with a promise from the Word. In a Sabbath evening routine each of us takes one of these promises and reads it aloud in turn.

Do you have a promise that is especially dear to you? Jesus Christ says yes to that promise. Paul tells us that God guarantees each promise because of what Jesus did for us. His life, His death, His resurrection, and His intercession assure that the promises will have their answer. In Christ, God is the hearing and answering God.

The text says something else. It tells us that Christ is the answer to every promise. To be satisfied in Him is to be satisfied indeed.

"Accept salvation as the gift of His grace, believing the promise because He has spoken it" (Selected Messages, *book 2, p. 248*).

17

JOINING THE ESTABLISHMENT

Now he which stablisheth us with you in Christ, and hath anointed us, is God. 2 Cor. 1:21.

If the promises of God are yes in Jesus Christ, why should we ever doubt our placement among the established and the saved?

The great shrine of Guadalupe lies across a huge cobblestone square. A cloak, Mexico City's most holy object, hangs in a glass case. In the 1500s a peasant supposedly received a vision of the virgin Mary. Suddenly made photosensitive, the tattered garment the peasant wore appears to have the shadowy outline of a human figure on it.

I came with tourist camera at the ready the day the pope presented a gold rose for the 450th anniversary of the vision. Crowds thronged the plaza, pressing into the shrine.

Not all walked. One man inched his way across the coarse stones on his knees. Two small children spread rags under knees already bloodied from the ordeal.

To those who reach out to God through faith in Jesus Christ, salvation raises no question marks over the future, but establishes them in Christ. How despair overwhelms the one who begins his quest for life hearing only a maybe when God wants him to hear the loud yes of Calvary!

"With the rich promises of the Bible before you, can you still give place to doubt? Can you believe that when the poor sinner longs to return, longs to forsake his sins, the Lord sternly withholds him from coming to His feet in repentance? Away with such thoughts. Nothing can hurt your own soul more than to entertain such thoughts of our heavenly Father" (*Testimonies*, vol. 5, p. 633).

Listen to what the text says: we belong to God; He establishes us in Christ; He anoints us as His. The word *christ* means "anointed." Christ shares His anointing, His setting apart with us.

For us there should be no bloodstained lurch across the cobblestones of doubt and despair. The cloak of salvation does not hide at the end of some hideous pilgrimage. As Paul asserts in verse 23, God has sealed us and given us the guarantee of the Spirit.

If such is the power of God's yes, should it not drown forever the whispers and deceits of the devil?

"We will rest in the rich promises of God. He will never fail us, but be to us a present help in every time of need" (Selected Messages, *book 2, p. 250*).

NEW DEPARTURES

Now the Lord had said unto Abram, Get thee out of thy country, and from thy kindred, and from thy father's house, unto a land that I will shew thee. Gen. 12:1.

In farewells in international airports, the traveler zigzags his way through barriers that finally hide him from the sight of tearful loved ones, and past the impersonal appraisal of immigration officials. He trundles his way to the line at the departure gate. The final moment of parting is short and sharp, though hardly sweet.

Twice our family departed for new lands in the grand style of the ocean liner. Relatives and friends explored our cabins, hustled off the ship at the last possible moment, and then caught well-aimed paper streamers. On our end we held that last tenuous link until the streamer ran out fluttering into the widening gap between wharf and ship.

Even then the farewell might not yet be over. Once my sister and her husband rented a small motor cruiser and followed our ship in its sedate passage through Sydney Harbor until forced back by the rolling swells beyond the Heads.

The point about Abram's departure has little to do with tears and waving hands. He made the greatest of beginnings when he left Ur of the Chaldees and began a life of faith. His beginning sets the mark for every person who begins with God.

Abram had the good fortune of taking wife and relatives as far as Haran. Jesus warned more than once that the kingdom of heaven may leave us alone at the departure gate to eternal life. At times, He said, we may even have to force our way past the opposition of friends and loved ones.

The point the Bible makes about Abram it makes for all who would follow God. The beginning with God matters far more than the route followed or the destination proposed. Abram knew neither route nor destination. He boarded a flight without number, stopovers, or entry visa.

Because we know what happened to Abram, how he became Abraham, father of the faithful, we feel a little more comfortable about beginning with God. Yet, though we may certainly trust our Lord, who of us would dare predict or even want to timetable the route over which His love will take us?

"God leads His children by a way that they know not, but He does not forget or cast off those who put their trust in Him" (Patriarchs and Prophets, *p. 129).*

SPRINGS OF JOY

Then those who sing as well as those who play the flutes shall say, "All my springs of joy are in you." Ps. 87:7, NASB.

When I was 9, our family crossed Australia by automobile. Today a paved road runs the 1,700 miles of what is largely desert between Adelaide and Perth. Then a two-wheel track wound its way between the poles of the transcontinental telegraph system. The wires of the system saved more than one life. Stranded travelers, in danger of starvation or dehydration, would scramble up a pole or chop it down, cut the wire, and await the repair crew!

Such maps as we had showed another life-saving system. Concrete tanks dug into the ground every 50 to 100 miles stored water from infrequent rains. Windmills pumped artesian water to supplement the supply. The desert conditions could easily trap the unwary traveler, and these man-made springs made successful crossings possible.

We saw kangaroos and emus galore, and occasionally an aboriginal family complete with camels. An endless succession of flat tires and a cracked radiator added variety. But nothing remains more fixed in my mind than meals around those tanks, the washing away of grime, and singing evening worship hymns in the wilderness.

In Bible times, desert crossings also had their risks. Bible writers picture the people of God trekking through a wilderness world. A land of milk and honey awaited ahead, but first one must cross these stony wastes. Yet refreshment came along the way. Out of the Rock of Providence flooded the water of life. Even the bitter springs of Marah sweetened under God's hand. The people pressed on, refreshed and rejoicing. Forever after, the people of God measured their closeness to God against those wilderness days.

Many years after the psalmist David, Jesus offered life to His followers as a stream of living water in a parched land. We drink of His saving life and our lives overflow with joy. Like the water tanks of a desert crossing, we may bless and sustain others as God has blessed and sustained us.

For all of us the springs of life and joy wait along the track to Canaan. No great distance separates them. All we need for today bubbles fresh and invigorating from the Source of our life. He invites us to drink and be satisfied.

"The grace of Christ in the soul is like a spring in the desert, welling up to refresh all, and making those who are ready to perish eager to drink of the water of life" (The Desire of Ages, p. 195).

LAUGHTER IN HEAVEN

A merry heart doeth good like a medicine: but a broken spirit drieth the bones. Prov. 17:22.

Norman Cousins, longtime editor of *Saturday Review*, reported on his successful bout with a collagen illness that threatened to lock him into a hospital bed until he died. Collagen illness is what happens when certain muscle fibers start turning into gelatin. The body starts falling apart. Cousins rented a stack of programs from the TV series *Candid Camera*, bought books of humor, and dosed himself with long hours of laughter. He finally developed his own formula: 10 minutes of laughter produced two hours of sleep. After months of the merry-heart medicine, he returned to work and even to his favorite sports.

God wants His people to be holy, healthy, and happy. Perhaps holiness and healthiness would grow more speedily if we laughed more. The God who created ducks and platypuses had to have a sense of humor. In fact, the Bible talks of the Lord laughing. Jesus exuded joy. People flocked around Him to hear His witty, wry comments on life.

Remember His humorous comment about the lily that beautifies the earth without trying, while mankind tries so frantically? You might like to remember other incidents from His life that showed His sense of humor. At times He wanted us to see the ridiculous situation so that we might relax and receive His Word better. Think of Zacchaeus up that sycamore tree!

Cause for a merry heart today might be found in one of the following:

1. In Jesus Christ God has forgiven your sins. What a great start to a new day!

2. You are worth so much that even for you alone God would have sent His Son Jesus to die. Now there's something to make you feel good about this day.

3. A lot of funny things happen in life. Just as long as they don't hurt someone else, make the most of today's doses of laughter.

If the angels shout with glee when Satan loses control over one more sinner, God meant you to rejoice too. Today, whistle a tune, at the very least inwardly. Hum a melody—out loud is best. Let your joy at being alive in Christ show.

"Have you not had some precious seasons when your heart throbbed with joy in response to the Spirit of God?" (Steps to Christ, *p. 117*).

SUCH NEED OF JOY

And the angel said unto them, Fear not: for behold, I bring you good tidings of great joy, which shall be to all people. Luke 2:10.

Christ brought His message into a world of religious thought that focused on despair and doubt.

For more than 300 years Stoicism had dominated much of Greek and Roman thinking. In this philosophy Greek thought reached its pinnacle. Yet its emphasis on personal morality and the endurance of evil forced people back into themselves and clouded society with negative, unhappy judgments about people and the possibilities of the human race. Devoid of joy, it cultivated pessimism.

Epicurus had many followers. He taught that the gods lived totally separate existences from mankind in their own happy paradise. Mankind, left to itself, had best try to rid itself of religion and the fear of death. His teachings had no place for joy.

The mystery religions with their orgies and ecstasies sought reconciliation with the gods and union with the divine. Their pathetic attempts highlight the desolate wasteland over which thought wandered in its quest for happiness in that age.

Hebrew thinking did little better. All the desperate attempts of the Jews to activate the divine promises of deliverance had failed. Neither in the Pharisaic righteousness clubs nor in the separatist communes of the Essenes, had salvation come. Though hope still lived, it had lost any sense of joy. God had either forgotten them or was demanding something that they could not hope to deliver.

Into this world came the conquering, newborn joy of the infant King. Luke saw the great significance of the angel's message to the shepherds. From faraway Britain to the north to Tarshish in the west, from Ethiopia to the south to Persia in the east, the whole world clamored for a message of hope and joy. Joy, the Word says, which shall be to all people.

It hasn't changed all that much. The ecstasies of Hinduism and the moralism of Buddhism still shackle multitudes away from true joy. Marxism and Islam offer diverse but restrictive world views.

But you, you have the better way. In a world that has such need of joy, you have been given it in essence and in substance.

"Heaven and earth are no wider apart today than when shepherds listened to the angels' song" (The Desire of Ages, p. 48).

WATER IN THE WELLS

Therefore with joy shall ye draw water out of the wells of salvation. Isa. 12:3.

Bazega presses against a man-made lake some 50 miles south of Ouagadougou, the capital of Burkina Faso (formerly Upper Volta). Here the church has built and operates an agricultural training school. This is the sub-Saharan savanna belt, so it is subject to drought and famine.

From Bazega I was taken a few miles to a village. The dry season raised questions as to whether this land could ever give crops. Yet bottle-shaped storage bins, made of mud and straw, told of past and future harvests.

Villagers had dug a well. School staff had supervised the installation of concrete liners and caps for the well.

Peter Wright, the English missionary at Bazega, explained to a few of the villagers that I had been involved in the decision that made their well possible. They talked eagerly among themselves. Then a shout went across the village. The people came running. Someone brought a drum, someone else a single-string gourd guitar. In moments they were singing and dancing around me.

No longer did the women trudge nine miles to the lake, sleep for a few hours at its edge, and then struggle home with huge earthen jars brimming with water on their heads. A well had come to their village. Joy could begin.

Thus, says Isaiah, with salvation. The village that has dug and found water will laugh and dance. The soul that has found salvation will let down its vessel of need again and again.

Herein appears one of the great secrets of superior living for the Christian. So many people wait for joy. They strive for it. Yet it waits for them in the Word, in prayer, and in meditation. Joy begins in the knowledge that the well of saving grace has never run dry or even been plumbed. Those that thirst find refreshment.

As I watched, women came and drew water. Cattle appeared to drink. Life focused at the well's rim. So much good from such a small act.

We possess the means to draw the water of life today.

Oh, the wells of salvation! How good, how refreshing, how vital! Draw a drink today and let the joy begin!

"Our Redeemer is an inexhaustible fountain. We may drink, and drink again, and ever find a fresh supply" (The Desire of Ages, *p. 187).*

TO EAT THE WORD

Thy words were found, and I did eat them; and thy word was unto me the joy and rejoicing of mine heart: for I am called by thy name, O Lord God of hosts. Jer. 15:16.

I once had the privilege of traveling for six weeks with H.M.S. Richards and his wife, Mabel. I imagine that only a preacher would really know what that meant in its fullness. Most English-speaking Adventist ministers regard him as the dean of preachers.

He read at least two books a week and in addition continued his annual reading of the Bible. His basic, inner joy never failed to lift my spirits. I also watched night after night as he encouraged and blessed his congregations.

I once asked him what he looked for in the Book now so familiar that he could recite large sections of it. My notes say something like this:

"I have never had a day reading my Bible when I have not come across some new thought, some new promise, to encourage me. It goes on and on, day after day, and never fails to amaze me. I will never know enough about this Book."

Some books, even serious books, contain so much chaff that they need much winnowing to yield a little grain. The Bible is whole grain: nothing taken out, no additives; the Word of God, whole, pure, and simple. Compared with books about the Bible, it is the Book of books.

Eating the Word means reading the Word, knowing the Word, obeying the Word. Be thankful that you have the Word to read. Hundreds of thousands of your fellow Christians cannot afford it; thousands more cannot read it; thousands have difficulty getting copies.

Pick up a Bible of a faithful reader and you can soon find the worn pages, the places used to feed and sustain faith. What tale does your Bible tell about you? Gold-edged pages still unmarked? Whole sections just like new? H.M.S. Richards wore whole Bibles out! God invites us to devour the Word, to enjoy it as you would a banquet. The promise above is a delicious snack right from the broad table of God's promises. There's so much more where that promise came from.

"Let the Bible be received as the only food for the soul, as it is the very best and most effectual for the purifying and strengthening of the intellect" (Fundamentals of Christian Education, *pp. 379, 380*).

FOND FATHER

Ye have received the Spirit of adoption, whereby we cry, Abba Father. Rom. 8:15.

Paul borrows this name for God from the practice of Jesus. As adopted children of the heavenly Father, we have the right to use the same term of fond affection that Jesus used of His Father: Abba.

If you could eavesdrop on a Jewish family in the time of Christ, you would hear them talking Aramaic. A son would call across the room to his father, "Abba, please come and help me light this fire." A daughter would snuggle up to her daddy and plead, "Abba, tell me a story."

The meaning of *abba* approximates our "daddy." As a term of fond endearment, it describes both the relationship between the child and the father, and the feeling of love and respect the child directs to him. As a word for the heavenly Father, it first appeared on Jesus' lips. No other writers of that time use it. Christians adopted it as their special word.

Villagers used abba for the village elder or for a person for whom they wished to show respect or affection. This usage Christians appropriated for God, whom they loved, honored, and respected, and for whom they felt holy affection. When we roll these attitudes into the "Dear Father" of our prayers, we follow the example and command of Jesus.

"Father" packs into one word many important ideas:

1. God has adopted us as sons and daughters through the sacrifice of His Son.

2. Our child-Father relationship extends from Jesus as the only begotten of the Father, and our Brother.

3. God has a special care for each of His human children.

4. When we accept the sacrifice of His Son, the Father may activate His love for us in a special way.

5. God accepts Jesus as Son and in Jesus accepts us.

6. Our status changes from disobedient sinner to redeemed child.

7. The Father assures us of a place in His house.

When Jesus gave the pattern prayer to His disciples, He told us to begin, "Our Father." By beginning our prayers this way we declare who God is for us. The prayer that follows and the answers God gives affirm that He is Father, our "Abba," and each of us, His child.

"Our heavenly Father has a thousand ways to provide for us, of which we know nothing" (The Desire of Ages, p. 330).

HOW SMALL IS SMALL?

Behold, I have graven thee upon the palms of my hands. Isa. 49:16.

In these words God sent answer to the complaint of ancient Israel: "The Lord hath forsaken me, and my Lord hath forgotten me" (verse 14). In reply the Lord says, "I have taken a hammer and chisel and cut your name into the flesh of My hands."

Feeling sorry for ourselves because someone whom we think ought to care for us seems to have forgotten us troubles us often enough. In the face of neglect and isolation God presents Himself as the God who cares, the God who knows all, personally and individually.

According to sociologists, the lost-in-the-crowd syndrome contributes to crime, social ills, and a whole raft of personality disorders. Many "little me's" are lost in earth's 5 billion people. Even today you may feel too insignificant for notice. Can God actually count us off so personally that He keeps tabs on the hairs of our heads? Yes, He says.

Edward Wolf, an electrical engineer at Cornell University, claims he can etch a billion dancing angels on the head of a pin. Another scientist says he could spell out the entire *Encyclopaedia Britannica* on a postage stamp. Another proposes that if the human brain ever reached its full potential, all the sum of human knowledge could be stored in one cranium.

At this point we should certainly stop worrying about how God keeps track of each of us and our individual doings. God not only knows but keeps record. It's humanly possible to do this, though at great expense and effort. God does it with ease.

Then you can start right in talking to God about all the things that interest you—what you have done, what has happened to you, what you hope to do. The good, the bad, the sad, and the glad—tell Him about them.

The flow of information to Him is complete and continuous. Your acknowledgment that He knows, your sharing with Him, will steer you away from feelings of isolation and "little me-ism."

One more thing. On Calvary the chisel and hammer of our sin and rebellion etched our guilt, our need, into Jesus' living flesh. He carried your sin identified against your name. No wonder Heaven demands to know your every move, each response. Jesus paid the price to buy you back from sin. He asks for your confidence, your love.

"Every soul is as fully known to Jesus as if he were the only one for whom the Saviour died" (The Desire of Ages, p. 480).

WHEN THE WIND FANS THE CHAFF

Whose fan is in his hand, and he will throughly purge his floor, and will gather the wheat into his garner; but the chaff he will burn with fire unquenchable. Luke 3:17.

At harvesttime in the Sahel in North Africa, farmers bring musicians to where the crop has been gathered. With pan pipes, flute, and a simple violin, they play the traditional rhythms of the winnowing. Young men with flails beat the heads of grain in unison. The village women urge them on with songs and dancing.

Clouds of dust and chaff billow up from the hard earth as the flails separate grain from husk. When the flailing is done, grain shovels toss the piles high in the air. A mountain of husks grows on one side, a mound of grain on the other.

Villagers load the grain into earthenware jars and tip them into bottle-shaped storage bins, handmade of mud. Wooden caps, also covered with mud, keep out moisture and vermin. Then, at the touch of a torch, fire flares through the accumulated trash.

The Word presents the Spirit as the conscience of the world. The Spirit goes between the world and the will of God, convicting of sin, righteousness, and judgment to come. He prepares the way of the Lord, as He did once before through the ministry of John the Baptist.

John the Baptist looked around in his day and saw an infection of moral sickness. The Holy Child of God already waited to open His ministry. Who would be ready to enter the kingdom that would now set its boundaries?

To prepare the way of the Lord means to repent and trust in Jesus. Those who repent, like the grain, nourish the world with their witness and righteous lives. When they are safely stored in the kingdom, the fire of the judgment cannot touch them.

The Spirit continually tosses us in the winds of conviction. Not that one day we are chaff and the next grain; rather, He seeks the pure grain, free from the useless and unnourishing. In every life the Spirit gathers grain and blows off trash. Thus He assures us of a corner in the heavenly garner. He goes between us and the coming judgment to prepare a people for the Lord.

"It is the Spirit that makes effectual what has been wrought out by the world's Redeemer. It is by the Spirit that the heart is made pure" (The Desire of Ages, *p. 671*).

THE WIND WITH A MIND OF ITS OWN

The wind bloweth where it listeth, and thou hearest the sound thereof, but canst not tell whence it cometh, nor whither it goeth: so is every one that is born of the Spirit. John 3:8.

At burning-off time in the inland of Australia, farmers test the wind. A fire lit in the wrong place and caught by an unexpected breeze has destroyed crops and homesteads. Only when the wind has set in do farmers fire the stubble or light a windrow of dead trees and stumps.

At times wind has a mind of its own. Sailors dread the wind that cannot make up its mind. Which sail should they set? When will the wind hold steady?

Jesus said the Spirit blows beyond our control. What did He mean? Does that make life uncertain? Do the Spirit-led become unpredictable? Hardly. The most stable people, the ones you can be sure about, walk closest to God.

Jesus was talking to Nicodemus, a member of the Jewish council. Nicodemus found Jesus a puzzle because He did the unlikely; He taught strange, new truths. Nicodemus now had an opportunity to share in the actions of Jesus. Born into the new life Jesus offered, he would appear as Jesus appeared to those around Him: possessed of different motives, marching to the sound of a Drummer others did not hear.

As the apostles reflected on what Jesus had said, they saw how much the gift of the Spirit changed their lives. He entered their daily existence, turned them around, gave them gifts they thought they would never have, asked the impossible of them. Are you ready for that, Nicodemus? Jesus asked.

The Spirit has a mind of His own. He knows what is in the mind of God. He knows God's will for every one of His children. Divine will may have little to do with earthly, secular expectations, though it may radically alter them.

The Spirit goes between us and the plan of God, guiding us into the truth about ourselves. To others, our obedience—our way of life—may appear directionless, even pointless, a wind with a mind of its own. But it isn't that way at all. When we have the Spirit, we have God's will for us.

"The work of the Spirit upon the soul will reveal itself in every act of him who has felt its saving power" (The Desire of Ages, p. 173).

WHEN THE SPIRIT COMES DOWN

But ye are not in the flesh, but in the Spirit, if so be that the Spirit of God dwell in you. Now if any man have not the Spirit of Christ, he is none of his. Rom. 8:9.

It began so well for Simon. He had watched Philip at work. What he saw thrilled him. He would like to have a part in it.

In his community he operated right at the top. He had more influence than rulers and priests. People flocked to him.

But Simon knew that he was a fake, or at least was operating under false pretenses. What the people thought was of the power of God he created from magic and sorcery. Philip had another Power working through him. Simon saw that this Jew who talked so much about Jesus of Nazareth accessed the very power of God, something he had always wanted to do.

Simon gave up his sorcery and followed Philip, professing his faith in Jesus. But then an even greater wonder occurred. With the arrival of Peter, the Spirit came down on Philip's converts. If only Simon could lay hands on people and give them the Spirit!

Simon offered Peter money for the ability to confer the Spirit on others. Such an idea showed Peter that Simon still had his league with evil. He would perish with his money.

In the early Christian church, experience taught that no one could profess Jesus Christ and not possess the Spirit. To Simon it appeared mechanical. He had seen the Spirit come on others through the laying on of hands. In his mind this was a sorcerer's trick. He thought that, as with any other magical trick, he could buy it if he offered the right price.

When the Spirit comes down on God's people, it encourages acceptance of Jesus as Saviour. To think that some special route or action must precede the giving of the Spirit traps us as Simon was trapped. If you have Jesus, you have the Spirit, Paul said. Or, if you don't have the Spirit, you don't have Christ.

In Romans 8, having the Spirit is equated with being under His control. He leads us. We obey Him rather than the flesh. The lifestyle of obedience that grows out of saving faith proves that the Spirit is with us. The Spirit governs the life of the believer. From such a life the fruit of the Spirit develops. To such a life come His gifts.

"To all who have accepted Christ as a personal Saviour, the Holy Spirit has come as a counselor, sanctifier, guide, and witness" (The Acts of the Apostles, p. 49).

LET THE HOLY WIND BLOW!

Suddenly there came a sound from heaven as of a rushing mighty wind, and it filled all the house where they were sitting. Acts 2:2.

Living in the British Isles, one quickly learns that the measuring of wind force has great importance. Radio and television announcers talk of winds of force 5 or 7, or even 10 or 11. Those who use the Hovercraft between Dover and Calais know that when the wind lifts past force 7, the skimmers have to stay put on the beach. Island dwellers understand the power of the wind.

Luke knew about winds and gales. With Paul he experienced the shipwreck on Malta. The fishermen that made up the bulk of Jesus' disciples remembered the Wind of Pentecost. Luke records that the Spirit came with the sound of a rushing mighty wind.

Why did the Lord send the Spirit? The New Testament gives several answers. He takes the place of Jesus. He goes between the church and the world, convicting of sin, righteousness, and judgment to come. He leads the Christian. He reigns over the lifestyle of the born-again. He baptizes the believer. These are just a few of the reasons given.

The upper-room occasion inaugurated the Spirit for the Christian Era. At first glance He came to give foreign languages to the 120. After His descent they could witness to the polyglot crowd of Pentecost. But that is too simple an answer.

Before Acts closes, the Spirit has moved people from place to place, confirmed new categories of believers from Samaritan and Gentile sources, made Barnabas a great soul winner, and urged Paul to Rome. From Paul's own writings we learn how the Spirit works in the life, how He affirms Christ to us every day.

We also learn that the Spirit moves freely in the church, but that we may block ourselves off from the Divine Breeze. Sometimes He moves gently; at times He roars through history, affecting events to match God's plan.

The one important thing to know about the Spirit is: Let the Holy Wind blow. Don't close the windows, don't shut the door, don't furl the sails. To the heart open to the Breath of God came the great Wind of Pentecost. Whether He breathes gently or comes like a gale, let the Holy Wind blow!

"The Spirit will take the things of God and stamp them on the soul" (The Acts of the Apostles, *p. 53*).

LET THE SPIRIT RULE IN ALL THINGS

It seemed good to the Holy Ghost, and to us, to lay upon you no greater burden than these necessary things. Acts 15:28.

We stood in a group in Geneva, leaders from various denominations come to attend a meeting. What issues were interesting our church members? one of them asked me.

At that time, Adventist leaders from around the world had just returned from a conference on righteousness by faith at Palmdale, California. "If you want a good discussion in any of our churches, start them off on justification and sanctification," I said.

One of the others started to shake his head in amazement. "How lucky you are. I wish I could get our members excited about righteousness by faith. Most of them wouldn't know what I was talking about, let alone find their way through Romans."

In the heady days of the 1840s and 1850s, when our pioneers were hammering out fundamental Bible teachings, they spent days and even weeks coming to a final conclusion. That we still take time to consider and discuss should not surprise anyone. If the Spirit would rule us in all things, then the Word must also rule us in all things.

The Spirit goes between us in the church to protect from error and to open new paths to truth. Less than 20 years after Jesus ascended, the church let the Spirit rule in the Jerusalem Council. Harmony and progress followed. He did not overwhelm them with a heavenly video cassette or a pamphlet written with the finger of God. They discussed and prayed, and discussed and prayed again. Only then did it seem "good to the Holy Ghost, and to us."

The Spirit will guide us in the study of the Word of God. He will direct as we pray and seek His help. Those who hide away from truth until they have sorted things out cut themselves off from the very Source they need.

The Jerusalem issues are largely alien to us. Keep from sexual immorality, yes; but the strangling of animals and the eating of food offered to idols hardly rank in the top 10 of modern-day temptations.

However, do not ever disparage the principle involved. In the kingdom of God we subject ourselves to the Spirit. He writes the epistle of the new life in Christ. To be "in Christ" lets the Spirit rule in all things.

"We cannot use the Holy Spirit. The Spirit is to use us" (The Desire of Ages, *p. 672*).

YOUR THOUGHTS ARE NOT YOUR OWN

The Spirit also helpeth our infirmities: for we know not what we should pray for as we ought: but the Spirit maketh intercession for us. Rom. 8:26.

Twins know what it is like. So do long-married couples. Even good friends experience it: someone makes a suggestion or a comment and another person says, "You stole my thoughts." Or "I can't even have my thoughts to myself anymore."

In a more sinister way hypnotism may invade a person's thought world. Unscrupulous intruders use drugs to pry open innocent minds.

Mostly, however, our thoughts are our own. Not even Satan can read our minds, though he observes our reactions and may often work out what we are thinking.

God knows our thoughts, whatever we raise as a barricade against Him. Therefore, we should not resent the help God wants to give. To yield to the Spirit means to welcome God's presence in our thoughts.

God deals very carefully with the free will. He may know intentions but He does not intrude or take over. His Spirit may offer counters to temptations and to control by evil thought. However, His help always arrives in the context of free choice.

The devil exerts domination over patterns of thought. The Spirit convicts and guides toward what accords with the Creator's will. The truly human alternative comes only from the One who made us and fully knows us.

It should come as no surprise that even prayer may lose its grip on reality. The Spirit brightens the future. He goes between our prayers and God. He asks for what God knows we need.

But don't think that our prayers are passive, that whatever we pray for the Spirit will make right. The follower of Jesus knows God's will in many things. The Bible transmits that will. A conscience that is tender to the Spirit opens the way to obedience.

All too often, however, the future clouds over. Fogs of doubt and uncertainty hide the pathway to choice. We pray in bewilderment. This way? that way? we cannot tell. At that point the Spirit guides us to the will of God. God's supreme will for us is complete trust in Him: to that end the Spirit continually works.

"There is comfort and peace in the truth, but no real peace or comfort can be found in falsehood" (The Desire of Ages, *p. 671).*

THE FREEDOM TO SAY YES

Now the Lord is that Spirit: and where the Spirit of the Lord is, there is liberty. 2 Cor. 3:17.

The world challenges with the almost impossible. Many things lie totally beyond us. We happily look at them and then go on to the possible. But some things tantalize by being just beyond our reach. A little more effort, a little more time, another day, and they could be ours.

When Roger Bannister was straining to crack the four-minute mile barrier, the world of athletics strained with him. What a day it would be! We shared his achievement vicariously.

When the summit of Mount Everest beckoned Edmund Hillary, he knew how near to impossible the ascent was. Yet he and Tensing Norkay pushed their bodies past the limits of their training. Mountaintops are achieved through such commitment.

Today the nearly impossible lies ahead. A day in which we could say yes to goodness, to obedience, to God. Will we have the freedom to say yes?

Jesus said that His freedom is real freedom. He meant that He gives us grace and power to be what we know we should be. Satan would have us dance, like puppets on their string, to the tunes of temptation and habit. But the Spirit works in our lives to give us freedom.

The truly free person is not the one who lets passions rule or habits control. The truly free person says yes to the better life. In another place Paul talks of the mastery of sin. We yield to sin and find it a slave driver. When we submit to righteousness as our master, the chains fall off.

The question is Who will be master? Will it be sin? Will it be righteousness? Not that sin and righteousness have personalities; rather, they indicate the trend of our life, the direction we are taking. The person who seeks after rightdoing in the Spirit's power has freedom not found any other way. He can choose right actions and attitudes that formerly yawned like chasms without a bridge.

In Christ we set patterns of righteousness that show whom we have made master. The rule of the Spirit liberates us to freedom of choice—an impossibility without Him.

"Under the influence of the Spirit of God, man is left free to choose whom he will serve. In the change that takes place when the soul surrenders to Christ, there is the highest sense of freedom" (The Desire of Ages, p. 466).

GRAND CANYON ASCENT

For thou art my hope, O Lord God: thou art my trust from my youth. By thee have I been holden up from the womb. Ps. 71:5, 6.

Roaring Springs gushes from the walls of the Grand Canyon more than 4,000 feet below the North Rim. As we descended the path, a young man jogged past us, whistling. He was attempting to set a new speed record for traversing the trail from North Rim to South Rim. We panted rather than whistled!

Neal Wilson, General Conference president, encouraged us. This was not his first view of the serial story of the great catastrophe that laid down these sedimentary deposits. We noted the intrusion of a lower layer up through higher layers, the inversion of layers, and other evidences of sediments being deposited in a short time period.

That was on the descent. Going up was something else.

Elder Wilson, an experienced mountain climber, paced us—five minutes climb, one minute rest. And he told us of a previous occasion, when three senior church officials had to be dragged, pushed, and half carried to the rim. On this occasion none of us needed such help; we even stayed awake during the evening geology lecture!

Perhaps such an experience in the canyons and gorges of Palestine had taught David that sometimes help must be accepted. Perhaps he had put his arm around a wounded soldier and exhorted and borne him to safety.

To be "holden up" means to lean on. From this verse and similar passages comes the hymn "Leaning on the Everlasting Arms."

Reflection taught David that his God might rightly be called "God of Hope." When it seemed impossible to reach safety, God's arms encircled him. When sin crippled his struggling morality, forgiveness sustained him. When doubt undermined his faith, he felt sustaining power.

For David, hope represented the continuing, sustaining presence of God. It had never left him in the past, it would never leave him in the future. Such hope had saved him and would save him yet again.

David saw his life as a pattern formed by an attending Providence. Just how long it took David to realize this, we do not know. For you and me, the sooner we know it the better, for in such knowledge we know also the God of hope.

"It is not the capabilities you now possess or ever will have that will give you success. It is that which the Lord can do for you" (Christ's Object Lessons, *p. 146).*

THE CHRISTIAN CELEBRITY

I am as a wonder unto many; but thou art my strong refuge. Ps. 71:7.

Have you ever wondered what it must be like to be a celebrity? A Ronald Reagan, perhaps? or a Napoleon Bonaparte? or a Joan Sutherland? You could not go shopping without being recognized; no caption would be needed to identify your picture in a history book; your fans would know your every whim.

Was that what the psalmist meant? David the shepherd, now king over Israel! Once famous for his harp, now holding the scepter of power! Victor over the Philistines, trader with a score of nations, scourge of the idolatrous! The small-town boy made good!

Every so often a famous person accepts Christianity. A few weeks ago I spoke with a man who had been a member of a state legislature for 13 years and was thought to have a good chance to be premier of his state. He gave it away in favor of his Lord.

David had no such escape. Samuel had anointed him in the name of the Lord God. Some would remember him as shepherd, some as consummate musician, some as Jesse's lad. But now he was king, and more than king.

Israel still thought of itself as a God-ruled nation, a theocracy. Much of the outpouring of the psalmist spills from the tensions created by being human and yet trying to govern the nation as though God Himself sat on the throne of Israel.

So while his subjects were numbering off his talents, remembering his skills, extolling his victories, David had other thoughts. How could he think like God? act like God? Impossible. Yet God had anointed him and assured the kingdom to him and his children.

Sensitive souls crack under such tensions. The insights of the Psalms show only too well how David sensed his insufficiencies. In many ways he has given us the true confessions of a saint.

A world exists where each of us is a celebrity. A few friends, the family circle, our schoolmates. They know us, read us, understand us. To them we are "a wonder." To meet what they expect of a Christian, to live as Christ lived, seems all too much, impossible. Except, as with David, God is your "strong refuge." Then all is possible, even the declaration that God made of David when He called him perfect, a man after His heart. Yes, even that!

"It is not enough that the sinner believe *in Christ for the pardon of sin; he must, by faith and obedience,* abide *in Him"* (Patriarchs and Prophets, *p. 517).*

"PLEASE HURRY, LORD!"

O God, be not far from me: O my God, make haste for my help. Ps. 71:12.

During a crowded fiesta in Bogotá, Colombia, I had my camera poised for the procession of a stone statue of Mary, mother of Jesus, through the streets. Brown-robed, barefooted monks staggered their way past as all around knelt.

Then she was at my side, beautiful, young, intelligent. "You do not worship the virgin, I see?"

"Me? No, I'm not a Catholic."

I could see the questions race through her mind. Doesn't everyone worship the virgin? What does being a Catholic have to do with that?

"If you do not worship the virgin, how can you get help? Do you have a saint?"

The thought gap was widening. Time to try a question myself. "Why have you come today? Do you come to fiesta every year?"

"Oh, no! I live way off in the mountains. But my mother is ill. She will die if God does not help. I tell the virgin to hurry!"

How often we cry out in our distress, "Please hurry, Lord!" He, the only solution to our helplessness, must act immediately or all is lost. Though we would shun the bended knee in Bogotá, our thinking borders on that of my anonymous teenage friend. Things can change, be turned around, only if we can impress God with the priority of our need. Thus David prayed, "Make haste for my help," a few scant minutes after he had declared God the one on whom he leaned.

But David knew God very well. Hurry, Lord, but let me lean while You are coming, he prayed. You are not giving up on me, Lord, and I will not give up on You.

"Do you think God knows where you live?" I asked my black-eyed friend.

"Why yes, of course."

"Does He know your name? your mother's name? your mother's illness?"

"Of course."

"Do you think you really needed to come here to tell Him your needs?"

She bowed her head and was quiet for a long time. The crowds moved us apart. But she caught my eye and I read her lips, "Thank you, senor. Thank you very much."

"At this very time He is inviting us to come to Him in our helplessness and be saved" (Patriarchs and Prophets, *p. 431).*

"I WILL HOPE CONTINUALLY"

But I will hope continually, and will yet praise thee more and more. Ps. 71:14.

Psalms 70 and 71 have at least two things in common. Both call on the Lord to hurry. In Psalm 70:5 David calls on the Lord not even to stop for a drink or a breath; "make no tarrying," he urges.

But the other thought that is common to the two chapters is puzzling: God will have to hurry or David's solutions will be impossible; yet "let such as love thy salvation say continually, Let God be magnified" (verse 4). God will have to hurry to sort things out; yet "I will hope continually, and will yet praise thee more and more" (Ps. 71:14).

Then, says the Christian, Hurry to my help, Lord, but I will praise You, whatever happens. Make things right, Lord, but I will hope without a break.

Our streets house the chapels of blighted hopes—gambling parlors, casinos, bookmakers, one-armed bandits, bingo halls. Our newspapers offer the prayer scrolls of the gambler's dreams—lotteries, art unions, raffles, and lucky draws. Gambling is hope turned into vice.

David had no such thought about God. To hope continually in God had foundation in fact. God had nurtured him from his birth (verse 6); He had guided and delivered His people. For David, to hope was "to go in the strength of the Lord" (verse 16). Hope did not speak about what God might or might not do in the future, about whether David might be the lucky one in some divine lottery. Not at all. Hope spoke of God's certain action for the benefit of His people, and more specifically for the benefit of David.

The haste the sweet singer asks of God may add to the innumerable saving acts he already knew (verse 15). On the other hand, there may be nothing that he as a human can discern that has changed the situation. Except for one thing: past experience of the God on whom he had leaned from birth assured him that that God was still acting for his salvation. Nothing could change that. Therefore he could declare continually how great is the name of God; he could wait in hope continually.

To wait in continual hope means to go with God both to the green pastures and to the valley of the shadow of death, and in all things to give praise and thanks.

"God loves to have us trust Him, loves to have us have confidence in His promises" (Selected Messages, *book 2, p. 247*).

GOLD IS FOR 50

And ye shall hallow the fiftieth year, and proclaim liberty throughout all the land unto all the inhabitants thereof: it shall be a jubile unto you. Lev. 25:10.

In the world of anniversaries, every five years and each decade has been assigned a precious stone or metal to commemorate to it. Gold is for 50. An appropriate choice. Anyone who can celebrate 50 years of marriage has golden memories in store. It is a long, long way from year one to year 50! No wonder the media love stories of people who live to be 100, or who celebrate anniversaries spanning many decades.

In the time of Israel 50 years lasted just as long as today. It must have crept toward anxious families as slowly as it does today.

You see, year 50 filled the future with hope. "That which especially distinguished the year of jubilee was the reversion of all landed property to the family of the original possessor. . . . Such were the provisions made by our merciful Creator, to lessen suffering, to bring some ray of hope, to flash some gleam of sunshine, into the life of the destitute and distressed" (*Patriarchs and Prophets*, pp. 533, 534).

In that year Israelites in slavery were set free. In that year the Lord provided for the people of Israel without their having to plant or reap. What an occasion to look toward!

Viewed from another angle, the year of jubilee reminded the wealthy and the landed that all belonged to God. It taught them to understand the rights and needs of the very poor and the oppressed.

In that year we perceive a type of what God does for His children. Jesus came to proclaim liberty. In Him the bonds of sin break. In Him God restores Eden and gives dominion to His people. In Him God provides for our every need.

All that is of spiritual value comes from His hand. He giveth, and giveth again, as the old hymn says. The yield of that year was to be free for the stranger, the fatherless, and the widow, and even for the creatures of the field.

Jesus came to give a perpetual year of jubilee to the world. Each day is a page in the calendar of His gracious love. This very day is such a day. If gold is for 50, then the year of jubilee is golden with its vision of what God wants to do for us.

"Christ connects fallen man in his weakness and helplessness with the Source of infinite power" (Steps to Christ, *p. 20).*

NO ONE TO LEAN ON

I will go in the strength of the Lord God: I will make mention of thy righteousness, even of thine only. Ps. 71:16.

Who will ever forget the women's marathon at the 1984 Olympics. Watchers sat appalled as Swiss marathon runner Gabriela Andersen-Schiess weaved and hobbled her way to the finish. The last mile remains a blank in her memory. Officials and coaches agonized over whether to lead her from the course; others walked beside her, keeping her on track and urging her on. Her body twisted grotesquely to one side and slanted forward as if she would stumble and crawl the last few paces.

She finally crossed the line. A huge cheer rocked the stadium. No hand had supported her, no arm had lifted even an ounce from her feet. She had done it alone. Alone in her mind, with her body obeying the urges of years of training, she found reserves of strength and struggled on to a personal victory.

But, I will go in the strength of the Lord!

You remember Paul's victorious shout, "I have finished my course, I have kept the faith," and his urging to look to Jesus, the author and finisher of the course set before us.

If only that Swiss runner had had someone to lean on for those last terrible yards! Someone to support her and renew her strength.

That renewal is yours today. In our text the Lord does not offer a spiritual monitoring system that drip-feeds us with a squirt of divine power to supplement our strength when it seems to falter. This isn't a me-plus-God situation. All the strength comes from the Lord.

God asks us to learn one great lesson about Him and about ourselves: He alone can give spiritual strength; we can only receive it. If the line is crossed at last, it will be because He has crossed it for us. If we run with patience the race of holy living, it will be because He has run it for us. His strength, His life, is our all.

The moments of today will fill with His strength as you go with Him. David had his own way of remembering God's strength and his weakness. He remembered and counted off the righteous, saving acts of God. In the victories of the past he knew the victory of today. As with Israel, so with you. To go in the strength of the Lord alone brings triumph.

"There should be hundreds where there is now one among us, so closely allied to God, their lives in such close conformity to His will, that they would be bright and shining lights, sanctified wholly, in soul, body, and spirit" (The Sanctified Life, *pp. 40, 41*).

39

THE SIMPLICITY OF SALVATION

All that the Father giveth me shall come to me; and him that cometh to me I will in no wise cast out. John 6:37.

Numerous figures of speech describe God's gift of salvation. Even the idea of saving is a metaphor that tries to describe God's acceptance of humanity in the terms of a battle, or a flock of sheep, or a purse of coins. What might be lost is found or preserved, and so "saved."

Paul offers a rich list of metaphors. They come from differing human experiences to which we may liken God's salvation. Justification originates from the court of law. So does acquittal. Sanctification pictures the process of making a person or object holy. Redemption buys us back as a pledge is bought back. Propitiation provides one who stands in place of another.

Jesus had His own wealth of language. He called for our conversion or turning around. In the Spirit we are born again. He puts the kingdom of heaven within us. He asks us to become as little children.

John speaks of those who have washed their robes, of names written in the Lamb's book of life, of the victory that overcomes the world, of walking with Christ in white.

So we might go on. The more one understands and reads, the larger the list grows. Paul assures us of completeness in Christ, of the new creation, of righteousness that comes from Christ.

One might think that the matter therefore must be complex. And at least one caution should be given. Just as a parable scarcely provides a secure base for doctrine, so we may well leave others puzzled and ourselves misguided if we take one or two of these figures of speech, no matter how rich in meaning, and build our whole understanding of salvation on them.

Today, think of the simple basics. Jesus says, You do the coming and I will do the saving. When the yes of your faith meets the yes of God's grace, you are saved. Even your coming and your yes is of Him and not of you. You do not need five steps, or four, or even three, in order to have God accept you. The New Testament teaches one-step salvation: "Believe on the Lord Jesus Christ, and thou shalt be saved."

No matter how important what follows after may be, here it begins. Salvation is of the Lord. From that axiom the Christian begins every new day.

"You cannot change your heart, you cannot of yourself give to God its affections; but you can choose to serve Him" (Steps to Christ, p. 47).

THE ENGLISH PUMPKIN PATCH

Who against hope believed in hope, that he might become the father of many nations, according to that which was spoken, So shall thy seed be. Rom. 4:18.

You really have to be an Australian to understand the importance of pumpkins. After potatoes, pumpkins rank number two as the staple vegetable on the island continent. The flavor and richness of Queensland blues, ironbarks, and triambles evoke homesickness among Aussies just as easily as a stand of eucalyptus trees or a toy koala bear does.

Therefore imagine my delight when I found similar pumpkin varieties on display in fairs in the United States. Yes, they could and did grow in Washington, D.C. But imagine my frustration in England when seed from Sydney sprouted and flourished but could not beat the winter deadlines there.

But hope has its devices. Seeds grown inside a sunny window gave plants a head start. Once more the delights of buttered mashed pumpkin, roasted pumpkin, and pumpkin scones were ours.

The hope that God gives in Jesus Christ trusts the fruits of God's promises as if they were ours today. Abraham did not just hope; he "believed in hope." For him, the promised son already lived; the many nations already flourished.

How this contrasts with ordinary human hope! Sarah was an octogenarian, but Abraham refrained from her mocking laughter. He still carried the serene trust in God that sees the promise as already fulfilled, though not yet happening.

In recent years theologians have talked about realized eschatology. By this they seem to mean that Jesus Christ and the early church viewed those things that are decidedly future as already happening in part. The kingdom of God is yet to appear, but it shows itself among us by the activity of the Spirit. The Second Coming still approaches, but we possess eternal life in Jesus Christ.

Certainly, Adventist Christians live in the presence of the Second Coming and bring it forward into their lives. We live differently because we live in the time of the end. The blessed hope conditions and motivates our lives.

To defy human definitions of hope and accept God's promises as already ours is to believe in hope as our father Abraham did.

God calls us "away from human influences and aid, and leads [us] to feel the need of His help, and to depend on Him alone" (Patriarchs and Prophets, *p. 127).*

THE FORGET-ME-NOT GOD

And have put on the new man, which is renewed in knowledge after the image of him that created him. Col. 3:10.

One spring in England we bought a tray of forget-me-not seedlings. I never really had been sure of the reason for the name, but now I know. Once you've planted forget-me-nots, you have forget-me-nots forever after.

Not that the spring carpet that turns earth into a patch of sky should have a word spoken against it. But they will remind you of their presence as surely as spring arrives. Our compost heap carried them to the vegetable garden, and each year we had patches of sunshine among our lettuce and peas.

God doesn't turn off and on as the seasons do, nor is He a sometimes splash of color against the drab of our lives. He continually renews us to provide us with the completeness that only Christ can give.

After Kadesh-barnea, Israel turned back into the wilderness for their predicted 40 years of wandering. But God had His way of telling them every day that He had not forgotten them.

Something happened to their clothes and shoes. Each day God renewed the wearing threads and the thinning leather so that they did not wear out. Unlike the manna, this almost imperceptible miracle must have taken months to catch their attention.

In his Epistle to the Colossians Paul uses the figure of the putting on and off of clothes to speak of our continuing life in Christ. We put on the new man; we put off all kinds of unholy living and disobedience. Take a moment to read the third chapter and see how much Paul makes of this idea.

In verse 10 he takes up the problem of how the new man retains his newness, how the Christian remains complete in Christ. God commands holy living as the appropriate response for the Christian. He knows our weakness but still gives us hope. God gives continuing completeness. The garment of righteousness shows no tatters or tears no matter how long we wear it. Because it is Christ's righteousness, it remains ever new.

Today, as you again claim completeness in Jesus Christ He renews you with His righteousness. And so all the future fills with the certainty of hope.

"Your hope is not in yourself; it is in Christ. Your weakness is united to His strength, your ignorance to His wisdom, your frailty to His enduring might" (Steps to Christ, p. 70).

LESSONS IN LIVING

If it bear fruit, well: and if not, then after that thou shalt cut it down. Luke 13:9.

Did you know that there are at least three different ways in which apple trees produce the tiny spurs from which fruit develops? Probably you'll never need that little piece of knowledge, but at least once it saved an apple tree from the executioner's ax.

On the grounds of the house that the church provided for our use in England were two apple trees. One bore loads of Cox's Orange Pippins—an apple direct from the Garden of Eden! The other, although a much larger tree, struggled to produce a dozen Golden Delicious apples a year.

My last attempt to help the big nonbearing tree, as in the parable, consisted of buying a book on pruning and learning about fruiting spurs. Book in one hand and pruner in the other, I went over that tree, scrupulously following instructions. There are people in St. Albans and at Newbold College who can testify to the embarrassment of apples that followed!

The point in Jesus' parable teaches that God never gives up before the judgment. Israel met its judgment as a nation in the way it treated the Son of God. The final digging, the final fertilizing, brought no national response and it was "cut down."

The fruit each Christian should bear awaits the flowering of the Spirit through the power of Christ. None of us lacks in fruit-bearing potential. Like that apple tree, we just need to have the right skills applied.

Now, we are neither apple trees nor fig trees nor even vines, that we should wait and wish for the fruit of the Spirit. The transformed rational being applies will and purpose to the task of bearing fruit. The will accepts its weakness and admits the power of God. Relying on God's power, the life puts forth fruiting spurs and fruit follows.

The hope that travels with us through life never tires of the pruning hand of God. It expects God's action, not just in forgiveness, nor alone in repentance, but also in a changed way of life. The New Testament teaches victorious living as surely as it teaches acquittal before God.

Today you may expect God's action in your life. You want the fruit of the Spirit to appear; so does He. But it must be His way. He calls for you to submit totally to Him.

"True sanctification is an entire conformity to the will of God. Rebellious thoughts and feelings are overcome, and the voice of Jesus awakens a new life" (The Sanctified Life, *p. 9).*

PERSEVERANCE AND HOPE

And shall not God avenge his own elect, which cry day and night unto him, though he bear long with them? Luke 18:7.

Just what brought the woman to court we are not told. Perhaps a land dispute. Disputes of this nature occurred frequently in the days when marker stones walked during the night and the powerful oppressed the weak.

The judge had no reason to bother with her. She had no clout. She had no bribe to offer. So he forgot her request and went on to other business.

But she came back, waiting again and again in the line of those seeking his help. Finally he gave in and heard her case. Jesus reported the judge as saying, "By her continual coming she wearies me."

The original Greek suggests that he feared for his reputation. Her complaints might "give him a black eye." In other words, his position of power would weaken. Just by standing in line she forced his hand and received justice.

Now the Bible makes it clear that the unjust judge in no way represents God. Quite the reverse. Jesus puts God in contrast with the judge. The story has two main points. First, the perseverance of the widow in the face of unconcern and callous treatment. Second, God's assurance that He will deliver His children.

The story comes just after Jesus has discussed the delay in His second coming and how people will react to that seeming delay. Some will cry, "Look, there He is! Look, here He is!" In other words, they will offer human solutions to the divine promise. Many clergy today see the coming of Christ in the living of a moral life, or by improving social conditions.

Others go to the other extreme and eat, drink, marry, and gather possessions as if the Son of man will never return. Hope also dies for them.

The widow instructs us by her constancy. The Lord encourages us by His commitment to us. Hope that continues neither chases after false leads nor relaxes in complacency. Hope knows the truth about God—He will act to redeem His people.

Jesus' great concern for us is that we will give up on Him and the kingdom and so lose faith and hope. Today live for the Lord who hears. He never forgets, never overlooks, never ignores the child of faith.

"The children of God are not left alone and defenseless. Prayer moves the arm of Omnipotence" (Christ's Object Lessons, *p. 172*).

RECONCILIATION AND HOPE

And he arose, and came to his father. But when he was yet a great way off, his father saw him, and had compassion, and ran, and fell on his neck, and kissed him. Luke 15:20.

The parable of the lost son offers models in reconciliation. Perhaps Jesus intended this as the basic lesson. After all, Pharisee and scribe needed the change of attitude that would reconcile them with tax gatherer and sinner. Unless reconciliation could come now, how could they hope for it in Messiah's kingdom?

Do you seek reconciliation with brother or sister, mother or father, husband or wife, friend or acquaintance? Examine the parable at the moment of reconciliation. How much the father hoped for reconciliation! He runs toward the distant figure.

What lifted his feet faster and faster? Hope for a new relationship, hope for a new start. Reconciliation grows out of hope. The hope of the father demanded no explanations, asked no questions, sought only to make the new beginning possible. A robe, a pair of shoes, a ring, and a party—practical help to make hope a reality.

And the tattered refugee who forced his reluctant steps up the track toward his former home? Yes, he too hoped for reconciliation. No great expectations filled his mind. He had sold his birthright. At best he might serve his father, see him every day, and so express his love— he knew he could never again be called "son."

The story teaches us to hope in each other. Those who wish reconciliation swallow pride, expect very little, provide for the other, make no demands, do not count themselves too high to do the humble thing.

In the story the other person's worth assumes importance. The son has worth to the father even though to us he does not appear worthy. And the father's presence has worth even though no material gain seems to await the son. Thus Jesus sought to teach the crowd around Him lessons of reconciliation.

Rightly, we see ourselves as the lost seeking our heavenly Father's presence and rejoicing in His provisions of grace. But today it might be worth the effort to relate the story to you and others. Its lessons may teach you to hope for and work for reconciliation with someone you care for.

"In the parable there is no taunting, no casting up to the prodigal of his evil course. The son feels that the past is forgiven and forgotten, blotted out forever" (Christ's Object Lessons, p. 204).

THE JUST AND THE UNJUST

That ye may be the children of your Father which is in heaven:
for he maketh his sun to rise on the evil and on the good, and
sendeth rain on the just and on the unjust. Matt. 5:45.

Do you feel good about a God who acts with equal concern toward the good and the bad? Sends them all rain? Gives them all threescore and 10 years? Shouldn't God play favorites, at least with those who put their trust in Him?

Of course, He does in Jesus Christ. Not that He gives us an umbrella to keep us dry when the rest of the community is soaking wet. Not that He injects a superantibiotic to keep off ills and chills. But in Christ He welcomes us into the sphere of His grace and gives us its benefits.

The God of hope has also offered the world the riches of His grace so that all may benefit.

If we profess Jesus Christ, that presents us with one of this day's greatest challenges. God expects us also to continue to hope in others. When Peter thought another beyond hope, Jesus said to forgive up to 70 times 7. That's the kind of hope we should show toward others!

Jesus demonstrated it in the way He reached out to Peter. He showed it in His refusal to drive Judas away. He gave His love freely and without discrimination.

Much of the Bible teaches about human interrelationships. The entire book of Proverbs is on the subject. More than half of Paul's writings deal with personal problems.

Our text for today lies at the heart of the Sermon on the Mount, Jesus' own expression of how people should relate to each other. In it He makes the dramatic demand that we love our enemies.

The demand overwhelms us. The command to be perfect like our Father in heaven (Matt. 5:48) relates specifically to this matter. To be perfect like the Father means to love even those who hate and despise us, and to act for their welfare just as God acts for the just and the unjust.

God loves without self-interest. What could He gain from us, after all? And we too should love without self-interest. Jesus' command isn't the most comfortable He could give to a world torn by racial, communal, and international strife. Yet could we expect any lesser command from the One who gave us His own Son?

"God is love. . . . It is His nature to give. His very life is the outflow of unselfish love" (Thoughts From the Mount of Blessing, p. 77).

THE WORTH OF YOUR SOUL

Wherefore I say unto thee, Her sins, which are many, are forgiven; for she loved much: but to whom little is forgiven, the same loveth little. Luke 7:47.

No story about Jesus illustrates better how He can change a person's view of what he might become through His power than the story of Mary and Simon.

Mary enters Simon's house with many counts against her:

1. She had lived from the proceeds of an immoral life.

2. A prostitute had nothing to bring as a religious offering. The law forbade the priests from accepting either money or animal sacrifice from her.

3. Her life defiled her in such a way that she could have no normal place in society.

4. Ellen G. White reveals that Simon himself had been involved with her.

Current customs permitted local people to come to a feast that was in honor of a special guest and stand around observing and listening. However, her lifestyle would keep her from that.

Yet she came, this woman of low esteem, forgetting all the barriers so that she could express her gratitude for what Jesus had done. All who were present knew of her sinful life, but Jesus Christ had made her anew, truly born of the Spirit. As God's new creature she recovered her self-esteem. It no longer mattered that the Temple gates were barred to her. She could come boldly to Jesus, her high priest, and pour out her gifts of love.

The disdaining looks from those at the feast meant nothing to her. Christ had made her a whole person again, and she could meet the world forgiven and rejoicing.

The confidence that faith and forgiveness bring helps us live in God-given honor in the very place where our sin and failing is known. The soul that alone would have created Calvary need not fear to walk in this world. For one soul Jesus would have died, yes, for you alone. In that love, hope begins and continues, whatever we have been, whatever under God we may yet be.

"It was the love of Christ that constrained her. The matchless excellence of the character of Christ filled her soul. . . . It was the outward demonstration of a love fed by heavenly streams until it overflowed" (The Desire of Ages, p. 564).

CELEBRATE! CELEBRATE!

The morning stars sang together, and all the sons of God shouted for joy. Job 38:7.

Those who make bobbin lace do it for the joy of creating. Many times I have watched my wife's nimble fingers working 30 or 40 pairs of bobbins to create the most intricate of tracery! At the end of a run the straw-stuffed pillow used for lace-making will bristle with pins like a porcupine.

How we joy in creating things! To be without any hobby, art, or craft that involves creativity almost puts one outside humanity! God has given His children the Godlike ability to create. In this we shadow His image in a pale, weak way.

How good to write an article or a book, read it over, and say, Enough, that's it. Any further tampering will make it poorer, not richer! Or to shape a chair or a quilt, or even to create the perfect typewritten letter!

On that distant Sabbath heaven hurrahed with an exuberance of song and exultant shouts. A new world was born that day, and the universe sang its beauties.

For me the Sabbath means celebration more than remembering. I hear and know the command "Remember the Sabbath day, to keep it holy." I obey it as the Lord gives strength. But the celebration and joy of the Lord's day attracts me strongly.

Celebrate because God has made a beautiful world in which to live. If I let Him show me its beauties, I will surely find glimpses of Eden.

Celebrate because I find divine order in the cycle of seven. Divine law governs the cells of my body and the molecules of all matter.

Celebrate because God has given me rest in Jesus Christ. The Sabbath talks to me of that rest and brings my heavy burden to Him.

"Remember" gives us the anchor of history and assures us of a past when God created and set a world in motion. "Celebrate" goes with us through time, giving contemporary dimensions to what God did so long ago.

Every time we create some lovely or useful object, we are bringing into our lives the celebration of the Sabbath. We create because the Lord created us. In this He has given us of Himself. To celebrate the Sabbath reminds us of what high hopes God has for us.

"They [Adam and Eve] would be constantly gaining new treasures of knowledge, discovering fresh springs of happiness, and obtaining clearer and yet clearer conceptions of the immeasurable, unfailing love of God" (Patriarchs and Prophets, *p. 51).*

FILL THE LIFE WITH DAY

For, lo, as soon as the voice of thy salutation sounded in mine ears, the babe leaped in my womb for joy. Luke 1:44.

The New Testament begins with a joy that reached the unborn John in Elisabeth's womb. Thus Luke records the power of the joy Jesus Christ brought to this world. This is the "all-conquering, newborn joy," to quote poet Matthew Arnold, that "filled her life with joy."

The various Greek words for joy occur 326 times in the New Testament. The first act of the New Testament creates joy. The angel said to Zacharias when he announced the birth of John, "And thou shalt have joy and gladness; and many shall rejoice at his birth" (Luke 1:14). John and Jesus were bringers of joy to a dark world. The angel brightness that surrounded them lit a light for the world that has never gone out.

You know how a simple act can brighten a whole day. Someone lets you ease your car into the traffic when every other morning you have waited and waited. The boss says thank you. You catch a smile from a fellow rider on the elevator. A stranger says hi.

But what if you had to fill the life of the world with joy? I write this at the height of one of those horrid, tense times when terrorists have control of a group of hostages. What we would do to bring joy and freedom to these innocents! Can you remember the torment and anguish of the Iran hostage crisis?

With a world held hostage to sin, with Satan in control, no simple act would suffice. Yet from the moment of Jesus' conception the joy began. Night had passed and day had begun.

Guides to the Carlsbad Caverns in the U.S.A. seek to give a sense of absolute darkness by switching off all the lights in one of the deepest caves. While we felt the darkness press heavier and heavier on us a voice beside me urged, "Please, please, turn on the lights."

The world of Jesus' day had entered such a cave of darkness that only the intervention of God and the coming of the Light of the world could show a way into the future.

True joy began with Jesus. True hope began with Jesus. Where else could they begin? And how else might they continue?

"To those who are seeking for light, and who accept it with gladness, the bright rays from the throne of God will shine" (The Desire of Ages, p. 47).

YOUR STRENGTH

This day is holy unto our Lord: neither be ye sorry; for the joy of the Lord is your strength. Neh. 8:10.

If you ever have the privilege of attending Sabbath services in one of our churches in Poland, you will observe a difference from Western congregations. The day begins with Sabbath school and is followed by a church service. But that doesn't end it. There will be another sermon after lunch (perhaps even during it, on a special day!); and then another, and another.

Ezra and Nehemiah would have liked that. Take time to read Nehemiah 8, and you'll understand why. A call went out for Ezra to bring the law of Moses and read it to the people. Ezra, a scribe or theologian, began to read in the morning and kept on till midday. Then a group of preachers took over. You can read the names of 13 of them in verse 7.

How long the marathon went on we do not know, but "the people stood in their place," absorbing every word. As in the great cathedrals of the Middle Ages, the people crowded around the speakers; no one sat.

Then something happened. Overcome by the warnings of the law, the people wept. Dismayed at this reaction, Ezra and Nehemiah turned weeping to joy. "Mourn not, nor weep," they said. The people were told to prepare a feast and take food to those who had none. This was a day "to make great mirth." Why? "They had understood the words that were declared unto them."

While the Bible may, at times, remind us of our weakness and humanity, from its center glows a warmth of joy that may cheer the saddest of hearts. God gave the Word in His joy at finding a way to escape the sin dilemma. His Word is joy. That joy is our strength.

You may have differing reasons for reading and studying God's Word. A quest for knowledge may push you deeper and deeper into its study. Or you may simply like the flow of its language. Or it may give comfort. But when it creates true understanding and you see God's provisions for you, the moments of tears soon give place to joy.

Joy in God's Word may not make you want to stay at church all day waiting for a further round of sermons, but it will go with you from morning to midnight and from midnight to morn. The joy of the Lord is your strength.

"Faith in God's love and overruling providence lightens the burdens of anxiety and care. It fills the heart with joy and contentment" (Patriarchs and Prophets, p. 600).

FOR THE JOY OF TITUS

Therefore we were comforted in your comfort: yea, and exceedingly the more joyed we for the joy of Titus, because his spirit was refreshed by you all. 2 Cor. 7:13.

Beware the wizened, shriveled souls who offer nothing to the world but gripes and grudges. They're out there, inside the church and out of it: second-guessers who tell you how much better your life might have been if you'd done this or that; armchair critics who call the shots from the sidelines but never even heft the weight of the ball you are carrying, let alone try to run it to the goal line.

Welcome the hopesayers, the joybringers, who find gladness in another's joy. They're out there too, inside the church and out of it. Titus brought joy to Paul just when he needed it.

Have you ever noticed how shoulders straighten and steps grow firmer with the greeting "You're looking great today"? And what if someone really beams at you, showing genuine joy?

At the New Orleans General Conference session in 1985 a circlet of exhibits surrounded the main arena. The path to the delegates' section led past one particular booth. Early in the session my eye caught the attention of a teenage attendant. Her smile infected my day with joy. I never found out her name, but each day I sought her gladness. Not too strangely, I found myself reflecting that smile and getting grins in return.

Now, you and I know enough about life to know that you can't go through life with a perpetual smirk, let alone a grin or a smile. Yet your joy can inoculate your job, your home, even your community, with happiness.

Paul needed a boost from Corinth. That church had grumbled and complained, whinged and whined. Then Titus came bouncing in from his visit, full of good news. What millions of people would give "for the joy of Titus" today. Perhaps you need it yourself—that essential good news that God is changing lives and circumstances for others.

Refreshed by joy: taking a drink from the wells of the Lord's joy. Passing that joy along. If not your own, then another's. Firsthand, secondhand, thirdhand, joy from the Lord spreads its contagion wherever someone shows it.

"Those who in everything make God first and last and best are the happiest people in the world" (Fundamentals of Christian Education, *pp. 83, 84*).

THE STERN JOY

Rejoice, and be exceeding glad: for great is your reward in heaven: for so persecuted they the prophets which were before you. Matt. 5:12.

What must it have been like for that church in Central America when armed revolutionaries entered the sanctuary? How would you react to a demand that the elders, Sabbath school leaders, and other church officers line up? And how about when the shots split the Sabbath air?

We are never far from the Christians and lions of the Roman circus, nor from the Inquisition. Tyranny and force may catch up the Christian or the congregation in both blatant and subtle ways. Yet in the face of persecution Jesus asks us to remember two things:

1. God's people in all ages have felt its chilling force. Even God's special messengers, doing God's business under His assignment, received no protection. How then should ordinary, humble Christians expect exemption?

2. Beyond the persecution awaits the freedom and security of heaven. The greatest reward waiting us in heaven isn't its streets of gold or its gates of pearl. Rather, we shall have freedom from sin, freedom from oppression, freedom from death. If Christ makes us free, then that freedom neither tapers off nor fails.

In most communities Christians, including Adventists, benefit from the open attitudes of present-day society. The dreaded midnight door knock could never happen to us. No one would force on us the yellow armbands the Nazis imposed on Jews. Yet we also know that the end time will bring everyone to the test.

Therefore, Jesus says, learn today to share in the suffering of those who are persecuted. Understand what sustains them. Accept the stern joy that comes from identity with those who do suffer. Know that God links the suffering of His people directly to the reward He will provide.

Subtle forms of tyranny and oppression occur in all societies. While avoiding paranoid attitudes, the Christian will sense the snubs, the exclusions, the innuendos, that stem from the same source as more violent forms of assault. Recognize them for what they are. And rejoice. You are in good company both with the past and the future.

"A man whose heart is stayed upon God is just the same in the hour of his most afflicting trials and most discouraging surroundings as when he was in prosperity, when the light and favor of God seemed to be upon him" (Thoughts From the Mount of Blessing, p. 32).

THIS HAPPY DAY

It was meet that we should make merry, and be glad: for this thy brother was dead, and is alive again; and was lost, and is found. Luke 15:32.

Only one who has been lost can know what it means to be found. Only one who has searched with desperation can know the joy of finding. For this reason we are at one with the parable of the lost son. We have been lost and then found. We have searched desperately and have joyed in finding.

Not long ago the news carried a story about a Jewish refugee from the Nazi extermination camps. He believed his family dead. Then, 40 years later, he found two brothers alive in Sweden! Such a story puts us in touch with Jesus' story.

What interests us in this story today is the emphasis on festive joy. Four times in the story's climax Jesus speaks of merrymaking, or the joy that accompanies a banquet or feast. You can read it in verses 23, 24, 29, and 32.

Perhaps you can remember the "smilie" badges that appeared in restaurants and on car bumpers in the early 1970s, wishing everyone, "Have a nice day." The parable does not seek to convey that kind of constant positive spirit that urges smiles on everyone, whatever the circumstances. The father in the parable makes merry because of the very nature of the event. This once-in-a-lifetime experience catches up the father and the household. This joy goes beyond the ordinary good cheer with which we try to greet each new day.

Jesus wanted us to know that, for Him, joy links with finding of the lost. A few chapters later He actually demonstrates in real life the same festive joy. He calls Zacchaeus down from the tree; in other words, He finds him. Then He shares the festive table with Zacchaeus: for the Son of man has come to seek and save the lost, Jesus explains.

Philip Doddridge has caught the true response of the one whom Jesus finds:

"Happy day, happy day, when Jesus washed my sins away!

He taught me how to watch and pray, and live rejoicing every day;

Happy day, happy day, when Jesus washed my sins away."

"Even before the prayer is uttered or the yearning of the heart made known, grace from Christ goes forth to meet the grace that is working upon the human soul" (Christ's Object Lessons, *p. 206).*

A REBUFF TO JOY

And he was angry, and would not go in: therefore came his father out, and intreated him. Luke 15:28.

What should we think about the older brother in the parable of the prodigal son? Perhaps you share a sneaking suspicion that he had a right to feel badly done by, that the father should have shown more restraint in welcoming the prodigal. Wouldn't it have suited the situation better if attitudes might be tested and motives evaluated?

Whatever we may think, the audience around Jesus would have recognized the failure of the older son. They would have noted the following:

1. His angry accusations against his father. Both custom and the law of Moses demanded respect at all times. The younger son had broken the fifth command by neglecting his obligations to his father. Now the older son breaks it by accusing his father of wrong actions.

2. The older boy had the attitude of a servant, not a son. He expected to be paid, sooner or later, for his hard work. He kept a personal account of the growing herds and resented the killing of the fatted calf.

3. He did not have the will to make merry with the father. If the father had given him the kid for which he asked, he would not have known how to enjoy it. He would have worried about the capital loss to the farm.

4. He went so far as to deny kinship. He called his brother "your son," not "my brother." Thus he placed himself on the side of Cain, who demanded of the Lord, "Am I my brother's keeper?"

In the whole story, at no point does the older brother see how he might have contributed to the younger's departure or participated in the joy of his return.

How easy to snuff out the joy of another! How simple to justify ourselves rather than see our own need of justification! How easy to deny the Father's entreaties!

The Pharisees and scribes saw themselves in the story. All too soon they would kill the Joy that God had given the world. The older brother—the ultimate killjoy—has his descendants today. How careful we should be not to rebuff the joy that the Lord entreats us to share!

"When you see yourselves as sinners saved only by the love of your Heavenly Father, you will have tender pity for others who are suffering in sin" (Christ's Object Lessons, *p. 210*).

THE FRINGES OF HIS POWER

At his breath the skies are clear, and his hand breaks the twisting sea serpent. These are but the fringes of his power; and how faint the whisper that we hear of him! Job 28:13, 14, NEB.

Breathe on me, Breath of God,
Fill me with life anew,
That I may love what Thou dost love,
And do what Thou wouldst do.
—Edwin Hatch

A life lived in the doldrums will move onward only as the Spirit of God fills its sails with hope and joy. Spanish galleons and merchant ships driving under full sail for South America would at times lie "as idle as a painted ship, upon a painted ocean." In futile efforts to reach the wind, some captains even sought to tow their ships with ropes tied to longboats.

Ocean charts still note the areas and times of the year when the wind fails. The era of steam and diesel has made such areas desirable for fast, efficient passage. However, the occasional yachtsman may still drift for days and weeks, waiting for the wind.

The Breath of God, His Holy Spirit, blows through the cities and suburbs, fans ranch and homestead, moves the thatch of a million villages. He is everywhere, the Spirit sent from God to catch the sails of faith and move forward the barque of trust.

Let us not forget His mighty power. The Holy Wind hovered over the chaos of the unformed earth. This heavenly Agent, active in giving form and life where none had existed, joined in Creation.

The Hebrew suggests the fluttering of hovering wings at Creation, not the force of a driving gale. He spread over the formless void when nothing else existed. Thousands of years later He would hover over the young woman Mary. And, soon after that, blow with the wind of power through the upper room of Pentecost.

To pray "Breathe on me, Breath of God" opens the unfurled sails of life to the presence and power of the Holy Spirit. For the life that drifts without onward motion, the heavenly wind shifts course toward heaven's haven.

Sails of faith may catch the Breath from God today. Not one of us has, as yet, felt more than the faintest whisper of His power.

"The Lord is more willing to give the Holy Spirit to those who serve Him than parents are to give good gifts to their children" (The Acts of the Apostles, *p. 50).*

55

"SO SEND I YOU"

As my Father hath sent me, even so send I you. And when he had said this, he breathed on them, and saith unto them, Receive ye the Holy Ghost. John 20:21, 22.

Perhaps you have heard the voice of the singer, soaring and challenging, "So send I you." At the General Conference session in Vienna, Charles Brooks sang his way into the hearts of thousands as the Spirit challenged us to fulfill the mission of the church.

Think of the widowed John Andrews, with his two children, setting off for distant Europe. From across the Atlantic, a whisper of interest had drifted. He went to turn a whisper of inquiry into a shout of faith.

Or remember Captain McLaren as he anchored off Emira and Mussau, to the north of New Guinea. Facing the village and the curious people, his crew sang. How could he know that the Spirit would totally take over these notoriously wicked islands? Not too many years later Christ would breathe and from these islands hundreds would go as missionaries.

To the disciples Christ gave a mission and the gift of the Spirit. They go together like computer and software. In the plan of God, you can't have one without the other.

At the beginning of His ministry the Holy Spirit descended on Jesus. The Gospels declare Him "full of the Spirit." Jesus immersed Himself in the Holy Spirit. In the same way He will immerse His people in the Spirit. The baptism of sending is the baptism of the Spirit.

Among those upon whom Jesus breathed the Spirit, some would go to Rome, or to India, or, if the old stories are true, as far as China. Today, all over the world, volunteers and paid missionaries are ministering because the Spirit sent them. But the Spirit also opens the eyes of others, and they will find mission next door, or in the next street, or at the village market.

God's sending Spirit gives eyes to see, ears to hear. We look, not across the Atlantic, but across the street to hear the whisper of inquiry. We transport ourselves, not to exotic tropical islands, but to islets of ignorance and despair that wait for us downtown, uptown, or even right next door.

"Wherever there is an impulse of love and sympathy, wherever the heart reaches out to bless and uplift others, there is revealed the working of God's Holy Spirit" (Christ's Object Lessons, *p. 385).*

HOW CAN WE KNOW THE TRUTH ABOUT ANYTHING?

When the Comforter is come, whom I will send unto you from the Father, even the Spirit of truth, which proceedeth from the Father, he shall testify of me. John 15:26.

Mount Egmont rises in a perfect cone from the Taranaki plains of north New Zealand. Not too many centuries ago lava spilled evenly down the sides to give it symmetry and height. Egmont rivals Japan's Fujiyama for snowcapped beauty.

But here's a thought about Mount Egmont. A final barrier lies between the most informed person and absolute knowledge of the mountain. Analyzing, measuring, and computing give just so much knowledge, and they stop short.

A dividing line separates the truth *about* Mount Egmont from the truth *of* the mountain. A scientist may describe and discuss, tabulate and test, and fill the mind with data without end. That is knowing *about* the mountain. But only as the mountain impacts with its size, beauty, and perfection can anybody *know* it.

Theologians, Bible students, archaeologists, historians, fill their books with truths *about* the Bible. But only as the truth *of* the Bible impacts on anyone can it change the life or bring a message of salvation.

The Holy Spirit testifies of Jesus. Whatever we know *about* Him, only as the impact of who He is, what He did, and what He can now do strikes home to us can we *know* Him. The specific and vital work of the Spirit is to testify of Jesus.

As the divine Enhancer, He goes between us and the knowledge we may or may not have and enlarges and magnifies it so that Jesus effects salvation.

The barriers that separate the human from the knowledge of God continually rear themselves. How may we know that Jesus hears our prayers? How shall we determine whether this is truth or not?

Every person desperately desires the assurance that God is for him or her. We want to know that God understands us individually and the situation we face. We want that knowledge. We cry out for it. The Spirit answers on God's behalf. In Him the hopes and joys that we know *about* enter the life and break through barriers to give us truth and the faith *of* Jesus.

"A knowledge of the attributes of the character of Christ Jesus" "is learned from the great Teacher alone" (Fundamentals of Christian Education, *p. 343*).

THE BEST WAY TO TALK OF GOD

His name shall be called Wonderful, Counsellor, The mighty God, The ever-lasting Father, The Prince of Peace. Isa. 9:6.

In a class on writing that I took years ago, the professor offered to "buy" our manuscripts from us. Her price list read like this:

Nouns and active verbs: $1.00

Passive verbs and pronouns: 50 cents

Adjectives: 25 cents

Adverbs: 10 cents

What was she trying to teach? She wanted us to understand that adjectives limit a noun. If we describe a rose as red, we immediately limit it to that one color. No one will imagine a white, yellow, or pink rose. But with no adjective the full truth of the rose lies available to our imagination. Memories of roses of many colors, of scented roses, of places where roses grow, all lie open to us.

The best way to talk about God is through nouns. The truth *about* something is like a string of adjectives, but the truth *of* something must always be experienced as a noun or its substitute, a pronoun.

But is this really important? We need to know that we have a kind, merciful, loving, heavenly Father, do we not? Indeed, yes. But to call God Love, Mercy, or Father adds so much to what we know of Him.

Isaiah strung together a list of nouns because they speak of God in a way that adjectives cannot. Adjectives help us understand how we respond to God. But the best thing about God is not how we describe Him but what He truly is. We respond to *Him*, not to the adjectives that describe Him.

For John to say God is love means far more than to say we have a loving God. We know too well that love, as an attribute of a person, comes and goes. But when that person *is* love, then he transcends human mood and doubt. Love that is God continues.

Today, why not string together your own Isaiah-style list of nouns that define God for you? As they come to your mind, you will understand again what the Holy Spirit is doing for you. Because you can define God by giving Him your choice of names, you may know that the Spirit has guided you in your quest for truth.

" 'Our Father.' This name signifies His true relationship to us, and when spoken in sincerity by human lips, it is music in the ears of God" (Fundamentals of Christian Education, *p. 309*).

NOT WHAT THE WORD TELLS US

Beloved, now are we the sons of God, and it doth not yet appear what we shall be: but we know that, when he shall appear, we shall be like him. 1 John 3:2.

In the moment of truth we whisper to ourselves, "The Word of God says this about me, but I know it is not true. It calls the church the body of Christ, but like me, it too falls short."

Yet this faulty church, this weak and failing "I," the Lord would use to win the world for Him. The Spirit sustains our essential difference as Christians. Some would try to tell us that the Christian should live like anyone else, submerged in the society that surrounds, indistinguishable from others. Yet if those who help God with His work cannot be distinguished, how will they help?

In the weakness that we show to the world, the Spirit has opportunity. He knows the trust and faith we possess. If we let Him go between us and the other person, then we become what God intends. Through the Spirit we are what the Word says we are.

Those who help God direct others to where they will find satisfaction. We may very well be "one beggar telling another beggar where bread may be found." Yet the very fact that we have found the Bread of Life offers hope to the world.

Visitors to West Africa remark on the great vigor of the church in Ghana and Nigeria. They also feel somewhat disappointed that Sierra Leone has only a small, weak community of faith. What they may not realize is that Sierra Leone evangelized West Africa. When Adventists arrived in West Africa, they took evangelists from Sierra Leone to help start the work along the coast.

When the Spirit leads on, He makes more of us than we could ever make of ourselves. At this moment, by faith and through grace, I am a son of God. What I will be has not yet appeared.

John knew that only too well. He accepted the declaration of his sonship. God had said it of him; why should he deny it? He was not one to call God a liar. But what he could not say was what the Spirit would make of him.

The Christian knows that what God has said about him, he is. The Spirit makes of him something good, a witness, a hope in a needy world.

"When divine power is combined with human effort, the work will spread like fire in the stubble" (Selected Messages, *book 1,* p. 118).

THE SPIRIT LEADS ON

When the brethren heard of us, they came to meet us as far as Appii forum, and The three taverns: whom when Paul saw, he thanked God, and took courage. Acts 28:15.

So Paul came to Rome. Not quite the way he had once expected to arrive, but there nonetheless. Thus far he had spent all his efforts in the lands between Jerusalem and Rome. But he had a dream. He longed to bring the gospel to Spain and the western Mediterranean. Rome, he had hoped, would surely propel him westward.

When James J. Aitken began to dream of an international shortwave station that would beam the Advent message around the world, he had to settle for something less than what he'd hoped for. His "Rome" was not a church-owned 500-kilowatt facility, but the leasing of time from a German-run station in Portugal. So began Adventist World Radio.

In 1987 the church began broadcasts from its own facility on Guam. Pastor Aitken had long since left his responsibilities with the General Conference Radio-Television Department. In fact, that department no longer even exists. Paul never saw Spain, but the gospel did.

One short life can do much, but not everything of which it dreams. But if it has no visions, it will achieve little or nothing.

The Spirit creates the future from the stuff of our dreams and visions. Paul, led on by the Spirit, went via Jerusalem to prison in Rome. His two imprisonments there gave the church a far greater heritage than a missionary journey to Spain might have done. In prison he wrote the grandest of his Epistles and fed them out to the churches he had founded.

God taught Paul quite early to be satisfied with what came to him. Flight to Arabia, troublesome brethren in Jerusalem, the traffic policeman of his vision in Troas—all must have brought some frustration. But in all the changes that came his way, he saw the leading of the Spirit and "took courage."

In 1969 and 1970 we had high hopes of establishing a shortwave radio station in Monaco. For various reasons it did not happen. What waited ahead, undreamed of at that moment, had far greater potential. The Spirit, the giver of visions, always has His plans. Time will show us what He has made of our dreams.

"All heaven is waiting for men and women through whom God can reveal the power of Christianity" (The Acts of the Apostles, p. 600).

"NOW, THAT WAS SURPRISING!"

When they were come up out of the water, the Spirit of the Lord caught away Philip, that the eunuch saw him no more. Acts 8:39.

The water still dripped from the eunuch's robes as he clambered up the bank, followed closely by Philip. The chariot stood ready to press on to distant Ethiopia. The eunuch stepped up into it, taking the reins into one hand. He looked around and raised his other hand in farewell to Philip. He blinked. Looked again. Shook his head. Philip had vanished!

Was it all a dream? Had he really talked those hours with that stranger? No doubt, really. His clothes still dripped. He glanced at the scroll, and what had puzzled him not too long before now spoke clearly about Jesus Christ. Jesus Christ? He had hardly heard of Him until the stranger had told him. He smiled; dream, vision, or reality, God had given him such joy that he would never be the same again. There would be much to tell back in the Candace's palace!

Philip had obeyed instantly when the Spirit had told him to head for the south road. No reasons given. Just go south toward Gaza. Then he had found that Black man. Of all things, reading a Hebrew scroll!

An hour or so they conversed in the chariot as it jolted over the ruts and cobbles. Not the best place for a Bible study, but this stranger had intelligence and quite a knowledge of the Scriptures. Then the sudden and unexpected question: "There's water here. Would you baptize me?"

Philip had followed the eunuch up the bank, water streaming from his clothes too. He watched as the man stepped into his chariot. A blurring. He shook his head. Where had the chariot gone? He looked around. This wasn't the road to Gaza. That town over there? "Please, sir, what is the name of yonder town? Azotus. Thank you, I'll be on my way then."

Thus for two men the Spirit led on. What would it mean for Ethiopia? Was it from the eunuch that the church there adopted the true Sabbath? What would it mean for Philip? and for his family? Those four daughters, so precious, so devoted?

What can you say about the Spirit when He takes control? He may be totally predictable. Or He may leave you gasping, "Now, that was surprising!"

"As we cherish and obey the promptings of the Spirit, our hearts are enlarged to receive more and more of His power, and to do more and better work" (Christ's Object Lessons, p. 354).

THE MAN AT THE CENTER

For I determined not to know any thing among you, save Jesus Christ, and him crucified. 1 Cor. 2:2.

The morning had dawned with crystalline charm at the church-run clinic in Banepa, Nepal. And so we had set out for a two-hour walk that would take us over a ridge where we hoped to view the distant summit of Mount Everest. Somewhere I have slides that prove the success of that walk.

Trudging back through the town of Banepa, we met a crowd of people who blocked the path. We strained and stretched to see the object of their interest. A man squatted on the dirt track. He had spread a cloth before him, and on the cloth he had displayed a multicolored collection of pills, tablets, and capsules.

He would listen to a few words from one of his customers, nod sagely, and for a few cents hand over one of the brightly-colored capsules. The only experience he possessed in pharmacy he had learned by observing his customers on his previous round!

The irony of it for us was that walking with us was Dr. Sturgess, highly qualified, an excellent diagnostician, and down the track a few hundred yards our clinic offered expert advice and treatment!

The man at the center of that crowd could offer nothing but foolish hopes, while, powerless to intervene, a man who might help had to pass on by!

Jesus moved continually at the center of a crowd. The Bible tells us that people trod on each other's toes to be near Him. He attracted people. Paul sensed that attraction and used it to spearhead his evangelism. Whatever Corinth might think it needed, from Paul they would receive only Jesus Christ. He turned from his learning to the One in whom his own life centered.

At the heart of almost any crowd, someone will be attracting attention. The Gospels, the Epistles, the Acts, and the Revelation place Jesus at the heart of the story they tell. He is the Man at the center. He is the One who must attract.

Do you want to witness today? Do you want to attract someone to the gospel? The formula is clear and simple. Offer no human nostrums, but only Jesus. He is the Man at the center of all true hopes and endeavors.

"There is marrow and fatness in the gospel. Jesus is the living center of everything" (Selected Messages, *book 1, p. 158*).

A CONTAGION OF JOY

He went throughout every city and village, preaching and shewing the glad tidings of the kingdom of God: and the twelve were with him. Luke 8:1. ·

"And the twelve were with him." What a privilege to journey with Jesus as He infected Galilee with the joy of the gospel!

The people never forgot it. The command to rejoice that echoes through Paul's writings, the songs of victory from the scenes in Revelation, have their origin in this Man of joy. Luke especially takes pains to establish the personality of Jesus as one who created joy. For this reason some call his story the Gospel of joy.

Why did Jesus attract such crowds? We might create many lists. No one had ever spoken like Him. He spoke with authority and simplicity. He healed people. He taught them about God in a way that made Him real to them. He offered them hope when they thought themselves hopeless. Once started on its way, the joy traveled with Jesus all the way to the cross and then on through the Resurrection to the ends of the world, where today it touches you and me.

No wonder the poet protests:

> "Man of sorrows, what a name,
> For the Son of God who came
> Ruined sinners to reclaim."

That He wept and sorrowed we know, but these contrasted with the "glad tidings" and "great joy" that flowed from His ministry.

In many ways Mahatma Gandhi tried to model himself on Jesus Christ. He moved through India at the center of great crowds. He taught a gospel of hope. He loved people and tried to uplift the outcast and the despised, as Jesus did. Yet he never could do what Jesus did.

The bullet that ended Gandhi's life did nothing to redeem sinners, but the nails that pinned the Sinless One to the cross provided life for all.

Jesus had the right to preach glad tidings because He could provide the power to make joy everlasting. Forever after, the disciples remembered. And after His death, they found His joy continued not just in their hearts but in its power to attract and change lives everywhere.

"We can impart only that which we receive from Christ; and we can receive only as we impart to others" (The Desire of Ages, p. 370).

63

THE CHRIST OF GOD

He said unto them, But whom say ye that I am? Peter answering said, The Christ of God. Luke 9:20.

The words ring strangely in our ears: "The Christ of God." Could there be any Christ except that God anoint Him? Why should Peter say so specifically that God had His Christ?

Near our church headquarters in Lagos, Nigeria, lights shine brightly every night from a huge complex of buildings. They house the devotees of a cult that believes their leader to be a new Christ.

In my mail, every so often, come letters from one of the Australian states declaring that the writer's son is Jesus Christ reincarnated.

We dare not ignore the warnings or the threat in such delusions. If Jesus be the Christ of God, then there are also "false christs." At the time of the end they will prove overwhelmingly attractive to vast multitudes. Satan himself will delude millions, providing a new man who will demand the world's allegiance.

The New Testament offers specific ways of distinguishing the true from the false. In John's First Epistle he tells us that any who did not confess that Jesus had come in the flesh was antichrist. Paul warned of the enemy who would perpetrate the lie and draw many from the truth.

While we have no shortage of religious quacks, or of fools who will believe them, the Christian may face far greater danger from more subtle forces. How we think of Jesus makes a great difference in the development of Christian maturity.

Do we remove His humanity from Him so that we think of Him as God moving among men but not truly part of humanity? Do we remove His divinity from Him so that we think of Him as a man yet not truly God? The Christ of God, who attracts the world to His throne, is truly man so that we might know He has gone before us on the way we tread. He is truly God so that we might rest assured of His power to create and sustain His kingdom both now and eternally.

While we sometimes think of Peter as impetuous, the answer he gave reflected careful thought. He had observed and he knew Jesus for what He truly was: the Christ of God sent to save man.

"If today we would take time to go to Jesus and tell Him our needs, we should not be disappointed; He would be at our right hand to help us" (The Desire of Ages, *p. 363).*

DESPERATE MEASURES

Because of the multitude, they went upon the housetop, and let him down through the tiling with his couch into the midst before Jesus. Luke 5:19.

Luke rather likes these stories about Jesus that show how people went to extreme measures to get Jesus' attention. The story of breaking open the roof has a parallel in the story of Zacchaeus climbing the sycamore tree.

On a visit to an African nation, I needed to meet a state government minister to discuss a broadcasting possibility. Naive and trusting, I went to his office and asked to see him. I still am not too sure how many layers of bureaucracy protected him.

"Have you made an appointment?"

"No, that's what I've come to make."

"Have you written a letter?"

"No, I just want an appointment."

"But you must write a letter."

We finally did make and keep an appointment, but only after hours of cajoling and pleading and tedious ascent through the bureaucrats who ran his department.

Not for the tile remover the delay and the waiting for another day. Can you imagine the dust, the insects, and the shower of rubbish that forced aside the crowd and thus made room for the couch as it descended through that hole in the roof? Perhaps Luke also had a sense of humor!

He succeeds in driving home his point, however. Forgiveness and healing come from one Source. Do not fear to come to that Source.

The daily nature of our spiritual needs sometimes discourages us from coming to the Source of healing and forgiveness. Paul died daily to sustain his relationship with Jesus.

The tiles of pride, of failure, of doubt or discouragement, must not keep us from Jesus. Nor must we hide our need with self-sufficiency, self-conceit, or self-justification. This day too we take the desperate measures that give us access and lay ourselves at Jesus' feet. The man in the story points the way. Not only is it worth the effort; it is the only way.

"Each morning consecrate yourself to God for that day. Surrender all your plans to Him, to be carried out or given up as His providence shall indicate" (Steps to Christ, p. 70).

DRAWN TO THE CROSS

And I, if I be lifted up from the earth, will draw all men unto me.
John 12:32.

The double play on words does not really come through well in
English. John has chosen a word that in the Greek has two meanings.
In this text it means to lift up a person on the cross for the purposes
of execution. It acquired that technical meaning as the gruesome
practice of crucifixion spread through the Roman Empire.

But the word has a second meaning. The emperor's enthronement
was also spoken of as a lifting up. Thus the word has the meaning of
exalting or lifting up of a ruler for crowning.

Did John have this in mind as well? Yes, it would appear that he did.
Jesus saw the cross as a path to the glory He would share with the
Father. Exalted through the cross, He would unite with the Father and
reign with Him.

With such a glory in view, He prayed, "Father, glorify thy name"
(John 12: 28). The Father's voice replied, "I have both glorified it, and
will glorify it."

Because Jesus' act on the cross would pass judgment on the world,
Satan had lost his dominion (verse 31). In the cross Jesus received the
right to rule. He would share the glory of the Father and the adoration
of His people. The cross would attract, not as a horror spectacle, but
because through it the true King of the world now reigned.

When we consider the cross, remember that it stood alone and
unused a few hours later. When we think of the garden tomb,
remember also that it lay open and empty a few hours later. The cross
carried the guilt of the world, but it also ignited the glory of
resurrection and deliverance.

The drawing power of the cross continues. The cross bridged the
way to heaven. Now our Lord draws men to Him through His sacrifice
and through the glory of His resurrection.

As self dies at the cross, one knows what the future may hold.
There, too, the way to glory appears for each of us. Like Jacob's ladder
that spanned from earth to heaven, the cross raises us to heaven itself
so that we might reign with the Lord.

*"Christ looks upon His people in their purity and perfection, as
the reward of His humiliation, and the supplement of His glory—
Christ, the great Center, from whom radiates all glory"* (The Desire
of Ages, *p. 680*).

THE CHRIST OF THE MOUNTAINTOP

And I looked, and, lo, a Lamb stood on the mount Sion, and with him an hundred forty and four thousand, having his Father's name written in their foreheads. Rev. 14:1.

On the South American continent two huge statues of Christ have been erected. One looks out over the city of Rio de Janeiro; the other marks the border between Chile and Argentina.

Rio needs Jesus Christ. Its infamous *favellas* breed crime and poverty. Chile and Argentina have fought and refought over their territorial boundaries. Yes, they too need Christ.

But a statue will not do. John's vision looks over a world torn by the machinations of the dragon, the beast, and the false prophet. All except the faithful remnant have wondered after the beast. In such a world, we live today. This time, this day, represents a day when the rampaging of apostate and counterfeit forces seems to go unchecked. I say "seems," for the vision of John intercepts the disasters of chapter 13 with a view of the Lamb on Mount Zion.

What a statue cannot do, the living Lamb does for a perplexed and perishing world. He gathers to Himself those who would share His concern for the world and makes them His witnesses to that world. Here we fit into His program. With the world ensnared by the delusions recorded by John, the Lamb sends angel messengers from His side to warn and encourage.

Adventists see both mission and message encapsulated in Revelation 14:6-12. Yet to understand these verses fully and know their source and motivation, we look to verse 1, where the Lamb stands drawing the world to Himself.

What we need today isn't an interpretation for the mystical 144,000, but Jesus the Lamb as center and ruler of the life.

You see, the Lamb on Mount Zion rallies the faithful to their pure and true witness. He calls the wicked world to repent, to come out away from the system of corruption and apostasy. He stands over against all who despise and destroy His grace and calls to His side. There the loyal and true people of all nations find identity. There God prepares a people for the last great climax. There the witness of the last days originates. That is where God is calling you today.

"All who follow the Lamb in heaven must first have followed Him on earth" (The Acts of the Apostles, *p. 591*).

67

A NEW SONG

Thou art worthy to take the book, and to open the seals thereof: for thou wast slain, and hast redeemed us to God by thy blood out of every kindred, and tongue, and people, and nation. Rev. 5:9.

In Revelation 5 John describes a vision in which Jesus, the Lamb, occupies center stage. Everything focuses on Him. "Every creature" acclaims Him.

The vision makes an important point. To talk of Jesus redeeming and saving means nothing unless He possesses the power to do it. The glorious scenes of the Apocalypse assure us that when Jesus takes the throne of heaven and sits at the right hand of God, He possesses all the power and authority that go with that throne.

Just once have I had audience with a king. In Ouagadougou, capital of the African nation of Burkina Faso, the king of the Mossi received me. He seemed a very ordinary person to me, anxious to chat about mundane things, pleased at the work of the church in his country. It soon appeared that he carried no real power except what tradition accorded him.

The very ordinariness of Jesus of Nazareth must have puzzled many as they heard early Christians talk of Him in terms of kingship and power. Some would remember Him as the carpenter turned itinerant teacher and healer. A succession of historical events strengthened the claim of the church. Jesus had risen. Pentecost startled the people of Jerusalem. Stephen saw Jesus at the right hand of God. Paul heard and saw Him on the road to Damascus.

That Jesus reigns at the center of the universe must encourage every follower of the Lamb. But it helps little unless that power affects our attitude and lifestyle. A whole chain of arguments that run through the New Testament goes something like this: Jesus stands (or sits) at the right hand of God; therefore our lives on earth change as we give our allegiance to Him. To acclaim Him Lord and Saviour makes a real difference because we then fall within His royal domain. He can do for us what a monarch might do for his subjects.

If Jesus reigns at the center of the universe and at the center of your life, what a difference it makes! You are, in truth, redeemed. We are, in verity, saved.

"By faith we may stand on the threshold of the eternal city, and hear the gracious welcome given to those who in this life cooperate with Christ" (The Acts of the Apostles, p. 601).

OVERFLOWING HOPE

Now the God of hope fill you with all joy and peace in believing, that ye may abound in hope, through the power of the Holy Ghost. Rom. 15:13.

Some Christians have no plug in their engine of faith. Whatever is poured in runs out just as fast. They pour in the oil of peace, and while they're pouring, the powerhouse of faith runs sweetly. When they take the pitcher away, squeaks and rattles start up. They fill the tank with joy, and while the pump is working the machinery of faith ticks over. But they send it down the road a few yards and have to run after it with a can full of gas.

What makes Christianity tick? What makes it take over and run the life when it is successful? Or what causes it to fail? Paul saw the problem only too well. The two Epistles to the Corinthians recount how the trip of faith can turn into a nightmare round of spiritual tow trucks and journeys to the gospel repair pit.

His answers to this problem appear in all his Epistles. In Romans they begin in chapter 12, verse 1: "I beseech you . . . present your bodies a living sacrifice . . . which is your reasonable service." He continues in the next verse, "Be ye transformed by the renewing of your mind."

How does this work in practice? The Christian casts off the works of darkness (Rom. 13:12). He makes no "provision for the flesh, to fulfil the lusts thereof" (verse 14).

Paul puts confidence in the Holy Spirit to strengthen and sustain the will of the follower of Jesus. The renewed mind submits to the will of the Spirit. It avoids the places of temptation.

Paul knew that human performance fluctuates. The life that seemed so full of good at one moment can fill with evil the next. The Holy Spirit will make sure the vessel of faith has a plug in it. Through the Spirit, the will retains joy and peace until the life fills and runs over.

To use yet another figure of speech, the greenest places in the desert surround a spring that has bubbled over. God needs your will to make His plan work. Joy, peace, and hope in your life exhibit to the world what Christ seeks to accomplish for it. The God who gives hope creates peace and joy, and they create the hope that overflows in blessing of the world.

"There is nothing that the world needs so much as the manifestation through humanity of the Saviour's love" (The Acts of the Apostles, *p. 600*).

THE DROUGHT HAS BROKEN

The parched ground shall become a pool, and the thirsty land springs of water; in the habitation of dragons, where each lay, shall be grass with reeds and rushes. Isa. 35:7.

The great drought that gripped Australia from 1978 to 1983 broke while we were in the far west of New South Wales. This part of the great Australian outback suffered severely. The small ponds the farmers had dammed had dried up. Skeletons of sheep and cattle whitened in the searing sun.

Then a once-in-a-century event turned things around. A cyclone approached the northwest coast of Australia. Instead of veering along the coast before turning back to sea, it swept inland across the Great Sandy and Simpson deserts. Huge areas of the inland that may not see rain for a decade reported floods and bursting riverbeds.

It reached the town of Bourke on a Sabbath. The rain continued through the night and into the next day. When it finally stopped, the miracle of renewal began. The sheep had not licked up all the seeds from the ground after all! A veil of greenness showed everywhere, thickening as we looked. The dams filled; dry creek beds ran. Places that had supported only a few goannas, the dragonlike lizards that roam those parts, now boasted kangaroos and great flights of cocka-toos and lovebirds.

In the story of the Bible, rain sometimes symbolizes the Holy Spirit. Luke records how the drought of the Spirit broke at the coming of Jesus. In chapters 1 and 2 you can read the Spirit-inspired songs Luke knew. In Acts he recounts the descent of the Spirit at Pentecost as God gave the early rain to empower and equip the infant church.

Yet once more He will send the rain, the Word tells us. The latter rain will fall on a parched spiritual desert. It will quicken the waiting church. It will spread out across the barren and dry lands of wickedness, and life will appear where before only death had reigned.

For those who experience it, as at Pentecost, this singular event will forever change the future. Beyond it lies the *end,* and beyond that *end,* a *beginning,* as God gives the kingdom to His followers.

At times it seems that drought will never yield to the Water of Life. Yet the seed still remains, waiting the quickening of the heavenly rain. As it falls, it will find response first among such who pray and long for its coming.

"The great work of the gospel is not to close with less manifestation of the power of God than marked its opening" (The Great Controversy, *p. 611).*

70

LIVING WATER *

*The woman saith unto him, Sir, give me this water, that I thirst
not, neither come hither to draw. John 4:15.*

This Samaritan woman had the same practical bent as Martha. Even
today the women of Africa carry great clay waterpots atop their heads.
The Samaritan thought of the vast material benefit for her if only she
didn't need to come twice a day to that well. Martha, like her, saw the
importance of practical things, such as getting food ready. As in the
case of Martha, Jesus succeeded in making the woman understand
about spiritual values.

A few years ago a farmer in Tasmania, the island state to the south
of the Australian continent, noted water trickling out of a rock face in
a remote part of his property. He tried some of the water and found
that it fizzed on his tongue.

Several years and countless tests later, one of the great international soft drink companies bought the rights to the spring. Now that
naturally sparkling mineral water quenches thirsts in a score or more
countries. Similarly, the famous springs of Perrier in France offer
refreshment just about everywhere. How much one overflowing hole
in the rock can mean!

Jesus applied this idea to the spiritual world. The Samaritan woman
had the potential of being a powerful witness in her city. He spoke
patiently with her as He explained that the water of life now bubbled
out in her very presence. Look at Me, Jesus said, I am the water of life.
He had judged her rightly. Within the hour a great crowd came out of
the city to hear Jesus.

Who knows what springs of hope lie dormant within you, awaiting
the infilling of the Spirit to burst forth into the world? Who would have
judged Mother Teresa capable of producing such blessing? Who
looking at the wan and wasted Ellen Harmon would have thought her
capable of inspiring a world movement?

Overflowing to bless a community, a family, a nation, may be God's
plan for you. Don't think it impossible. Listen to Jesus speak to you
about what He sees in every one of us: "The water I shall give him shall
be in him a well of water springing up into everlasting life" (John
4:14).

The woman found it true. In her relationship with Jesus hope flowed
for herself and for her community.

"He who drinks of the living water becomes a fountain of life"
(The Desire of Ages, *p. 195*).

WATER FROM THE ROCK

Behold, I will stand before thee there upon the rock in Horeb;
and thou shalt smite the rock, and there shall come water out of it,
that the people may drink. Ex. 17:6.

In their fear and anxiety the people of Israel "tempted the Lord"
(Ex. 17:7). Angry and fearing death by thirst in that hot desert, they
threatened to stone Moses. We have only the bare outlines of the
crisis, but it must have been critical. It certainly marked itself into the
history of the people.

Centuries later the Lord reminded Israel of the event through the
psalmist David: "Thou calledst in trouble, and I delivered thee; I
answered thee in the secret place of thunder: I proved thee at the
waters of Meribah" (Ps. 81:7).

During World War II conditions for a small Adventist village on the
island of Bougainville worsened alarmingly. The Japanese had secured
control of the northern Solomon Islands. Short of food, they raided
local gardens just as produce reached maturity. Villages feared for
their lives as fighting broke out between the invaders and local people.

Christian leaders remembered a high plateau on one of the mountain ranges. One night the entire village slipped away noiselessly
through the jungle. The plateau stronghold kept them hidden, and
their stocks of food seemed adequate until gardens matured. But as
the dry season wore on, the water supply began to run out.

The villagers searched for a spring and found a damp place under a
rocky cliff face. Gathering around it, they prayed for water to come
from the rock. At the end of the prayer season they watched with awe
as the damp spot became wetter and wetter and then began to drip.
Soon the villagers could fill pitchers with water. For more than two
years that spring dripped without stopping; it supplied all their needs.

Jesus saw in human hopelessness His opportunity. Those who could
see no hope for themselves found hope in Him. You have the right to
call on Him in trouble. The water that flows in answer to our need may
be as practical as that thirst-quenching flow at Horeb, or it may be as
intangible as a quickening of our faith and a renewing of our hope.

"He in whom Christ is abiding has within him a never-failing
fountain of grace and strength" (Patriarchs and Prophets, *p. 412).*

HE WILL SPEAK PEACE

I will hear what God the Lord will speak: for he will speak peace unto his people, and to his saints: but let them not turn again to folly. Ps. 85:8.

In this marvelous praise poem the psalmist creates images of contentment about the way God treats us. Mercy and truth meet each other as the Lord shows His saving power. Righteousness and peace kiss each other.

For the Hebrew mind, peace meant more than the absence of conflict or turmoil. It included ideas of well-being and wholeness. The greeting "shalom" is actually a prayer for the well-being of the one greeted. Peace may rule the inner life even though times go badly and external conflict threatens the individual.

When the angels proclaimed peace on earth and goodwill toward men, they did not expect that war would suddenly cease. Rather, they predicted that Jesus would provide spiritual health and wholeness. The desperate conditions from which Psalm 85 emerged found Israel surrounded by its enemies, its existence threatened. When the angels sang, the civilized world was approaching disintegration. Moral anarchy reigned. Spiritual confusion had eaten away at certainty and had exposed the skeletons of despair.

At the height of the Battle of Britain, bombs blasted London day and night. Even Buckingham Palace had its share of destruction from the skies. Two figures lent calm and confidence to the city's citizens. Emerging from the palace, King George and Queen Elizabeth toured the bombed areas. Fearful officials urged the king and queen to leave London and find refuge in the countryside, but they elected to stay. They risked their own personal safety to visit the bomb victims and speak words of support and sympathy. The queen even quipped that she was glad a bomb had hit the palace because now she could trade stories with East Londoners.

One serene person can influence a city or a nation. In the life you will live this day, you will meet distressed and fearful people. Your inner calm can have an immeasurable influence.

Today, remember and cherish the gift of peace God has placed in your life. It isn't meant for you alone. You can let it speak for God at home, at school, at work. The peace Jesus brings finds its most powerful evidence in the life that shows the wholeness of that peace.

"The peace that Christ left His disciples is internal rather than external and was ever to remain with His witnesses through strife and contention" (The Acts of the Apostles, *p. 84).*

THIS LIGHT OF MINE

They saw not one another, neither rose any from his place for three days: but all the children of Israel had light in their dwellings. Ex. 10:23.

Plague number nine almost persuaded Pharaoh. A darkness that no light could penetrate spread over Egypt. Commerce halted. Schools closed down. The first hours of darkness registered inconvenience, but inconvenience rapidly gave way to concern, concern to anxiety, and anxiety to panic.

Those who lived through the great electrical blackout of the northeastern United States in the 1960s remember how panic grew more and more extreme as the hours ticked on and still the electric switches remained dead. The deadly fog that settled over London in the early 1950s left hundreds dead.

Egypt's plight echoes faintly the coming disaster of the fifth of the seven last plagues. In the panic and terror of that plague, the Word records, people will gnaw their tongues in pain.

Even now a plague of spiritual darkness blankets communities and nations. The perplexity of national leaders shows how greatly the world needs the light of divine hope.

In contrast with the dreadful blackness of those Egyptian nights, candles and oil lamps burned brightly in the homes of the children of Israel. When midday came to Egypt God blindfolded its people, but light shone in Hebrew homes. Have you ever wondered what it would have been like for a Hebrew to take his candle into that Egyptian darkness, or for an Egyptian to stumble through the barrier into the light that the Hebrews enjoyed?

In this story we see two nations that faced diverse destinies. Probation had closed for Egypt. A bright future opened for Israel. We have not yet come to such a parting, though the end-time will surely separate the righteous from the wicked. The darkness that we see around us has not blocked off our witness. The light that shines in Christian homes does not yet mark them off from the plague of darkness that will surely settle over the rebellious last-day world.

Today, polish the windows of witness; turn up the light in your life. Let your dwelling place beam to the world the saving love of God while there is still time.

"The spirit and work of Christ must become the spirit and work of His disciples" (Patriarchs and Prophets, *p. 278*).

ROARING WATERS

And I heard a voice from heaven, as the voice of many waters, and as the voice of a great thunder: and I heard the voice of harpers harping with their harps. Rev. 14:2.

Thus the prophet attempts to describe the swelling sound of joy and praise that fills heaven from those around the throne of the Lamb.

On a still autumn night Niagara Falls announces its presence for many miles around. The mists thrown up by Victoria Falls in Africa block out the morning sun for great distances. Far downstream from the Iguassú Falls, on the border between Paraguay and Brazil, the waters still throb with the force of the torrents that create the mightiest of waterfalls.

The book of Revelation echoes again and again with the sounds of heaven. Sound, light, and beauty filled the eyes of the aged disciple John as vision after vision showed him what God had in store for the faithful followers of the Lamb.

One of the features of prophecy is that it shows the future as a magnification, or expansion, of something we already know or perceive today. Thus we can understand something of what the immorality of the last days will become because we stand appalled at today's moral collapse. We know that the gospel can go to every creature because even today it reaches to the corners of the world.

John had heard the singing of Christian communities. In his vision their praise to the Lamb and to the Father was amplified a thousandfold. His insistent repetition of the presence of song in heaven shows his great interest in music.

How he thrilled at the hallelujahs of the angel voices! at the anthems of the redeemed! at the massed voices of victory around the throne of God! As the sound of great waterfalls announces their presence long before the traveler comes upon them, so our song of praise foretells the song of Moses and the Lamb.

Somewhere in his ministry John must have heard a massed choir singing. It had poured sound over him. Such singing showed what heaven will be like. Even today we can begin the song of victory.

"Through the beloved Son, the Father's life flows out to all; through the Son it returns, in praise and joyous service, a tide of love, to the great Source of all" (The Desire of Ages, p. 21).

REJOICE WITH ME

And when she hath found it, she calleth her friends and her neighbours together, saying, Rejoice with me. Luke 15:9.

The tiny brick-and-mud house has only a door for an opening. Freshly laid rushes cover the hard dirt floor, providing warmth underfoot and comfort when sleeping. One room serves as kitchen, bedroom, and workplace. Busy around the room, the housewife lays aside her headdress. Ten coins hang from it: the dowry to her marriage. Not for her the dowry that so loads the headscarf that it must be kept in a safe place. Ten coins had strained her parents' resources.

Picking up the headdress again, she fingers the coins. Her heart leaps. She counts again. Nine! One has fallen off. The lost one must be somewhere in the house. Somewhere in the reeds and dirt lies one tenth of her dowry.

Jesus has us by the ears with this story, just as He must have charmed His listeners so many years ago. We know what it is to lose something precious and to search desperately for it.

The woman lights a lamp, an extravagance at any time, justified now only by the importance of the quest. She peers into corners, bends to examine the rushes. Then driven by desperation, she pulls the reed mats out of the house and shakes them, watching all the time. Nothing. Now she takes a bundle of twigs. Dust flies out the door. The whole village knows her plight.

A dull gleaming in a corner. A shout of joy. She has found the coin. And for this one coin she throws a party! How could she share her joy without food or drink? Unthinkable. The party costs far more than the value of the coin, but no matter. The joy of finding must be shared.

Magnify this woman's desperate search to God-size and you will begin to understand how earnestly God searches for the sinner. He lights the lamp of His love. He scrambles among the dirt and trash of the human home. Turning from a universe of riches, a galaxy of adoring subjects, He searches for this one lost coin as if it were all He possessed.

You are that one lost coin! At your repentance, at your finding, God and the angels shout for joy.

"At the foot of the cross remembering that for one sinner Christ would have laid down His life, you may estimate the value of a soul" (Christ's Object Lessons, *p. 196*).

THE RIGHT TO REJOICE

*Let us eat, and be merry: for this my son was dead, and is alive
again; he was lost, and is found. And they began to be merry. Luke
15:23, 24.*

The shriveled, malignant soul of Satan finds no joy in those who live
for God. The evil one sneered at the status Job enjoyed with God. "You
have put a hedge around him and his house," Satan claimed. "You have
blessed the work of his hands and have made him prosperous" (see
Job 1:10).

What Job had been before he found God, we do not know. We do
know that he sensed deeply his sin and need of God. We know that,
like all God's children, he sought the obedient, faithful life (see verse
1). Satan's scorn left Job vulnerable, but at the end his faith
triumphed.

In the parable of the lost son, the older brother scorned his
brother's repentance, grew angry at the favors the father gave him,
and demanded to know what right the father had to treat the younger
brother thus. He raised the same excuse as Cain did when he
murdered Abel. He had no responsibility for the prodigal. The
wayward one was "your son," not "my brother." In *Christ's Object
Lessons* we learn that the older brother showed by his attitude that he
needed reconciliation with the father as much as did the prodigal.

In the repentant attitude of the wayward son, we understand the
secret of the father's joy. In order, the prodigal declares: (1) his sin
against God; (2) his sin against the father; (3) his loss of sonship; and
(4) his determination to serve faithfully in the father's house.

On such contrition the father based his hopes for the future. He saw
in the son that which he had always wanted for both his children—a
desire to serve from the love they had for him.

In the parable the father represents God; the younger son, all who
repent and seek reconciliation. The father's joy as he prepares to
celebrate the son's return matches the heavenly Father's.

God's joy over Job appears in the final chapter as Job understands
how much he owes to God and God gives His blessing. In the parable
of the lost son, the father who "makes merry" helps us understand
what it is that makes the heart of God glad.

*"All the resources of heaven are at the command of those who
are seeking to save the lost"* (Christ's Object Lessons, *p. 197).*

THE GOING-OUT-OF-BUSINESS PEARL MERCHANT

A merchant . . . , when he had found one pearl of great price, went and sold all that he had, and bought it. Matt. 13:45, 46.

In 1985 divers in the Arafura Sea, to the north of Darwin in Australia, brought to the surface an oyster containing the "world's most beautiful pearl." Described as perfect in shape and of incredible luster and depth of color, the pearl awaited a wealthy buyer. Custom provides the original owner the right to give a name to an exceedingly precious gem. Thus the very rich came to examine, and perhaps to bid for, the Victoria pearl.

In about the year A.D. 30 a similar event occurred, which Jesus tells us about. An expert found an exquisite, unique pearl and decided he must own it. The Master makes the point that this man went out of business to own that gem. He gave up his merchant stock and perhaps his future as a pearl trader to own and keep that rich and precious object. He was not buying to sell again but buying to own and keep. That, said Jesus, should instruct you about the value of the kingdom. That should teach you that nothing you own or cherish should keep you from availing yourself of salvation.

To sell all and receive the kingdom means to give up the lifestyle of sin and seek the kingdom of God and His righteousness. What He gives back in exchange for total surrender has value far beyond what we can sell.

God finds joy in those whose total commitment to Him compares with the total commitment He made in sending Jesus. He is the Pearl of great price. Made precious in suffering, He is of value beyond estimate because of what He means to the repentant sinner.

What buys the Pearl? How can we "purchase" the kingdom? Only through faith in Jesus Christ. In the paradox of the kingdom we may say both that the kingdom is God's free gift and that it costs our all.

The merchant, content with its beauty and value, scraped together all his possessions to buy that pearl. We too scrape together all that we think has value and surrender it to God. That it has no real value we know, but transformed by faith in Christ, He may yet use it to bring glory to His name.

Who would not go out of the business of self-righteousness to own the Pearl of great price?

"In the market of which divine mercy has the management, the precious pearl is represented as being bought without money and without price" (Christ's Object Lessons, *p. 116*).

JESUS REJOICED IN SPIRIT

In that hour Jesus rejoiced in spirit, and said, I thank thee, O Father, Lord of heaven and earth, that thou hast hid these things from the wise and prudent, and hast revealed them unto babes. Luke 10:21.

On one occasion Jesus "groaned in the spirit" (John 11:33). Distressed that the death of His dear friend Lazarus should bring sorrow to his sisters, He showed His power by raising Lazarus to life.

On the other hand, the return of the 70 from their successful mission brought joy to Jesus. Because we would like to bring Him joy, note what made our Lord rejoice:

1. The disciples had subjected themselves to Jesus' will and gone out witnessing in the towns and villages.

2. They had preached the kingdom with urgency and conviction.

3. They had been sustained by Jesus' presence, even though He was not physically with them.

4. The forces of evil met defeat through their faith in Jesus.

5. God had written their names in heaven.

6. By trusting and witnessing they had shown true knowledge and wisdom.

7. They had fulfilled God's mission by proclaiming the nearness of the kingdom.

In the victories of His followers Jesus saw the defeat of Satan confirmed. He saw the deceiver fall as lightning from heaven. Satan had lost his position of authority over these redeemed witnesses. No longer could he claim the dominion he had achieved in the Garden of Eden.

In terms of the kingdom of heaven, those who turn to God must be born again, or become as babies. They lose whatever power they might have had and must now depend on the help of Another. The very ones who seem so powerless achieve victory over evil and succeed in claiming others from the clutches of the devil.

You might like to check the seven points above to see if your life causes Jesus to rejoice in spirit. The key to every spiritual victory lies in total surrender to Jesus and complete reliance on His power.

"The more we contemplate the character of Christ, and the more we experience of His saving grace, the more keenly shall we realize our own weakness and imperfection, and the more earnestly shall we look to Him as our strength and our Redeemer" (The Sanctified Life, *p. 83).*

JOY IN THE TEMPLE

And they worshipped him, and returned to Jerusalem with great joy: and were continually in the temple, praising and blessing God. Luke 24:52, 53.

You can imagine the mutual joy that prevailed when the friends of Jesus met Him after His resurrection. John tells us that He prepared a simple meal to celebrate their togetherness. Luke tells us that He put His hands on them in blessing.

When Jesus died, the joy went out of the disciples' lives. In their sorrow and despair they finally returned to the shores of Galilee and despondently determined to take up fishing again. But Jesus had other ideas. He knew that His resurrection had created such a stir in Jerusalem that the prospects for successful witnessing there were great.

We do not know anything about their trip back to Jerusalem from Galilee. But you may be sure it went quickly and with singing and praise. As the small band retraced the steps of former journeys, they remembered this incident and that. Their courage and confidence grew.

Luke likes to note parallel events. His Gospel begins with joy at the prospect of the Spirit-endowed child who would prepare the way for Jesus. His story ends with joy at the soon-to-come Spirit birth that would send the disciples as messengers to the whole world.

The joy Jesus brought runs throughout the gospel story. It continues today. Joy expresses hope. The opposite to hope is doubt. The expression of doubt is despair. Just as hope brings the promises of God into our lives and confirms them in Jesus, so doubt questions the promises and denies Jesus' power to make them real.

The joy that brought the disciples to wait in Jerusalem for Jesus' gift of the Spirit spread like a contagion through that city. Acts records how Solomon's Porch became the evangelistic center for the infant church.

Can we know that joy today? Yes, if, like the disciples, we understand how Jesus fulfills prophecy and meets contemporary needs. Yes, if we meet with Him and pray for His Spirit to descend. Yes, if we tell each other about what He has done for us.

"The true, joyous life of the soul is to have Christ formed within, the hope of glory" (Steps to Christ, p. 47).

THE ULTIMATE PRIZE

I have seen his ways, and will heal him: I will lead him also, and restore comforts unto him and to his mourners. Isa. 57:18.

Suffering and joy partnered each other in Jesus' life. Sufferings made Him the perfect and only salvation for humanity (Heb. 2:10; 12:2). Joy came as He took His place at the throne of power and began to give to those He saved the benefits achieved through His ordeal.

Joggers know the pain barrier that some must hurdle if they will run on, rather than falter short of their goal. If you want to know what it means to endure and achieve, talk to marathon runners. Just to finish represents such an achievement that they will not keep quiet about it.

Soberly we contemplate the sorrow and suffering of our Lord. Whatever you may endure today finds its answer in what Jesus endured. When tempted to ask about the pain the innocent bear, remember that the innocent Lamb of God suffered also. If God could not spare His Son, how can reason demand that He spare us?

Perhaps Ellen White wanted us to meditate each day on the closing scenes of Christ's ministry because there we see gathered into one Person all human tragedy and despair. There our own guilt and suffering meet with Jesus' sacrifice.

In *Pilgrim's Progress* all kinds of companions join Christian as he moves steadily but painfully toward Celestial City. They taunt him, tempt him, seek to divert him. At other times different companions walk with him. They sustain and strengthen his determination to press on.

Jesus met opposition, the "contradiction of sinners" (Heb. 12:3), but He kept on and won a glorious victory. So may we.

At the end of the parable about the widow and the unjust judge, Jesus asks the question "Nevertheless when the Son of man cometh, shall he find faith on the earth?" (Luke 18:8).

The same question meets us today and every day: If I begin this day with my faith fixed on Jesus, will I end it that way? If I have begun the life of faith, will I complete it in faith? The joy of Jesus rises not alone from ministering the benefits of His atonement but also, as Finisher of our faith, by giving the grace and power needed to begin and end with Him.

"All that Christ was to the disciples, He desires to be to His children today" (Steps to Christ, *p. 75*).

JOY IN THE UNSEEN

Whom having not seen, ye love; in whom, though now ye see him not, yet believing, ye rejoice with joy unspeakable and full of glory. 1 Peter 1:8.

The Taj Mahal glistens and glows under the Deccan sun, near Agra. Only in seeing can you understand its beauty and symmetry. One of the great achievements of the late Italian Renaissance, it attracts thousands of tourists day after day. My one day in Agra found me drawn to it. How can I describe the marble, the minarets, the reflecting pool, the skill and artistry? You have to see it to understand.

And if you could see the magic of it, as I did, as the full moon outlined its form against the midnight velvet of an Indian sky, it would live forever in your memory. To me it represents the very best of human endeavor in architecture.

Yet as I write, my mind immediately goes to that masterpiece of English building arts, Henry VII's chapel at King's College in Cambridge, England. Many times we went to hear the chapel choir sing in that singularly proportioned and ornamented tribute to God. I wish I could write so that you understand its effect on me. To see means to know.

Peter did not try to describe Jesus to the churches, though he could have. He gave no word about how tall He was, what He wore, how He walked, how His voice sounded, though all these lived in his memory.

Instead, Peter went to the essentials of faith. The power of the Spirit was sustaining their faith; therefore they knew Jesus. They had passed successfully through trial and temptation; therefore they saw Him. They could love Jesus because they knew His presence in the difficult and troubled lives they lived.

In Peter's mind, faithfulness in trial and difficulty proved that a Christian knew and saw the One he loved. Belief in the power of Jesus to sustain through such trial created rejoicing. Peter could no more write the words to describe that joy than the Taj Mahal can be described in words. But like that building, the "unspeakable joy" really exists. Peter could tell it was there. So can you. So can the world that sees you. Joy expresses your hope, and hope captures the world for Christ.

"If we are clothed with the righteousness of Christ and are filled with the joy of His indwelling Spirit we shall not be able to hold our peace" (Steps to Christ, p. 78).

PUTTING LOVE FIRST

Now these three remain: faith, hope and love. But the greatest of these is love. 1 Cor. 13:13, NIV.

Members of the lily family have one thing in common. Many parts are to be found in a pattern of three. Petals, seed pods, stamens, and stigmas have this neat arrangement. As in so many of God's creative acts, the lily has a theme that the Maestro composes in thousands of variations.

Take one example, the Easter lily. Look at the flower. Beginning with the bud, the flower hides inside three sepals. Touches of green distinguish them from the three creamy petals that unfold with them. Look at the pollen sacs, arranged in packages of three. The pistil has three plates, or stigmas, to catch the pollen. At its base the seed pod divides into three chambers to carry three rows of seeds.

Paul pictures love in somewhat the same way, except for one difference. The flower of God's grace has three parts: faith, hope, and love. Love forms part of grace, and yet is much more. Love is also the whole flower.

In another passage Paul describes the fruit of the Spirit: love, joy, peace, longsuffering, gentleness, goodness, faith, meekness, temperance. But the English language hides the meaning of the Greek. The fruit of the Spirit *is* love—period. The others in the list *describe* love. Faith and hope have meaning and fulfillment only through love. Alone, they are nothing. Love does not represent a progression from faith or hope, it works alongside and with faith and hope.

Paul's discussion began quite a few verses before this. He is talking about spiritual gifts. He creates a list from his experience. From Acts and the Epistles we know how the gifts of the Spirit operate in the church. By the end of chapter 12 he has finished his listing.

What a formidable list it is! All the way from administration to prophecy, all of them vital elements in the developing church. But wait a minute.

Dear Spirit, you can almost hear Paul praying, give the church all these things when and as they need them, but don't leave out faith, hope, and love, and especially love. Of all Your gifts, they must have love for their faith and hope to flower. Love is Your greatest gift; without love no flower will form.

"Reader, He loves you. Heaven itself can bestow nothing greater, nothing better. Therefore trust" (The Desire of Ages, *p. 483).*

WHILE WE WAIT

For we through the Spirit wait for the hope of righteousness by faith. Gal. 5:5.

As a child I lived on Billygoat Hill. Who among the people of Cowra, a small town in New South Wales, gave it that name, I'll never know. Huge granite boulders made it a boy's delight. From a thousand hiding places Indians could swoop onto prairie trains and cowboys could protect their ranches. Early on, I learned one thing. Granite is mighty hard and rough! I can still point out a scar or two from close encounters with granite boulders.

Perhaps for this reason I love the stonemason's taming of granite. How the back of the hand glides along the satin-smooth surface of a bank or insurance building! Skill turns the rough and the shapeless into the smooth and the lovely.

In his discussion of righteousness by faith, Paul has gone on from the action of God in Jesus Christ. Now he comes to the practical. What will that righteousness mean in the life?

Some have surely gotten it wrong: They are looking for a physical symbol to show the world that they belong to God's chosen people, and therefore to the righteous. Not that way, says the great apostle, circumcision isn't the answer. What we need is faith working by love.

God gives us faith to claim Christ's righteousness. That we need. But a hope remains. That hope expresses itself in the outworking of love.

At this point Paul departs into a discussion of a lifestyle growing out of love for God and for each other. The Spirit directs us to a way of life every bit as moral and upright as the most meticulous keeping of the law. God does not fall short in the imparting of righteousness.

Through faith that works by love—in other words, through the leading of the Spirit—we shun the disobedient path and follow right living.

My brother and I used to imagine those boulders as enemies or allies. We would even divide them up just that way. Those rough, coarse companions left their mark on us! But someone took some of them. Loved them. Worked at them. Polished them. Transformed them. Anyone can tell the difference between a boulder and a polished stone! We hope for such a life change through the righteousness that is by faith.

"Through faith we receive the grace of God; but faith is not our Saviour. It earns nothing. It is the hand by which we lay hold upon Christ, and appropriate His merits, the remedy for sin" (The Desire of Ages, p. 175).

GIVING DIRECTION TO FAITH, HOPE, AND LOVE

Since we heard of your faith in Christ Jesus, and of the love which ye have to all the saints, for the hope which is laid up for you in heaven. Col. 1:4, 5.

To hear some people talk, faith is a feeling of confidence in God; love, a good feeling about life in general; and hope, a formless anticipation that things will turn for the better. Of the dozen or so places where New Testament writers link faith, hope, and love, this one in Colossians gives specifics.

Today you are going to have to go out into the world and put faith in people. Some, we know from experience, will turn out to be totally trustworthy. Others will let you down. On any busy street corner, at a bus depot, or a metro station, the let-down people wait and wait.

In Delhi I talked with a Jain. We tested our understandings of faith for a good half hour. He squirmed away from any confrontation over Jesus Christ. He had no person to put faith in. His best prospect? the nothingness of nirvana. The world needs the trustworthy Person, Jesus Christ. Is it hearing about your faith in Him?

The love that God gives is not just letting the Sun of righteousness bathe you with warm happiness. He directs our love toward others. Like Jesus Himself, we are to see need and meet it in love. Love brackets you with your neighbor. You cannot escape the confines of acquaintance and friendship. Within those circles love works for the best good of the one it neighbors.

Hope, the kangaroo of emotions, leaps over the chasms of doubt and the fences of discouragement to land among God's promises. I have a nephew who owns a cattle ranch next to some of the largest national forests in Australia. At both dusk and dawn the kangaroos and wallabies emerge from the forests to graze along the river flats. No farmer has found a way to fence a kangaroo out. Thus with hope. No one has found a way to fence out the hope of a follower of Jesus.

Rally the saints, Paul says. Let's give a cheer for faith, hope, and love. Between them they give support and direction to life. Faith toward Jesus Christ, love toward others, hope toward heaven, a formula for complete living, all available in the here and now.

"Into the hearts of all who are united to God by faith the golden oil of love flows freely, to shine again in good works, in real, heart-felt service for God" (Christ's Object Lessons, p. 419).

"DID YOU SEE ME DO THAT, LORD?"

Remembering without ceasing your work of faith, and labour of love, and patience of hope in our Lord Jesus Christ, in the sight of God and our Father. 1 Thess. 1:3.

Paul came up with his faith, hope, and love formula very early. Most scholars say that the first letter he wrote went to Thessalonica about A.D. 54. For the apostle, how others followed his example mattered. His assessment of the church reflected how trust in Christ would show.

Paul knew that God was looking at him. He knew it from his rabbinical studies of the Old Testament. He knew it from experience. The finger of God singled him out from the many who were persecuting the Christians.

Paul did not separate the abstract world of ideas from the concrete world of action. While, like David, he could meditate on the works of God, he did not isolate faith and contemplate it apart from some action it grew out of or prompted. God watched to see what faith, hope, and love would produce. What they caused to happen provided a better description than all the adjectives a philosopher might give them.

The New International Version says, "Your work produced by faith, your labor prompted by love, and your endurance inspired by hope." Paul denied works any part in salvation. Faith and faith alone would suffice for eternal life. Yet he insisted, above all, that faith produce work.

God had labored long and hard for His Paul. Paul knew that. He remembered 14 years in Arabia, where he had had to rethink so much. How easily God might have given up on him. But He did not. Love labors for its beloved. If we have love for others, nothing will keep us glued to our seats while they perish without Jesus. Love cannot be love unless it works for another's good.

At Thessalonica the church members puzzled over the passing of time. So much was happening that pointed to Jesus' return. How much longer would they have to wait? So, Paul says, hope without patience will die. The essence of hope is that it waits. If it inspires patience, then its work is done.

Meanwhile God is watching it all, noting with satisfaction the results of faith, hope, and love in His children's lives.

"Love cannot live without action, and every act increases, strengthens, and extends it" (Testimonies, *vol. 2, p. 135*).

BODY ARMOR FOR THE LORD'S BATTALIONS

Let us, who are of the day, be sober, putting on the breastplate of faith and love; and for an helmet, the hope of salvation. 1 Thess. 5:8.

I was lying in bed one night in Lagos, Nigeria, while rifles cracked in the streets around me. A coup had toppled one leader and replaced him with another, and some people wanted to fight over it.

The crisis over Solidarity in Poland proved a bit more nerve-wracking. On a long motor journey southward, I passed many checkpoints, where rifles covered every movement. The trained weapons of the North Korean Army at Panmunjom were even more chilling. If such be the life of an unknown preacher, no wonder statesmen and celebrities wear body armor and hire guards.

More than once in his life Paul would have liked armor. A breastplate and a helmet would have done wonders for him on the three occasions his enemies tried to dispatch him with stones. And the "thirty-nine stripes times five" would have left little damage had he had a vest of body armor. He could write with conviction about helmets and breastplates! No wonder, too, that he saw the world as basically antagonistic to the Christian message. He remembered how Israel had suffered at the hands of enemies. He knew, too, how just being Jewish would provoke persecution in some quarters. With so much personal suffering to remember, he could reach only one conclusion: Satan was marshaling forces, not just against him but against all who confessed the name of Jesus.

Having survived beatings and stonings, rods and shipwrecks, Paul did not see physical violence as necessarily a threat to faith. But he had known times when the whips of self-doubt and the rods of discouragement had lashed at his faith. He knew what pulled him through those rough times.

God had fitted him out with faith. His Lord had encased him in love. He had lifted the visor of hope and seen God at his side. The wrath of men might hail their rocks on him or tie him to the scourging pole, but God had provided armor. Not wrath but salvation was God's intention. Faith, hope, and love, His protection.

"If Christians were to act in concert, moving forward as one, under the direction of one Power, for the accomplishment of one purpose, they would move the world" (Testimonies, *vol. 9, p. 221*).

NOTE WHAT GOD NOTICES

God is not unrighteous to forget your work and labour of love, which ye have shewed toward his name. Heb. 6:10.

Jesus told two versions of the parable of the talents. In Matthew the story focuses on making the most of the varying abilities and responsibilities God gives. One servant receives ten talents; another, five; the third, one. The servant who fails to venture in service for the Master does not see his gifts multiply.

In Luke the story unfolds differently. Each of ten servants receives one talent. How you deal with the same responsibility others have decides whether you will receive added responsibility. What you do with the one thing that God gives all His children is what He notices.

Jesus taught what Hebrews teaches. God notes the labor of love in Christ's name. He has given us the gospel to cherish, nurture, and minister. The servant who does not accept responsibility for the priceless gift of faith and hope, but treats it carelessly, can never expect the Master's approval.

In Hebrews we look back at those whose faith and patience were approved by God. Names such as Moses, Abraham, Isaac, and Daniel immediately come to mind. They had the qualities of the servants who received ten and five cities. God could give them added responsibility because their faith and hope did not fade away.

God gives us faith, hope, and love. They are not really three different things, but aspects of the one saving grace. Faith and hope show our response to God's love, but themselves are God's love in action for us.

Faith says yes to God as His love reaches out to save us. Hope says yes to God's love as it calls us into the future and the coming kingdom.

What about our love for God? Does it also share in the faith, hope, and love trio? Yes. God's love and our love cannot really be divided. We love because He loves. Is there nothing, then, that is truly our own? Does all come from God? Not quite. In the parable the servants accepted responsibility for the gospel and used it to the Master's glory. This God notes. But the sobering thought advises that even the talent of the gospel given by the Lord has no other source but Him.

"Learning, talents, eloquence, every natural or acquired endowment, may be possessed; but without presence of the Spirit of God, no heart will be touched, no sinner be won to Christ" (Christ's Object Lessons, p. 328).

"NOBODY TOOK THE SLIGHTEST BIT OF NOTICE"

Who by him do believe in God, that raised him up from the dead, and gave him glory; that your faith and hope might be in God. 1 Peter 1:21.

After he'd been drinking sea for 10 days, Don Allum set the emergency beacon going. Every day, 30 to 40 aircraft passed overhead. "I honestly think nobody took the slightest bit of notice of it. In the end I just kept going until I got to Nevis and rowed into the harbor."

Allum had paddled alone for 114 days across the Atlantic. He reached the Caribbean successfully only to have wind and current push the 20-foot QE3 away from island after island. Back in England, his brother Geoffrey had announced that he was presumed dead.

What kept him going? "I knew that if I let myself despair, I would die. I kept telling myself, 'Despair kills.' I had to believe I would come through, and keep working to make that happen. It's all down to determination, really."

Former Australian prime minister Malcolm Fraser once tried to calm the citizens by telling them, "Life wasn't meant to be easy." But it can get far too difficult for any of us, especially when we set high hopes for ourselves.

Peter saw purpose in the resurrection of Jesus. Through His presence with God, hope and faith transferred away from this world to God. How many times Peter had looked to Jesus for hope. He could remember nearly drowning. He recalled the great haul of fish. How he now cherished the compassion of Jesus that turned the despair of his denial into repentance and hope.

Too many people signal "Mayday" to a world that ignores them. Alone, unanswered, they row on, tossed and pushed this way and that. For them the time for despair has come. Nobody takes the slightest bit of notice when they are hurting and desperate.

But in the world where faith lights the beacon of hope, things go differently. Jesus once rowed through perilous passages to victory and glory. He knows the dangers, understands the loneliness and despair. He recognizes the signals before we even send them. And He is where it really matters, at the emergency center of the universe.

"No man is safe for a day or an hour without prayer" (The Great Controversy, *p. 530).*

THE CROWN JEWELS

The eyes of your understanding being enlightened; that ye may know what is the hope of his calling, and what the riches of the glory of his inheritance in the saints. Eph. 1:18.

Before the time of Ayatollah Khomeini, visitors to Tehran could view the crown jewels of Persia. The shah had arranged them in a room where the tourist might wander around, taking in the bowls of pearls, diamonds, and rubies. It all seemed so casual, so accessible, but all who visited knew that keen-eyed guards watched through slits in the walls, checking every movement.

Without doubt this must have been the most impressive array of jewels on display anywhere in the world. It far outdid the crown jewels of Denmark, and even left behind the royal jewels of England.

It took only a little imagination to picture a Persian princess picking her way through the treasure and selecting a diadem or a necklace.

But consider the crown jewels of the King of kings. Paul talks in more than one place of the riches of His glory. By this he means at least two things. First, the great and abounding love that God has shown us in sending Jesus Christ to redeem and justify the sinner.

No human mind can measure that grace. In Jesus Christ, God has established a positive action toward every sinner. His attitude seeks always to save. God is interested in saving all whom He can because of the price He paid.

If that is the case, then the second truth operates. You, whom Jesus has bought back at fearful price, assume a value far beyond any human estimation. Paul declares the saints to be Jesus' glory. The price paid suffices, and therefore God is glorified in the eyes of the universe. We are "to the praise of his glory" (Eph. 1:12).

The host of heaven watches anxiously as the human race walks in a redeemed world full of such riches. The impetus of heaven seeks not to bar but to have you reach out and pluck from God's grace the very things you need to adorn the life with righteousness.

Then today let God strengthen your tentative, trembling hand that reaches in hope toward His riches. Are you unworthy? Take His worth. Are you unclean? Take His purity. Are you weak? Take His strength. Array yourself with His riches.

"Calvary! Calvary! Calvary! will explain the true value of the soul" (Testimonies, *vol. 3, p. 188).*

AFFIRMATIVE ACTION

And the Pharisees and scribes murmured, saying, This man receiveth sinners, and eateth with them. Luke 15:2.

The words spoke of a past most would sooner forget. Written into the deeds of the house were two clauses. First, while the owner might employ Negro servants, they must not live on the premises. Second, when the time came to sell, the house could not be sold to a person of Negro descent.

Of course, by 1975 the law of the land had long since made such blatant racism not only illegal but punishable. We had never seen the deeds until our transfer to England occasioned the sale of the house. We read with fascination and horror. What had we been party to, even for a few short months?

To the credit of the United States, such evils have largely passed from society. Affirmative action has sought to give true cultural as well as legal equality to its citizens. But injustices that need to be redressed will probably always be with the human race. As one wrong is righted, in some other place a new one is created.

Jesus operated on similar principles. He deliberately sought out the underprivileged, the despised, the discriminated against. Hence the scornful aside of His critics, "This man receiveth sinners!"

In Jesus' time, sinners represented many whom, for one reason or another, the religious establishment had declared unworthy. It could happen because of occupation: to physicians, because of contact with sickness; to tax gatherers, because they were assumed to be invariably crooked; to tanners, because of contact with carcasses. Society often conspired against certain groups.

Why did Jesus work harder for such groups? Because they had little hope or self-esteem. In the irony of the Gospel narratives, the very ones who seemed furthest removed from hope of eternal life became, not just the prime object of divine love, but its most successful outreach.

When the gap is widest, God's love reaches furthest and with greater intensity. The measure of God's love may be read in how Jesus sought those in greatest need. In bridging the far-reaching chasms of human discrimination, Jesus spanned every gulf that separates man from his God.

"Precious Saviour! His grace is sufficient for the weakest; and the strongest must also have His grace or perish" (Testimonies, *vol. 1, p. 158*).

WHO NEIGHBORS?

Which now of these three, thinkest thou, was neighbour unto him that fell among the thieves? Luke 10:36.

The parable of the good Samaritan condemns any system that asks its followers to cut themselves off from the need of fellow human beings. The story judged against Pharisaism because that philosophy precluded the priest and Levite from helping the wounded man.

The priest risked too much if he went near the body. Some scribes even ruled that if a person's shadow fell over a dead body, that person was rendered spiritually unclean. For the priest the risk of pollution probably loomed larger than the threat of brigands.

Over against the poverty of such a system, Jesus offered the actions of the Samaritan. Though his religion also sought to avoid pollution, he never hesitated, but went into action.

The story paints a picture of extravagant action in favor of the needy one. The Samaritan placed the wounded man on his own donkey. He laid him down, as it were, on the back seat of his limousine while he himself rode along in the pickup truck. There's a difference between an animal trained to carry a rider and one used to loads of merchandise!

Though the "two pence" of the story sounds insignificant, it represented board and lodging for a number of weeks. Besides which, the Samaritan spent the night at the side of the wounded man and wrote a blank check against any future expense.

The English language frequently turns nouns into verbs with scarcely a pause. For example, in the matter of a year or two the word *parent* shifted from being always and only a noun to being either noun or verb.

The issue of the parable lies in whether you will live with *neighbor* as noun or verb. The lawyer wanted it to define a particular group; Jesus made it a mode of action. Not "Who is my neighbor?" but "Who neighbors?" the Christian must ask. Not "Whom will I cut off and whom will I include in my outreach?" but "How shall I neighbor in the face of this present need?"

For our example we have the Great and Good Samaritan who saw humanity wounded and dying of terminal sin and shed Himself of honor and glory to lift and heal.

"Our neighbor is every soul who is wounded and bruised by the adversary. Our neighbor is everyone who is the property of God" (Testimonies, *vol. 6, p. 294).*

THE MANY SINS

And when they had nothing to pay, he frankly forgave them both. Tell me therefore, which of them will love him most? Luke 7:42.

Did it really happen as Jesus told it? Was there a moneylender of His day who wiped off the slate the loans made to two customers? The parable says so. One man owed 50 silver pieces, the other 500, and the lender forgave them both their debts.

The second amount equaled a man's wages for 500 working days. No small sum in any economy. No wonder the man had reason to show love for the lender! Today such a debtor would face bankruptcy and disgrace. Back then he faced enforced service, which was a kind of slavery, or everything he owned would be sold and he would live as a beggar.

What was Jesus teaching through this parable? It nestles at the heart of the story about the woman who came to the house of Simon and washed Jesus' feet with her tears. Was Jesus saying that when we love much, then God can forgive much? Not at all. At the end of the story Jesus says that her faith, not her love, saved her. He also commented that the one who has had little forgiven loves little. The sequence, therefore, goes like this: sins, forgiveness, love.

What Jesus asked Simon to do had him looking inside himself to see how he thought of sin. He didn't ask Simon to total up his sins in comparison with Mary's. Rather, He wanted the Pharisee to understand the terrible nature of sin and the great gulf it creates in every life between man and his Creator. Simon, like Mary, was a 500-silver-piece debtor. Only as he saw this could he know how greatly he needed the grace offered by Jesus Christ and have the gulf bridged. The story teaches what Paul says in Romans about all having sinned and fallen short.

Mary saw how much she fell short. She recognized how greatly God had loved and provided for her by sending Jesus.

The only love for God that answers His love for us sees too well how unworthy and helpless we are. When we contrast the enormity of sin, however we wish to list or quantify it, with the greatness of God's forgiveness, then we begin loving as Mary did. Then we act in response to that love in a way that honors the love given us.

"All that was lost by the first Adam will be restored by the second" (Patriarchs and Prophets, *p. 67*).

HONORED GUEST AMONG US

I entered into thine house, thou gavest me no water for my feet: but she hath washed my feet with tears, and wiped them with the hairs of her head. Luke 7:44.

The Sabbath day had been difficult and tiring. A minister reminds himself occasionally that, while the Sabbath day may bring rest to some of God's people, for him and others in the church it means heightened activity and increased stress. For me, that day brought a preaching assignment in the large tent on the conference campground. In the afternoon I participated in an ordination service. Temperatures hovered around 100° F.

Hot, thirsty, and tired, I arrived at a friend's home to share the evening meal. My host took in my situation at a glance. In a moment a glass of fruit juice was cooling my throat. I sat in the lounge room for a few minutes. Then he offered, "Take a shower. Freshen up. Then come and have another drink."

Jesus might have expected similar treatment that Sabbath day when He responded to the Pharisee's invitation. Courtesy toward honored guests required three things: the kiss of peace, a drop of attar of roses on the head, and a basin of water to wash the feet. Simon provided none of these simple but very welcome acts.

So Jesus compares Simon and Mary. Tears provided the water Simon had failed to give. Women never let their hair down except in the inner privacy of their own homes. Yet Mary, in her loving gratitude, concentrated totally on service to Jesus.

Simon could not bring himself to give the customary kiss of peace. Was he, perhaps, afraid of being ritually defiled by contact with Jesus, who did not hesitate to eat with sinners? He did not even send to the kitchen for cooking oil, let alone perfumed essence. Mary kissed not Jesus' head, but His feet! She poured not just a mere drop of perfume, but the whole flask.

The lesson emerges clearly. Our love in response to Jesus' love must show itself in action. The observing world knows how much we love by how we act and how we live in response to Jesus' forgiveness.

Love to God "is full of gratitude, humility, long-suffering. It is self-sacrificing, forbearing, merciful, and forgiving. It sanctifies the whole life and extends its influence over others" (Testimonies, vol. 4, p. 223).

GO IN PEACE

And he said to the woman, Thy faith hath saved thee; go in peace. Luke 7:50.

I have my own way of measuring how much I like a painting or a poem or a piece of writing. I like to feel that the creative mind I am observing has let me in to it. I look for a space where I can come in and be at home.

Of the Gospel writers, Luke probably had the greatest talent for leaving space within a story for you and me to enter, look around, and examine. In this I am sure he captured Jesus' intention. I doubt that our Lord ever told a story that did not invite the listener to be a participant.

In the story about Simon the Pharisee and Mary, we may enter at any one of a number of points: as the Pharisee, who sees advantage in having Jesus with him but fails to respond in the right way; as one of the guests who recline around the table, at first embarrassed but then involved as the scene unfolds; as Mary, who forgets the world around to show her love; as one of the debtors at the heart of the story.

As you come into the story and look around, you begin to understand how Jesus wants you to participate. This story, like so many others in the Gospels, deals with relationships between people and between an individual and God.

Jesus never lets the reader escape the twin commands: Love your God, and Love your neighbor as yourself. Thus we may be Simon, comparing ourselves with Mary. Or an observer, comparing ourselves with both Simon and Mary. We compare our attitudes with theirs and learn how to love our neighbor.

We look at Simon and Mary and suddenly we must check how we respond to God's love, what we should do when we say we love Him.

Like so many of Jesus' stories, not only does this story let you into it, it also shows you the right way out. At the end of the story we have no doubt about who has responded correctly to Jesus. We know what we must do, how we must see ourselves. We know that we must forget the world around us and see only Jesus; we must serve Him and do His will.

The exit sign from the story stands clear and sharp against the darkness of self-righteousness: "Thy faith hath saved thee; go in peace."

"If the soul is not baptized with the heavenly grace of love to God and one another, we are deficient in true goodness and unfit for heaven" (Testimonies, *vol. 4, p. 224*).

TRULY BEYOND MEASURE

And ye are complete in him, which is the head of all principality and power. Col. 2:10.

The sheer abundance of life sometimes leaves us breathless. On the road south of Addis Ababa, capital of Ethiopia, you may see the lakes and decide that the white border that runs for miles along the shores is sand. But stop the car and walk toward it and at a particular point the shoreline will disintegrate into a soaring canopy of pink as thousands and thousands of flamingos take flight at your approach.

You know that with patience you could count them, yet who would seek to know the number when such abundance exists? Or consider the fossil beds of the western United States. Square miles of wall-to-wall fish. Cliffs 30 or more feet high made of millions of seashells. Try to comprehend the abundance of life that went into the coal we burn and the oil that feeds the petrochemical industry.

It appears from a study of the Word that God may actually know not just the number of sinners who have lived, but also the total number of sins committed. Humanity has carpeted this planet with a seamless roll of sin. God knows it all. He can take your life and in a moment discover all about you—all the insufficiencies, all the weaknesses, all the mistakes.

In Jesus Christ, God chooses to forget our weaknesses and make us complete in Him. In fact, He seeks to do that for the whole human race! For that reason alone Jesus Christ reigns supreme over all.

To be complete in Christ does not only mean that we have received His completeness into our lives. It also means "putting off the body of the sins of the flesh" (Col. 2:11). "Having forgiven you all trespasses" (verse 13), Christ lifts you up to a new life of obedience. We then live complete lives. By this Paul means that we lack nothing needed to qualify for the eternal inheritance.

One thing we cannot count, Paul reminds us: the riches of God's grace. It outmeasures any human form of reckoning. In practical terms, this means a new start, a new self-esteem, a new creation. The completeness of Christ goes with you today, always there to sustain your will and renew your faith.

"All power, all wisdom, are at our command. We have only to ask" (The Ministry of Healing, *p. 514).

HOW TO KNOW WHEN YOU ARE FREE FROM SIN

And ye shall know the truth, and the truth shall make you free.
John 8:32.

In the 1950s and 1960s Africa raised the cry *"Uhuru!"* (freedom). Nation after nation, set free from colonial rule, expressed itself through vote and referendum. Those were heady times. Dreams of a United States of Africa flourished. President Nkrumah of Ghana promoted a unified continent.

If you go to those countries today you will find that their situation has improved little materially. Some are worse off than they were before independence. Development and relief agencies speak of the world's rich north and poor south. The First and Second Worlds of Europe, Asia, and America grow richer, and the poor of Africa and South and Central America grow poorer.

But would the poor nations like their colonial masters back? Without exception they will answer no. They see a truth in political freedom that overwhelms any argument for more prosperity and less independence.

Jesus offended the Jews of His day by telling them that they were in slavery. They answered back that they had Abraham for their father. Who could challenge their freedom when they were the God-chosen? They did not see how sin had enslaved them. They could not imagine what it was like to be truly free. Jesus offered them truth about God and the kingdom. Later He told His disciples that He was the way, the truth, and the life. Through knowing Jesus and His kingdom the Jews would find freedom.

The Bible again gives us a figure of speech for salvation. To know truth is to put our trust in Jesus. Coming to God in Jesus, not a system of belief, brings salvation.

Today in our world we will have to discern between truth and error. We do it as we drive careful and safe courses along the city streets. Our computers remind us how easily the human may err. Accountants wrestle with figures to give a true balance. Knowing truth frees us from mistaking error for truth. And that, Jesus said, is freedom.

How unfortunate if we should produce a perfect balance sheet, compute a faultless software program, or notch up a lifetime of fault-free driving and miss out on the greatest truth of all—the truth about Jesus.

"The only condition upon which the freedom of man is possible is that of becoming one with Christ" (The Desire of Ages, *p. 466).*

THE SON ABIDES FOREVER

The servant abideth not in the house for ever: but the Son abideth ever. John 8:35.

Pity the employee when the owner's son wants his job. What chance does he have? At the chosen moment he will have to yield to the heir. He can expect kind words, perhaps a golden handshake, but little else.

Jesus' words stand in contrast with such partiality. The Jews thought themselves the privileged owners of the house of truth. God had given them the law. In fact, they believed that the Lord had offered the Torah to other nations but that only Israel had welcomed and fulfilled its conditions. Therefore they expected to occupy that house forever.

Jesus brought them down to earth. Only the free can occupy the house of truth. Sin had enslaved the people and their rulers. They eyed the future messianic kingdom and gloated at the prospects of supremacy. Just wishful thinking, Jesus said.

The Egypt of sin had them in its grasp, and Pharaoh (Satan) ruled them without mercy. Now came the Son of man, Jesus, God's life-giver. This new Moses would give them freedom from the evil one. "If the Son therefore shall make you free, ye shall be free indeed" (John 8: 36).

Being servants of sin excluded them from the promised kingdom. But the kingdom belongs to the Son forever. God intends to incorporate into the kingdom those who accept the gift of life in the Son. They will no longer serve sin, but the Son.

What a marvelous thought! God gathers us into the Son's kingdom. He loves the Son, and therefore loves us. He gives the kingdom to the Son, and therefore gives the kingdom to us.

Every so often a magazine article will tell of the fantastic wealth and property holdings of Britain's prince of Wales. Thousands live on his properties and earn their livelihoods through his enterprises. They look to the son of the monarch to provide for them.

But think of the wealth of the Son of God. His grace cannot be bought, but is yours for the asking. His words of life and truth apply to each and all. He provides spiritual sustenance. Earthly princes cannot secure the future for any person. But the Son abides with us forever. Here is a truth to put a smile on your face big enough to last all day!

"To learn of Christ means to receive His grace, which is His character" (Christ's Object Lessons, *p. 271).

GOD LEADS TO FREEDOM

Thou in thy mercy hast led forth the people which thou hast redeemed: thou hast guided them in thy strength unto thy holy habitation. Ex. 15:13.

These refugees from Pharaoh's oppression had a dangerous start to their flight. Untrained in war, taking with them women and children, the old and the very young, they trekked off toward the Red Sea. In a matter of hours Egyptian armies raised dust on the western horizon. Would Israel's flight be nothing more than an excuse for slaughter, plunder, and rape, before their former masters herded them back to the clay pits and brickkilns?

Relief workers among the Cambodian refugees in Thailand talk of the terror of escape and the torture of those captured. The media have documented the atrocities performed against the Vietnamese boat people as they flee to freedom.

We know how God redeemed Israel. For generations their prophets and poets sang of that deliverance. Egypt came to epitomize spiritual oppression by satanic forces. God still called His people out, but now He would deliver them from sin.

As the song of victory went up on the far side of the Red Sea, the people chorused in unison, "The Lord is a man of war." Later they would remember this. The prophets urged the people to let God fight for them, spiritually as well as physically.

When Jesus came, He came as deliverer. He would set the captives free. He would save the people from their sins. The imagery of escape and deliverance dominates what the Bible says about salvation. Word pictures record the universal plight of a race captive to its own inadequacies and weaknesses.

Only as we realize how strong the shackles that bind us to sin, how awful the slavery to which disobedience condemns us, can we understand how great is the deliverance God has given. Joy breaks out among the redeemed when they see how great their escape, how hard-won the victory.

The enemy waits to savage our souls today. He lusts for our submission to his will. Every day the Lord sets our feet on the other side of the Red Sea and reminds us that He has defeated the foe. In the joy of redemption we walk toward the land of promise.

"He who died for the sins of the world is opening wide the gates of Paradise to all who believe on Him" (Prophets and Kings, pp. 731, 732).

AFFIRMING THAT GOD HAS FREED US

When Peter was come to himself, he said, Now I know of a surety, that the Lord hath sent his angel, and hath delivered me out of the hand of Herod. Acts 12:11.

Luke chuckled over Rhoda. Young, innocent, but very much involved, her prayers had joined those of the other disciples in Mark's home. When the knock on the door came, she left the prayer circle and ran to check the door.

She knew the voice. She had heard him preach many times. He had visited this house frequently. She scampered back to tell the others, but left Peter standing outside, still knocking.

We smile at the incident, which turned out so well. Luke tells us a little more about Rhoda. When they called her mad, she would not keep quiet. "She constantly affirmed that it was even so" (Acts 12:15). He also says that the reason she failed to open the gate was "for gladness" (verse 14).

Often God does the impossible. He frees from sin when all had thought the handcuffs unbreakable. In a Melbourne jail a murderer serves out his time. He writes his friends to tell them that now he is free. An Adventist prison chaplain brought him to the Lord. Now the prisoner who is free prays for the free who are prisoners.

Rhoda teaches the lesson of affirmation. Jesus sets prisoners free. We must tell it over and again. To bear witness to the Lord who redeems and delivers fills the life with gladness. We have seen God work; we must tell others.

Sometimes the first love for Christ begins to wane. What can revive it? When you have told everyone about your own experience of God's deliverance, remember Rhoda. If you want to renew your love for Christ, remember Rhoda and tell of how He has set others free.

The praying church had pled for God to open Peter's prison. But when one of their number brought the glad news, they would not believe her. She insisted that God does work this kind of miracle and that it had happened. Her insistence brought gladness to the whole church.

One person's conviction that God is working and changing lives, one person who has evidence that a prisoner of sin has escaped, can bring joy to all. Rhoda broke up the prayer meeting and made it a testimony meeting. We need more like her!

"Reveal to the desperate, discouraged sufferer that he is a prisoner of hope" (Testimonies, *vol. 6, p. 279).*

TO SING A NEW SONG

Let us be glad and rejoice, and give honour to him: for the marriage of the Lamb is come, and his wife hath made herself ready. Rev. 19:7.

At the 1980 General Conference session in Dallas, Texas, the evening reports from the various sections of the world church provided many touching moments. When Northern Europe brought their report, the choir from Poland was featured first.

For a few minutes chaos reigned. People with cameras flooded to the stage. Applause began. The narrator, blinded by the footlights, could hardly see what was happening. Only when the choir finished and had retreated off stage could the program proceed.

What brought such a reaction? One could not question the music; it was superb—but so were many other musical offerings. The color of the Polish national costumes made them a photographer's delight, but every General Conference catalogs the colorful dress of a hundred nations.

The delegates bore in mind the difficult times that Poland had endured: the food shortages, the political crises, the stories of hardship. Now they wanted to show solidarity with their brother and sister Christians. As the choir poured out songs of joy, the crowd affirmed their oneness in that joy.

The solidarity of the saints in the new earth has a special poignancy for God's people in difficult times. The victims of oppression in Colombia in the 1950s, those who have died in the southern Philippines in recent years, the Christians who starved with their fellow countrymen in Ethiopia, those who have fled persecution in Uganda— for them the song of deliverance will rise with added meaning.

Songs of deliverance are as new as each day. If we add nothing to our experience today, then the song turns sour. Freedom is not just event; it is also process. Christ not only sets us free but continues to set us free.

Our hymnals provide us with hundreds of songs of Christian experience. Every one confirms the continuing presence of the Redeemer. He was with you when you first sang your song of freedom. He is with you this day as you sing it again. But the song has changed, because of today. This day He has again given you the joy of freedom.

"Praise Him for the heavenly inheritance, and for His rich promises; praise Him that Jesus lives to intercede for us" (Patriarchs and Prophets, *p. 289).*

HOW TO LOSE YOUR LIBERTY

Stand fast therefore in the liberty wherewith Christ hath made us free, and be not entangled again with the yoke of bondage. Gal. 5:1.

Every day the farmer would put a special harness around his horse. At his command the animal would walk off to a distant shed. It would position itself against a pole and begin to push. Around and around it would walk, turning the cogs that drove a variety of machines in the shed nearby. At lunchtime, without any further command, the horse would stop work, walk to the stable for a feed of chaff, take a rest, and then return to its task till evening.

The place was Tasmania, the island to the south of the Australian continent. You can visit that farm and see the track worn by the plodding of that faithful animal.

In a way, Dobbin was free. He came and went to his task without any lead or bridle. But the halter of ingrained habit had him under as tight a rein as any rider ever held.

How should we relate to the freedom that Christ gives us? Paul talks of the bondage of legalism. He warns against anything that would lead us to believe that our actions bring God's acceptance.

Having laid the specter of legalism to rest, Paul proposes that it may sneak up on us and again bind us. How comforting patterns of behavior become! To know that an action is right and to have the habit of doing it gives a feeling of goodness.

But watch out! If you start to think that you are qualifying in the sight of God through your deeds, you are back in bondage. The worst forms of legalism are those that we create ourselves. Any time we attach merit to human action, we have made our own brand of legalism.

It can be done a hundred ways. Consider, for example, the group from a country town in Australia who took themselves off to the forest to practice a translation diet! The more bizarre forms of legalism should not hide the more subtle ones.

God's grace will give us freedom and lead us to obey. But the obedience that comes from love for God faces the opposite direction from obedience that seeks to have God love us. Learning that basic lesson holds the secret of true joy in living for Christ.

"The Christian's life is not a modification or improvement of the old, but a transformation of nature" (The Desire of Ages, p. 172).

NOTHING WORKS LIKE LOVE

For in Jesus Christ neither circumcision availeth any thing, nor uncircumcision; but faith which worketh by love. Gal. 5:6.

In this text Paul makes a subtle point: to put your trust in externals leaves you lost, true enough, but to put your trust in no externals can also leave you lost. Put your trust in Christ alone, he says. The systems of uncircumcision can hold in bondage as fiercely as circumcision ever could.

The one who trusts in Jesus lets love govern actions. What did Paul mean by love? Love climaxes the trio that manages the life: faith, hope, and love.

Love works continually to guide relationships to God and to other people. The Christian loves even his enemies. That everyone might know what that love meant, our Lord quoted the Ten Commandments.

Love that avails does not create its own rules but expresses itself in obedience to God's will. Love let loose without a governor quickly becomes license. Paul deplores the concept that freedom from works righteousness gives freedom from any righteousness.

He calls us to a faith that works by love. Faith has its works, but love for God and for others motivates them.

In Ghana, often troubled by drought and shortages of medical supplies, a relief agency has provided large quantities of life-saving medicines. If you look closely, you will see that those who disburse them wear uniforms. They are Pathfinders. The government trusts them. They share without creating a black market or taking selfishly. Thus faith that works by love governs morality.

In Nicaragua a pastor leaves his home and heads into guerrilla country. He takes a risk. But love for God guides him as he seeks to spread the gospel.

In Christ we have the freedom to choose good actions. We do not have the freedom of inaction. Love from God makes the Christian active. He obeys the commandments.

Paul saw legalism closing off the Galatians from freedom to love as Christ loved. They had things around the wrong way. Love for God and His will does not create saving faith. Saving faith creates love in action.

"Love to Christ cannot exist without corresponding love to those whom He came into the world to redeem" (Testimonies, *vol. 3, p. 396*).

HOPE WITHOUT MOCKERY

And hope maketh not ashamed; because the love of God is shed abroad in our hearts by the Holy Ghost which is given unto us. Rom. 5:5.

Greek proverbs spoke of hope as mocking those who expressed it. Paul turned around the common wisdom of his age. The hope that "maketh not ashamed" never mocks the one who holds it.

In a well-known story the Greeks told how the gods had given mankind a closed box full of blessings. The box had to remain closed. In his curiosity man opened the box, and all the blessings escaped and flew back to the gods. All but one; when the lid slammed shut, hope remained in the box. Hope is a mockery, the Greeks taught, that lures the foolish into the future and then deserts them and laughs at their discomfort.

Paul denies this of the hope he is expressing. This hope never mocks. Hope in Christ differs sharply from ordinary secular hopes. Like the Greeks, we have our sayings about foolish hopes, false hopes, and blighted hopes. Every secular hope raises a question mark over the future—the thing hoped for may or may not happen. Even the secure hope of the passengers on the *Titanic* did not prove enough.

The bright hopes that fill our lives as the Spirit renews and blesses us have a different character. Paul has explained how they differ in his references to Abraham. For that patriarch a promise from God assumed the nature of a fact. Because it waited in the future, it could be called a hope, but it remained a future fact. Abraham lived in the present with these hopes surrounding him. He never questioned them, only waited for them to happen.

Paul builds the chain that produced in Abraham this kind of hope. Abraham waited and trusted through difficulty. His patience had its reward when he saw promises fulfilled. Experience of fulfilled promises brings certainty to our hope.

As the example of the fulfilled promise that we all may share, Paul reminds us of the love of God that fills our lives through the influence of the Holy Spirit. God fulfills this promise for all of us. What has not yet happened still remains a promise, a hope. But this hope will never mock us. It will surely happen, because Christ has died and risen again, and so sealed God's love for us. For this reason we may dare to act as if all the future God has set before us has even now begun.

"The Lord is disappointed when His people place a low estimate upon themselves . . . They may expect large things if they have faith in His promises" (The Desire of Ages, p. 668).

WHEN SHOULD THE PARTY BEGIN?

By whom also we have access by faith into this grace wherein we stand, and rejoice in hope of the glory of God. Rom. 5:2.

The bright double-decker buses of London demand attention. So did the face of the middle-aged man grinning hugely from a poster along the side of the upper deck. Apparently this gentleman had won a huge sum in a gambling enterprise that is legal in the United Kingdom.

He could grin, all right; but what of the millions of others whose money he had taken? For them a little less food for the children, a little less saved for a rainy day. No joy for them, nor any hope. The advertisement suggested that this gray-headed man's exultation could be anyone's. Only a fool would go and buy a ticket in that lottery and then start rejoicing. But then, gambling is for fools.

In our text for today Paul chooses a very strong word for the rejoicing in the hope that God brings. The closest English equivalent would be "exult." Right now, Paul says, the singing can begin. Right now we can start the anthems of praise. Right now we can exult in hope of the glory of God.

Hope and joy depend on each other. Joy comes only from the secure hope we have in Christ. Today that hope is yours, and therefore joy is yours.

We should sing about our hope. The theme song for the General Conference sessions for 1975 and 1980 expresses it for us: "We have this hope that burns within our hearts, hope in the coming of the Lord." In 1985 the session had as its motto "Christ Our Hope."

All over the world, anniversaries of the church's activities create times of reflection and rejoicing. We have reason to celebrate the power of Christ that has created a community of faith reaching into every part of the earth. We may exult in the millions who share our hope in Christ.

Yet the singing must begin in one heart: yours. The celebration of hope brings the glory of God into your life today. You stand as free before your God, your guilt taken by Jesus Christ, your justification assured by His resurrection.

Therefore sing. Therefore exult.

"If we would give more expression to our faith, rejoice more in the blessings that we know we have—the great mercy, forbearance, and love of God—we would daily have greater strength" (Selected Messages, *book 2, p. 243*).

THE ANCHOR OF HOPE

Which hope we have as an anchor of the soul, both sure and steadfast, and which entereth into that within the veil. Heb. 6:19.

Let me tell you about Mousehole. The unusual name goes back to when this small fishing port was used by Phoenician traders seeking tin at about the time of Solomon. A narrow inlet parts two steep hills on the coast of Cornwall, a few miles from Land's End. A place of picturesque beauty, it offers the first haven for trawlers and small ships beating their way into the English Channel.

Two deep and wide breakwaters reach toward each other from the opposing shores of the hills. Once through a narrow entrance, a ship has found safety.

Such a harbor Paul had in mind when he wrote "we . . . who have fled for refuge to lay hold upon the hope set before us" (Heb. 6:18).

Tied up in the haven at Mousehole, with anchors set, ships could survive the fiercest gale. Thus with the life that lays hold of the One who anchors us in the haven of His love.

If the soul is like a ship in a stormy sea, forced at last into a place of refuge, what is the hope that anchors the soul? It seems impossible to escape the example of Abraham. "When God made promise to Abraham, . . . he sware by himself " (verse 13). In Romans 4 Abraham shows how to hope in the promises of God. Here he receives the promise that secures his faith.

Hebrews 6 charts some of the rocks and reefs we face. In verse 6 we observe the irretrievable plight of the soul that will not seek the refuge of forgiveness and power. Those who bear thorns and briars will burn as trash is burned (verse 8). Failure to maintain hope to the end (verse 11) cuts off inheritance of the promise.

God made a promise and sware by His own name. That promise we share. That promise anchors us.

This day your soul will rock in the storms of life. Currents of doubt will pull this way and that. In your weakness, you will seem unable to resist the storms the tempter raises. But your anchor holds strong. Christ has entered within the veil to the presence of the One who made the definitive promise. He is the Man on your side, the High Priest of your calling, who has fulfilled the oath and promise made by God.

"The righteousness manifested in the character of Christ was forever to be the anchor, the saving hope, of the world" (Selected Messages, *book 1, p. 348).*

HOPE THAT PURIFIES

And every man that hath this hope in him purifieth himself, even as he is pure. 1 John 3:3.

Who would put at risk the marvelous hope that we have in Jesus Christ? Yet we do it so often. Not that He fails us. Today He is with you as always, ready to answer your need, hear your prayers, give you grace and power. Yet all too often our trust in Him falls short and we disappoint and disobey.

John saw into the future and looked to the day when we shall be like our Lord. To be like our Lord means to live above sin. Because this will have happened when Jesus appears, even now we should purify ourselves. Thus we respond in the right way to the love that makes us children of God.

How does this work in the life of the Christian? The Bible teaches victorious living. John himself proclaims faith as the victory that overcomes the world. Paul calls on us to put off the works of unrighteousness.

Nothing we do adds to the purity of the robe of righteousness Christ gives repenting sinners. Attempts to establish our own righteousness provide rags instead of spotless garments.

Obedience, pure living, begins not with sets of rules or with commandments, though these stand over against our lives as standards of judgment and measures of morality. Rather, right living begins in knowing what God has done for us in Jesus Christ. He provides the path of love and light, and we respond to His saving grace by walking in those paths.

John saw a path of darkness and a path of light (1 John 1:6, 7). When we walk in the light, we know we are sinners (verse 8), yet we still follow righteousness.

Years ago, with a group of young people I was lost in the valleys around Sydney. In the pitch dark of a moonless night we bumped and tripped our way, we knew not where. But when a search party found us and brought light to the path, what a difference!

The Christian never fails to seek the path of righteousness. He loves God's commandments. He looks to Christ for victory over sin. He goes on in the path of light. He expects victory. He knows forgiveness.

Hope that purifies knows a future in which God will provide spotless characters. In Christ that future meets us and grace gives us victory.

"Remember that working with Christ as your personal Saviour is your strength and your victory" (Testimonies, *vol. 7, p. 39).*

RIVER RED GUMS

Blessed is the man that trusteth in the Lord, and whose hope the Lord is. Jer. 17:7.

When European explorers first broke through the eastern mountain barrier of the Australian continent, they picked up the beginnings of the inland river system. In almost every case these streams led them out past the well-watered fertile western slopes of the mountains into dry, parched land.

The riverbeds, some of them dry in the fierce summers, meandered across the landscape between avenues of huge river red gums. This majestic eucalyptus surpasses the oak in girth and spread of branches, and produces even harder lumber.

Rooted deep in the rich soil of the river plains and tapping the flow of artesian streams, they survive years of drought, flourishing and flowering unhindered.

Jeremiah understood what would happen to Judah if she failed to trust the Lord. If hope in the Lord's saving acts faded and died, the nation would wither and die like the ephemeral plants of a desert rain. But if she revived her trust, knew again the sustaining hope that had seen the nation through many crises, she would stand unmoved, like trees drawing water from hidden sources when the river runs dry.

As with the nation, so with her people. Jeremiah saw little to encourage in the nation but sought individuals who would trust and hope. Thus too for us. The rivers of human hope all too often sink into the desert of failure and disappointment. Our lives run dry of trust in others, and hope turns to despair.

At that moment God comes closest to us. When we feel our helplessness, then we stand most ready to receive divine help. Turning our despair over to God leaves us open to accept alternatives that God can govern. Disappointment in others may remind us of the happiness that trust has brought in the past. Our own failure may point us to the infinitely successful Lord, who has won victory for all who trust Him.

Through the haze of the summer heat, the traveler sees the river trees from afar and knows that shelter and refreshing await. In the same way, the life that trusts and hopes in the Lord draws others to its strength.

"The Christian is in the world as a representative of Christ, for the salvation of other souls" (Christ's Object Lessons, *p. 67*).

HOPE FROM DISASTER

And I will give her her vineyards from thence, and the valley of Achor for a door of hope: and she shall sing there, as in the days of her youth, and as in the day when she came up out of the land of Egypt. Hosea 2:15.

Really, did the Lord mean what He was saying? Israel's day of shame turned into a door of hope? The defilement of the valley of Achor an entrance to joy and singing?

You will remember Achor. It lay close by Jericho. The singing soldiers of Joshua had shouted the walls of Jericho into rubble. Elation filled the camp. Despite the distrust that had turned the Israelites into cowards at Kadesh-barnea 40 years before, God was now fulfilling His promises. He would drive out the people of the land and give it to the Israelites. How could anyone disobey a God who dealt so wonderfully?

And yet one man did. At Achor God revealed the despicable greed of Achan. He had polluted Israel and brought defeat and death instead of the bloodless victory the Lord planned.

For a Babylonish garment, some silver, and a handful of gold, one man cost the people of God the fulfilment of God's best plan for them. Now they had to settle for second best. God would be with them, but the people of the land, remembering the rout at Ai, would no more melt away from the advancing Israelites.

How could such a memory be a door of hope? The purposes of God may fail because we fail Him. How often the servant of the Lord has told us of the delay in the climax of God's plans because of the church's unfaithfulness.

If, then, we can learn that lesson and submit in obedience to God's will for us, the very best plan God can devise will operate. He preserves our freedom but still gives us His love and care. Such a hope Achor taught.

In our weakness we all too often fail in obedience. The results may thwart God's optimum plan. But all is not lost. If we learn our lesson, the new plan God offers will see us through.

In our repentance and turning to Him, God takes the mistakes we have made and in His wisdom uses them as the bases for a new start, a new plan. God never leaves us without a way to Him and His future for us. If God never gives up on us, should we ever fail in hope and trust?

"Reach up your hands for help. In your weakness lay hold of infinite strength" (The Ministry of Healing, *p. 513*).

SECURE IN CHRIST

Likewise reckon ye also yourselves to be dead indeed unto sin, but alive unto God through Jesus Christ our Lord. Rom. 6:11.

The Christian can never say, Secure but sinning. Sin destroys hope. It fights against the future that God has for us. It raises to life the very despair and guilt that Jesus came to defeat.

What went wrong for the Pharisee who boasted of his right acts but received no word of justification (Luke 18:11)? No one would question the morality of the life he professed. He failed, however, to understand the fierce grasp that sin takes of the life. While concentrating on obedience to the listed requirements, he did not sense pride, self-exaltation, and worst of all, self-righteousness.

Sin, the cruel master, leers at us from around the corner of every right and good act. It invites us to feel good about ourselves, measure ourselves against others, count off the victories won, number the hours spent without transgression.

In Romans 6, Paul gives personhood to sin. Sin may "reign in your mortal body" (verse 12). We may "obey it." Our members may come under its direction, yield to its control.

Therefore, says the apostle, in Christ you die to the master, Sin. Once dead, a slave no longer fears his old master. Now that you are alive to God, Sin can claim no dominion over you.

Jesus Christ defeated sin in two ways. First, He removed from us the guilt of the broken commandments. Sin could no longer claim us as slaves. Second, He made us alive to God, aware of the power of grace, secure in the knowledge that Jesus saves the lost.

Safe in Jesus Christ, we do not need ever again to know the hopelessness of sin's dominion. Your very sense of weakness God uses to strengthen you against disobedience.

Righteousness becomes the new master, obedience (verse 16) and holiness (verse 19) the way we respond to its reign. Today you have this Lord, Jesus the righteous.

As sin seeks to tempt to wrong action, righteousness offers the alternative of obedience. Today, because of Jesus you have a choice you never had before: obedience that comes through God's grace.

"It is all offered us in His Word. If we receive the Word, we have the deliverance" (The Desire of Ages, p. 320).

JOY IN THE FATHER'S WORLD

Consider the lilies how they grow: they toil not, they spin not; and yet I say unto you, that Solomon in all his glory was not arrayed like one of these. Luke 12:27.

In Western Australia the Creator has splashed color through the bush, the forest, and the plain. A riot of blue, pink, gold, and red lures the wanderer from plant to plant, field to field.

Imagine, if you will, a field of spider orchids—cream on top, deep red or purple underneath, their petals spanning ten or eleven inches. The breeze lifts them in waves of color and turns the landscape into sheer enchantment.

Or follow a patch of sky-blue shrubbery until it merges with the distance, creating the illusion of a sky with no horizon. Bend to admire the unique blossoms of the kangaroo paw, one of the many quaint and unusual shapes that flowers take in this garden of the Lord.

What shall we say of a God who has given us more than 20,000 species of orchids and the same variety in the daisy family? With such a wealth of beauty, who could ever deny the possibilities of His power?

Smile at the pansy. Lift your eye to God with the rose. Gather His goodness to cloak you like the blossoms of the azalea. For those who will see it, the world will never lack in beauty.

Solomon relied on his tailors and jewelers to provide his raiment. Gold and silver thread flashed from his robes. The choicest of fabrics bedecked the great sovereign of Israel. What did he lack? Beauty that resulted from the Lord's giving.

If God can give each of the hundreds of thousands of plant varieties a singular and special loveliness, will He not also give to all who trust in Him that unique clothing to fit them for the kingdom of God?

Imagine the surprise of a West Australian farmer when his plow turned over a strange plant. Stepping from his tractor, he discovered a completely new kind of orchid, one that carries out its cycle of life completely buried under the topsoil humus. In the most negative of situations God provides not just for plants but for people, too.

Each flower seeks its purpose in seed, and fresh life for its world. Thus when God clothes the sinner. The new creation from the seed of the gospel fills the earth with delight.

"God has bidden us wear the richest dress upon the soul" (Testimonies, *vol. 4, p. 643).*

PRAISE FOR THE SNOW

He sendeth forth his commandment upon earth: his word runneth very swiftly. He giveth snow like wool: he scattereth the hoarfrost like ashes. Ps. 147:15, 16.

Christmas Day 1968 formed a fairyland of snow and color. Winter rarely clothes Washington, D.C., in a blanket of powder snow. But that yuletide 12 inches fell. Traffic halted, for many Washington motorists have had little experience in dealing with heavy snow.

In the early evening an unearthly quiet spread over the city. Were all the snowplow drivers enjoying Christmas supper? Clad in boots, gloves, caps, and hats, we were scarcely touched by the cold. The snow flew in fat clouds as our feet kicked their way through. By now the fall had stopped. Streetlights and Christmas decorations reflected and glowed in the white world.

For a family newly arrived from "down under," where Christmas means mangoes and cherries and a day at the beach, such a day would never be forgotten. In fact, we never have quite understood the Northern Hemisphere's impatience with snow.

Picture the ugly landscapes of the world. Slagheaps spewed from the earth by generations of mining. Ruined towns, sad reminders of men's hopes gone sour. Battlefields spawning metal memories of past cruelties.

Now give them the white wool of God's snow. Even an automobile graveyard assumes a beauty of its own when snow caps the rusting hulks.

In the year of the Lord's favor, in which we now live, God proclaims new hearts for all who repent. Wherever the ruin of sin has decayed a life, His word runs swiftly, commanding the gift of holiness.

But the change gives not only Christ's righteousness. The life that God clothes extends into the world in response to such love. Obedience is the snow of grace blanketing a sin-scarred landscape with prospects of renewal.

When the light that is the church in the world reflects from lives of obedience, the world is transformed. It knows that God has commanded and the obedient have said yes. Thus the Light of the world shines through the light of the world and gives light to the world.

"The princely dignity of the Christian character will shine forth as the sun, and the beams of light from the face of Christ will be reflected upon those who have purified themselves even as He is pure" (Testimonies, *vol. 4, p. 357*).

AN EXTRAVAGANCE OF BEAUTY

And stood at his feet behind him weeping, and began to wash his feet with tears, and did wipe them with the hairs of her head, and kissed his feet, and anointed them with the ointment. Luke 7:38.

God's love of the extravagant gesture dances before us in the gaudy wings of the butterfly. The splash of color as a parrot screeches through the forest, the elaborate tail feathers of birds of paradise, and the bejeweled body of a hovering hummingbird delight the senses. They must have brought joy to their Creator.

The same God went beyond the minimum in making provisions for our salvation. He "spared not his own Son," who was the "brightness of his glory." No wonder Paul exults in "his riches in glory."

The pouring out of His love for sinners climaxed in His death on the cross but continues to flood into this world in response to human need. God goes out into the wilderness to seek the one lost sheep. He searches the corners of the human hovel for the one lost coin. And having found them, He celebrates His acquisition with joy and singing.

Mary, weeping at Jesus' feet, answers for all who have ever been touched by the wealth of heaven's grace. Her tears, the kisses on His feet, the unbound hair, the spilled vial of precious perfume, speak for the grateful heart. She has not held back. As God has given abundantly, so she gives beyond any necessary response.

In the outpouring of God's love He challenges the selfish spirit of sin. He acts always for our benefit. Will we do the same for the world of need around us? As she left Simon's house that day, Mary had spent all on the Master. She had poured out a year's saving on Jesus' feet. More than that, she had humiliated herself in the eyes of the diners at Simon's table. She took with her the joy of forgiveness, and that was more than enough.

Was it worth it? She would say yes, yes. Love does not mete and measure. Love gives and gives again. We know this from the way God forgives and forgives again.

God has given us the extravagance of nature to remind us that beauty in the human spirit lies in willingness to give itself. Who gives totally displays the true response of love to God's extravagant Gift.

"Those who feel the constraining love of God do not ask how little may be given to meet the requirements of God" (Steps to Christ, *p. 45).*

AS BIRDS FLYING

As birds flying, so will the Lord of hosts defend Jerusalem;
defending also he will deliver it; and passing over he will preserve
it. Isa. 31:5.

The great meadow of Port Holme links the towns of Huntingdon and
Godmanchester in central England. Rated as the largest meadow in
England, it hosts numerous species of meadow plants. Living creatures that love the flowers and tall grasses of its summer flourish in its
lushness. Hares, rabbits, and many other small mammals build their
nests and dig their burrows in this fertile environment.

On a summer day the air never lacks the skylark's song. If you look
carefully into the soft blue of the English sky, you can see the tiny
form fluttering high above.

The song drifts down to join the warm buzz of bees and the chatter
of crickets. Watch carefully and you will see a skylark plummet to the
earth to rest and feed, while another climbs high to begin its song. The
combination of flower and flight charms the senses with the abundance of God's provision for us.

In the hovering, soaring birds God shows us His care. As the eagle
with its keen eyesight watches its nest from afar, God can discern us
and our need. And as the eagle swoops into the nest, bringing food, so
the Lord descends to our aid.

Is the God who soars above the earth a cause for joy? For the sinner,
the ever-watchful eye of the Lord, the Redeemer, presents the Spirit
with opportunities to convict and turn away from sin. For the saints,
His provident care lifts through present crisis and difficulty toward
the goal that God has for us.

Isaiah also assures us that the people of God will have His
protection. The Lord sees the threat to His people and flies to their
aid. In the conflict waged by the church, evil lays siege to truth,
seeking to fill the earth with lies and subterfuge.

God and the church share a common cause. God sees conflict and
descends to preserve His people and prepare the world for judgment.
A bird in flight knows the threat to nest and nestlings below. God has
the same knowing eye, but infinite power comes from Him. He will
preserve His name and His people. They are His and He their only
Hope.

"He is speaking to us still by His Spirit and His providences"
(Testimonies, *vol. 5, p. 235).

SO MANY TO REACH OUT FOR CHRIST!

Behold, I will send for many fishers, saith the Lord, and they shall fish them; and after will I send for many hunters, and they shall hunt them from every mountain, and from every hill, and out of the holes of the rocks. Jer. 16:16.

Drifting with snorkel and mask, I found the coral reefs of the tropics brushing my senses with enamel blues, golds, and browns. Fluorescent corals and fishes dance and swim across the pastels of an underwater landscape.

Through such extravagance the Lord lets us know that He holds no small designs for this world. Humbug fish flash past in baked-enamel black and white. Fluorescent blue wrasse drift above their anemone haven. The mind wrestles with the profligacy of beauty and shape.

Shoals of fish swim ceaselessly in the Mediterranean and the Sea of Galilee. The prophet saw in them a picture of the God who thinks big. To Abraham He had said that His people would be in number as the sands of the sea.

In his poem "The Hound of Heaven," Francis Thompson likens the heavenly quest for receptive hearts to a hunting dog that will not let the quarry escape.

God wants to fill eternity with an overflowing of the redeemed. He hunts each prospect with skill and persistence. God sends His faithful followers as fishers and hunters to find and gather the people to Him.

The quest Jesus undertook to save humanity models our quest for souls. Like the shepherd after his one lost sheep, we go out from comfort and security to confront the world's need and bring it to Christ. Like the woman searching for her lost coin, we peer into the world for those who will respond to Christ's salvation.

The Lord who filled the reefs with darting, colorful creatures wants His kingdom full of the redeemed. He sends His people as fishers to fill their nets to breaking point. With the dogged persistence of the tireless hunter, we join Him as He goes on the mission of salvation.

He has no ideas of small numbers or little remnants. The abundance of nature helps us understand how much He longs to people heaven with the hosts of the redeemed. To this end we "fish" and we "hunt" with the gospel as our commission while God makes up the number of the redeemed.

"We are not to wait for souls to come to us; we must seek them out where they are" (Christ's Object Lessons, *p. 229).*

THE CROWN OF THE YEAR

The pastures are clothed with flocks; the valleys also are covered over with corn; they shout for joy, they also sing. Ps. 65:13.

The checkerboard of the Canadian spring stretches endlessly across the broad plains of Manitoba and Saskatchewan. For a time, the combine harvesters lie silent, the great disc plows and seed planters are at rest. Man has done his part, now God does His.

The traveler's road parts fields of blue flax, golden rape, the white daisy pyrethrum, and great stretches of wheat, barley, oats, and rye. From the slightest rise, one can see the fields stretching to the horizon, broken only by ranch house and the occasional clump of trees.

Half a world away, puffy white sheep spot the endlessly green hills of New Zealand. Everywhere man's skill and providence demonstrate the fulfillment of the ancient promise of seedtime and harvest.

Our great urban complexes relegate farm and pasture to picture postcards and *The National Geographic*. Reduced to envelope size, they have their beauty and charm. But if you want to know how fertile this world, how generous our Creator, walk the hills among the flocks, or stride the length of a Dakotan wheat field.

The supermarkets of the cities concentrate in one place the joys of God's goodness. Fruit and produce, cans and freezer foods, show how fully God has provided.

In the time of the psalmist all people lived among that which kept them provided with food. They could watch the seed germinate, the sheep drop their lambs. Each season produced its songs and ceremonies. The technological society reserves the pleasure of food production to fewer and fewer. We perforce must focus on temperamental house plants and visits into the nostalgia of the agricultural world.

Could not this be the day to sing a psalm to the God of the supermarket? the One who makes those mountains of grapes, those cans of juice, those stacks of eggs and shelves of bread? Without Him, where would we be?

The supermarkets' stuffed aisles spread field and farm before you. See what God has given. Share in the miracle of plenty and the God who provides for your needs. Sing to God with joy, just as the psalmist heard pasture and valley shouting and singing to the Lord.

"Let us praise Him, not in words only, but by the consecration to Him of all that we are and all that we have" (Testimonies, *vol. 6, p. 480*).

GOD GIVES DOMINION

O Lord our Lord, how excellent is thy name in all the earth! who hast set thy glory above the heavens. Ps. 8:1.

In the ancient world the hierarchy between God and man frequently dominated thought. How did God regard mankind? Did He deal directly with him, or did He structure layers of authority that must be penetrated before one could reach the throne of the universe?

History records how paganism established whole rankings of good and evil spirits, gods, and demiurges. Each activity of human existence had its own supernatural force that demanded sacrifice or appeasement so that life might go on satisfactorily.

Israel knew better. But a single step separated mankind from God. True, God had angels to serve as His ministers, but they did not occupy a level through which man must go to God. Man did not go to God via angel or spirit but related directly to Him. In the Bible order, God creates man and woman and then delegates authority over the rest of His creation to them. "Thou madest him to have dominion over the works of thy hands; thou hast put all things under his feet" (Ps. 8:6). Land and sea animals, plant life, everything that has life, God has given into the hand of mankind.

Every day reminds us how terribly we fail this responsibility. One day God will call humanity to account for its stewardship of Planet Earth. Even this day all of us share responsibility for the ecology and environment around us.

Sin has not taken from mankind dominion over life. For sure, yielding to Satan reduces the ability to manage the resources God has given. Selfishness and greed distort the plenty of nature into poverty and hunger. But, nonetheless, the world belongs to humanity, and we must care for it.

God has made the world not just for this generation but for all life to the very end of time. Therefore we must monitor and measure our use of resources. Every being who sees stewardship as the only right relationship with the world is recreating the pattern of Eden.

The profligate plunders and destroys. The provident nurtures and preserves. To use wisely and well creates joy in this our Father's world.

"As we behold these works of nature we should let the mind be carried up higher, to nature's God" (Testimonies, *vol. 2, p. 589).*

DRAWN TO THE CROSS

So must the Son of man be lifted up: that whosoever believeth in him should not perish, but have eternal life. John 3:14, 15.

In the New Orleans Superdome, 30,000 Adventists collectively held their breath as the tally for the 1000 Days of Reaping mounted higher and higher. As I mentally added figures given by the presidents of the world divisions I wondered, *Have we reached out so that "whosoever believeth in him . . . should . . . have eternal life"? Had we done enough? Could we ever do enough? Was this text on the other side of a coin reading "Preach the gospel to every creature" (Mark 16:15)? Were we dealing in the true currency of the kingdom of God? Had the lifted-up Christ been the theme of our work? Was He lifted up so that all might see Him and come to Him?*

To walk the streets of your community and feel the need that emanates from houses and apartments, to think of the "every creature" that your neighborhood alone represents, puts you up against what seems an impossible mission. Yet here is the promise: The lifted-up Lamb of God will open the way for "whosoever" to believe and live.

John's record of Jesus' teaching makes it clear where our responsibility lies. "I have chosen you, . . . that ye should go and bring forth fruit." "The branch cannot bear fruit of itself, except it abide in the vine" (John 15:16, 4).

In this figurative language Jesus asks us to join Him in sharing the gospel with the world. In Him we too are lifted up before the world. In Him we share the redemptive process.

Jesus spoke of His lifting up on three occasions. Each time it stood over against human need. The cross would answer that need.

In the lives that come to the cross to find salvation, God beholds the true glory of the cross. Because the Son of man saves through His sacrifice, God's glory shines ever brighter.

The hands of infamy and injustice that lifted our Lord upon Golgotha's tree never knew the power they were unleashing into the world. But we know; we understand. Christ has drawn us to the cross. Today, pray that you may abide in Him. Let Him provide you with sustenance so that the weak shoot that represents your faith may grow into a branch bearing much fruit.

"While logic may fail to move, and argument be powerless to convince, the love of Christ, revealed in personal ministry, may soften the stony heart, so that the seed of truth can take root" (Christ's Object Lessons, p. 57).

GLORY IN THE CROSS

God forbid that I should glory, save in the cross of our Lord Jesus Christ, by whom the world is crucified unto me, and I unto the world. Gal. 6:14.

A common invitation begins this way: "Let me pick you up in the morning, you must see . . ." The "must sees" of the world include just about everything that mankind can conceive or that God has put in place. A water fountain in Medellín, Colombia; the Taj Mahal; Impressionist paintings at the Louvre; the midnight sun; the crown jewels of England; the Opera House in Sydney. Some of them, such as the Statue of Liberty or a Dutch windmill, achieve the fame of a kind of national logo.

For the Christian, the most notable object ever constructed by human hands hung the Saviour between earth and sky. Not that we worship two planks of wood, but there our Lord died, and it forever calls us to consider God's saving action.

Paul's opponents gloried in circumcision. They claimed the right to inherit the promises made to Abraham. To lack this sign was paramount to being cut off from the seed of Israel.

What did Paul mean when he gloried in the cross of Christ? The cross is everything that righteousness by works is not. The cross totally excludes anything you can do to find salvation. Only God could make the cross of Christ the glorious route to life. Man could make nothing of the cross, but God made everything of it.

The world crucified Jesus, but God made the cross His glory. In the cross the world loses its hold on those who walk by the Spirit. Because of the cross the world dies for the justified.

Righteousness by works counts on what man can add to what God has done. God cannot work that way. But the cross has only God as its authority. To glory in it means to trust totally in what God is doing through what Jesus did on the cross.

But that is not all. The cross affirms God's saving grace and makes the world dead to those who say yes to what God is doing. When we know this, the plight of those whom the world still controls calls us to the cross to give ourselves, as He did, for that world.

Then boast about, exult over, glory in, the cross of Jesus Christ. Take a journey every day to this "must see" of salvation.

"Those who would put their trust in Christ should begin to study the beauties of the cross now" (Testimonies, *vol. 4, p. 493).*

WHO WILL DISCERN THE GLORY OF THE CROSS?

Now when the centurion saw what was done, he glorified God, saying, Certainly this was a righteous man. Luke 23:47.

Two brothers listened to their father's orders for the day. Making the farm productive needed careful management. Every day the list of things to do stretched longer than the hours provided.

"No problem with that, Father. I'll get right on with it," said the older of the two.

"Wish I could help you Dad, but I really have too many other jobs I want to do," said the younger.

By the end of the day the younger had changed his mind and had finished all the father asked. The older brother had done nothing with his list.

At the cross the world divides. The people who had thought to make Jesus their coming king looked and looked again. They could not believe how quickly things had gone wrong. Finally they turned from the cross, mourning their loss.

The rulers derided Jesus, asking mocking questions about how the Chosen of God could find Himself crucified. The soldiers took up the jeering, scoffing at the title "King of the Jews." One thief joined the rulers and the soldiers in their taunt "If you are the Christ, save yourself and us."

The second thief saw the cross as salvation. Even as the others mocked, he asked for eternal life.

The Gentile centurion would not join his soldiers in their insults. He found glory in the cross.

With his picture of typical reactions to the Crucifixion, Luke shows how the cross judges those who behold it. Of all those who watched Jesus die, one saw it as the road to glory for him. A second gave glory to God for what he had seen.

The Gentile had heard Jesus ask forgiveness for His tormentors. He had heard the assurance of life to the thief. He listened while Jesus talked to His Father. That was enough. He did not need the knowledge of Scripture that had proved so useless to the rulers.

The Man of the cross asked for his trust. From those who had no knowledge of God's way, one found life, while those who should have known better spurned the moment of truth.

"The followers of Christ and the servants of Satan cannot harmonize. The offense of the cross has not ceased" (The Great Controversy, *p. 507).*

HOW THE FOOLISH BECOME WISE

For the preaching of the cross is to them that perish foolishness; but unto us which are saved it is the power of God. 1 Cor. 1:18.

Paul knew what he was talking about. His mission to Corinth came directly after the visit to Athens. In the intellectual capital of the world he had shown his learning.

His parents had given him a remarkably broad education. At times he used Greek fluently. Probably he could switch to Latin when needed. His Hebrew flowed so sweetly that crowds stopped their rioting when he spoke.

His education included a detailed knowledge of the Old Testament and its methods of interpretation. He understood the culture of his people. At Athens he showed another side of his erudition. He quoted Greek poetry. He interacted with considerable skill with the two major schools of philosophy, the Stoics and the Epicureans.

Ellen White records how Paul's preaching in Athens disappointed and discouraged him. He arrived in Corinth wondering if the gospel would work among the sophisticated pagans of that city. If his skills had not brought the expected results in Athens, how would the gospel fare in Corinth, famed for its licentiousness and wealth?

Paul did not throw away his education. How could he? He still remained a great linguist, theologian, and scholar. But in Corinth he switched strategies. In Athens the way to the cross developed out of his learning. In Corinth the cross came first, and he devoted his skills to the glory of the cross.

We know how well it worked. Corinth produced the first Christian community whose base was almost totally pagan, with little support from converted Jews or Gentile adherents to Judaism.

At times we think it wise to approach the secular world from its own thought system and gently lead it to consider Christ. Some results came in Athens, despite Paul's second thoughts on his methods. However, witness that fails to confront the sinner with the cross simply isn't Christian.

Once we confront the cross, it enters our experience. We go past it faced with decision. In retrospect the cross will become either foolishness or power. That possibility meets the Christian every day as he considers the call of God to obedience and holy living.

"Let us educate our souls to be hopeful and to abide in the light shining from the cross of Calvary" (The Ministry of Healing, p. 253).

RESCUED FROM EVIL POWERS

Who hath delivered us from the power of darkness, and hath translated us into the kingdom of his dear Son. Col. 1:13.

Those who study primitive societies sometimes deplore the coming of civilization. They imply that the people of these cultures would live in happiness if other, more advanced peoples would cage them off from development.

Without doubt, primitive social structure has its charm. No one would question how contact with the sophisticated disrupts and destroys patterns of behavior.

What role should Christian missions play? Those who work closest to pagan societies tell of the terrors that fill day and night. Many pagans live in fear of each other. One society in Papua New Guinea teaches its young men to shun women. For a woman to cross their path means disaster. They live in single-gender clubhouses and mix with the opposite sex only under carefully prescribed conditions.

Walking with Kukukuku tribespeople in their mountainous homeland, I learned that sticks and stones hide evil spirits. Each journey risks devil possession or the sorcerer's witchery.

In a moment of rare privilege, I participated in the very first baptism of the Kukukuku people. They had come direct from paganism to Adventist Christianity. No other denomination had contacted them. Communicating through translators, I learned how they felt about Jesus. He had rescued them from a world of frights and fears. The powers of darkness no longer held them in their power. They lived free in the kingdom of the Son.

Could similar terrors kidnap the sophisticates of western society? Does the devil hold millions of hostages with machine pistols of suspicion and ignorance? The answer has to be yes. The world sits with its back to the wall lest something dark or strange assail it unawares.

Many pay ransom to the occult and mystic, looking for freedom from the horrors that rise in lost souls.

All around us people are accepting strange and inadequate answers to the power of sin. To the glory of God He offers rescue for pagan or philosopher, the simple or the sophisticate. That rescue comes from the victory of the cross.

"Our only safety is to lie low at the foot of the cross, be little in our own eyes, and trust in God" (Testimonies, *vol. 4, p. 608*).

MISSION AND THE CROSS

For we are unto God a sweet savour of Christ, in them that are saved, and in them that perish. 2 Cor. 2:15.

When the Saviour was crushed on the cross, the world filled with the perfume of salvation. Those who trace the incense of sacrifice to its source will find life.

In Saint Albans, England, the town council has planted a garden for the blind. They have made it a bouquet of fragrant flowers and shrubs. Blossoms drift their aromas upward. Leaves wait to release their scented oils as hands reach out to crush them.

When cruel hands thrust the cross into the rocks of Golgotha, they planted a life-giving tree. "He was wounded for our transgressions, he was bruised for our iniquities: the chastisement of our peace was upon him; and with his stripes we are healed" (Isa. 53:5).

The bruising of the Suffering Servant infuses and heals. The repenting sinner breathes the oxygen of eternal life.

When a jumbo jet drifts me down toward one of the world's great cities, I often remind myself that the city lies under a foul blanket of pollution. I ask myself, How will I ever breathe down there? How can life exist in such a stench?

Viewed from eternity, sin has spread its fetid miasma over Planet Earth. The sin factories of the cities pollute the atmosphere. Media machines exhaust their deadly gases into every home. Souls gasp for breath. Can anyone find life when evil pervades all?

There is breathing space at the cross. When Jesus died, the earth filled with darkness; but when He arose, light flooded out from the grave. His sin-free sacrifice drove back the pollution of sin. No trace of evil taints the zephyrs of grace that spring from His death.

In the imagery of Paul, the pollution-free zone grows wider as more and more breathe life from the Saviour. Because we are Christ's and He has given us His righteousness, the pure air of grace flows from us. In such an atmosphere our homes will thrive. With this sweet incense our churches will fill.

The greatest glory of the cross is the life that has breathed its air and carries its atmosphere with it into the world that is dying for want of the breath of life.

"All incense from earthly tabernacles must be moist with the cleansing drops of the blood of Christ" (Selected Messages, *book 1, p. 344*).

HE CARRIES THE SCARS OF SLAUGHTER

And I beheld, and, lo, in the midst of the throne and of the four beasts, and in the midst of the elders, stood a Lamb as it had been slain. Rev. 5:6.

Shaking thousands of hands in a lifetime of ministry gives insights into people's professions and interests. In working-class Poland thick muscular hands reach out. In Silicon Valley the delicate fingers of computer wizardry offer themselves. A mother's lifetime of work shows in bent and gnarled joints. A child's timidity puts out its tentative fingers. A teenager's disinterest flicks past with scarcely a touch.

Someone has said, "Show me your hands, and I will show you your life." Old hands carry the history of the body written on them. They show its triumphs, defeats, and scars.

Jesus took carpenter's hands to the cross; they could shape and fashion. He took a physician's hands; they knew how to heal and save. He took a teacher's hands; they had trained and directed. He took a Son's hands; they obeyed and kept the Father's will.

Nails pierced and wounded those hands. When the Resurrection gave life to our Lord, His hands became sources of infinite power. But they are forever scarred.

John's vision puts Christ at the very center of divine authority and power. Around stand the ministers of God's might. Thus the figurative language of the Apocalypse links together the wounding at Calvary with the throne of power. Because of the cross, Jesus has power. His hands are the instruments of that power.

But all is not vision and symbolism and mystery. John's vision invites you to think of your own need of help. Angels, elders, and living creatures make strange reading but practical sense. The hands that went to the cross now work for those who cry out for help. Jesus can point His heavenly ministers this way or that to send assistance.

The scarred Lamb, with His court, shows the glory of the cross. In this vision God tells us how much the sacrifice means to the carrying out of His plan. It also shows us where we must go for strength and healing. The practical hands of His ministry, which did so much for the people of Palestine, wait to serve us in our need today.

"Expressing our gratitude for His great love, and our willingness to trust everything to the hand that was nailed to the cross for us" (Testimonies, *vol. 4, p. 462).*

JESUS IS OUR TEMPLE

Jesus answered and said unto them, Destroy this temple, and in three days I will raise it up. John 2:19.

Jerusalem knelt at the foot of the Temple. The lesser buildings of the city paid homage to its grandeur. From time to time Israel reminded itself that this structure did not equal Solomon's Temple. Yet, though they despised Herod as an Edomite converted to Judaism, they did not regret what he had done for their house of worship.

On one occasion Herod had donated a golden cluster of grapes for the holy place. Josephus states that it stood taller than a man and was of solid gold. Later, rampaging Roman soldiers would tear the place apart in their search for its treasures.

Daniel had written of the abomination that would threaten the function of the Temple. Now came Jesus threatening its existence. The Jews hounded Him all His life for this threat. The disciples would inherit the accusation.

But Jesus used this provocative statement to direct His hearers forward to the Resurrection. "He spake of the temple of his body" (John 2:21). He knew that the Temple in Jerusalem had no further value. What it had signified He would now fulfill. The hope now fixed in ceremony and sacrifice He would gather totally into Himself.

The Temple had raised false hope in Israel. It led the people to think that the fulfillment of the prophecies must accommodate the Temple. While they despised the Gentiles who worshiped man-made objects, they came very close to Temple worship themselves.

If Jesus is our temple, how do we worship? When the Resurrection gave to the Lord the body He now has, He took to Himself all the functions of the Temple.

Jesus is sacrifice. The Lamb slain from the foundation of the world offered Himself once for all. The cross broke His body for us.

Jesus is veil. Through His body we approach the throne of God.

Jesus is atonement. His blood removes the guilt of sin. Over His sacrifice we confess our sins and claim cleansing.

Jesus is high priest. With Him we enter the courtroom of heaven. He offers His body as atonement for our sins. His blood sets us apart as His people. Thus the Resurrection gives birth to hope and then sustains it.

"All who are one with Christ through faith in Him gain an experience which is life unto eternal life" (Selected Messages, *book 1, p. 302).*

SALVATION HAS A SHORT HISTORY

And unto the angel of the church in Smyrna write; These things saith the first and the last, which was dead, and is alive. Rev. 2:8.

Political coups come swift and sudden. A flourish of weapons, a count of who controls whom, and the former leader may just as well take the next plane out. Pity Bolivia, which has counted more coups than years of independence!

During one of my stays in Ghana, the military moved with speed to topple the civilian government. A rumble of tanks, a crackle or two of gunfire, and that was that.

God's coup against Satan lasted just three days. Though the planning had begun with time itself, the execution of the plan had the swiftness of a well-planned military takeover.

Satan's topple from power came at the very moment when all appeared well for him. He had plotted cunningly. Even Christ's disciples had forsaken Him and fled. Political and religious leaders performed on cue. Not even Pilate, convinced of Jesus' innocence, could hold off His execution. With Jesus in the grave, the devil had reason to think that he had achieved victory at last.

But all had not gone just as he might have wished. The weight of sin had not turned Jesus from the agreed plan. Even on the cross, Jesus had offered Paradise to the dying thief. In one swift blow the veil of the Temple was rent, showing that God had marked the moment of Christ's death.

Once before, Satan had argued over the body of Moses, one of God's saints. Only the rebuke of the Lord Himself had released Moses. Now he claimed the right to keep Jesus in the tomb. If Jesus had died for sin and sinners, then He must continue to pay the price.

But death cannot hold the sinless. Jesus rose as He had died, the Innocent One. The battle ended in victory for Christ. On Friday the death of Christ, the first salvation act on that memorable weekend, set in place a door of hope for humanity. On Sunday the second act, the Resurrection, flung that door open.

The righteousness we receive from Christ turns hope into reality. In His sinlessness He led the way out of death. In His sinlessness we will follow on to everlasting life.

"Christ became one with humanity, that humanity might become one in spirit and life with Him" (Selected Messages, *book 1,* p. 302).

EVIDENCE ENOUGH TO CONVINCE

Whom God hath raised up, having loosed the pains of death; because it was not possible that he should be holden of it. Acts 2:24.

Have you ever wondered why Peter didn't march the Pentecost crowds out of the city to the garden tomb and challenge, "There you are. See? It is empty. You tell us where the body of Jesus is"?

Nothing will convince like seeing it for oneself, it is said. But wait a minute. Would an empty tomb have convinced that crowd? It might have helped some. Others would have fallen to arguing about what had happened to the body. Accusation and counteraccusation would have risen. Result? Confusion, not conviction.

Instead, the apostles offered three proofs of Jesus' resurrection:

1. "We have seen Him ourselves." Not even the rulers of the Jews could suborn 500 witnesses to the living Lord. Delusion may play tricks with a few, but not the widely dispersed and independently minded members of the Resurrection people.

2. "You can see how different we are." That is because Jesus has sent us the Holy Spirit from heaven itself. Pentecost cried for an explanation. One hundred twenty people calling for belief in Jesus in as many languages as were present at the feast—how did that happen? Had someone started a language school in Galilee?

By claiming Jesus as the giver of the Spirit, the apostles challenged the world to find another explanation. After all, the Old Testament had promised a Spirit event in the last days. It was more than coincidence that Pentecost followed hard on the Resurrection.

3. "The prophecies declare that Messiah would suffer and die, but that death would not hold Him." In the lineup of Scripture proofs, the apostles linked the Messianic psalms of David with the servant prophecies of Isaiah—a new and convincing approach.

Where did Peter and the others receive such insights? Doubtless from the Lord Himself as He taught and instructed them between His resurrection and ascension.

Convincing proofs indeed. Just as convincing today, if you are yourself convinced. Hope springs from the evidence. Jesus lives; therefore, all that the New Testament promises is true.

"He lives to make intercession for us. Grasp this hope, and it will hold the soul like a sure, tried anchor" (The Desire of Ages, p. 794).

RESURRECTION AND MISSION

Behold, I see the heavens opened, and the Son of man standing on the right hand of God. Acts 7:56.

In the late 1970s Adventist missionary outreach claimed two new prizes. The nations of Gambia and Benin, in West Africa, received their first missionaries, properties were acquired, evangelism begun, companies organized.

For Claude Lombart, to be first in Cotonou, the capital of Benin, and set about the task of establishing the work—what a privilege! The Spirit used him to find a meeting place, ferret out a few migrant Adventists, encourage their faith, and run a crusade. Events tumbled over each other as tentative approaches solidified into solid achievements.

No New Testament chapter says more about the mission of the church than Stephen's sermon. For him, Cotonou would have seemed logical and necessary as the church meets its Master's commission.

Step by step, Stephen outlined a biblical basis for reaching out to the ends of the world:

1. God does not restrict Himself to one geographical location. He appeared to Abraham in Mesopotamia, Joseph in Egypt, Moses in the wilderness of Sinai. Draw the conclusion, then: God will sustain His church wherever it goes with the gospel. Each new center can be as much a focal point for God's power as Jerusalem itself.

2. The glory of God is not the great institutions in Jerusalem but the witnesses who carry out His commission.

3. Faith now focuses on the Son of man at the right hand of God. His resurrection has moved hope from earth to heaven. Power will go from Him to any and every place where the faithful give their witness.

Stephen's theology of mission makes good sense today. Where we live, God will sustain. The solitary witness, who has no one to stand alongside, will remember Joseph in Egypt and expect the Son to sustain. However marvelous and effective the institutions of the church may be, only its people truly give glory to God.

Such a vision could not be possible without the Resurrection. Because Jesus lives, power will accompany even your witness.

"The disciples were to begin their work where they were. . . . God often uses the simplest means to accomplish the greatest results" (The Desire of Ages, p. 822).

HOW JESUS MAKES YOU RIGHT WITH GOD

Believe on him that raised up Jesus our Lord from the dead; who was delivered for our offences, and was raised again for our justification. Rom. 4:24, 25.

In the world before the Flood, Ellen White says, precious jewels gleamed in the soil like crystal flowers. Paul has filled Romans with jewels of truth. Every text has its diamond, its ruby, its pearl.

Paul draws on one figure of speech after another to help us understand how Jesus gives us righteousness. Some words he uses interchangeably with others. Some he uses for shades of difference.

What he says about the Resurrection proclaims the supreme hope of the New Testament. Because Jesus lives and reigns with God, He will justify, or acquit, the sinner.

The cross removes the offense of our sin. We therefore come before God without guilt. But what of our standing with God? How can Jesus make us right before God? This He does through the Resurrection. Because Jesus lives, we may also live, not just now but eternally. Jesus stands in our place and claims His righteousness on our behalf.

The resurrection of Jesus is a reality. God has said yes to you in Jesus Christ. When you put your trust in Jesus, you say yes to God's saving work. Justification expresses the coming together of these two yeses—God's and yours.

Paul has several other ways of talking about how God saves you, but justification is one of his key ideas. Because it has a legal background, it implies that the human race has lost legal right to life. Sin passes the sentence of death on all. Sin offends the Ten Commandments. God restores our legal right to life through Jesus Christ.

But we must not push any figure of speech too far. For example, we cannot say, "Once acquitted, always acquitted." Nor can we say, "Once righteous, always righteous." Because we go on sinning, God continues His saving work. Not so that we may sin and live, but so that we may live for Him and show His righteousness to the world.

The hope of the Resurrection provides the assurance of life. If God can bring Christ to life, He can provide power so that we may both live in Him and for Him.

"Christ is sitting for His portrait in every disciple. Every one God has predestinated to be 'conformed to the image of his Son' " (The Desire of Ages, *p. 827*).

RAISED WITH JESUS

Buried with him in baptism, wherein also ye are risen with him through the faith of the operation of God, who hath raised him from the dead. Col. 2:12.

A life that serves its own interests hates the death that awaits it in the realm of faith. Only with Christ's power can self die. The will may say yes to obedience and holiness, but without Jesus, there will be no death to sin.

To die to sin is one thing; to live in Christ, another. Again, the impossible takes on reality as we rise to the life of faith accompanied yet again by Jesus. Only in Him can we live victoriously.

The working of the plan of God raised Jesus to life, Paul says. God, with the Son in death as well as in life, brought Him out from the tomb. Jesus, who brought death to sin, now brings us out from the tomb where sin lies buried and raises us to the new life of faith.

All is of God and nought of self. That does not mean that the self is powerless or has no will to do right. The will to do right draws on the power of the indwelling of Christ to prompt right action and to ensure victory.

The new life of faith exists only in union with Christ. It cannot survive if we turn again to the dominion of sin. The greatest hope that comes from the resurrection of Christ is not the physical resurrection that will come to the faithful at the last day. The hope that faith holds in sight unites with Christ. Through Him it perceives and obeys His will.

When a Pharaoh died, a whole retinue of servants was buried with him. In the afterlife they would care for their lord.

The Chinese refined the idea by using clay models of servants and soldiers to line graves of the great. A few years ago Chinese archaeologists unearthed a whole army of horsemen. That age believed that after death the statues would come to life and serve their master.

While Paul does not have this in mind as he talks of burial and resurrection of the believer, it does illustrate his teaching. In baptism, self dies under sin's rule. Christ goes with him to that death. As a new creature, he rises from baptism. Jesus rises with him to provide grace and strengthen faith.

"All who consecrate soul, body, and spirit to God will be constantly receiving a new endowment of physical and mental power" (The Desire of Ages, *p. 827).*

GOD'S SURE MERCIES

He raised him up from the dead, now no more to return to corruption, he said on this wise, I will give you the sure mercies of David. Acts 13:34.

In one of those turnarounds in which our loving God delights, David offered to build the Lord a house, but the Lord promised to build the house of David. God has a greater interest in people than in temples, for which we should thank Him.

The logic of a temple encouraged David to plan for it. Israel had secure boundaries. No longer need the people move the tabernacle to the best-defended part of the nation. In Jerusalem such a structure might arise that would outshine the temples of the heathen and show the nation's gratitude for God's goodness.

God said, Why do I need a house? Since Israel left Egypt I have walked in a tent. Not once have I asked for a house. God reminded David how He had taken him from following the sheep, had gone with him wherever he went, had made his name great. The hidden question was Did David want to tie God down? Would such a house answer Israel's needs tomorrow and a thousand years thence?

In one of the happiest lessons of the Bible, God now gave David not what he asked for, but what he and the people really needed: a promise that would secure them to the Lord for all time.

God's covenant with David established the throne of David forever. Far more important to have the promises of God working for you than to offer God human promises!

When the prophets remembered the covenant, they saw it as God providing the people's needs. All who thirst, all who hunger, might come and receive from God (Isa. 55:1). To those who hear the voice of God and obey will come the sure mercies of David.

When Paul preached his great sermon of Acts 13, he took his Jewish hearers away from Temple, land, and law to Jesus, in whom God was affirming the covenant He had made to David. He took his Gentile hearers to God's demand for trust in His Son. With that trust the promise made to David would belong to the new Israel, Gentile and Jew alike.

In the resurrection of Christ the Father assured the true Israel that the King of love would always reign.

"Nothing will so build up the Redeemer's kingdom as will the love of Christ manifested by the members of the church" (Testimonies, *vol. 5, p. 168).*

131

COURAGE COMES FROM HOPE

Be of good courage, and he shall strengthen your heart, all ye that hope in the Lord. Ps. 31:24.

The land had not yet yielded to law and order. Lions and bears hunted in the uplands. Vipers and asps slithered in the wilderness. Brigands and raiding Philistines terrorized the isolated and the traveler.

In this land the poet called the Lord fortress and rock. He opened space for David. His enemies did not tie him hand and foot; the Lord gave him a large room.

Some had even forgotten David lived. If they knew, they sent assassins after him. Yet in that untamed and violent land, the future that lurched toward him, uncertain and unfriendly, had God watching it.

Today you will walk in your own land. Human predators seek the moment to loot your mind and your faith. Media manipulators slide past with fingers clutching for your will. The robbers of the right life and the marauders of the spirit shoulder weapons against the lonely and the uncommitted.

In this land, call God your safe house and strong room. Let Him open safe space around you. Let Him give you the wide room of His grace and freedom.

Can we truly identify with the poet of 1000 B.C.? He spoke courage for those who feared as Saul sent soldiers after the shepherd prince. His call to hope sounded to those who hid their grain at harvest and guarded their sheep and cattle from raiders.

For 3,000 years people who know God have read Psalm 31 and said, "Yes, that is the way it is with me. Thus God has dealt in my life. What David knew, I know."

Would a modern David sing to the Lord as his traffic controller, his bank? Would he call Him programmer? modem? security fence?

In a land where violence to the mind ambushes the unwary, and forces outside your control threaten the future for which you hoped, the Lord says again and again, "Be of good courage."

Stress and tension, discouragement and despair, speak from the past. But so do the confidence and strength of a thousand deliverances.

"Cease to talk discouragement. Take hold of the arm of Infinite Power" (Testimonies, *vol. 6, p. 474*).

WHEN NOT TO GIVE UP

And let us not be weary in well doing: for in due season we shall reap, if we faint not. Gal. 6:9.

The women flex from the waist, legs straight, bodies supple. The rice paddies stretch endlessly around the contours of the valley. Feet inch forward through the water while fingers thrust rice seedlings into the fertile mud.

In the eye of the visitor the task looks totally boring, the least to be desired of a thousand professions. But step a little closer and listen. The planters are singing in the paddies. If you wait, the song will turn to chatter and laughter. Why? The seasons have rolled again. The singers in the fields already see the harvest coming. They create the cycle of life itself in the rhythm of their planting.

In the word picture of Paul he has already told of the danger of planting tares rather than corn. He has spoken of the certain harvest that follows any planting, and how that will bring joy or sorrow. He wants us to think of judgment and reward. He wants us to understand that sometimes the judgment against us is self-imposed. The harvest of joy is the gift of the Spirit to the life that trusts Him.

But that is not all. The life of faith has many days ahead of it. In the moment of conversion we sense the Spirit very near. At a time of crisis, faith urges us to total trust, simply because we do not see any other solution except God's.

At this point, this trust is not Paul's concern. He has seen a life give up on good deeds, tire of the right and of moral action. He has known those who would fasten on their own actions as a source of hope rather than on the actions of the Spirit.

He looks at the church and notes those who sow to the Spirit in spurts and those who do it consistently day after day. From the paddy fields of faith he hears the steady sowers' song rising toward God.

The hope that continually stretches out its hand from the future urges us to continue in faith. It will place in the contours of time opportunities for good, and there we will plant, and plant again. This is the true response of our faith.

"Faith and activity will impart assurance and satisfaction that will increase day by day" (Prophets and Kings, *p. 164*).

"ARE YOU COMING WITH ME, JESUS?"

Looking unto Jesus the author and finisher of our faith; who for the joy that was set before him endured the cross, despising the shame. Heb. 12:2.

Time had separated us for 34 years. The blue eyes still twinkled with intelligence and good humor. His happiness about life showed as we chatted.

In the distant past I had been pastor and he a bank manager attending evangelistic meetings. He faced the loss of his position as he related to the claims of Jesus Christ. One night we talked it over. As a young pastor I had offered him Jesus and the Word of God.

"Christ will go with you if you trust Him. He has promised never to leave or forsake you. When you feel discouraged, look around; Jesus will be there beside you."

Nothing had come easy after his decision. Demoted to a clerk, salary slashed, wife angry at his decision, children unsure about what it all meant. But his faith? As strong and sure as that evening when he first decided to depart into the future with Christ.

Jogging, running, walking, stumbling—the Christian life has many gaits. No one has ever suggested that running with Jesus would be easy. But the companionship is great. Jesus fires the starter's gun, paces Himself beside you all the way, cheers you at the finishing line. He is the Christian's very own support system—Bread of Life, Water of Life, Light of the world, Balm of Gilead. Whatever you need, He has a supply.

Hebrews lists names of those who started and finished with Jesus. Faith sustained them from the moment they committed themselves to God's will. Abraham's cross-country marathon stressed him to the limit. He tripped. He fell. But he never doubted the Friend running with him.

No one handed Jesus a laurel wreath as He finished His course. Instead, the soldiers forced a crown of thorns on Him. Not for Him the winner's embrace, but the arms of a cross. The referees of that day disqualified Him. Yet He won the race, and so bought victory out of defeat.

Jesus runs with you. He had His own journey through this world. He knows, far better than any of us, all that can discourage and go wrong. What He has begun in your life, He will complete—if you run with Him all the way.

"Have faith in God. He knows your need. He has all power" (Prophets and Kings, *pp. 164, 165*).

BECAUSE IT WILL BE SO BEAUTIFUL

Being confident of this very thing, that he which hath begun a good work in you will perform it until the day of Jesus Christ. Phil. 1:6.

Black miners plucked it from the diamond pipes of the Transvaal. From the moment of its discovery, experts destined it for the diamond studios of Amsterdam.

In the distant past, fierce heat and enormous pressure grew this million-dollar crystal. Slight impurities gave this diamond a subtle tinting, making it the largest "black" diamond ever discovered.

In Holland three years were needed to cut and polish the precious stone. What formed thousands of years ago, and now received exquisite attention, went on the market in June of 1986, called Black Rembrandt. The weight of this child of God and man was 42.27 carats.

After all the care and effort, the jewel gleams with a muted yet brilliant ambience. Its depths catch the slightest light and bounce it toward the eye with a loveliness that echoes the Song of Solomon: "I am black, but comely, O ye daughters of Jerusalem" (S. of Sol. 1:5); "A garden inclosed is my sister, my spouse; a spring shut up, a fountain sealed" (S. of Sol. 4:12).

Man snatches a lustrous carbon crystal from the soil and makes of it a king's ransom. God, the patient miner in the soiled earth, pays a King's ransom to bring to light and perfection just one sinning soul.

In the day when He comes to judge the earth, He will come to make up His jewels (Mal. 3:17). Through the purity of His Son's righteousness, the Father sees all who trust in Him as jewels already, fit for the crown of glory. But His treasure-house of jewels will show how patiently and tenderly He has fashioned and refined.

Two things to remember about God's persistence with us: First, while God does all of the saving, that does not mean that we are left with nothing to do. Second, while we have clear duties to do for God and our neighbor, not one thing we do will qualify us for God's treasure chest.

Diamond cutters worked years on that gem from Africa. God persists with the character of you, His redeemed child. Diamond or child of God—patience and persistence have the same motive: because it will be so beautiful.

"It is our lifework to be reaching forward to the perfection of Christian character. . . . The efforts begun upon earth will continue through eternity" (Testimonies, *vol. 4, p. 520*).

MIRACLES FOR OTHERS, BUT NOT FOR MYSELF

And he said unto me, My grace is sufficient for thee: for my strength is made perfect in weakness. Most gladly therefore will I rather glory in my infirmities, that the power of Christ may rest upon me. 2 Cor. 12:9.

Consider Paul, the miracle worker. His prayers shook the Philippian jail and saved himself and the jailer. He cast out demons and healed the sick. Euroclydon, a strong northeastern wind, drove his ship toward certain disaster, but Paul's prayers protected all on board.

Miracles for others but not for myself, Paul might have thought. Three times he asked the Lord for freedom from his infirmity. Three times God said no.

No miracle for the miracle worker! Did it handicap him? He thought so. He saw himself as more efficient, more effective, if freed from this hindrance. But what did God think? He based Paul's mighty witness on his need to depend on Him.

Edward Shiflett thanks his wooden leg for his life. In May 1986, storms swamped his boat in the Gulf of Mexico. He managed to grab a flotation pillow. Coast guards rescued him two days later. They found him floating face down on the pillow, good leg hooked over his artificial limb.

He had lost his leg as a result of a car accident some years before. He had thought his artificial limb a nuisance. "I resented losing my leg, but today I can thank my balsa buoy for my life."

Paul reflected on God's negative answer. He looked for God's purpose in it. He concluded that what might have discouraged him as a "thorn in the flesh" had allowed God to give him greater strength. What had seemed a crippling hindrance God turned to His good.

While on earth, Jesus found the greatest response among those whom the rulers despised. The poor, the outcast, and the weak received Him gladly. In their weakness they saw no power in themselves and relied wholly on Jesus' power. God taught Paul the same lesson.

When you see miracles for others but none for yourself, remember Paul. "Therefore I take pleasure in infirmities, in reproaches, in necessities, in persecutions, in distresses for Christ's sake: for when I am weak, then am I strong" (2 Cor. 12:10).

"Christ connects man in his weakness and helplessness with the source of infinite power" (Patriarchs and Prophets, *p. 184*).

HAVE YOU SEEN GOD'S GOODNESS LATELY?

I had fainted, unless I had believed to see the goodness of the Lord in the land of the living. Ps. 27:13.

The writers of lyric poetry use the scalpel of words to lay bare their souls. They let you see yourself in what they experience. They capture the common feelings of humanity and magnify them, drawing you into sharing hunger, fear, awe, beauty, love.

David, perhaps the greatest lyricist ever, wrote much of his poetry while fleeing from Saul or hiding from Philistine marauders. Some psalms came from bitter regrets for his sins and mistakes. Others soared as glad paeans of victory and worship.

Always his searching "I," "me," and "my" reach out to God. For every experience, he probes for the God link that will express his faith. No circumstance lies outside his faith or beyond the ken of God.

David's sensitive nature heightened his awareness of the enormity of sin and evil. He perceived how evil men affronted his Lord. God saw the evil and took account of it. God then moved to continue His name, His people, and His purposes among the nations. When David failed God it tore at his heart, and bitter remorse followed. When his armies won or he escaped ambush, a song would pour out his praise.

Things went wrong at times. Evil appeared to be the victor. Vicious persons had their day of boasting. David felt trapped by the marching forces of wickedness, and cried to God to remember him.

When Israel won he sought beautiful and intimate word pictures from nature and the pastoral society of his youth. His poetic self-analysis lets us see more of the real person behind the words than any other Bible writer.

With total optimism he looked to the future for God's good deeds. When one has slain the monstrous Goliath with one smooth stone, one may expect great things of one's God. Not for David the fainting away at the crunch of defeat. Not for him the luxury of despair. God had not given up on him, nor would he give up on God.

The malignant influence of discouragement never took hold in him. Like all true leaders, he faced forward with optimism. One time of divine presence and victory outdid a score of defeats.

"Only in the name of the mighty Conqueror can you gain the victory" (Testimonies, *vol. 4, p. 259*).

THE CALLING AND THE COMING

Faithful is he that calleth you, who also will do it. 1 Thess. 5:24.

Apparently, in Thessalonica the Christian church had begun to ask whether God could do as He had promised. They were asking:

1. Will God save those who die before Jesus returns?

2. Once we have put trust in Jesus for salvation, what kind of life should we live?

3. If God wants us holy when Jesus returns, will any be saved?

It took Paul two letters to straighten them out. It takes no more than 30 minutes to read the two books to the Thessalonians. Because of our belief in the soon return of Jesus, they are well worth reading.

Paul made clear the people-keeping power of God. He had not paid such a dear price for these people just to let them slip through His hands. Don't mourn for believers who die. God plans to bring them to life. He takes them to heaven at the same time as those who are still living at the return of Jesus.

If God has that kind of power, you should not worry about the power of God to keep the living believer faithful to Him. In Thessalonica, church members were heading down two wrong tracks. Who can live without sinning for any length of time? they asked. If Christ should not come soon, no one would be left with the purity of life to which God called them.

Others had taken a different tack. God had accepted them in Christ; should they therefore give much thought to how they lived? Christ would come and save them, whatever they did.

Paul's first letter to them gives clear answers. The immorality of the Gentiles must have no part in the Christian life. The calling God gave would produce a holy life. Also, God would preserve a people blameless at His coming.

God offers His solutions in Jesus Christ. God doesn't deny us forgiveness when we confess our sin and repent. In Christ He continues to hold out the robe of righteousness.

When we offer Him our wills, He gives us grace to respond to Him in obedience. He both calls us to holiness and provides holiness. But it is always and ever the work of our Saviour, for us and in us.

Every Christian must "remember that to gain the victory Christ must abide in him and he in Christ" (Testimonies, *vol. 5, p. 47).*

WHO BUT JESUS CAN WIN THE BATTLE?

For whatsoever is born of God overcometh the world: and this is the victory that overcometh the world, even our faith. 1 John 5:4.

Did John remember that day when Peter, James, and he came down the mountain with Jesus? What a night they had had! Glory on the mountaintop! A vision of Moses and Elijah! To see Jesus as truly the Son of God! He never forgot that day.

Of all the writers in the New Testament, John most fully portrays Jesus as the Son of the eternal Father. His Gospel and the book of Revelation give us the glory of Jesus. Glory in the past with the Father, in prospect while on this earth, and in the present at the Father's side.

The other disciples had waited at the base of the mountain. When the descending group reached them, a man stepped out of the crowd. He told the story of his son and his dumbness. The disciples, Jesus' agents, could do nothing about the spirit that had invaded the lad's mind.

What had the disciples lacked? Prayer and fasting, the works of a faithful generation, Jesus said.

In his Epistles John did not argue or persuade; he declared what experience had taught him. Through no other method could the born-again Christian defeat the world, he said, except through faith.

What did he mean by "the world"? He meant the forces within and without the follower of Jesus that prevent complete obedience to the commandments of God. He linked love with faith. Sometimes people stop to measure their love for God or for others. John had a simple formula. If you would know how much you love, then ask how well you obey.

Had those disciples at the foot of the mountain failed to obey? In their unconverted, self-centered natures they had sought to exercise power without reference to the One who gave it. Defeat routinely afflicts the one who relies on self.

John remembered the voice of God speaking to the Son on the mount. But he also remembered the voice of a son as he spoke his first words. He remembered the joy of the father as the two went their way home.

Out of his experience John speaks to us today. When we show faith, when we say yes to Christ's power and authority, then and only then comes the joy of victory.

"Obedience to God is sure to bring the victory" (Testimonies, *vol. 4, p. 27*).

WHO SHALL RULE OVER US?

I will not rule over you, nor shall my son; the Lord will rule over you. Judges 8:23, NEB.

No wonder Gideon inspires the modern Israeli general. With a tiny band of warriors, meticulously trained and disciplined, the ancient Hebrew captain defeated a huge army. The precision of the attack, the surprise factor, the excellent communications, would impress any military leader. The broken pitchers, the trumpets, and the great shout might seem poor weapons, but the tactics remain superb.

Behind this doughty fighting force lay another dimension. Gideon began by reformation at home. He dismantled his father's altar to Baal. He chopped down the sacred pole that stood beside the altar. His father called his son Jerubbaal. The issue over worship would have to be settled by Baal himself. If he could not defend himself against Gideon, then he wasn't much of a god. In his father's reaction we discern how false worship had taken over in the homes of ordinary people. Gideon's action put him squarely on the side of Jehovah and against idolatry.

The young captain-general defeats the hordes of Midianites with his valiant 300. Very little help comes from the rest of Israel. Fearing reprisals, two cities ravaged many times by the enemy refuse to give food to the little band.

But at the end of the battle, the Israelites rally to the side of Gideon. They clamor around him. "You be our ruler, you and your son and your grandson" (Judges 8:22, NEB).

Gideon rejects the offer. How could he be their king when God had worked out the victory? That would be false pretense.

Daily we face the same question: Who shall rule? Self demands to be king. Especially when we tot up some small victory. One victory over sin won through God's help and self wants the throne. Self looks ahead and says, "I did it once. I can do it again."

A Christian needs an excellent memory. He remembers that the Spirit led into past victories. He recalls the past defeats when self tried to wield the sword. The very moment when we think we might rule is the hour to declare the Lord king.

"Get them to look away from their poor, sinful selves to the Saviour, and the victory is won" (Testimonies, *vol. 6, p. 67*).

THE JOYFUL LAODICEAN

To him that overcometh will I grant to sit with me in my throne,
even as I also overcame, and am set down with my Father in his
throne. Rev. 3:21.

Anyone who knows even a little about Adventist religious thought
will see a contradiction in the title of this reading. Somewhat like
playing an Irish jig at a funeral, or the "Hallelujah Chorus" at a
graveside. After all, the True Witness describes Laodiceans as
"wretched, and miserable, and poor, and blind, and naked" (Rev. 3:
17).

The ancient city of Laodicea shared a part of Asia Minor with
Ephesus. Paul wrote a letter to Laodicea, no copies of which exist.
Like Ephesus, the city had wealth, and delighted in fine clothing.
Warm springs in the area attracted many who sought cures at these
waters.

Though the Firstborn had scarcely a good word for this church, He
did provide a way for joy to break through. Wherever God's word
comes to man, hope comes with it, and through hope joy may appear.
The devastating attack on the complacent church carries with it the
assumption that the church may correct its ways and turn to its Lord.

Members of the Laodicean church felt blessed by God. Their
doctrine bore the divine stamp of approval. The system of church
support provided an astounding array of institutions and services.
Personal prosperity gave the members an appearance of being
God-blessed. But their faith lacked commitment.

For this and all its other failings, the Lord who knocks gave
remedies. Forget prosperity and seek the gold of true faith. Despise
the fine clothes of conformity and put on the white raiment of My
righteousness. Brush away the mask of self-satisfaction and rub in the
eyesalve of the Spirit.

All this divine counsel fingerposts its way to the heart of twentieth-
century belief. The suburbs of Laodicea spread through the church,
turning commitment to complacency, sacrifice to self-interest, wholeness to hypocrisy.

Yet this church will also overcome. Those who know their desperate
need will open the door to Jesus. He will fellowship with them. He will
turn bewilderment and uncertainty to joy and fulfillment. Laodicea
needs its Lord. Let Him share your life today.

"Christ is the depositary of all graces. He says: 'Buy of me' "
(Testimonies, *vol. 4, p. 89).*

REJOICING WITH A PERFECT HEART

Then the people rejoiced, for that they offered willingly, because with perfect heart they offered willingly to the Lord: and David the king also rejoiced with great joy. 1 Chron. 29:9.

David watched as the people bearing gifts paraded past him. They represented a moment of great significance. Secure borders, defeated enemies, and growing prosperity brought the belief that God had fulfilled His ancient promise. Israel dwelt in the Promised Land. It flowed with the milk and honey of wise administration, internal peace, growing markets, respect among the petty kingdoms of the area.

The gold, the silver, and the wood stacked high in the king's treasury promised one final tribute to the God who had made all this possible. Solomon, David's son, would build a house for Jehovah.

David understood very well how such good times had come to the nomad tribes of Israel. "Thine, O Lord, is the greatness, and the power, and the glory, and the victory" (1 Chron. 29:11). The quantum jump from shepherd to monarch never failed to amaze and humble David. Would the people remember that what they saw happen to their ruler had also happened to them? God had done it all.

In this marvelous outpouring at the end of his reign, David and his people truly understood the source of all prosperity. The victories of Israel belonged to God. The wealth so freely given came from God.

True joy begins with a true relationship to God. In the centuries that followed, Israel and its kings left the way of true joy. The shouts of triumph and the choruses of praise gave way to mourning and lamentations. As the nation consorted with pagans and exalted their idols, times of will-o'-the-wisp, ephemeral joy came and went. But the joy of the perfect heart almost always escaped them.

In this condition Jesus found the nation a thousand years later. In the remarkable parallels of Scripture, the humble, devout, and blameless people of Luke's Gospel began the rejoicing that went with Jesus all His life.

Elisabeth, Zacharias, Mary, Joseph, Anna, Simeon, the shepherds—all of them God's own children—had that perfect heart through which God can do great things. A further two thousand years later, nothing has changed. True joy begins with true relationships.

"Thank God we are not dealing with impossibilities. We may claim sanctification. We may enjoy the favor of God" (Selected Messages, *book 2, p. 32).*

BOLDNESS, THE RESULT OF VICTORY

Preaching the kingdom of God, and teaching those things which concern the Lord Jesus Christ, with all confidence, no man forbidding him. Acts 28:31.

Was there any sign from the Lord? Ellen Harmon, James White, Joseph Bates, and the pitiful few around them asked that question again and again on October 23, 1844.

The bitter bile of disappointment had sent the thousands of yesterday scurrying into hiding, fearful and ashamed. The bold and the free of Miller's band had cowered and cringed in bewilderment.

But within hours God was comforting and reassuring the faithful remnant. Step by step He led them from dismay and near despair to hope and joy. History gives many examples of defeat as the father of victory. None amazes more than the creation of the third angel's movement out of the nothing of complete defeat.

As that small group saw Christ enter the Holy of Holies in the heavenly sanctuary to begin the closing phase of His mediatorial work, bewilderment turned to boldness, despair to joy, defeat to victory.

Christians remember that the world forced this pattern of defeat on their Lord and His followers at the very beginning. Herod, Pontius Pilate, the Gentiles, and the people of Israel conspired against "thy holy child Jesus" (Acts 4:27). The church has known many seeming defeats, but as its Lord rose from the defeat of death, so His church body renews itself and goes on with boldness.

Just a few years ago the government of Idi Amin banned the Seventh-day Adventist Church in Uganda. Every appeal failed. The church went on, but with reduced power and success. Amin came and went; so did Obote. And then God created His own surprise. Just as the rulers could not keep the apostles from their task, no more could the authorities in Uganda keep the church from theirs.

In Kampala the government found one of our Sabbath school teachers, Dr. Kisekka, and made him prime minister of the country.

Boldness breaks out whenever we remember how God is working for us. The early church saw God working deliberately on their behalf. The 1844 movement discerned the same God at work. When faith meets its greatest test, it produces its greatest witness. And that is true for everyone who perceives God's action in his favor.

"Christ dwelling in the soul is a wellspring of joy" (Christ's Object Lessons, *p. 162*).

THE JOY GOES ON FOREVER

And they sing the song of Moses the servant of God, and the song of the Lamb, saying, Great and marvellous are thy works, Lord God Almighty; just and true are thy ways, thou King of saints. Rev. 15:3.

In heaven God will have two songs for us to sing. Moses composed the first after the safe crossing of the Red Sea (Ex. 15:1-19). For centuries the Jews sang this song of victory at every Sabbath evening service.

At any synagogue service today you will hear the Shema, or creed, followed by two prayers. One of them refers to the song of Moses: "A new song did they that were delivered sing to Thy name by the seashore; together did they praise and own Thee King, and say, Jehovah shall reign, world without end! Blessed be the Lord who saveth Israel."

In the imagery of Revelation, the Red Sea gives way to the sea of glass. The song rises, not for the greatest victory in all Israel's history, but for the conquest of the apostate forces of evil. Like Israel, the saints had seemed hemmed in as Satan and the world stood against them. But God gave the victory, unlimited and eternal.

The second song celebrates the victory of the Lamb. Look carefully at this song. Not one single word boasts of human achievement. In this lyric outburst, every word concentrates on the great deeds of God.

Those who sing on and on in heaven have forgotten self. They remember only God and His goodness. Heaven and its wonders totally absorb the attention of the redeemed. In God's presence they see the whole scheme of God's action and the part they have played. God's purposes have always surrounded and directed them.

At certain national shrines burn eternal flames. There gather patriots and statesmen to honor the past and its defeats and victories. At one such shrine in Warsaw, Poland, at every hour around the clock a detachment of soldiers marches to the shrine. As the guard changes, even at the midnight hour, the nation affirms its history and expresses confidence in its destiny.

Thus with the Song of Moses and the Lamb. It comes to us from the future to tell us where true victory lies. It calls us to that future in which Christ's victory on our behalf will give us a song to sing forever.

"Let self be put out of sight. Christ alone is to be exalted" (Christ's Object Lessons, *p. 162).

VICTORY WON—CELEBRATION DELAYED

God having provided some better thing for us, that they without us should not be made perfect. Heb. 11:40.

The crowds pressed at the barriers long before dawn. These positions offered the best view, and no one could deny them this time of rejoicing. Later that day Charles, the prince of Wales, and his bride, Diana, would pass in their coach, going to and coming from Saint Paul's Cathedral.

The million or so who thronged the streets to see their future monarch were eager to give their tribute of love and affection. But the barriers held them back, and though they would have loved to touch and talk, they could do no more than shout and wave.

As the Bible looks to the final victory, it tells of the barriers death has erected. Only through faith can we feel the touch of the King's hand or hear His voice. Hebrews imagines the faithful of the ages pressing against those barriers, waiting the resurrection, when all will burst through together to the presence of God and the Beloved Son.

The crowds sang and chanted before the gates of Buckingham Palace, hoping for a glimpse of the royal couple. How the sound surged as they finally appeared! Such a celebration the people of Britain will wait many years to enjoy again.

In a parable, Jesus told of a farmer who needed help with the labor. Hour after hour he went to the marketplace and hired more workers. At the end of the day each received the same wage as the others. The parable puzzled those who listened. Where had fairness gone? If the farmer represented God, didn't He take any notice of time?

In God's plan the celebration and the rewards wait till the end. He does not dribble the redeemed, minute by minute, through the gates of glory. For all their faith and for all that God did through them, the faithful of the past wait the promise of the future. As one people we shall go through the gates of the resurrection to the victory parade of the ages. Not even the living will precede the resurrected.

But we do not have to wait till that day to begin the singing and the joy. The celebration of redemption rises from each heart that has seen its King and known His salvation.

"Even here Christians may have the joy of communion with Christ; they may have the light of His love, the perpetual comfort of His presence" (Steps to Christ, p. 125).

WORDS OF HOPE AND BEAUTY

*A word fitly spoken is like apples of gold in pictures of silver.
Prov. 25:11.*

After His baptism and the bout with the devil in the wilderness,
Jesus spent several Sabbaths visiting the synagogues in Galilee and
preaching in them. "A fame of him" went through the region. He was
"glorified of all."

In the synagogue at Nazareth, His hometown, folks heard Him
through. They "wondered at the gracious words" He spoke. Where had
He learned to speak like this? Not in the carpenter's shop down the
street! What could they conclude except that God was with Him?
Throughout Jesus' life His flow of language, His wit, His forceful
arguments, and His figures of speech crackled through the air with the
electric spark of life. He cut loose from the platitudes and clichés of
religion and spoke with freshness and vigor.

He virtually invented the parable. He constructed two-line verses in
Aramaic so that the people would remember what He said. He made
up catchy sayings and proverbs. No wonder the scribes, that age's
word wizards, both dwelt on every word He said and greatly feared the
power of His speech.

He said to the people, Here is a saying about the kingdom. Hold it
in your mind like you would hold in your hands an apple made of pure
gold. Treasure it. Give it the silver frame of memory.

In Jesus' teachings, words press on each other, urging the beauty of
salvation.

God wants us to take the Word of life seriously. He filled its pages
with words of hope and beauty. The wonderful words of life point the
finger of truth and say, This is what you are. They point again and say,
This is what God will give you. Yet again they urge, This is what I will
make of you.

The Word is *for* you, not *against* you. Its words are wonderful
words of life, not fear or death. When the dark shades of the negative
line its word pictures, they serve only to highlight the positive.

This, then, is the Bible: the word of life, the word fitly spoken,
beautiful and valuable, the golden apples of eternal life in the silver
frame of love and hope.

*"We should gather the jewels that come from [Christ], that, when
we speak, these jewels may drop from our lips"* (Testimonies, *vol.
6, p. 174).*

ABOLISH: WHAT THE CROSS CANCELS

Then cometh the end, when he shall have delivered up the kingdom to God, even the Father; when he shall have put down all rule and all authority and power. 1 Cor. 15:24.

During the first half of the nineteenth century, first in England and then in the United States, there began a movement to abolish the slave trade. Abolition drew support from all kinds of people.

In England the emancipation of all slaves came quicker than in America. But an anomaly developed. The English freed their relatively few slaves but continued to supply slaves to American slave markets!

Emancipate! England said. Abolish! the more perceptive countered. A slave could have his individual freedom, but thousands of others continued in bondage. In the end, the only solution was abolition.

In our text today the word translated "put down" has the meaning of abolish, do away, cancel, or bring to nothing. Paul, especially, makes it a key word in describing how Christ removes hindrances to life in Him. Abolition pulls down the walls of restriction. It opens prison houses. Sets free.

But what does Christ abolish? He pulls away the veil that hid His glory. We do not look for a veiled Moses to show us God's presence among His people. In the Spirit, face-to-face communion changes us from glory to glory.

Christ does away with the ministration of death and gives the ministration of the Spirit. He writes the epistle of obedience on the heart rather than on stones.

Christ does away with the sinful self, that sin-dominated nature that was ours in Adam. In its place the Spirit guides. The new nature takes over.

God will remove the man of sin. Christ will put down all forces hostile to the kingdom. Life will go on into eternity, secure from all danger.

Through Jesus the chains of sin-slavery are falling away. The slave market is going out of business forever. The auction block has been chopped for firewood. The slavemaster will fall to the abyss and his own millennial chains. Let freedom reign. Christ has put down all that would rise against His people.

"The means He employed with which to overcome evil were the wisdom and strength of love" (Testimonies, *vol. 2, p. 136*).

REGENERATION: BACK TO SQUARE ONE

Not by works of righteousness which we have done, but according to his mercy he saved us, by the washing of regeneration, and renewing of the Holy Ghost. Titus 3:5.

What if you could play the game of life over again? Go back to square one and reconsider each decision, each situation, that led you to where you are now? What if the transplant merchants put on sale a way to turn back the effects of time and give a new beginning?

The symbol of a new creative act that lets us begin again describes God's saving action in Jesus Christ. God had spiritual regeneration in mind when He told Ezekiel to tell Israel that He would give them a new heart. So did David as he asked for a clean heart. The failing of the Flood people afflicts all mankind. The thoughts and intents of the heart are evil continually. Only God can begin us again.

In the pagan religions of the East, the world passes through cycles; regeneration comes according to a pattern. Such religions also tie humanity to a cycle of life from which only nirvana, the loss of self-awareness, provides release.

Such ideas have no place in Christian faith. Just as God will make a new heaven and a new earth, so He regenerates man through the "kindness and love of God our Saviour" (Titus 3:4).

Paul creates a figure of speech to describe the divine act of salvation. God has created a fountain of grace. In its waters He regenerates the believer. In today's text, regeneration and renewal go together; so do washing and the Holy Spirit.

Baptism and the receiving of the Spirit are a unity. To speak of baptism as separate from the giving of the Holy Spirit misplaces one of the great emphases of the New Testament. The Spirit renews and regenerates the life. Baptism signifies that regeneration.

But the Spirit does not move the marker on the game of life back to square one. He does not put us on a time machine that lets us have new chances at old mistakes. As God's futurologist He makes today square one. The Spirit implants a new heart and so gives a new start.

"Christ has given His Spirit as a divine power to overcome all hereditary and cultivated tendencies to evil, and to impress His own character upon His church" (The Desire of Ages, *p. 671*).

BORN AGAIN: A NEW START FROM GOD

Them that believe on his name: which were born, not of blood, nor of the will of the flesh, nor of the will of man, but of God. John 1:12, 13.

When we turn to God He gives us a new point of origin. We begin from Him and go into the future, growing and maturing under His will. John, more than other writers, uses birth language for turning to Christ.

The new birth does not begin with man, but with God. In Jesus Christ we begin and end. In the New Testament this new beginning is called "born again," "begotten of God," "born of the Spirit."

Nicodemus came at night. Did he fear the watchful eye of the group of Pharisees to which he belonged? Was this the only time when he was sure he could find Jesus alone, free from the huge crowds that always surrounded Him? It was worth the effort and the risk. Jesus held hope for him. He had listened and watched, full of questions about the teachings of Jesus.

What Jesus told Nicodemus mystified him. He couldn't see that being "born again" was necessary before he, an Israelite, could have a right relationship with God. But he was not stupid. He soon grasped the aptness of the figure to his own need.

Out of the interchange between Nicodemus and Jesus came the promise of John 3:16. God's gift of His Son offers new birth with water and the Spirit. The child of this birth does not face eternal death, the lot of all who live in sin, but has begun everlasting life.

Peter attaches rebirth to the resurrection of Jesus. In 1 Peter 1:3, 5 he calls this rebirth a living hope, made possible through God's great mercy and power. No one can lay it aside and pick it up again at will. Being born anew lies totally within God's province. A child looks back at parents and grandparents and discovers how heredity has affected him. In Christ we have a divine genealogy. We have no more control over it than we do over our ancestors.

In Christ, God has removed once and for all the reality of death. He has crossed out and erased any claim that life as we know it is real life. He has brought near to us another stream of life. It lies so close to us through Christ that we can reach out, grasp the new life, and let go of the old. With this living hope we lay hold of eternal life.

"Wherever a soul reaches out after God, there the Spirit's working is manifest, and God will reveal Himself to that soul" (The Desire of Ages, p. 189).

WHEN JESUS SURRENDERED HIS LIFE

Almost all things are by the law purged with blood; and without shedding of blood is no remission. Heb. 9:22.

Two ideas from the Old Testament join together in this text. Blood equals life. For this reason the law forbade Israelites to eat or drink blood. When Cain killed Abel, his brother's blood (life) cried out from the ground.

In the sanctuary service, blood belonged to God for the purpose of cleansing. The priest poured it out at the base of the altar. Because it represented life, the high priest sprinkled it toward the congregation. In the Day of Atonement ceremonies and on other occasions, blood purified and cleansed.

In the figure of blood we have symbolism of both cleansing and life. To be washed in the blood of the Lamb means to be both cleansed and alive in Christ. As we drink the wine at the Lord's Supper, we acknowledge that forgiveness and eternal life come through the shedding of His blood.

Because Jesus did not sin, His blood (the taking of His life) gives life to others. Sin demands the life (blood) of all who sin. The death of the sinless Son of God substitutes His life (blood) for ours.

But the story does not quite end there. We also must "shed blood." Forgiveness comes through the surrender of life. We surrender our lives to God. We die to Christ. With the hold broken that this life has on us, the new life in Christ may take over. It isn't easy to deny the value of the life we live without Christ. Yet if we do not surrender that life, He cannot give us His life.

What does the blood of Christ (His death on the cross) do for the people of God? By His blood, Christ ransoms and frees the church from the power of evil. His blood justifies all who accept His sacrifice. God blots out all our sin because of the blood of Christ. Through the blood we have a clear conscience toward God.

But we have not exhausted what the surrender of Jesus' life means to us. His blood sanctifies and conquers, transforms and renews, gives access, and establishes the new covenant. It makes peace, reconciles, and purifies. All these are ours when we appropriate the blood of Jesus to our need.

"Jesus is officiating in the presence of God, offering up His shed blood, as it had been a lamb slain" (Selected Messages, *book 1, p. 344*).

THE GOD WHO IS

Thus shalt thou say unto the children of Israel, I AM hath sent me unto you. Ex. 3:14.

In the recesses of the great temple in Madurai in the south of India, a sketch hangs on the wall. At first it looks like a plan for a piece of furniture. Look closer and you will see that it lays out a design for a humanlike figure. An even closer examination reveals a detailed plan for the Hindu god Vishnu. Each of the multiple arms has its precise angle. The head tilts appropriately. The legs poise in dance. A skilled craftsman could take this and make his own god. That, incidentally, explains how one overcomes the problem of making an important deity when he has more than 3 million gods to reckon with.

Behind paganism lies a certain way of thinking about divine beings. Though a god has much freedom and tremendous power, he can be controlled through his image—which you possess. God avoided that danger completely. Even the Shekinah glory hovered in the open space between the cherubim above the ark of the testimony, free to come and go, not confined within the golden box itself. Nothing that suggests that man might control God was permitted. In the symbols, in His name, in the system of worship, His freedom remained intact.

Behind the mysterious I AM lies the assurance of the living God, who knows and cares about His creation. He did not want Israel to think that they could capture His image in wood or stone. He asked them to accept Him as the invisible God, radically different from the gods of neighboring nations.

He has lived with our past and knows our future. We do not go to visit Him in a temple or shrine, for He travels always with us. We do not kneel to an idol, for He accepts the secret worship of our heart. No one owns Him, for He is sovereign Creator. He remains ever free to act for the benefit of all.

Yet His freedom to act for our good has limitations. We impose them. His offer of salvation depends on our choice. His intercession in answer to our prayers depends on those prayers. The guiding and power of His Spirit waits the surrender of our will. He is the I AM, the very God we need: the free God who gives us freedom, but also always remains free to redeem us.

"When His laborers do the very best they can, God does for them that which they cannot do themselves" (Testimonies, *vol. 5, p. 400).*

GOD ON OUR SIDE

The Lord is on my side; I will not fear: what can man do unto me? Ps. 118:6.

"Plenty," Paul might have answered to that question. At the Spirit's direction he went to Jerusalem. The very thought of arriving at the nation's capital thrilled him. For years he had traveled in Gentile lands. What could brighten his life more than the prospects of Zion with its Temple and history of God's providences?

More than that, he had with him a band of Gentile converts. Isaiah had predicted Gentiles coming to the light of Israel. Now Paul brought these men, like a tribute to a ruler. They showed that God was working to do what the prophets longed for. The Lord was creating a new Israel out of all nations.

Added to these things, he had with him donations from Gentile churches to support the center of Christianity in Jerusalem. How his steps quickened as he climbed the hilly ramparts and finally caught sight of the great city!

Yet things went so wrong. James and the others asked Paul to protect their interests at his personal risk. They told him what to do; after all, their converts in Jerusalem numbered many thousands and had to be protected. Paul would have presumed that the same Spirit who guided him had control of the decisions of James.

In a matter of days he barely escaped lynching; the Sanhedrin turned against him; Roman guards hustled him off to Caesarea to begin a period of custody there that lasted more than two years.

What are we to think when our best intentions go awry? When others' decisions put us in danger? When things go horribly wrong and disaster piles on disaster? Today could be that kind of day.

David's answer you can find in other psalms. Paul lets us know what he thought of it all. Nothing could separate him from his Lord. Not even the stupidity of those who might have known better. Not even lynchings and floggings.

God has declared Himself on our side, which puts us on His side.

"God will not fail His church in the hour of her greatest peril. He has promised deliverance" (Prophets and Kings, *p. 538).*

WHEN JOHN PRESENTED HIS MIRACLE LIST

There stood by me this night the angel of God, whose I am, and whom I serve. Acts 27:23.

Every few weeks I meet John. Since we last met he has been keeping record. He even numbers them off on his fingers. God operates at a very personal level for him. In little and big things he reads the providence of God.

The people who service his car had a special on a tune-up; Johnny Junior made it onto the honor list; Mary, his wife, picked up a bargain in shoes for the children. Every day has its miracle, and John remembers them.

Once we fell to talking about prayer. He reeled off answers to his petitions in a truly amazing recital. It couldn't all be that good, could it? Did he blame God when things went wrong?

He smiled a smile I won't forget. "I count them only when I can see the answers. Some of them I wait a long time for."

Would that kind of attitude do for me? for you? Not all of us are made that way. We do not see God in simple things. Because a supermarket chain has slashed prices on canned peaches, should we praise God? Especially if we use only a can a month?

Miracle lists don't offend me; they make me feel guilty. I know only too well that I ought to give thanks more often; remember better; see God at work here, there, and everywhere.

The feeling coming from Paul's writings has a somewhat similar effect. "Rejoice evermore." "In every thing give thanks." Paul would have understood John.

Not too many people can face a vision of shipwreck, know it comes from God, and still boost the spirits of all aboard. Paul knew his guardian angel. When he heard the whisper that all would escape, right away he began to praise God.

Of course, God didn't let Paul off without problems. He had more than his share. That is where his greatness as an example begins. No one has a life any worse than Paul's. Remember, he finally faced a Roman executioner, from whom God did not deliver him.

John is right: God is on our side, and because He is, the good times have already begun. All we have to do is count, and remember.

"God has provided divine assistance for all the emergencies to which our human resources are unequal" (Prophets and Kings, p. 660).

THE MOVES YOU MAKE TODAY WILL COUNT

So that we may boldly say, The Lord is my helper, and I will not fear what man shall do unto me. Heb. 13:6.

Any time a text says "so that," it invites a look back through the previous verses to see what causes the writer to come to his conclusion.

In the very old editions of *Bible Readings*, three wood engravings show life as a board game against Satan. In the first picture, an angel stands between the players, intently watching the progress of the game. In the second, the Enemy wins, and the angel turns aside in tears. In the third, the young man wins, and the angel rejoices.

If you look in Hebrews 13, the tests of life also appear. The Lord does not help us move the pieces in the game of life unless we seek His help.

In the New Testament, relationships matter for the Christian. The brothers need our love (verse 1). That is obvious to anyone who understands the Christian way, but it is often foreign to our actions. The Lord cannot help us if we move onto the squares marked selfishness and greed.

If hate or indifference rules in the church, how will we treat the strangers who happen by (verse 2)? And what if those strangers have a divine purpose for us? if God has sent them to minister to us?

Our brothers and sisters in faith, and even strangers, serve God on our behalf. They teach us patience, brotherly love, gentleness, forgiveness. Through them God's hand reaches out to guide.

The list of positives that show God's help continues. We must empathize with those in trouble, as if we had the same trial (verse 3). Put yourself in their place and suffer with them. Why? Because then we will know that God is our helper.

What the Christian must deny himself is covetousness. Whether sexual or material (verses 4, 5), wanting what we have no right to leaves us powerless in the final assessment of the game.

In rapid succession the writer says three things about God: "Our God is a consuming fire." "God will judge." "The Lord is my helper." Those who trust in Him will always win through His help. He is judge, yes; but, oh, how He loves to help!

"Do not neglect secret prayer. Pray for yourself. Grow in grace. Advance. Don't stand still, don't go back. Onward to victory. Courage in the Lord" (Testimonies, *vol. 1, p. 663*).

GOD IS OUR CHAMPION

The Lord shall fight for you, and ye shall hold your peace. Ex. 14:14.

In the fierce wars of the Middle Ages, terrible bloodshed might be avoided by a contest of champions. Like Goliath and David of the Philistine wars, two selected individuals would battle to the death, and entire armies would accept the result.

In the cosmic sense, the great conflict of the ages pits the Lord of heaven against the lord of darkness. In the day-to-day issues of our human existence the Lord of heaven champions our cause.

Not that we are pawns shuffled about by two titans. Rather, our choices show who is enlisting us in his service. Whenever the push of the evil one moves us away from the divine will, trust in the Lord brings Him to our side.

The Lord said to Israel, Walk on toward the Red Sea and leave the Egyptians to Me. In trusting Me you have accepted My peace; you need never war again.

Some would have run for the hills that hemmed them in on two sides. Others might have begged for mercy. Still others fingered shepherds' crooks, testing them as possible clubs.

Moses gave the Lord's directive to Israel, but was this the counsel of despair? March on, yes, but what other choice did they have?

Israel obeyed and walked through the Red Sea, then watched as God finished off the Egyptian soldiers.

How could one ever compare the little crises of today with the situation of Israel? Does not God rule and triumph at the cosmic level, where the big issues reign? Yes, but not just there. Your skirmish with the enemy also requires His attention. What happens to His followers projects the great controversy into the personal arena. Defeat there would mean loss at the very level where it matters most—the saving of those for whom the Son died.

The Lord, your champion, allies Himself with you. Today's "Egyptian threat" will pass. The way into the future will open for you. Tomorrow you will look back from the other side of the "Red Sea" and joy in your Deliverer.

"To all who are reaching out to feel the guiding hand of God, the moment of greatest discouragement is the time when divine help is nearest" (The Desire of Ages, p. 528).

EVERYTHING A CHRISTIAN SHOULD KNOW ABOUT GOD

Then said they unto him, Where is thy Father? Jesus answered, Ye neither know me, nor my Father: if ye had known me, ye should have known my Father also. John 8:19.

Everything-you-should-know books continue to top the best-seller lists. How-to-do-it manuals give us inside information, the latest research, the experience of years.

Isaak Walton wrote *The Compleat Angler*, the first modern-day how-to-do-it book, in the seventeenth century. It helped fishermen improve their luck. The charm of fishing, mingled with folksy insights into life and glimpses of English landscape, created a masterpiece. Excuse enough for even nonanglers to niche his book into their shelves.

God exists; we know that. But what do we know about Him? How can we know about Him? Is there a manual that tells us all we need to know about Him?

The Bible pulls down shutters so that we can never have complete knowledge of the Infinite. No one can approach God (1 Tim. 6:16). All we can learn of Him is simile, metaphor, and analogy.

In the Old Testament, God descends from on high to range Himself against Israel's enemies. He exists in eternity but moves to His people's aid as they call on Him.

Yet we can know Him through the Living Witness, who is Jesus Christ. Everything the Christian should know about God is Jesus. To speak of Jesus speaks of God. To talk about God talks about Jesus.

In sending Jesus, God came to share humanity. The Gospels help us understand God. In Jesus, God's power, love, grace, and justice come to our aid. He seeks and saves mankind through His sacrifice and love. He is both with us and of us.

We talk of Father, Son, and Spirit because that helps us understand relationships. However, using these words helps us little in knowing the exact nature of the members of the Godhead. Only as we know Jesus does the Father-Son relationship take significance in our lives. Only as we see Jesus at work in the Gospel story do we comprehend what the Spirit means to us.

We cannot know enough about Jesus. A thoughtful hour each day will help our quest but never exhaust what we may learn. To know Jesus is to know God. In Him God is of us and with us.

"In Christ we become more closely united to God than if we had never fallen" (The Desire of Ages, *p. 25).*

HOW GOD GIVES HIMSELF TO US TODAY

Ye have heard how I said unto you, I go away, and come again unto you. If ye loved me, ye would rejoice, because I said, I go unto the Father. John 14:28.

The grave of John I. Tay rests neat and tidy on a Suva hillside. How he came to die in Fiji is one of the great stories of Adventist missions. A layperson, he conceived the idea of taking the Advent message to the descendants of the *Bounty* mutineers. In October 1886 he arrived at Pitcairn.

Within three months he had changed the course of Pitcairn's history. The whole island accepted the Sabbath, and to this day maintain their faith. Tay's death in Fiji in 1892 came as he was pursuing the purpose of taking the message to all the South Sea Island groups.

All the intelligence tests and aptitude evaluations have failed to measure what one person may do for the world. Jesus showed us what changes take place as people enter the kingdom of God. He taught us that what we are now is not what we might yet become.

The Holy Spirit, the divine futurologist, perceives potentials within the most unlikely that none of us could ever discern. Just as Jesus could take a James and a John, fisherfolk, and turn them into apostles, so the Spirit may take any person's potential and develop it.

After all, John knew what the Spirit had done for him. No wonder he remembered and told us so much of what Jesus said about the Spirit. Pentecost had changed him beyond anything he had imagined the day he heard Jesus talk of the coming of the Comforter.

You remember how Jesus spoke of coming again to receive us to Himself? The promise of the Second Coming lives brightly in the hearts of all Christians. But Jesus comes in another way. He comes to us in the Holy Spirit. To concentrate on the Second Coming and overlook the coming of Jesus through the Spirit bypasses one of the great provisions of God's grace.

The Spirit makes the Johns and the Tays of the church. He carries out the will of Jesus that His gifts and fruits should be in all His disciples. Spiritually the Spirit does not replace Jesus; rather, He is Jesus continuing among us. Jesus did so much for His followers, and for the needy world. He will also do great things for us as the Spirit comes to refresh and bless.

"It is not you that work the Holy Spirit, but the Holy Spirit must work you" (Testimonies, *vol. 6, p. 57*).

NO REVERSE GEAR

Create in me a clean heart, O God; and renew a right spirit within me. Ps. 51:10.

His face twisted with anger, the man in the red shirt shoved and yelled at the bus, trying to push it back out of the way. Not that he hadn't been told. The driver had said it five or six times.

"Reverse gear doesn't work on this old bus. I can't make it go backward."

But some VIPs were arriving from the airport to cross on the ferry to the capital city. Red Shirt had the responsibility of giving them priority.

"You had better make it go backward!" he commanded. "Let me see you try."

He leaned into the cab to make sure the driver tried, then jumped around to the front again. "Now let your clutch out!"

The driver shrugged and did so. Only nimble footwork prevented the angry man from being run down.

The game went on for more than 30 minutes, until common sense ruled and the bus advanced onto the ferry.

Each new day gives us opportunity to use the reverse gear in our lives, an opportunity to:

1. Go back as far as we can and take a new direction.

2. Forgive those who have hurt or misunderstood us, and start a new page in our relationship with them.

3. Claim God's forgiveness and ask for that new heart that permits us to start over again.

4. Submit the will to the Spirit of God, and not let it drive us into rebellion.

To back up means to repent and start afresh. It means to let God take us out of the tangled web of sin and mistakes.

> Dear Lord, take up the tangled strands,
> Where we have wrought in vain,
> That by the skill of Thy dear hands
> Some beauty may remain.
> —Mrs. F. C. Burroughs
> (copyright 1920, Homer A. Rodeheaver).

"Trusting, hoping, believing, holding fast the hand of Infinite Power, you will be more than conquerors" (Testimonies, *vol. 7,* p. 245).

REPENTANCE HAS A PRACTICAL SIDE

Are there not with you, even with you, sins against the Lord your God? 2 Chron. 28:10.

In all the history of the divided tribes of Israel, nothing like this had ever occurred. Pekah, king of the northern tribes, attacked Ahaz of the southern two, and killed 120,000 soldiers "because they had forsaken the Lord God of their fathers" (2 Chron. 28:6).

Following the custom of the times, the victors rounded up captives to take away—200,000 in all. Women and children, with mountains of spoil, formed a sorry procession northward toward Samaria.

We can picture it readily enough. Mass media depictions from Thailand and Ethiopia imprint the plight of the refugee. For the captives of the two tribes, no relief agency waited to offer help. No ships loaded with grain came out of Tarshish or sailed from the Phoenician colonies with medical teams and supplies.

Slavery waited for the captives. The victors conveniently forgot the divine command against enslaving fellow Israelites, and rubbed their hands at the thought of the value of their spoils.

But then appeared Oded the prophet. He stopped the procession in its tracks. What they were planning stank to high heaven, he said. Unless they set these captives free, the judgment of God would fall on them.

He reminded them that they too were sinners. Did they not also need God's forgiveness and favor?

They heard Oded. But they did nothing at first. Then four men took Oded's side (you can read their names in verse 12). They persuaded the soldiers to abandon their plan.

On behalf of the whole people they repented, found clothes among the spoil, put the weak on donkeys, turned the whole procession around, and headed it back south. Down the Jordan Valley they guided and guarded their brothers and sisters from Judah until they came to Jericho, and turned the multitude over to their brethren.

What price repentance? Giving up wrong action is one thing. Undoing mistakes, another. True repentance measures how the past has wronged both God and others and seeks to make things right. It never exults in any sense of superiority. It understands its own mistakes, accepts forgiveness and hope, and seeks that hope and new life for those it has hurt.

"True repentance is more than sorrow for sin. It is a resolute turning away from evil" (Patriarchs and Prophets, *p. 557).*

TOO GOOD TO BE TRUE?

Behold, Lord, the half of my goods I give to the poor; and if I have taken any thing from any man by false accusation, I restore him fourfold. Luke 19:8.

In a world that never existed, Ferdinand and Imelda Marcos said to their accusers, "You are right. A president's salary never could produce such wealth. We are giving back to the nation every penny we have hidden in Swiss bank accounts and invested in foreign property."

In the same world, Baby Doc Duvalier confessed to bleeding his nation for his own gain. He boosted Haiti's economy by leading its bankers to his hoarded dollars. About the same time, the beer barons and liquor lords closed their factories and turned their profits over to the rehabilitation of alcoholics. Not long after, the cigarette moguls sold off their tobacco factories and set about, with almost unlimited resources, the business of cancer research.

Do you begin to understand what the impact of Zacchaeus' repentance was? No one would ever believe a tax gatherer who claimed repentance if he continued to live in opulence. In a world governed by pastoral concerns, he applied to himself the law that dealt with sheep stealers. The law of Moses required repayment on the basis of four for one. After Zacchaeus had spoken, everyone in Jericho knew what it meant to repent!

Immediately afterward the people began to ask whether Jesus would set up the kingdom of David again. Only in the Messianic kingdom might one expect sinners to repent as Zacchaeus had. Jesus was creating the kind of response that the prophets had foretold. Under ordinary circumstances, the people thought this impossible, given the greed and hypocrisy of the rulers of the Jews.

No one should underestimate the hope that true repentance creates in the world. When a greedy, grasping person changes course and generosity takes over, people take note. Such a life goes up before God as a sweet perfume. It calls others to consider their lives and also repent.

In the days before the end of time, God will have a people prepared for His coming. They will show through their lives that they walk according to His will. Through them God will let His glory be seen. In them all peoples will find hope.

"The world will be convinced, not by what the pulpit teaches, but by what the church lives" (Testimonies, *vol. 7, p. 16*).

HOW THE LORD REWARDS REPENTANCE

Repent, and be baptized every one of you in the name of Jesus Christ for the remission of sins, and ye shall receive the gift of the Holy Ghost. Acts 2:38.

She waited near the front of the tent after the evening meeting. The preacher had called for repentance. To her, the greatness of sin weighed so heavily that she dabbed continually at her eyes. Could she find forgiveness?

Then the greatest of her fears tumbled out. "I've sinned so badly that God will never forgive me. How could He? I have committed the unpardonable sin."

Most preachers have someone say that to them during their ministry. Sensitive individuals carry a huge sense of guilt. It takes all the persuasive assurance of the Word to convince them that God does forgive all that we bring to Him in confession. They argue inside themselves that God has a point beyond which He will not go in giving forgiveness. They surely must have passed that marker.

Those who heard Peter's sermon at Pentecost might have felt that way. Consider their sin. God had sent the Messiah to them, His own Son. They had deliberately conspired to do away with Him. They had even made Him look like a criminal by having Him nailed to the cross. Now He reigned with the Father in heaven. Surely He would seek revenge rather than allow repentance.

But Peter knew better. After all, he had rejected Christ himself, and knew how freely the Lord forgave. He said to those desperate souls, Acknowledge the authority of Jesus; confess His name before all. Not only will He accept you, but He will also give you the gift of the Holy Spirit.

Peter also knew the truth of that. He was not only thinking of the tongues of fire and the infilling of power, but remembering the healing touch of the Spirit as He restored him to faith and trust.

In this way the Spirit comes to all who repent and believe. He seals forgiveness into our hearts. He proffers divine power to aid our wills. Through Him the trusting life continues "in Christ." The one who repents does not go into the new life unsupported. The Spirit goes ahead, around, and within, that the child of faith may live in hope.

"If all were willing, all would be filled with the Spirit" (The Acts of the Apostles, *p. 50).*

THE LIFE AFTER REPENTANCE

Then put on the garments that suit God's chosen people, his own, his beloved: compassion, kindness, humility, gentleness, patience. Col. 3:12, NEB.

At Mardi Gras time in Rio de Janeiro and New Orleans, revelers don masks. In their bizarre clothes and makeup they shuck off the conventions that normally govern their lives. By putting on their festival adornment, moral restrictions fall away. As the music throbs and the liquor flows, inhibitions collapse and frivolity reigns.

The ancient city of Colossae hosted a pagan festival that lasted a month. For that period, groups of people would wear special clothes. While in those garments they were exempted by city officials from the normal laws of morality. Paul feared for the life of the Colossian Christians in such a culture.

He draws on the custom of the people by way of illustration; he talks of putting off the life of sin and lust (Col. 3:5) and putting on the life of Christian godliness. He calls us to purity in public and in private. What we are when we are alone tells how close we are to the Lord.

Yet Paul isn't afraid of talking about public appearance. He would want us to avoid hypocrisy, but he would also have us appear Christlike. The way we live gives the greatest witness in the world. The apostle would not want that witness stopped.

The robe of righteousness that Christ gives offers status and acceptance with God. We need that continually. His robe does not do away with right living. It should provide a visible expression of inner godliness.

Nothing can replace a character that shows its dependence on Christ. In Christ we show to the world the changes He makes. Without Christ we may expect "fornication, indecency, lust, foul cravings, and ruthless greed." In Christ we may show "compassion, kindness, humility, gentleness, patience."

A life that shows no contrast with the world has not forsaken the world. In Christ the masks and garments of sin's Mardi Gras fall away. Instead, the robe of righteousness displays a life of purity and Christlikeness. He gives new garments of goodness and love, so that there will never be any doubt as to whom we honor and serve.

"Put off the garments of earth in order to be clothed with the robe of heaven" (Christ's Object Lessons, *p. 318).*

HOW TO FORGET YESTERDAY

Take away the filthy garments from him. And unto him he said,
Behold, I have caused thine iniquity to pass from thee, and I will
clothe thee with change of raiment. Zech. 3:4.

Miss Tryhard came to college from a very poor family. She had no
beautiful dresses in her closet, no special skills to help her earn
money. What she brought with her she had made herself, from scraps
of material picked up here and there. Worse than that, she knew
nothing about making dresses, as anyone could see.

Then came The Invitation. Mr. Important was giving a party and
asked her to come. The flurry and anxiety in that little room in the
north wing of the dormitory defied description. Each shabby dress had
its moment of examination. But the mirror told the truth.

But she did have a little money. To the store down the street she
went and bought the best material she could find. This time she really
tried. She even borrowed a pattern and a sewing machine.

What a disaster! The old things she had brought from home were as
good as this. It sagged unevenly in the front and the back. One sleeve
gaped open, and the other threatened her blood supply. The waistline
slanted alarmingly upward from her hips.

Her tears and cries of desperation attracted Miss Bountiful, who
seemed never far away at this college. Out tumbled Miss Tryhard's
story.

"Now stop your crying," said Miss Bountiful. "Let's go down to the
store again. You choose the dress you really want, and I'll pay for it."

Finally she settled on a rack of exquisite dresses. At first Miss T
thought them all the same. But when she tried one on, it seemed made
only for her. It was just what she needed. Precisely right. She had
never looked so lovely. Miss B agreed with her. Only this dress would
do. But the price! Impossible. Miss T could not expect her new friend
to pay this price. But before she could open her mouth in protest, the
check was written and the dress was hers.

Back in her room Miss Tryhard looked sadly at her collection of
shabby dresses. What good would any of these be to her? Down the
incinerator chute went the lot. One perfect dress was worth a whole
collection of misfits. And she would look just right for Mr. Important's
party!

"He is waiting to strip them of their garments, stained and
polluted by sin, and to put upon them the white, bright robes of
righteousness" (Testimonies, *vol. 2, p. 453*).

THE LORD WAITS FOR REPENTANCE

The Lord . . . is longsuffering to us-ward, not willing that any should perish, but that all should come to repentance. 2 Peter 3:9.

Out of the Vietnam War come graphic images of the final escape of the American forces and their Vietnamese allies. In one picture, a stream of Vietnamese snakes toward a building, up a ladder, and across the rooftop. Hovering above the roof, a helicopter is reeling one person up into the body of the aircraft. Did the rest also escape? And how many others would have joined the line had they known escape was possible?

Peter's concern that all repent develops as he compares the last day with the time of Noah. Only eight survived that catastrophe. How many will survive the fiery flood soon to destroy the earth?

Looking back over the recent past, we can see that the end of time has come very close indeed. More than once Ellen G. White laments the lack in God's people that delayed the Second Coming. She would have us realize that we live at the very edge of time, when even small events may produce large consequences.

Time, the apostle reasons, stands still for God but rushes on for mankind. God sees the desperate need for repentance and waits for more to put their trust in Him. Humanity feels the wind of time gathering strength and wonders how much longer it has.

Repentance, escape, and deliverance stand over against intransigence, captivity, and enslavement. To know these choices makes salvation possible. To deny them leads on to perdition. To scoff at warnings, to ignore God's past and future action, blocks out any chance of hope.

Newscasts, the headlines of newspapers, the analyses of magazine and television commentary, tell the Christian one thing. The end approaches. Knowing this demands the turnaround of repentance.

How should waiting men and women regard the passing of time? Look on it as the long-suffering of God, Peter says (2 Peter 3:15). God is giving you this further opportunity to transform your life. He holds open the door of salvation just a little longer.

Time-bound, we wait the moment of God's action. Saving grace appears to all; some accept it, many reject it. Therefore, repent! Tell others! The time is yours. God may wait to fulfill His will, but you dare not wait to do God's will.

"The time has come when we must expect the Lord to do great things for us" (Selected Messages, *book 1, p. 111*).

FAMOUS LAST WORDS

I have fought a good fight, I have finished my course, I have kept the faith. 2 Tim. 4:7.

Though neither Paul nor Luke left on record the last words the great apostle spoke, these will surely do. A look over his life from the moment of his conversion shows how bravely and selflessly he labored for the Lord he served. Again and again he suffered without wavering. At times unable to choose between Roman law and synagogue law, he felt the rough justice of both. The Romans flogged him. The Jews rained stones on him.

But we don't need to go back to Paul to uncover lives that remained true in the face of persecution and adversity.

Whenever we went to Oxford, we made a point of passing the cobblestone cross set in the pavement of Broad Street. Here Hugh Latimer and Nicholas Ridley paid the ultimate price for their faith. On October 16, 1555, a flame lit the straw and wood of their martyrdom. Latimer called to his companion, "Be of good comfort, Master Ridley, and play the man. We shall this day light such a candle, by God's grace, in England, as I trust shall never be put out."

Sometimes I think to myself that it would be easier to face the large decision, the great challenge, than to meet the little temptations, the nagging irritations, that daily beset our lives. Under the pressures to publicly confess my faith, I would steel myself and be true.

Such a great test may never come our way. By the little tests our character will develop. Overcoming daily will show our trust in the Father's provisions.

Latimer and Ridley had their moment when they could have chosen not to meet their final fate. Those Protestant Reformers and martyrs set in motion a chain of decisions in favor of truth. This chain led them on and finally gave them the courage to meet the ultimate test of faith.

We may never have to face such moments, but we do have to choose for God. Such choices we must surely make this very day. Not necessarily large choices, but decisions in favor of our Lord. Decisions that truly confess His name and our faith.

"Only by acting upon principle in the tests of daily life can we acquire power to stand firm and faithful in the most dangerous and most difficult positions" (The Ministry of Healing, *p. 490).*

THAT STEADFAST JOY

His name shall endure for ever: his name shall be continued as long as the sun: and men shall be blessed in him: all nations shall call him blessed. Ps. 72:17.

Stonehenge, the ancient shrine of pre-Christian sun worshipers, now has protective fences. Not too many years ago the tourist could wander at will among the massive pillars and fallen capstones of the twin circles of the monument.

For as many as 4,000 years tourists have visited Stonehenge. They have left their mark. Graffiti carved into the stones stretches back through the centuries. Who was Alfred? And who was Catherine? When did they come to blazon their love to the world? Names of forgotten people rebuke the visitor to a cemetery—"You do not even know who I am," they say.

Caught up in the intensity of modern life, do you sometimes give the passing events of today eternal values? Do you want to write your experience, your event, into the eternal timetable?

A sense of proportion governs our mortal expectations. We know instinctively that time will pass us by. Only a very few people will remember us. Eventually only the seekers for roots will even want to know our names.

But God goes on forever. Calculations about the life of the sun project it forward for several billion years. To put time limits on the God of the universe borders on the ridiculous. Because He goes on, we go on.

The powerful of the world, the ones whom history may remember, often consider ordinary mortals as expendable, the stuff of election victories, fodder for cannons. God views us differently. None should ever think of himself as graffiti scratched on the corridors of time, or as an identification mark on a cross of a cosmic Arlington.

Today may stifle us with happiness, tomorrow smother us with tears. God transcends time. He assures constancy and guarantees remembrance. He loses track of no one.

Even Alfred and Catherine, Stonehenge scribblings of a past era, have their identity in God's memory banks. Steadfast joy, a gift from a true knowledge of God, sustains us in Him. And so we call Him blessed.

"Jesus knows us individually, and is touched with the feeling of our infirmities. He knows us all by name" (The Desire of Ages, p. 479).

SOW A HANDFUL OF CORN

There shall be an handful of corn in the earth upon the top of the mountains; the fruit thereof shall shake like Lebanon: and they of the city shall flourish like grass of the earth. Ps. 72:16.

Around the turn of the century, George Tenney made a trip from Melbourne to Sydney. He had arrived in Australia in 1887, to edit the *Bible Echo*, an early Australian version of *The Signs of the Times*. Missionaries had landed just a few years before that, to establish the Seventh-day Adventist Church in the down-under continent.

Tenney found a handful of believers meeting in the Sydney church. Around them spread the metropolis, wealthy, materialistic, prejudiced. Would anything come of this tentative beginning?

For his text Tenney chose David's promise, part of the psalm written especially for Solomon, the king's son and heir.

In Palestine, peasants plant their fields, beginning in the valleys and thence up the hillsides. Only the very optimistic, or those with grain to spare, would scatter even a handful of corn on the cold and barren mountain ridges. Yet in the providence of God, the mountain would outproduce the valleys. The handful of corn would grow lush and vigorous. As the cedars of Lebanon tremble when the wind moves their branches, so the corn would shake at the weight of its ears.

In the partnership of the Spirit God gives steadfast joy. A handful of seed planted at His will flourishes, and may exceed our hopes.

Nearly nine decades after Tenney's sermon, Sydney now has more than 7,000 members, worshiping in more than 50 churches and companies. What will God give us if this day we scatter a handful of witness? Who can measure?

But we miss the point if we talk only of the Spirit multiplying witness. He has other fruit to give us.

David knew the skills and potential of Solomon. A proud parent, yes; but also a skilled analyst of personality and character. The time was right for a good and wise king. David saw Solomon as a handful of corn. Possibilities, yes. Unproven, yes. Would he bear the fruit of love, joy, peace, long-suffering, gentleness, goodness, faith?

At times in the life of Solomon the fruit of the Spirit rustled like the cedars of Lebanon. We know some seed died, fruitless. Any human character is an unlikely place for the fruit of the Spirit to flourish. But with divine nurture and human willingness, it may.

"A man may have precious seed in his hand, but that seed is not an orchard. . . . The mind is the garden; the character is the fruit" (Testimonies, *vol. 4, p. 606*).

YOU WILL NEVER FALL

Wherefore the rather, brethren, give diligence to make your calling and election sure: for if ye do these things, ye shall never fall. 2 Peter 1:10.

The view from the top of the Khancoban Walls rivals anything, anywhere. To the west and thousands of feet below, the Murray River valley sweeps away to the blue waters of the Hume Weir; in the distance lies the haze of the Albury-Wodonga city complex. To the east and north, the climb continues, but at a more gentle slope, to the snowcapped Kosciusko massif, the highest mountains in Australia.

The hard-won slog to the top went on interminably. Just to place one foot in front of the other demanded as much mental as physical exertion. No four-wheel drive could climb these cliffs. No bus came down a road over the plateau. Only the climber and the will assured the joy of conquest.

Up the cliffs of Patience, helped and helping with the rope called Brotherly Kindness, at last we gain the summit of Love. And the view from there eclipses imagination.

Now add another word picture to Peter's upward climb. He calls it the Christian's escape route. Through the indwelling of the divine nature, an escape route appears. The bogs of lust and the trash heaps of corruption no longer block the view of the hills of righteousness. A spiritual look around, and the route up appears in front of us.

Any person who has performed a difficult physical feat remembers it with joy. Achievement brings joy. A sanctified character represents the Christian's goal. The Spirit advises what we should become. Will we reach the summit of true love?

I remember spraining my ankle once and having to wait halfway up a mountain while friends went on to the top. Despite all their attempts I could not fully enter their joy.

Character does not develop via another's achievements, as encouraging and instructive as they may be. It comes as the Spirit goes with our wills, now submitted to Him, up to the heights of Christian love. One who trusts Him to lead and help will not fall.

"True character is not shaped from without, and put on; it radiates from within" (The Desire of Ages, p. 307).

"BUT, I'M NO DANIEL, LORD"

He is the living God, and stedfast for ever, and his kingdom that which shall not be destroyed, and his dominion shall be even unto the end. Dan. 6:26.

These words Darius wrote in a letter to all parts of his empire. When his leaders in India and Arabia received them, what did they think? In their world every god had to belong to someone. The Bible has many stories of "the god of" this or that nation or individual. Darius defined the living God as the "God of Daniel."

That would help. Any person of importance knew the prime minister. But they also knew the Persian policy. The emperor played no favorites with national deities, a policy that kept the diverse conquests at peace with each other. What was the king doing, then? Breaking with his policy? Probably not. He wanted his subjects to accommodate the thought world of the Jews, now scattered throughout the realm.

Darius was not adopting Jehovah as the empire deity. He was affirming, from personal knowledge, that Israel had a God who went over and beyond the political fortunes of the nation. Others may rule Israel, but Israel's God ruled the future of His people.

To the command of Darius the Bible adds cosmic values. The escape from the lions' den created a new climate for Israel's fortunes. Eventually it resulted in their return from exile. Taken out of the immediate context and translated into the conflict of the ages, it showed that God does not forget His covenant promises.

Had the lions killed Daniel, Persian rulers might eventually have tried to obliterate Israel. Two centuries before, the Assyrians had decimated the northern tribes. But this one escape—a famous one for sure, but still just one miracle—produced an eternal consequence. Israel survived, the Messiah came, the covenant held.

The steadfast faith of Daniel met the steadfast concern of God. Miracles may happen when faith does not falter. Doubt gives God a risky base on which to build a miracle.

You may look into your life and see yourself beset in a lions' lair. Daniel's escape assures us that God's eternal purposes will prosper. From such an assurance the steadfast joy of God's presence grows.

"A man whose heart is stayed upon God will be the same in the hour of his greatest trial as he is in prosperity" (Prophets and Kings, *p. 545*).

RELATIONSHIPS CAN BUILD FOR LASTING JOY

Thou wilt shew me the path of life: in thy presence is fulness of joy; at thy right hand there are pleasures for evermore. Ps. 16:11.

Every so often, the *Adventist Review*, one of the other church papers, or a local daily will feature one of those longlasting relationships that delight the reader. A husband and wife married for 50, 60, or in one case that I read of recently, 75 years! Almost without exception the affection of the one for the other shows, not just in the photos but in comment and interdependency. Could it be that long life depends in part on good personal relationships with one special person?

All Seventh-day Adventists like those surveys that show that our health practices give us a longer life expectancy than others. But researchers note a factor that does not relate to diet or health habits. They talk about the dynamics of groups committed to a specific cause. Church members would reinterpret this and talk of commitment to a Man as well as to a cause.

The joy of having an abiding and real relationship with Jesus Christ can affect the life span, at least so it appears from some research. Not surprising, after all, because He is the Bread of Life.

How we relate to Jesus Christ affects our happiness and general attitudes. A life spent in fellowship with Christ will show as surely as 50 years together show in a married couple.

David's psalm carries a theme of positive thinking. The early Christian church called on it to support their claims about the resurrection of Jesus Christ. The words speak of what God does for us through Jesus Christ, and of what God did for Jesus Christ in raising Him from the dead. He reigns with joy in the presence of the Father. He carries out the will of the Godhead as He ministers blessings to His people.

All who place their lives in a right relationship with Jesus, He will lift to heavenly places and assure eternal life. He carries us with Him into the very presence of God, giving us peace and joy as we fellowship together. He pleases us with forgiving grace and overcoming power.

The message is clear enough. Life lived close to God can only get better and better.

"The relations between God and each soul are as distinct and full as though there were not another soul upon the earth to share His watchcare" (Steps to Christ, *p. 100).*

JOY IN THE GLOOM-DOOM WORLD

And when these things begin to come to pass, then look up, and lift up your heads; for your redemption draweth nigh. Luke 21:28.

In a recent interview Britain's Prince Philip voiced pessimism about the world in which his grandchildren would grow up. In a comment about population growth, he said, "It's inevitable that very grave damage is going to be done to this world in the next one hundred years."

Could anything be done? "Search me. I don't know. The older I get, the more cynical I get, in the sense that I just think things are going to get worse.

"I mean, there was a period in this country [The United Kingdom] when you could leave your car unlocked, your front door open, when you could trust anyone across the social scale. Now you can't even trust your neighbor."

The prince felt nuclear war unlikely, because of the horror of being responsible for such devastation. However, the interview predicted a continuing decline in social relationships and quality of life.

A comment not surprising to those who believe that Jesus will come at that very time when world leaders despair of the human condition. Surprising, however, from a figure whose commitment to various causes shows a belief that changes can be made for the better.

When the angels came to Bethlehem, they announced tidings of "great joy" to the shepherds. We do not expect angels to visit us again to announce the Second Coming. However, as an event of "great joy," it needs those who will spread the word.

Even Prince Philip need not despair, because a better world could be his for the asking. His children and grandchildren could share in it. Taking Jesus literally hallmarks the sincere follower of Jesus. If we believe that Jesus is coming soon, we will never join the world's doomsayers.

The great civilizers and best-loved leaders of the nations see through gloom and doom to a bright future. The Leader of leaders gives us steadfast joy to share with others.

People without hope have a corner on gloom. Let them keep it. Let us spread joy.

The true workers "help to swell the tide of His joy, and bring honor and praise to His exalted name" (Christ's Object Lessons, *p. 403*).

GOD CONTROLS TECHNOLOGY

Thy right hand, O Lord, is become glorious in power: thy right hand, O Lord, hath dashed in pieces the enemy. Ex. 15:6.

Consider the tyranny of technology. In his book *Future Shock*, Alvin Toffler regarded the technological revolution as the most taxing of all for the mind.

While grandparents watch bemused, their grandchildren manipulate computers as easily as they themselves once rode scooters. But it's one thing to feel good about a lad notching up records in an electronic game, quite another to know that your retirement check comes courtesy of IBM.

The song of Exodus records God's scorn for the technology of the Egyptians. Israel quaked as they heard the rumbling of chariot wheels. How could they handle metal shaped for war when all they had were handcarts and a few donkeys? But with the east wind and with walls of water, God tumbled the chariots to destruction. A touch of His power, and terror turned in on Pharaoh's armies.

The Shakers tried to lock technology at an acceptable level, but time swallowed them up and left only their handiwork. Closing the door may create a moment of calm, but the storm surely comes.

Three Mile Island and Chernobyl have taught us to dread nuclear technology. Politicians with their hotline telephones and generals with their fail-safe switches offer cold comfort measured against past experience. Mankind has never invented a technology of terror that he has not unleashed beyond his control.

But what of God's people in the midst of burgeoning technology. Paul saw divine technology lifting the faithful from Planet Earth and transporting them to the Father's house. The tyrant's technology has no more authority over God's people today than it did in Pharaoh's day.

It may seem quaint to think simple thoughts like these: God made the laws that make it possible to produce the wizardry of inventive science. If He made those laws, He can turn aside any system, or accumulation of systems, and make it useless. Quaint or not, the Red Sea proved it true.

What can a chariot do when God stretches out His right arm to save? What can an atom bomb do while God walls in His people as they wait for Jesus' coming?

"The path where God leads the way may lie through the desert or the sea, but it is a safe path" (Patriarchs and Prophets, *p. 290).*

174

WE ARE SO FEW, AND THEY ARE SO MANY

The Lord stirred up ... the spirit of all the remnant of the people; and they came and did work in the house of the Lord of hosts, their God. Haggai 1:14.

The idea of a faithful remnant who complete God's work against overwhelming odds grew out of Israelite history. In one long-remembered incident, the Midianites covered the plain like a plague of locusts. But 300 faithful and true men defeated them.

If God's people waited until their numbers matched those of their opponents, they would never act for God. Yet so many of us do nothing. "I'm the only Adventist Christian at my work." "Everyone around me worships on Sunday." "No one wants to hear about God anymore."

The French speak of *force majeure*; they mean the threat of superior power, which holds others in check. Satan would have us think that he has the superior force; God rules otherwise.

God stirs up the spirit of the remnant through unexpected opportunity or sudden threat. If there are 100,000 people in Zaire knocking at the church's door, we must answer the stirring of the Spirit. If God can add a thousand every day to His church, then the time has come for action.

In the face of a small band of dedicated people, the so-called superior force may suffer defeat. Only a comparatively small band of people continued their trust in prophetic truth following 1844 and its disappointment. But they were enough for God's purposes. Out of that small band has grown the globe-encompassing judgment-hour message.

Feeling small and isolated places us under a tyranny of fear. To overthrow this tyrant, look to the Spirit, who may give us powers we never imagined.

Pentecost turned a remnant into a city-shaking force. Prayer and the Spirit can do it again where you are, alone or few though you may be.

In the plan of God a faithful remnant will not only preserve His name in the earth, but will witness to the whole world. The operative word is *faithful*, not *remnant*. The faithful believe that God can accomplish wonders. Because He has done it for them, He can do it in the world, in the community, at home.

"God is always a majority" (The Acts of the Apostles, *p. 590*).

PUTTING ERROR ON THE SCAFFOLD

The kingdom and dominion, and the greatness of the kingdom under the whole heaven, shall be given to the people of the saints of the most High. Dan. 7:27.

"Truth forever on the scaffold,
Wrong forever on the throne."

In the last days God will reverse the poet's wisdom. He will judge error and destroy it. "They shall take away his dominion, to consume and destroy it unto the end" (Dan. 7:26).

The prophet also reveals how that will happen. He saw savage forces attacking God's people, God's truth, and God's law. A tyranny of error, apostasy, and corruption was ruling the earth. In the scandal of the cosmos, evil forces actually claimed the powers of God. They tried to determine what is truth, who are the righteous people, what rules will govern intelligent beings.

It takes the judgment to set the record straight. History would produce the Waldenses and record how error would grind them down. The Inquisition would arraign the true and the faithful and condemn them to torture and death, but the judgment will sit, and then the universe will know who was right.

Error hung the innocent Son of God on a Roman scaffold. No one could do anything to hold back that shameful event. In view of what befell Jesus, it should not surprise us that the tyranny of error still oppresses God's people and obscures His truth.

Error infiltrates the office, the workplace, our homes. The innocent find themselves declared guilty. Concocted rules make good actions appear wrong. The majority insists it is right, whatever the evidence says. The individual's life, all too often, echoes the cosmic situation.

The judgment consumes and destroys all error and wrong. The Innocent One, the Son of man, receives the kingdom from God and declares judgment in favor of God's people. Thus the future will take care of the grievance of God against the great accuser.

Today as you ask for God's grace, He will declare in your favor. Sin will no longer rule over you. Truth will take its place on the throne of your will. The tyranny of sin will be dead in Christ.

"While the followers of Christ have sinned, they have not given themselves to the control of evil. . . . The divine Advocate pleads in their behalf" (Testimonies, *vol. 5, p. 474*).

POLITICS PROVOKE THE POWER OF GOD

And now, Lord, behold their threatenings: and grant unto thy servants, that with all boldness they may speak thy word. Acts 4:29.

In these days of the Moral Majority, it pays to read the book of Acts. The early church had to deal with those who used political power for moral and religious purposes. Not too surprisingly, the politicians of Acts thought they were doing the will of God.

Consider the secular government of that day. The Herods featured largely in it. What an unsavory crew they were! Herod the Great tried to murder scores of innocent babies to make sure he killed Jesus, the infant king. Herod the Tetrarch stole Herodias, his half brother's wife. He also had John the Baptist put in prison and beheaded.

By the time the early church began its work, another Herod was conniving with the Jewish rulers. To secure their support he had James, the son of Zebedee, killed. Then he tried to make himself even more popular by putting Peter in prison, intending the same fate for him. Peter escaped and hid himself from this tyrant.

The early church saw, in the hideous end of this Herod, the proper fate of any ruler who combines with religious forces to destroy God's work. Herod dressed himself in silver. The Jews cried out that he had the voice of a god. He collapsed, worms devouring him, probably the victim of a burst hydatid cyst.

On the other side of the evil duo, high priests and rulers used every scrap of political clout they could muster to destroy the young church.

One would think that Acts would have taught its lesson for all time. Not so. Today both Protestants and Catholics do not hesitate to join hands with governments to attain their religious goals.

The end does not always justify the means. The Moral Majority speaks truly of moral decline and escalating depravity. The wrong lies in seeking legislative influence to govern the nation's spiritual habits.

To seek to achieve right living by self-improvement cannot have God's approval. He provides righteousness in Jesus Christ. Be right with Him so that right living might follow. The tyranny of right purposes with wrong means rules far too many. The only way to topple self from the throne is to give it to Jesus.

"Amid the working of evil, God's purposes move steadily forward to their accomplishment" (Patriarchs and Prophets, *p. 338).*

YOU CAN CHOOSE YOUR MASTER

Being then made free from sin, ye became the servants of righteousness. Rom. 6:18.

Paul gives us a choice of only two masters: sin or righteousness. He stresses the sinfulness of sin, how it separates us from God, how it offends Him, how it leaves us guilty and defenseless.

He also personifies it so that he may heighten our sense of its power. He knew just what a grip it could have. He tells how it takes advantage of every situation to "kill" us. Sin, the slavemaster, whips its victims toward destruction.

However, something happens when God justifies the sinner. Now he has a choice. The tyranny of sin has been totally shattered in the cross. In Christ the sinner dies to sin.

Paul sees us as possessing a sanctified will, which now has the right and the power to choose righteousness. Before this choice existed, sin had control. Now Christ sets us free from sin's dominion so that we may choose to live unto God.

The freedom to choose does not of itself suffice. God uses us as His instruments. We are alive to God, through Jesus Christ. Yielding says yes to the action of the Spirit. To know what is right, and to ask for that to happen, puts the resources of heaven on the side of the will.

Today the yielded life will correct itself against what it knows as the will of God. It will cry out to God for strength to choose what it knows to be right. It will not yield to sin. It will seek holy living.

In the dry outback of Australia the machinery of a century lies dead under the bright skies. Rub off a little rust from these machines, fill the tanks with fuel, swing the crank handle, and they would burst to life; at least, they seem that close to being in working order. But time has passed them by. Though they take scores of centuries to rust away, they will not know life.

Sin drains off the power of self-determination. The rust of habit eats at morality. The life looks passable at times, but it is a ghost of its Maker's intentions.

In Jesus, life comes again to the dead in sin. The road of righteousness waits open for travel. The Spirit gives power and the Lord points the way. And so we go toward heaven, carrying the gift of eternal life God has given in Jesus Christ.

"Yield yourself to Christ without delay; He alone, by the power of His grace, can redeem you from ruin" (Testimonies, *vol. 2, pp. 564, 565*).

THE DAY THAT DEATH DIED

He will swallow up death in victory; and the Lord God will wipe away tears from off all faces. Isa. 25:8.

As the prophet saw it, the day would come when the Lord would destroy the covering thrown over all people, the veil that covers all nations. He saw death as making a victim of all mankind, but he saw its certain end.

When a worker in a Swedish nuclear power station set off the alarm that alerted the world to the Chernobyl disaster, a pall spread over all the earth. The radioactive cloud carried death with it. But the fear went further. All saw how easily human error could pollute the whole planet. A veil of death may yet cover all people.

In the agitation that followed Chernobyl, the young looked into the future and saw it bleak and, perhaps, without hope. The words over the entry to the Hades of Greek myth might well apply, "Abandon hope, all ye who enter here."

But has hope heard its death knell? The Word of God says no. Rather, the bell has tolled for death. In the farseeing vision of the prophet, God will engulf death.

In Hannover, Germany, you can still see the tomb of an atheist woman. The inscription declares that no resurrection will open that tomb. The seed that spoiled the atheist's boast has grown large and tall. The Creator's pine tree mocks those who declare the finality of death.

Death died when Jesus rose from the grave. Until Jesus rose, sin could have no other result but the death of the sinner.

The death of death has another message for us. If death can be defeated, then those other situations that appear unalterable may also yield to Christ's power. Sin has a victor, Jesus Christ. Fear has a victor, Jesus Christ. Doubt has a victor, Jesus Christ. The Lord declares that in Him all things are possible. The resurrection of Jesus has changed forever what can be done for the sinner.

Who swallows up death in victory? Jesus Christ, we might answer. But Paul perceives more clearly than that. The victory is ours. Through Christ our own death has lost its finality and power.

"But thanks be to God, which giveth us the victory through our Lord Jesus Christ" (1 Cor. 15:57).

"Faith is a mightier conqueror than death" (The Ministry of Healing, *p. 62).*

THE DAY SATAN LOST CONTROL

The prince of this world cometh, and hath nothing in me. John 14:30.

Make no mistake about it. Jesus is talking about a defeated foe. In the previous verses, Jesus has talked to the disciples about the peace and comfort the Spirit brings. The promise of the Spirit looks to the future and what God will do for His children. Satan has fallen from his position of power. The moment Jesus began His ministry, Satan had lost. He found no toehold in the character of Jesus.

You can mark the point where Satan knew his defeat. When Jesus came out of the water of baptism, the voice of God acknowledged Him as Son. The Holy Spirit descended on Him. From that time forward the Victor had taken control.

Not only do the wilderness temptations show how Jesus triumphed where humanity failed, but they also show Jesus as victor over the devil. True, he will lie in ambush to menace Jesus. During His Passion, the evil one sought His destruction. But from the moment of His baptism the battle was joined, and victory has gone to Christ.

The cross led to the Resurrection. Satan could not hold Jesus in the tomb. He arose victorious.

Before the winter sun rises in Australia, the sky may take on extraordinary beauty. Brilliant shafts of blue and pink fan from the hidden orb and fill the heavens. The display lasts a few minutes and then vanishes as the sun emerges.

From the Resurrection, shafts of light fan with hope across the sky of faith. The Sun of righteousness has risen and brought life to all.

In the word pictures of the Bible, Satan rules in darkness. Those whom he controls sit in darkness. But darkness flees the rising Sun. The Word calls Jesus the Light of the world. The gospel declares that Jesus has brought light to all nations and dispelled darkness. The devil cannot abide the Light that lightens everyone who comes into the world.

Just as darkness cannot live with light, so Satan loses control when the Light enters. His defeat is known and published through the lives we live in the power of Jesus Christ. The tyranny is broken. Jesus lives. Jesus rules.

"They knew that the destruction of sin and Satan was forever made certain, that the redemption of man was assured, and that the universe was made eternally secure" (The Desire of Ages, p. 764).

KISSING GATE

Mercy and truth are met together; righteousness and peace have kissed each other. Ps. 85:10.

Walkers on the countryside footpaths of England will not go very far before they arrive at a kissing gate. Designed to stop cattle from using human trails, the gate takes its name from its unusual structure. Three posts sit in the ground in a narrow V. From a fourth post in the open end of the V swings the gate. To go through, the walker pushes the gate to the farther side and then sidles to the narrow end of the V. The gate then swings past him to the other side, and he can sidle out.

Couples coming to such a gate must go through separately. But if they follow each other closely, a moment comes when they are face-to-face. Hence the name "kissing gate."

In the thought world of David, four virtues travel together. Mercy joins hands with truth; peace embraces righteousness. For the sinner walking toward the heavenly Canaan, these couples meet in the kissing gate of salvation and open the way to eternal life.

To be at peace we must have righteousness. Unless God declares us just, we will always be in torment. If truth alone tests us, our fate is certain and horrible. For salvation's sake, mercy and truth must meet together.

This little bit of Hebrew poetry introduces us to a favorite device of ancient writers—parallelism. Not only do the four relate in the way the verse suggests, but the knowing reader would be expected to link them vertically so that mercy and righteousness function together, and so do truth and peace.

How unlikely such pairings are to our thinking! We would prefer to link mercy and peace and then put together truth and righteousness. But that is not God's way. Righteousness depends on the mercy of God. Peace comes because we have walked in the way of truth.

All four characteristics meet in the Saviour. On the road from Jericho the cry "Son of David, have mercy on me" received an instant answer. At Jesus' hands, blind Bartimaeus received his sight and forgiveness for his sins. Jesus alone lived as a righteous man among men. He is the only just man. He declares Himself the way, the truth, and the life. He gives the peace that only He owns.

"Both our title to heaven and our fitness for it are found in the righteousness of Christ" (The Desire of Ages, *p. 300).*

WHEN GOD CHOSE HIS CHILDREN

When the fulness of the time was come, God sent forth his Son,
. . . that we might receive the adoption of sons. Gal. 4:4, 5.

Those who had invaded the Galatian church and were rallying the members to an alien flag had crossed into enemy territory. At the cross, faith took over as the system of salvation. Fighting for an out-dated system meant the loss of salvation. God no longer lifted up the law of Moses as His standard, but called all to faith in Jesus.

When faith came, things changed. New relationships between God and man were set in place. The Jews might call themselves children of Abraham (Gal. 3:29), but in the Son, God adopts all the faithful as His children. When Jesus died in the fullness of time, the family of God included those from every race who would hear and accept His grace. Right now He has adopted you.

Ties of blood pale into insignificance as God accepts us as His children. Both what He does for us and what we should do for Him go beyond the normal father-son bond. The child of God values the link with the Father more than any earthly kin.

To be a son or daughter of God shows the freedom God has given us. Just as He chose us, so we choose Him. His will makes us His; we call Him our Father. In this way God tells us that He has committed Himself to us. We trust His will because He is our Father.

The adoption model of divine-human relationships goes one step further. It has a double aspect. On the one hand, we have sonship now. We cry Abba, Father (Gal. 4:6) through the Spirit. On the other hand, we wait for the adoption of sons (Rom. 8:23). Sonship is a goal of hope and a gift from the future. Paul creates an already-but-not-yet tension. We both have our sonship and wait for our adoption. What the Lord will give us in the kingdom we already possess through the Spirit.

Salvation is about relationships. Outside of Christ we have no saving relationship to God. In adopting us, God wants us to know that He has freely chosen us. Unlike in the usual adoption process, the child of God has a say. The Father adopts us as His children, with all the rights and privileges of a child of Heaven. We accept Him as our Father, and so He gives us eternal life.

"Faith will lift up the repenting soul to share the adoption of the sons of God" (Patriarchs and Prophets, *p. 754).*

A NEW GARMENT FOR THE WORLD

Thou art the same, and thy years shall have no end. The children of thy servants shall continue, and their seed shall be established before thee. Ps. 102:27, 28.

The Hebrew eye looked out on nature and saw it as clothing. Corn clothed the valleys and hills. Cedars crowned the hilltops of Lebanon. God had made garments for the world, and kept them fresh and beautiful.

Not too far from that thought emerged the idea that the world was growing old as a garment (Ps. 102:26). One could no more expect the clothing of the world to last forever than to have clothes that never wore out.

Yes, said Jesus, look around you. Mankind's spiritual hopes have worn threadbare. The theologians and religious leaders are trying to patch an old garment. But this age lies in tatters. You can attach nothing new to it.

Jesus came preaching the gospel of the kingdom as a new age for the world. The old was passing away. God was making all things new. In the future, God would give the physical world new garments. Right now He was giving the world the new garments of His salvation.

In this new age of the kingdom, no one puts on old garments, but clothes himself in the wedding garment of Christ's righteousness. Dressed in these new robes, the citizen of the kingdom joins the community of the redeemed.

In the kingdom of faith, the white clothing given by God provides security. In the ancient world, the cities and villages employed watchmen. If one of them was found asleep, he was stripped of his clothes and they were burned. The one who walks naked and whose shame is seen (Rev. 3:18) has not watched for the coming of the Lord.

In this time of Laodicea and the falling of the seven last plagues, the new age of faith in Christ comes under threat. Sharp divisions occur. The call to show allegiance to one cause or the other separates the peoples of the earth into two camps. Those who keep their garments (Rev. 16:15), who maintain their faith, will have joy and reward.

The gathering of the white-robed around the throne of God will prove to the universe that the new era of faith has achieved God's purposes.

"Faith, living faith, always bears upward to God and glory; unbelief, downward to darkness and death" (Testimonies, *vol. 1, p. 144*).

WRONG WAY! GO BACK!

For ye were as sheep going astray; but are now returned unto the Shepherd and Bishop of your souls. 1 Peter 2:25.

Not every driver reads freeway signs. Imagine the horror of finding yourself going the wrong way up an exit ramp. Yet it happens somewhere every day. The signs jump at you in scarlet, "Wrong Way! Go Back!" But that does not stop everybody.

When the signs of the Spirit shout "Wrong Way! Turn Back! Repent!" what do we do? Repent? Convert? Turn around? Go back?

To turn around is not usually easy. To do so makes a judgment on previous views and behavior. Some find conversion relatively simple, others find it difficult or even impossible.

Conversion always has a practical result. Theory and concept do not achieve change by themselves. When we turn around, the life changes. The converted person does not continue deliberately in sin but takes a new moral and ethical direction. To return to the Good Shepherd means to leave the trails of one's own choice and accept God's choice for us.

The converted person turns his will to God. He turns from the blindness and error of his ways and returns home to the Saviour. He does not concentrate on the old life, as if that were what had to be dealt with, but on Jesus Christ. Conversion is not God forcing His will on us, but us turning to Him in an act of the will.

In the figurative language of the book of Revelation, the Lamb stands on Mount Zion. From every direction the redeemed stream toward Him. Christ takes His stand where all ought to stand. Anyone who repents turns toward Him and takes his place with Him.

In the feudal system of the Middle Ages, everyone acknowledged another person as lord. The serfs bowed to the lord of the manor. The lords of the manors bowed to the dukes and earls. They in turn bowed to the king, who was supposed to kneel before God. Your immediate lord owned you, body and soul. He could command your services, march you to battle, change your status.

Jesus, the Lord of the converted, commands us in the new life. We yield to His will. Like the sheep of Peter's promise we return to the one Shepherd, the one Lord, Jesus Christ our Redeemer.

"The more we know of God, the higher will be our ideal of character and the more earnest our longing to reflect His likeness" (Thoughts From the Mount of Blessing, *p. 19*).

THE FINGER OF GOD

If I with the finger of God cast out devils, no doubt the kingdom of God is come upon you. Luke 11:20.

The abominations that fell on Egypt came to a climax when the magicians tried to counter the plague of lice. It was beyond them. To Pharaoh they said, "This is the finger of God" (Ex. 8:19). What lies beyond man's ability or comprehension may represent God's action.

In Jesus' day the source of His power came under question. Did it come from God? Had He formed a league with evil, like Pharaoh's lackeys? Jesus turned back the power of evil, reclaimed people from the clutches of Satan. No one had ever done such things before. Here, then, was the finger of God, the power of the Holy Spirit at work.

I suppose that every day countless people seek and accept new directions for their lives. In a sense, they convert. But this is not the repentance that the Bible asks for. Jesus called for repentance toward God. The repentance that claims God's saving action turns the life to Him. To those who do not seek salvation for themselves, the changes raise questions. To those who understand God's purpose, it is saving power—the finger of God.

In the Old Testament the call to repent sought a return to the purer, more obedient days of the past. John the Baptist called for repentance in the light of the coming kingdom. Repentance that answers Jesus calls us forward rather than directs us to a better past. We look to the future and prepare for it. We repent in order that we might share in that kingdom.

In the contrasts of Luke 18 and 19, Zacchaeus understands true repentance. He sees what life in the kingdom of God asks of him and accepts that request. The rich young ruler wants affirmation of his past success within the coming kingdom. The radical call to repentance passes him by.

The Pharisee, praying in the Temple, cannot repent. He has measured himself against the social demands of his culture and finds satisfaction in his progress. The publican repents because he knows that he falls so far short of any goodness that only God can offer him hope.

The simple basis for repentance is this: because God has turned to man in Jesus Christ, man can turn to God.

"He longs to clasp our hands, to have us look to Him in simple faith, permitting Him to guide us" (Thoughts From the Mount of Blessing, *p. 12*).

THE CROSS: THE TREE OF LIFE

O foolish Galatians, who hath bewitched you, that ye should not obey the truth, before whose eyes Jesus Christ hath been evidently set forth, crucified among you? Gal. 3:1.

In a future world of God's making, the tree of life will stand among God's people. God intended it that way from the very beginning. In Eden all paths led to the tree of life, where the first pair met God and where they plucked the fruit that kept death away.

With their shameful and hideous torture stake, the Romans thought they would end the story of Jesus. Instead they planted the tree of life anew in the midst of mankind. From that day on, the Christian proclamation has declared the cross to be central to life. All paths lead to it. There all may see Christ lifted up so that eternal life might be theirs.

What did Paul mean when he said that Christ had been set upon the cross among the Galatians? He was declaring the centricity of the cross.

The cross does not stand in the past, locked into history, something to point back to, marvel at, and adore. The cross moves with us as the word of the gospel is preached. Here, today, in our midst, stands the cross. Not that the Word of God asks us to describe over and over the nature of Roman execution and how Jesus died. It asks us to declare God's saving act in Jesus, to tell all that the Crucified One died for our sins.

The other tree, the tree of knowledge of good and evil, had brought death to the race. The tree of Golgotha reversed the loss of Eden. In the knowledge of the cross, the tree of life returns. Not everyone will see it that way. The cross still scandalizes; it still looks foolish to some. Yet it is the power of God unto salvation to them that believe.

The Galatian church had turned their eyes away from the cross. They looked to the past. God had given Moses a law; should not that also have priority? Did it not have the right to make demands of them? Did it not offer life through its provisions?

Anyone who wants to involve other than the cross in his salvation is out of his mind, Paul says. Once we see the cross in its glory, all our thoughts will flow to it. There and there alone God has provided life.

"In the matchless gift of His Son, God has encircled the whole world with an atmosphere of grace as real as the air which circulates around the globe" (Steps to Christ, p. 68).

THE CROSS: POWER AND WISDOM

Unto them which are called, both Jews and Greeks, Christ the power of God, and the wisdom of God. 1 Cor. 1:24.

"When the chips are down" has taken on a new meaning. Once it meant that something was really at stake. Now it means that the computer has gone wrong, or some program has malfunctioned.

Quality control rejects more silicon chips than it accepts. In fact, high memory and heavily programmed chips are very difficult to produce. The more one asks of a chip, the more likely that it will be thrown away.

Mankind's condition parallels that of chips, except that things are far worse. All humans are faulty. All are rejects. The cross teaches that the One "rejected of men" is, after all, the perfect One, in whom we may fix our hope.

Two things are wrong about man. First, all have sinned and come short of the glory of God. Not only do we each have a list of sins accumulated against us, but we also possess a depraved, basically sinful nature. It matters not whether one speaks of religious people, such as the Jews, or secular, pagan people, such as the Greeks. Self-seeking hostility against God permeates the whole race.

The second is perhaps more subtle. Salvation and grace flow from God to man. Salvation that comes wholly from God means that mankind is always receiving. Against this, we rebel. We want to have our religiosity accepted and then have God build on it. Or we would like our wisdom and education counted and then for us to be lifted to higher planes by the power of God. In other words, we say, Look what I have done. Now, Lord, carry me where I cannot go.

The cross stands over against human power and wisdom. In it God provides power to save. He gives us life in Christ. The old nature dies on the cross, and the new nature takes over.

The God who sees us as we truly are will have none of our self-seeking, self-improvement plans. Our wisdom just will not do. Any life built on a foundation other than Christ and Him crucified will surely totter and fall. The divine Quality Controller knows us better than we know ourselves. This is hard for the carnal heart to accept, but nonetheless it has been tested against time and proved true against any doubt.

"The spirit of Jesus Christ ever has a renewing, restoring power upon the soul that has felt its own weakness and fled to the unchanging One" (Fundamentals of Christian Education, *pp. 264, 265).*

COME TO YOUR SENSES

I will set off and go to my Father. Luke 15:18, NEB.

The youth stands by the pigsty, letting the pods fall slowly back to the snuffling swine. All the tracks out from the pigpen carry the sign "No Through Road." Except one. It means gulping down his pride, making the long trek back, apologies, an uncertain future.

He practices his speech and says goodbye to the kind Gentile farmer who kept him alive when his Jewish countrymen offered no help. He makes the final turn onto the home plantation. Suddenly he sees a distant figure running toward him. It is his father. He tries to read the expression on his father's face and sinks to his knees. But before he can kneel, his father catches him up and kisses him.

Words tumble out—the well-rehearsed speech, "Father, I have sinned, against God and against you; I am no longer fit to be called your son" (Luke 15:18, 19, NEB). But the father cuts him short. He never gets to say, "Treat me as one of your paid servants." The son's intentions mean nothing in this situation. Instead, the father declares his. Bring the best robe, put a ring on his finger, bind sandals on his feet, make a feast.

What he could not earn or reclaim, the father gives to him. In the story the father bestows more on the prodigal than he had before he packed his bags and left home.

Thus Jesus shows God's intentions toward the repenting sinner. Our plans have no real value. Instead, in Jesus Christ He gives us what we can never earn.

Can you imagine that middle-aged man racing down the path, dignity forgotten, sandals clacking, robe flying? Thus God shows us the eagerness with which He seeks and welcomes the lost.

The record states that there by the hogs the son "came to his senses." To know how sorry your circumstances and how desirable even a small corner of the Father's house is, is to come to your senses. To say "I will set off and go to my Father" is to come to your senses.

Are we not all, this day, prodigals asked to come to our senses? Every day, even the most holy of us wastes the inheritance of faith and sins against the Father. Only as we know ourselves as we truly are and come each day for the embrace of love and the Father's gifts can we be His obeying children. For such reunions Love spreads its feast.

"If you take even one step toward Him in repentance, He will hasten to enfold you in His arms of infinite love" (Christ's Object Lessons, p. 206).

CONTINUALLY AT THE KING'S TABLE

And he bowed himself, and said, What is thy servant, that thou shouldest look upon such a dead dog as I am? 2 Sam. 9:8.

When the kingdom had settled down a little after the deaths of his former monarch, Saul, and his friend Jonathan, David began to reflect on them. In the bitter days following their defeat, David's allies had sought out Saul's family and supporters, killing them. And yet, there still might be someone left alive.

David asked, "Is there yet any that is left of the house of Saul, that I may shew him kindness for Jonathan's sake?" (2 Sam. 9:1).

They found Saul's servant Ziba. Yes, he knew of a lad, Jonathan's son.

And so David found Mephibosheth. He was a pitiful figure. In the panic that followed Joab's feud with Abner, a maid had run off into the hills with the 5-year-old boy. She had tripped, throwing the child hard to the ground. His spine injured, he never walked normally again.

David gave the former lands of Saul to Ziba to farm for Mephibosheth. To the latter he said, "You shall eat at my table always."

How did Mephibosheth react when first told of the king's bounty? We have his words: "What is thy servant, that thou shouldest look upon such a dead dog as I am?"

A happy ending to a sad story! Yet like all Bible stories, the story is more than that. It speaks to us of the King who rescues the poor, lame souls of this earth and feeds them at the table of grace.

Through the grace of the Lord Jesus we come to the King's table. No matter that our value equals no more than a dead dog's; He calls us to His side and sets the banquet of love.

The story has in it some things that remind us of Jesus' parable of the wedding feast. To his table David brings the rejected fugitive and gives him the same status as his own sons.

We cannot measure what God has done for us in Jesus Christ. He poured out not just love but the very being and nature of heaven.

And what should we do in response? Move into His household as Mephibosheth moved into David's. Draw our chair up to His table and there eat of the goodness and plenty God has provided. Sit next to the King and count ourselves princes and princesses.

"He will bring you into His banqueting house, and His banner over you shall be love" (Christ's Object Lessons, *pp. 206, 207).*

THE EMPLOYER WHO WORKS FOR HIS STAFF

I say unto you, that he shall gird himself, and make them to sit down to meat, and will come forth and serve them. Luke 12:37.

The story has an improbable air to it. Did an employer in Jesus' day ever wait on tables and serve his staff? These days one could just imagine a boss doing it as a gimmick. Back then the lord treated servants like objects rather than people. Slaves could expect very little in the way of thoughtfulness or sympathy.

In so many stories that Jesus told, He turned around the common practice in order to make a point. What does He want to teach here?

In this chapter Jesus talks about money, anxiety for the future, and how God cares for His children. Inevitably that raises the question, What does God expect of us?

First, the follower of Jesus will wait faithfully for the Lord to return. Time will test faith and constancy. Having put your trust in Jesus, continue to keep it there.

Second, the disciple switches the center of hope away from this world to heaven. Because preparation for heaven has priority, attention will fix on spiritual values rather than material gain.

Third, watching for the coming of the Lord will bring the rewards of vigilance. Faith will remain intact. No thief will snatch it away.

Fourth, in all that affects faith in Jesus, patience will prevail. As a security guard will make the rounds hour by hour, so the faithful servant will count off the days and years, but not give up the blessed hope.

Servants in Jesus' day received small pickings from the master's table. He could scrape up the leftovers or stew the scraps from the butchering of an animal. If weevils had infested the grain, that would be his. The chief steward would count into and out of the kitchen every portion of food to make sure no hungry slave stole any.

In the incredible event of this parable, Jesus dons the servant's garb. He brings the portions He might have kept for Himself. What could not happen in the world of master and servant provides the bounties of love and grace in the world of faith.

The table is spread. He is serving. Take, eat, and live.

"We try too hard to take care of self ourselves. . . . And the Lord does not do much for them, for they give Him no opportunity" (Testimonies, *vol. 2, p. 196).*

DUTY DOES NOT NEED A REWARD

When ye shall have done all those things which are commanded you, say, We are unprofitable servants: we have done that which was our duty to do. Luke 17:10.

Pity the servant when the master had no one else to help with the work. Life for such could be short and brutish. During the day he might pull the plow while his master guided it, or if a little more fortunate, work alongside an ox.

The small holdings of the Jewish peasant could not support a large staff of laborers. Therefore, when a farmer acquired a slave, the unfortunate one must make every moment count. At the end of a hard day's work no one waited on the slave to trade slippers for his boots or to offer a cooling drink. No one listened sympathetically to the complaint, "I had a hard day at the office. You have no idea what the boss expects me to do."

Before the slave could gulp a few bits and pieces for his evening meal, the master had to have his meal. The slave had to stir up the fire, heat the stew pot, ladle out a portion, and take it to the master.

Two wrong conclusions can come from the commands of our Lord. First, we may think that doing His commands gives us the right to eternal life. This parable teaches what not to expect from obedience. It will not change or improve our status. Faith in Jesus places on us the demand to trust and obey. The saved serve not to receive reward but because salvation motivates them to respond in lifestyle and service.

Second, we may figure out that the purpose of obedience is to give smaller or greater rewards, depending on our faithfulness. Not so, Jesus said. Service represents duty. Do the commands of the Master because He asks, not for reward.

The parable stands in sharp contrast to the earlier one in which the master girds himself and waits table, serving his servants. The first parable declares God's provision for us. The second, our response to that provision. The new covenant contracts God to provide grace for every sinner who comes in repentance. The same covenant contracts the receiver of that grace to love God and keep His commandments. In the sphere of works, you can have duty without grace; but in the sphere of divine love, you cannot have grace without duty.

"Self is forgotten, merged in the life of Christ. To be rich in good works is as natural as their breath" (Testimonies, vol. 2, p. 465).

JESUS INVITES TWO DISCIPLES HOME

He saith unto them, Come and see. They came and saw where he dwelt, and abode with him that day. John 1:39.

In writing his Gospel, John quickly gathers an aura of mystery and divine purpose about Jesus. He declares Jesus to be the eternal Word who became flesh and dwelt among us.

Then he adds the prophetic figure, John the Baptist. We hear John describe Jesus as the Lamb of God, which takes away the sin of the world.

Then suddenly we are with the ordinary humdrum of life. Or are we? It seems a simple enough question as Andrew and John asked it: "Where do You live?" And a simple enough answer as Jesus replied, "Come and see." But John has purposes behind what he writes.

Jesus first asks, "What seek ye?" A few moments later He says, "Come and see." John chose these words carefully. They give us his motive for writing the Gospel. The Gospel of John puts Jesus on display. It explores His origins, records His teachings, documents His actions. Look, says John, this is Jesus Christ, the Saviour of the world.

In recording Jesus' teaching, John paid special attention to what Jesus said of Himself. "I am the bread of life." "I am the light of the world." "I am the bread which came down from heaven." The whole purpose of John's Gospel is to reveal who Jesus is.

Andrew and his friend went home with Jesus and spent the day with Him. Where was He staying? We do not know. What we know is that their visit made a great impression on the pair. They began to witness about Jesus. Andrew made up his mind immediately about the identity of Jesus. In the other Gospels we wait many months before Peter declares Jesus to be the Messiah. In John, Andrew perceived Jesus to be the Messiah after just a few hours.

John filled his Gospel with Jesus so that we might witness to Him. What Jesus said in invitation becomes the invitation of all His disciples. In his witness to Nathanael, Philip used Jesus' words, "Come and see."

Faith cannot be taught by logic or scientific reasoning. John the evangelist knew that. Farther on in his Gospel he calls all to "behold the Man." Faith comes from seeing Jesus, knowing what He is, what He does, how He can help. How better could He welcome us than to say, "Come and see"?

"It is through Christ, by the ministration of His heavenly messengers, that every blessing comes from God to us" (The Desire of Ages, *p. 143).*

HOUSE ON OFFER

If I go and prepare a place for you, I will come again, and receive you unto myself; that where I am, there ye may be also. John 14:3.

Scattered across Australia, New Zealand, America, and England the houses I have called home still stand. In Carcoar, people still draw water from the well that served my parents years ago. The Mandurama house graces the main street of that small village. There an angry husband tried to shoot my father after he baptized the man's wife and daughter.

Near the crumbled ruins at Scot's Creek grows a willow planted as a wand that my aunt once used as a skipping rope. The apricots still bear their luscious crop beside the house in Mooroopna. In Takoma Park, neighbors still lean across the fence and yarn Sunday morning away.

I love all those houses. In an ideal world it might be possible to stand them side by side or merge their better features into one magnificent tribute to nostalgia.

In John's Gospel Jesus talks so frequently of His life with His Father that it becomes a feature of the Gospel. He has a home, the Gospel says, with the Father. In that home He and the Father are one. He has left that place to do the Father's will, but He is going back.

Home with the Father has so many delights that He wants to share it with His earthly friends—to those who trust in Me I will give everlasting life so that they may dwell with Me and My Father.

Do not let the majesty of the language of John hide the simple nature of the appeal that Jesus makes. Heaven is My home. There I live at one with God My Father. We want you to join Us in Our home.

For Jesus, going away and coming again form two parts of one action. The going away has only one purpose—so that He may come again. While He is away He is preparing for His return. He longs to end His mediatorial work and receive to Himself those for whom He intercedes.

Mediation and intercession have no fulfillment in themselves. They hold open the offer of a house in heaven for those for whom the Father and Son have prepared it. We go to our Lord for forgiveness so that we keep our names on the list for a home in heaven. He is coming to receive us. While He waits that moment He prepares both a place for us, and us for a place in His Father's house.

"Hear the gracious welcome given to those who in this life have cooperated with Christ" (The Ministry of Healing, *p. 506).*

DWELLING IN THE PRESENCE OF GOD

Behold, the tabernacle of God is with men, and he will dwell with them, and they shall be his people, and God himself shall be with them, and be their God. Rev. 21:3.

The Sunday morning trip from the mission compound to the Addis Ababa airport passed a large Coptic church. A high fence enclosed the structure. Through the gates streamed the morning congregation. It looked so normal. But then something odd occurred. A woman, lovely in her pure white dress, stepped from the side of her husband and sons. Her daughters went with her. They joined a group of women similarly clad.

Some of the women simply stood and looked through the wire mesh. Others clung to it as if to press themselves closer to the house of God. A few knelt and prayed toward the entrance. Only male adults could enter.

Inside, a heavy curtain barred the way to its most holy room. In Coptic belief God comes to this most sacred place, and the priests commune with Him in prayer.

That which denies access to the presence of God plays on people's fears, permits manipulation of the ignorant and needy, and provides for one group to oppress another.

At the entrance to that security fence in Ethiopia guards sorted out who might enter and who must watch from afar. But that is not God's way. No Peter stands at the gate of heaven to turn on and off the welcome sign. Over each of the 12 gates to the New Jerusalem God has written, "Come in."

We know this is so because Jesus acted that way while on earth. He came to seek and save. He received and cleansed sinners. He called the world to come to Him.

In John's vision of heaven no ghettos marred the streets of gold, no privileged few controlled access to the Ruler. The family of God dwelt together as one people in one city.

Discrimination still bars some of God's people from full sharing in the benefits of the community of Christ. The fences that keep some people out collapse only as each one of us pulls down what we see between ourselves and others.

In a growing and increasingly diverse church it pays to remember how God welcomes all in Jesus Christ.

"Wherever hearts are open to receive the truth, Christ is ready to instruct them" (The Desire of Ages, p. 194).

ONE SACRIFICE ENOUGH

For by one offering he hath perfected for ever them that are sanctified. Heb. 10:14.

The document carries the heading "Inquiry for Enclosing a Woman." It tells of one Christine Carpenter who requested to "be shut up in a narrow place in the churchyard adjoining the parish church of Schire, that therein she may be enabled to serve God the more worthily."

On July 11, 1329, in the English village of Shere, an assembly of villagers and visiting churchmen watched. Masons bricked in the little enclosure at the side of the church. Inside was Christine. A small hole served for the local people to feed her. You may still see the slot, slanted toward the altar, which let her watch the daily round of service.

Apparently her penance became too much to bear. In 1332 she broke out of her cell, probably with the help of sympathizers. But an oath was an oath. With the authority of the pope himself, the local church authorities forced her back into her cell so that she might fulfill her solemn vow. Declared the pontiff from Avignon, "Christine shall be thrust back into the said re-enclosure. . . . You shall take care to guard her . . . that she may learn how nefarious was her committed sin."

A strange story out of a past we can scarcely understand. Can you imagine the longing for a holy life, the sense of sin, that would demand such a penance? You can almost hear the thoughts: *In there the devil won't get near me. In there God will see how sorry I am. This sacrifice of mine will wipe out all my past and future sins.*

She found, of course, that the devil follows the mind, not the body. The struggle for a pure life went on.

God's plan for us does not include the torture of mind or body to establish our worth or to attract His sympathy and forgiveness. The struggle ends when we place our wills completely at the disposal of God. The ultimate test is not over subduing this vice or controlling that emotion, but over submitting our wills.

The answer to our needs lies outside ourselves in the one sacrifice of Jesus Christ. This alone sanctifies and perfects us. The will that accepts its own inadequacy and Christ's complete sacrifice has made the giant step that can lead to holy living before God.

"The greatest battle that was ever fought by man is the surrender of self to the will of God" (Thoughts From the Mount of Blessing, p. 141).

A NAME FOR GOD'S DWELLING

And after that I looked, and, behold, the temple of the tabernacle of the testimony in heaven was opened. Rev. 15:5.

In a city I know, the Hall of Justice stands next to the Hall of Peace. But that nation knows neither justice nor peace. The citizens that pass those grandiose buildings make wry and sarcastic comments. When names represent propaganda rather than the true nature of government, unrest and scoffing are automatic.

In the vision presented in today's text John hears the name of the heavenly temple. It immediately thrusts us back into the halcyon days of God's relationship with Israel in the wilderness.

The victors of Revelation 15 have passed through their wilderness experience. The remnant have survived fierce attacks engineered by the devil and carried out by the dragon, the beast, and the false prophet. God has led with deliverance after deliverance just as He saved ancient Israel.

Yes, the vision says, God has a temple in heaven. But do not confuse that temple with either Solomon's Temple or Herod's Temple. Stephen the martyr summed it up when he accused the Jews of his day of worshiping the Temple and restricting the ability of God to work where and when He would.

The temple of God has the same character as the tabernacle in the wilderness. Those who look to it have God as leader and deliverer. They have not wandered aimlessly, but always under God's providence.

The heavenly temple also declares God's true character. He has given it the name "testimony." As Israel went into its wilderness experience, God wrote the testimony on tables of stone. It showed the people the character of their God.

Israel knew the tables as the tables of testimony, the ark as the ark of testimony, and the veil as the veil of testimony. Finally, they called the whole structure the tent or tabernacle of testimony.

God has not changed. We may still examine His character through the Decalogue. Our prayers and His mercy have their roots in the heavenly hall of justice and peace, from which hope and joy issue to God's people.

"Doing, not saying merely, is expected of the followers of Christ. It is through action that character is built" (Thoughts From the Mount of Blessing, *p. 149).*

THROUGH THE SHEDDING OF BLOOD

By faith Abel offered unto God a more excellent sacrifice than Cain, by which he obtained witness that he was righteous. Heb. 11:4.

Westerners may not attend the daily sacrifice of live goats in the temple of Kali in Calcutta, India. But once the slaughter has been finished, the bodies of the goats disposed of, and the blood washed away, one may wander at will. If one arrives early enough, the heads of the slain beasts still lie around while the devout offer their prayers.

At one visit a young couple had tied handwritten prayers into a tree, sacrificed an animal, and were pleading to the goddess for their first child.

A Christian, especially a Seventh-day Adventist Christian, could not visit such a place without mentally visiting the altar of burnt offerings in the ancient Jewish sanctuary. Was it like this? Did the smell of blood hang thus in the air? Were the priests as busy as the devotees of this pagan shrine?

One leaves such a place appalled at the sense of guilt and failure that brings a person to sacrifice an animal. What was God about when He commanded the first family to bring a sacrifice?

First, He imprinted on the penitent the affront of sin to God. If a prized animal from the flock must die, how carefully must one measure the future lest sin again offend.

Second, He forced the realization that sin had its penalty. The death of the animal spoke of the sinner's own death if sin remained uncleansed.

Third, the sinner participated in a prophetic rite. However dimly perceived, the sacrifice looked to the day when the Saviour would pay the final price for sin.

When God split open the Temple veil, He announced the end of the system of animal sacrifice as a way of dealing with sin. The death of the cross declares the enormity of sin as no animal sacrifice could. As the Innocent One, Jesus accepted the penalty of death for all who will put their trust in Him. He swallows up death with His victory.

But above all else, through the shedding of His blood Jesus makes all human sacrifices useless and valueless for salvation. He is fulfillment. He is hope. In Him death flies and life enters.

"Our ransom has been paid by our Saviour. No one need be enslaved by Satan. Christ stands before us as our all-powerful helper" (Selected Messages, *book 1, p. 309*).

CLEANSED FOR ALL TIME

And he said unto me, Unto two thousand and three hundred days; then shall the sanctuary be cleansed. Dan. 8:14.

In the tragic aftermath of the Chernobyl nuclear disaster, pictures of its widespread effects began to appear. In one series, cows in northern Italy showed symptoms of radiation sickness. In others, little children queued for iodine shots.

No one can tell precisely how many will die because of the escape of deadly radiation. All European countries predict that some of their citizens will sicken sooner or later from cancer caused by Chernobyl.

But no insult that man can offer to nature, or plague that he can bring on himself, compares with the all-pervasive pollution that has spread from the disobedience in Eden.

A concrete tomb may seal off the worst of the radiation at Chernobyl, but no structure or philosophy has protected from sin. Sin pollutes the earth. Sin pollutes mankind. Sin pollutes even those whose names God writes in the Lamb's book of life.

For ancient Israel the sacrifices of the Day of Atonement cleansed people and camp. In God's new Israel the sacrifice of Jesus Christ cleanses His people and the universe.

In Israel the faithful looked with hope to the Day of Atonement. The service over, the high priest emerged from the Most Holy Place to sounds of rejoicing. The day began in judgment and finished in joy.

In the antitype Jesus Christ marks each faithful child of God as His. Not one of them suffers the final judgment. They have stood all the tests through His grace, and none can take them from His hand. Thoughts of judgment turn from despair to joy as we look to Jesus the Intercessor and Saviour.

In Daniel's prophecy the attacks of the evil one appear to put all God's plans at risk. His truth, His people, His system for saving sinners—all come under threat. But the judgment declares in favor of God's people. The heavenly sanctuary and the atoning work of Christ prove more than sufficient.

To live in a time when this promise is meeting fulfillment fills us with hope. If Christ be for us, then who can deny us life in Him?

Christ *"asks for His people not only pardon and justification, full and complete, but a share in His glory and a seat upon His throne"* (The Great Controversy, *p. 484).*

OPEN FOR ALL TO ENTER

Having therefore, brethren, boldness to enter into the holiest by the blood of Jesus. Heb. 10:19.

The Spanish did not ship off all the Incan gold to Aragon and Castile. It is still being found at the sites of ancient cities and villages and in burial places. If you wish to see as fine a collection as exists, visit the vaults in the national bank in Bogotá, Colombia.

But go prepared to move fast and take in much in a short time. As the steel door swings open a group enters. The opening of the door triggers a mechanism, and a countdown commences. Five minutes, no more, no less, in which to absorb the skill and splendor of a civilization that deserved far better than it received.

The gold dazzles and intrigues. Why this shape? What did they do with that? How lovely! You whisper a hundred questions to yourself. And just as an answer or two offers itself, the lights begin to fade. Hesitate too long and two hours will pass before the cycle begins again and the door opens once more.

But if you want to examine the treasures of salvation, God has opened the door permanently. The High Priest of the heavenly sanctuary wears the robes of power and righteousness. The riches of His grace and glory adorn them. He beckons through the Spirit and bids you enter and feast on the splendor of His love.

The wilderness tabernacle taught the lesson of God's holiness and man's sinfulness. None might enter the holiest unless purified of all uncleanness through an elaborate and costly ceremony. Only by faith could the sinner accompany the high priest.

Cleansing through the sacrifice of Jesus gives access to the very presence of God. No doors that close. No time limits. No dimming lights. Yes, faith must go with you. Trust in what God does has always accompanied God's acceptance of His people. But Jesus leads the way and calls us to follow Him into the presence of God. Our faith goes with Him and finds cleansing, forgiveness, righteousness, and power.

Do not think that cleansing and purity precede our coming to the Father in Jesus. Not at all. We need no password, no code, no ticket. Through Jesus Christ God has opened to all His storehouse of mercy and grace. In absolute confidence we may go in and claim His salvation.

"The acceptance of the Saviour brings a glow of perfect peace, perfect love, perfect assurance" (Christ's Object Lessons, p. 420).

NEVER A TIME TO GIVE UP

Seeing then that we have a great high priest, that is passed into the heavens, Jesus the Son of God, let us hold fast our profession. Heb. 4:14.

Follow the reasoning of the author of Hebrews. Israel never achieved the spiritual rest God promised. They did not even have the land rest that God wanted to give them in Canaan. Joshua led the people, but he could not deliver what God had promised. Not that the record faults Joshua. Israel brought conflict and delay through their own unbelief.

Unbelief continually denies God's children their potential. The Word of God measures belief and, like a sword, determines motives as well as monitors deeds. Don't think that anyone can hide from God and His discerning Word. We all lie before Him like open books.

What should we do then? Take advantage of the new Joshua, who has already gone ahead to the promised inheritance of the saints. Jesus will lead His people into the presence of God, where true rest waits.

And so Hebrews brings us to the Great High Priest. Jesus our Captain not only defeats evil and provides a better hope but also intercedes at the right hand of God to give His people rest from sin.

From here on, Hebrews looks and looks again at the sanctuary service. If Jesus ministers in the heavenly sanctuary, what does that mean to those who put their faith in Him? From beginning to end the writer urges us to consider Jesus, the better one.

One by one the great of the Old Testament pass before us: Moses, Aaron, Joshua. Jesus gathers into Himself all the promises and qualities they represent, and goes beyond anything they could do or be.

He does the same with the Old Testament system of sacrifices and priests. Jesus offered Himself as sacrifice, and what can compare with that? He then takes His own sacrifice and ministers it on our behalf. He does this on His authority as God's appointed High Priest. His sacrifice excels because He knew no sin. His position excels because He reigns at the right hand of God. His authority excels because He holds the office of High Priest in the heavenly sanctuary.

In Christ you have the best God can do for you. With Him all is hope.

"Jesus has opened the way to the Father's throne, and through His mediation the sincere desire of all who come to Him in faith may be presented before God" (The Great Controversy, p. 489).

ATONEMAKER

But now hath he obtained a more excellent ministry, by how much also he is the mediator of a better covenant, which was established upon better promises. Heb. 8:6.

William Tyndale, Bible translator of the sixteenth century, coined the word to describe Jesus. He is the perfect Atonemaker. Through His sacrifice and ministry He conserves the interests of both parties for whom He acts. He makes at one God and man.

In no way should God contract any stain on His honor. Jesus secured this for God by His sinless life and impeccable sacrifice. In no way should the offender miss out on full rescue and reclamation. Jesus certifies our salvation through His resurrection and exaltation to the throne of God as our great high priest.

Jesus arches between God and man as the reconciling rainbow of promise. While His mediation continues, the way to life remains open. He is the Ladder joining earth to heaven. Through this Ladder man and God meet in reconciliation.

What He does occurs within the framework of the better covenant. The covenant relies on God writing His laws and commandments on our hearts rather than having us swear to obey them. Thus Christ secures the better hope.

Jesus not only seals the covenant through His sacrifice but also governs its operation. He makes us at one with God.

Not that the purpose of the new covenant differs from previous covenants. God has always promised to make to Himself a people and to be their God. The difference lies in the way God provides for obedience. Through the Son and the Spirit, who represent Him, God gives new natures, new hearts.

In the sanctuary, priest and people made good their shortcomings. Sacrifice and ceremony cast shadows forward toward the cross. But they were shadows no more. Whatever they produced in faith and obedience had its authentication in Jesus and the cross.

In the heavenly sanctuary Jesus offers Himself to atone for the shortfall of sin. In Him God confirms eternal realities. He is substance, not shadow. Whatever we do in faith and obedience comes from Jesus, Sacrifice and Mediator.

"He is our interceding High Priest, making an atoning sacrifice for us, pleading in our behalf the efficacy of His blood" (Fundamentals of Christian Education, *p. 370).*

THE JOY OF THE WEEK

Where wast thou when I laid the foundations of the earth?
declare, if thou hast understanding. Job 38:4.

In the days when ocean liners commanded media attention, huge crowds would gather to watch the launching of the blue-ribbon vessels. The ships gathered about them a mystique of national pride, luxury, romance, and intrigue. Shipbuilders vied for the honor of riveting their maker's plate to these vessels.

On the Sabbath day when the six days of Creation had ended, all made ready for review. Angels and created beings from other worlds came to inspect and to share the celebration of the Maker's masterpiece.

When He added Earth, how many new worlds had God already launched through space? One day we will know. Earth offered yet another opportunity to show God's love for fellowship and communication. And so He gathered the massed choirs of heaven, assembled the representatives of planet after planet, and staged an outpouring of joy and music. Fit hallelujahs for a new world born that day!

We remember the day in the past when God declared His work both finished and good. We look forward to the time when the Sabbath will bring us to the throne of the Lamb to worship and praise. But for the present the Sabbath brings the weekly joy of celebration.

God did not launch His spaceship Earth and leave it without a maker's plate. The Sabbath tells us that we travel through time and space on a world "Made by the Lord God." The Sabbath rivets that plate onto the ship that is the life of faith. In praise to the Manufacturer we join the chorus of praise as they did on that Sabbath so long ago. Like Job we are to remember and consider ourselves in relationship to Creation.

God gave us a model for Sabbath observance. Rest, yes. Worship, indeed. But also, celebrate! Let no shrunken soul steal joy from God's day. Be glad for God's power. Be glad for your humanity. Be glad for Earth. Be glad for the Love that made us, sustains us, and redeems us.

The Sabbath brings joy. As long as time lasts, God will use it to remind us of His power and our dependence. The weakness of humanity finds strength in knowing its Creator. The Sabbath is the joy of the weak, and also the joy of the week.

"God desires that the Sabbath day shall be to us a day of joy. There was joy at the institution of the Sabbath" (Testimonies, *vol. 6, p. 349).*

WE SHARE THIS TIME TOGETHER

This is the day which the Lord hath made; we will rejoice and be glad in it. Ps. 118:24.

We occupy space, but we share time.

Every created thing, every manufactured object, takes up a portion of space. The space your body occupies cannot be occupied by a tree, a bicycle, a flower, or another person. In the strictest sense, no person, animal, or thing can share space with another person, animal, or thing.

But we cannot cut out a chunk of time and make it solely and wholly ours. Whether we wish it or not, time is for everybody. We can limit the way we share time, but we cannot block other people off from time the way our bodies block off space from them.

As you read this, 5 billion other people are using the same time as you use. It passes by them as it does you. At Creation God made the Sabbath for sharing. He rested. Adam and Eve rested with Him. The angels and the created intelligences of other worlds shared the time of the Sabbath with God and His new creation.

Of course, any period of time may pass in isolation. You may choose not to spend your time awareness with anyone else. But God, through the Sabbath, would remind us that He made time. It measures all our lives. We cannot buy any exclusive right to it or deny it to anyone.

Because the Sabbath began as fellowship and worship, keeping the Sabbath involves sharing. We share it with God. God, who does not limit Himself to the human flow of time, enters earthtime to share the Sabbath with those who celebrate His creatorship.

We share it with other Christians. Adam shared the Sabbath with Eve. They both shared it with God's creation. No person can keep the Sabbath as well alone as at church. This excludes one of the purposes of the holy day: the sharing of time in worship and fellowship.

When the body moves from place to place it displaces air. When we swim we displace water. But time cannot be displaced, pushed elsewhere, or changed. It flows endlessly and ceaselessly.

In the flow of time God has given the Sabbath for sharing with Him and with others who want to share it with Him. Sharing the Sabbath centers on God. He meets us in this special portion of time. He has set it apart. He has made it for man!

"The Sabbath is the golden clasp that unites God and His people" (Testimonies, *vol. 6, p. 351).*

LIBERATION FOR THE SATAN-BOUND

Ought not this woman, being a daughter of Abraham, whom Satan hath bound, . . . be loosed from this bond on the sabbath day? Luke 13:16.

The map of the west coast of Scotland showed a clear route running south toward Fort William and Glasgow. Best of all, a ferry would cut short the journey and bring us to our hotel in time for some local sightseeing.

It did not trouble me that the ferry was waiting across the loch. Soon it would be on our side. But the waiting went on and on. Finally I opened the door and walked to a notice down by the ramp. The ferry had stopped running at the end of August, and this was October!

What if grace and salvation stopped each Friday evening at sunset? No calls to surrender, no journeys to the mourner's bench, no prayers of repentance. Hold them over, please, until Saturday sunset.

While the legalists of Judaism would not put it quite like that, Jesus could see the essence of their position no other way.

We distinguish sharply between physical illness and sin. The Jews of Jesus' day did not. Looking to the women's gallery, Jesus saw this woman bent over, pitiful, a hopeless case. Sabbath brought her shame, not joy. What great sin had caused this? Others asked this about her. She asked it about herself.

Jesus called the Satan-bound to Him and said to her, "Woman, thou art loosed from thine infirmity" (verse 12). In this miracle Jesus made clear how God regards the Sabbath.

If the Sabbath brings rest and worship only for the spiritually whole, then how will sinners find healing and fellowship? The Sabbath stands for liberation. It rebukes Satan and cuts the bonds strapped around sinners.

In the Sabbath, sin meets the Creator-Conqueror who sets sinners free. The Sabbath returns us to the garden of God. It reminds us of Christ's power to set free. It denies the tempter the advantage he gained over mankind at the tree.

After the crowd broke up that Sabbath, joy broke out. "All the people rejoiced for all the glorious things that were done by him" (verse 17).

"The power that created all things is the power that re-creates the soul in His own likeness" (Testimonies, *vol. 6, p. 350*).

THE DECISION TO OBEY

Many of the Jews and religious proselytes followed Paul and Barnabas: who, speaking to them, persuaded them to continue in the grace of God. Acts 13:43.

The story begins much the same as did the beginning of Jesus' ministry in Galilee. However, this time it was Paul beginning his ministry among the Gentiles. On both occasions Sabbath has brought them to the synagogue. Both times the rulers of the synagogue have asked for the visitor to speak.

Luke continually reminds us of what happened on the Sabbath. He saw it as the appropriate time for new beginnings, or statements about how God related to people. It was on the Sabbath that Jesus announced His ministry of liberation and reconciliation. It was on the Sabbath that Paul announced the provision of salvation for the Gentiles. By accepting Jesus they became worthy of everlasting life.

Rejecting Jesus involves a self-judgment, Paul says. Thus, the Jews judged themselves unworthy of eternal life. They decided against obedience. In accepting Jesus, the Gentiles also evaluated themselves. They decided in favor of obedience and thus of eternal life.

The Sabbath holds the core of human obedience. In the garden Adam and Eve showed their obedience to the divine will by keeping the Sabbath. It gave them their first opportunity to respond to their Creator. The Sabbath expressed the relationship between Creator and created.

Not that obedience to the Sabbath command bears down as a heavy weight on the Christian. Rather, it gladdens. That Sabbath day at Antioch in Pisidia joy broke out. Forever after, the Gentile converts would remember the Sabbath as the day they found the saving grace of Jesus.

Luke wanted to attach to the Sabbath the positive joy and freedom that Jesus gave it. Time and again our Lord moved to make the Sabbath a celebration of deliverance. Every time Jesus or the apostles reach out to others on the Sabbath, gladness erupts.

To believe on Jesus means to obey His command to trust Him for life. The Sabbath forever speaks of the God who gave life. Creation and redemption join in joy on the Sabbath.

"The demands upon God are even greater upon the Sabbath than upon other days. . . . God does not wait for the Sabbath to pass before He grants these requests" (The Desire of Ages, p. 207).

AFFIRMATION AND RESPONSE

I will cause thee to ride upon the high places of the earth, and feed thee with the heritage of Jacob thy father. Isa. 58:14.

When the snow-capped Himalayas lie cloudless below, the high places are yours. To stand at the foot of Everest and gaze toward the distant summit brings awe, forces humility, provokes challenge.

On a memorable occasion a daytime flight cruised us high over the mountains of northern India and Tibet. The pilot told us to look and look again. The Himalayas seldom escape a blanket of cloud. Everest lay stark and clear below us, with all the other giant peaks that provoke awe.

What did the prophet mean when he recorded God's promise about the high places of the earth? In the texts preceding our promise God calls us to turn from Sabbathbreaking to a joyful celebration of God's holy day. Make it a delight, give it wholly to God, keep out intrusions, let Him have all of you that day.

In these ways we affirm the relationship between the Creator and the created. Thus we declare God to be deliverer and sanctifier. In accepting this understanding about how God relates to us, we say yes both to our true humanity and to God's personal care for us.

All true relationships grow out of affirmation and response. How does God respond to our affirmation? First, through His goodness God places delight and reward within the Sabbath. Your delight may grow out of physical and mental rest or from the way the Sabbath marks God's liberating and sanctifying power.

The second response promises the heights for those who obey and affirm the Sabbath. To ride upon the heights means success and advantage. As God's people receive the Sabbath in their hearts, they receive the heritage of Jacob, the rest that only God can give.

In the world of action and reaction the legalist presumes that his action will bring a predictable reaction from God. This text does not propose rewards based on cause and effect. Rather, it describes a developing relationship born of experience.

Isaiah knew how the Sabbath could delight as Israel turned to God and He responded to them. Above all, they would find joy and delight in their heavenly Father, their Creator and Redeemer.

"Those who . . . sought to . . . honor God by calling the Sabbath a delight—these the angels were specially blessing with light and health, and special strength was given them" (Testimonies, *vol. 2,* p. 705).

LET REST ENTER YOUR LIFE

For he that is entered into his rest, he also hath ceased from his own works, as God did from his. Heb. 4:10.

From the experts in stress management comes the advice to make time once a week for a complete break. Stress is a response mechanism. Often the cause of stress cannot be pushed out of the life: another job isn't available, this qualification must be earned, late hours cannot be avoided. Life doesn't let us off easy. Modern technology and business procedures place enormous demands on all levels of activity. The routine worker in a calculator assembly line may have the same symptoms as the chief executive of a corporation.

Typical advice for people under stress includes the following:

1. Make sure of seven to eight hours of sleep each night.

2. Keep your weight within appropriate limits.

3. Exercise regularly.

4. Avoid alcohol, caffeine drinks, tobacco, and other drug dependencies.

The advice does not always stop there. Simply taking a complete break once a week may control stress better than anything else. The Friday evening sigh of relief and the Sabbath morning change of pace relax and fulfills.

But Hebrews looks at another aspect of the Sabbath rest. God had work to do. At the end of the Creation week He stopped work and rested. A Sabbath rest waits for God's people as it did for Him.

The primary focus of Hebrews 4 magnifies the spiritual rest that comes from placing our trust in Jesus. However, it also talks about correct response to the rest God offers.

To escape the deadly stress of sin, stop working on your salvation. Jesus did the work of re-creation on the cross. We can add nothing to it. Therefore, cease from works.

The peace and joy that come from Jesus' saving grace has a counterpart in the Sabbath. Keeping the Sabbath shows that we know what God has done for us. Our resting from work and self-centered pleasure has the same essential character as resting from works of salvation. Both show our trust in God and reflect our position in relationship to Him.

"The Sabbath is a sign of Christ's power to make us holy. And it is given to all whom Christ makes holy" (The Desire of Ages, p. 288).

GOD-MADE FOR HUMAN NEED

I say unto you, That in this place is one greater than the temple. Matt. 12:6.

In these words Jesus reordered the value system of His day. When the system assumes greater value than the people it serves, then God is finished with it.

And not only God. Though cruel and rapacious people devise ways of bleeding others of respect and resources, justice ultimately overturns these people and their designs. The very nature of mankind rejects systems that deny the intrinsic value of human life and liberty. For example, only sufficient time had to pass for the total wrong and injustice of slavery to evidence itself.

But good does not always triumph easily. Consider the Aztec empire, where the belief flourished that only through human sacrifice could their system survive. Or the Tahitian altars, where victims died to assure the future of that Polynesian paradise. Humanity owes a debt beyond estimate to Jesus Christ for His insistence that the person outvalues the system.

Jesus had many ways of making this point. His disciples had broken off a few heads of grain. As they walked on through the field they rubbed the grain and chewed it. An innocent enough event. Yet the system ruled otherwise.

The Temple governed attitudes toward things sacred. Even on the Sabbath the priests continued some of the sacrifices. But the freedom to use the system for the benefit of those the priests served, stopped short there.

Jesus put joy into the Sabbath. He declared it God-made. Theologians had distorted the purpose. They had so surrounded the Sabbath with regulations that it achieved a value system of its own—at all costs the Sabbath must be kept in fine, meticulous detail.

Jesus declared the manward purpose of the Sabbath. God would direct it toward our need, not toward its own glory.

It really comes down to a couple of basic questions about how we regard God and each other. If we love God, we will direct ourselves toward Him through the Sabbath. Our Sabbathkeeping will have a Godward direction. If we love others, then the Sabbath will flow with positive action for their benefit. God made it for us. Through the Sabbath we reach out to Him and comprehend how God would have us reach out to others.

"While [the Sabbath] calls to mind the lost peace of Eden, it tells of peace restored through the Saviour" (The Desire of Ages, *p. 289).*

GOODBYE TO DESPAIR

Who shall separate us from the love of Christ? shall tribulation, or distress, or persecution, or famine, or nakedness, or peril, or sword? Rom. 8:35.

To talk of Auschwitz is to talk of horror. Who can forget the piles of discarded spectacle frames, waiting to be melted down? And what of the room full of baby shoes? And the gallows, where difficult prisoners died? And the four horror chambers where millions gasped, convulsed, and expired as gas snuffed out their lives?

Yet in this place, where more than 4 million died during World War II, hope flowered. I spoke with a man whose father had survived the Nazi death camp. I asked him how a person could keep sane while death stalked the dormitories and work halls night and day.

"He had faith and he had good fortune. But it was hope that kept him alive. He never despaired."

Studies of survivors of concentration camps and labor camps, long-term prisoners, and hostages of terrorists isolate hope as the most effective survival factor.

Despair cannot take over when hope keeps its hold, however tenuous, on Jesus Christ. His love gives us hope, no matter how cruelly life treats us. And so we hold on.

Neither Acts nor the epistles tell us when Paul faced famine or nakedness, but we know he suffered more than most. This only touched the edges of his pain and privation.

But behind today's marvelous promise lies a deeper thought. When Jesus suffered in Gethsemane, He faced the bitterest of deaths. Totally innocent, He accepted the load of human sin. Forsaken, alone, distraught, He reached for the Father's approval.

But not even sin could keep a wall between the Father and Son.

The haunting trauma of pogrom and extermination reminds us that peril can take deadly and physical forms. However, for most of us, dangers will rise from within ourselves or from nonphysical sources. In these, too, Christ draws us to Himself and refuses to let the child of faith go from Him. The Father kept the Son within the circle of His love and power. He encloses us in that care also.

"He watches over His children with a love that is measureless and everlasting" (The Ministry of Healing, *p. 482*).

WHY DETERMINATION COUNTS

And from the days of John the Baptist until now the kingdom of heaven suffereth violence, and the violent take it by force. Matt. 11:12.

Totally unacceptable alternatives keep people going when all seems lost.

David Niemz was digging postholes on his 550-acre property near Robertstown, South Australia. He hopped off his tractor to kick some wire out of the way. The wire caught in the digger, dragging David's leg into the hole and amputating it just below the knee. Within minutes he should have died of shock and blood loss. Instead, he twisted his belt into a tourniquet, wrapped the stump of his leg in an old sweater, disengaged the digger, climbed onto the tractor, and drove 30 minutes to his farmhouse.

He struggled from the tractor to his pickup truck, backed the truck out of a shed so that he could use his CB radio, called his sister at a nearby ranch, and waited for help.

The doctors called it "remarkable." Niemz himself understated the epic with "I'm not quite ready to die."

In Jesus' day the kingdom of God offered an incredible contrast to the thought world of Pharisee and scribe. Humble people, despised and rejected by the religious elite, fought off fear. They rejected long-held inadequacies and made the kingdom of heaven their preserve.

Jesus Himself urged the absolute priority of the kingdom. Nothing should stand in the way of those who desired it. Limb or eye were better gone than to lose entry through the narrow gate.

For the sinner who desires life, Jesus offers the only hope. The counsel of despair calls it impossible. How can anyone live for God? Where will the strength to serve Him come from? Why bother trying?

Yet the alternative appalls. The voice of hope says, "You are not quite ready to die." Especially when sin signals on to eternal death.

Yet no person lifts himself into the kingdom by his bootstraps. The Son of Man seeks and saves the lost. Because He helps, the kingdom will surely open and receive those who desperately desire it.

"Christ has undertaken the work of saving all who trust in Him for salvation" (Selected Messages, *book 1, p. 178*).

LIFE ON THE OTHER SIDE OF DESPAIR

When my soul fainted within me I remembered the Lord: and my prayer came in unto thee, into thine holy temple. Jonah 2:7.

"I just sat there on the rocks in the darkness, listening to it break up. It sounded like a wounded dinosaur dying. It was really sad. There was nothing I could do but listen to its total destruction." Thus John Biddlecombe recalled the night his yacht ground itself to pieces on a reef off Tonga, in the South Pacific.

How did it happen? He was sailing solo, and knew that the coast was close. He reefed the mainsail, set a course to miss the islands, and catnapped. He awoke with the jarring of the ship as it rammed a reef. A shift in wind speed had driven him faster than calculated. He barely escaped with his life.

Jonah and disaster; the words almost stand for each other. He brought trouble to the ship he sailed on. He brought trouble to himself. He wanted trouble for Nineveh—he was a walking disaster area. But God used him in ways that He used no other Old Testament prophet. Jonah turned all in that completely Gentile city to the worship of the true God. Who would have thought it possible when the crew tossed him to the waiting fish?

The gourd of self-pity may shelter us for a while. But when it shrivels, God is waiting to point us on to the future.

In the belly of that great fish Jonah remembered the Lord. From this unthinkable place, prayer found its way to the very presence of God. In the temple of God the High Priest of our salvation hears the cries of the despairing. When life breaks up, when the very thing that means the most lies wrecked and beyond repair, Jesus waits to answer prayer. When mistakes close you in and friends desert, Jesus has you in His hand.

Life goes on even after the greatest disappointment. Jonah had to learn that truth the very hardest of ways. Life may teach us the same lesson. But whether or not we are taught a lesson, prayer holds the answer. God accepts our cries, wherever they come from.

Not only does life exist on the other side of disaster, but it may actually bring new opportunities, new successes that go beyond anything ever expected.

"God's plan [is] to grant us, in answer to the prayer of faith, that which He would not bestow did we not thus ask" (The Great Controversy, p. 525).

THERAPY OF JOY

In his favour is life: weeping may endure for a night, but joy cometh in the morning. Ps. 30:5.

When hope replaces doubt, then despair turns to joy. Jesus came to stop the mouth of doubt. He turned sackcloth and ashes into wedding clothes. He anointed the world with the oil of joy.

But will you join the joyful cries of those whom the Lord has saved? If you were King George II of England would you have brought the crowd to its feet as Handel's "Hallelujah Chorus" shouted its triumph for the first time?

The world has too many inhibited Christians. They sit on their hands, while the "little hills . . . on every side" clap their hands for joy.

I remember a brass band on Tonga that made the coral reefs reverberate with praise as the members performed the *Messiah* at a baptism by the sea. In Ghana I listened to massed choirs sing fortissimo of the Lord God who reigns. From the Albert Hall in London a thousand voices crescendoed, "Hallelujah!"

Norman Vincent Peale taught a whole generation the power of positive thinking. But we forget so soon. Come the first chilling winds of something gone wrong and hope melts away. It should never be that way. God has given the world infinite joy in Jesus Christ.

Bartimaeus waited for the crowd to come near. For some time he had heard them coming. At last they were near enough. "Who is it?" he asked, for he was blind. "Jesus of Nazareth," they replied.

The moment for which he has longed has finally come. He knows about Jesus. But, "Jesus of Nazareth," is that what they call Him? Not good enough. "Jesus, thou Son of David, have mercy on me" he calls. That's who He is: the One come to fulfill the promises of the covenant made with David. He is King and can do for me what no other can.

They urge quiet on him. He cannot know it, for his eyes forbid the knowledge, but Jesus heads a triumphal procession. "Not now, not now," they insist. But he will not desist. His voice rises to a yell, "Have mercy on me!"

Bartimaeus looks around, sees the crowd, sees Jesus. He begins to praise God. He pushes to the front. His voice has found a new power, an unstoppable praise.

"To praise God in fullness and sincerity of heart is as much a duty as is prayer" (Christ's Object Lessons, *p. 299).*

A NEW START FOR ALL

He that sat upon the throne said, Behold, I make all things new.
And he said unto me, Write: for these words are true and faithful.
Rev. 21:5.

The fear that things will never change, that there never will be a new start, drives people to despair.

The ghettos of our cities reproduce despair. The slavery of hopelessness has its own chains, its own slavemasters, its own slave shacks. For the very poor, the learning deprived, the unemployed sons and daughters of the unemployed, from where will hope come?

With all the awareness education gives, with all the philanthropy secure jobs may create, with all the concern and goodwill our Christian compassion urges, we do not and cannot fully comprehend the despair gripping whole communities, and even nations.

The "must do"s of faith create aid and relief organizations, send missionaries, equip health vans, build schools, and assure good nutrition. They help, but will we ever learn to share so that none may want food, knowledge, health, or hope?

Few who have worked to change such situations find complete solace in the promise of the earth made new. Will these people, so deprived, so hungry, even understand enough to make a decision for eternal life?

In the face of such need, concern turns to anger, but not against God. He has provided a world with enough for all, despite the ravages of sin and disease. Anger against greed, anger against systems that prohibit help, anger against evil men who fatten on ignorance and weakness. Jesus knew such righteous indignation as He saw the poor of His day robbed and manipulated by those who should have shared.

Yet the day is coming when all will be new. Best of all, God will renew minds and hearts of those who enter the new earth so all will truly love and care. That happy day waits just ahead. It calls from the future and beckons on to the promised newness.

Can we steal a little of that future and bring it back to give hope for hopelessness? Yes. By compassionate and sacrificial action, little pieces of time and place can be made new. Christianity proposes a creeping takeover of life and circumstance. If you have what only Jesus gives, then despair can give way to hope right where you are.

"He bids us rejoice because we are the heritage of the Lord, because the righteousness of Christ is the white robe of His saints" (Christ's Object Lessons, p. 299).

213

WHAT LIFE SAYS ABOUT GOD

Yea, though I walk through the valley of the shadow of death, I will fear no evil: for thou art with me; thy rod and thy staff they comfort me. Ps. 23:4.

What can life teach you about God? Trust in God and despair cannot live together in the one mind. Doubt fathers despair. Trust gives birth to hope and joy.

What had taught David to turn away from depression and anxiety to the One who gladdens and provides? Did he remember the moment when he went down into the valley to search among the pebbles for stones for his sling? That truly was the valley of death. Someone must die that day, and it might be he. The lessons of trust started early for this young man.

Or perhaps he remembered the whistle of the javelin as Saul sought his life. So near to death, and from a hand that had welcomed and advanced him. He came through, shaking his head in wonder that he had again escaped. Who else but God had done it?

Without doubt, memory would replay the temptation, the yielding, the remorse as he had shamed himself, his nation, and his God in the affair of Bathsheba. That day he looked into the valley of the shadow of the second death—final and absolute—and found the staff of his God guiding him out.

The high drama of David's life may not be yours or mine. Our lives most likely will play over the common themes of grief, alienation, illness, insecurity, anxiety, and fear. Yet they will have all the reality and fierceness of the trials the shepherd king faced. What will we learn from them?

David saw God as guide, shepherd, helper. He could have said, You give me a good job, plenty of food, prosperity, and I will worship and trust You. Life brings unemployment, mourning, illness, danger, and still I will trust You. Even when the world has formed in ranks against me, You help me forget their threats while I sit down and enjoy a banquet from Your table of grace and love.

Despair will never call you into its dark depths if in all things you see the goodness and mercy of God. But if despair strikes, remember the One who would shoulder you to safety. He protects as a shepherd protects. His rod and staff are forgiveness and the power of the Spirit.

"The perfect fruit of faith, meekness, and love often matures best amid stormclouds and darkness" (Christ's Object Lessons, p. 61).

ONE DAY AT A TIME

For which cause we faint not; but though our outward man perish, yet the inward man is renewed day by day. 2 Cor. 4:16.

"What you see of me now is not what I really am. You must look inside me to see the real person."

The words came from a respected friend, now dying of cancer. He wanted me to look past the disfigured face, the wasted form, the hospital bed with its tubes and meters, and remember him as he had been. His mind and heart expressed his real person better than his tortured body.

Do you know a person who bubbles over with vigor, strength, and assurance? You feel that such an individual could run a marathon. Or perhaps a handicapped person who grips life as strongly as his hands grip the wheelchair?

An indomitable spirit infected Paul. He got up from under a heap of stones and walked into the city of Lystra. He waded ashore at Malta and set about gathering firewood. When a viper bit him, he shook it off and went on stoking the fire.

He knew only too well the wasting of hunger, the agony of unjust imprisonment, the injuries powerful men inflicted on their victims. But the Paul inside that scarred and enfeebled body never lost his trust or confidence in God.

He sustained himself by always looking toward God. True, he had not forgotten the road to Damascus, or the confrontation over legalism, or any other of life's lessons. But he remembered them in order to reassure himself about the future. God would be waiting in the future to help and deliver him there.

He felt death in his body. The outward man was perishing. He knew the risks he had taken, how he had pushed physical strength to its limits. He knew his mortality. But God gave assurance that he would have life. Day by day he found renewal.

All too often we expect that the day God first gave spiritual life will suffice forever. Paul knew better. Not that what God had done in the past lacked in any way; but this very day he had to go to God for grace. He never let the external world distract him from the spiritual. Nor did he forget the power that day by day sustained and renewed him.

"Nothing is apparently more helpless, yet really more invincible, than the soul that feels its nothingness and relies wholly on the merits of the Saviour" (The Ministry of Healing, *p. 182).*

A THOUSAND WORDS, OR ONE PICTURE?

Thy word have I hid in mine heart, that I might not sin against thee. Ps. 119:11.

"One picture is worth a thousand words." So they say. But is it?

In the ordered and beautiful garden you come to an old peach tree, loaded with ripe fruit. A golden globe, flushed with pink, drifts its scented delight toward you, inviting you to reach and touch. Your fingers caress the soft down of the sunward surface. A twist, and it nestles, heavy with juice, in your hand. Your lips kiss the velvet skin. The juice bursts through the sweet cover and floods your taste with perfumed and tangy nectar. The flesh melts under the gentlest of pressures.

Such is a peach.

The lad steps into the gurgling brook. One hand divides the chill water while his alert eyes keep watch. Stone after stone he rejects, selecting only those whose smooth symmetry will ensure straight flight. Ah! This one will do. And this. He counts them. Four in the pouch, one in the hand. Enough. The young David climbs out of the brook and walks toward the towering giant. Carefully he slots a stone, wet from the stream, into his leather sling.

You cannot paint those words on canvass. A picture carries its own authority in paint and color, but words let loose memories, shared experiences. Imagination takes over. Your mind creates pictures no painter could capture.

So James had it right when he warned against the wrong use of words. Solomon had it right when he extols the beauty of appropriate words. And David had it right when he tucked away in his heart words that speak well of God. As we read the Bible words flow at us continually. They invite us to think of God and His love and care.

We remember a beautiful choice of words. We remember from childhood the encouraging words of parents and teachers. We count off the words that friends spoke long ago as they recognized our achievements. We cherish the words of comfort and hope.

We sometimes think that if it cannot be filmed or painted, it doesn't impress. But if you are sensitive you will discover today that the words you know about God, the words you learn about Him, do indeed bring life. They are the wonderful words of life.

"Hang in memory's hall the precious words of Christ" (Testimonies, *vol. 6, p. 81).*

PAUL , THE MATCHMAKER

I am jealous over you with godly jealousy: for I have espoused you to one husband, that I may present you as a chaste virgin to Christ. 2 Cor. 11:2.

In the world of arranged marriages, the supreme role goes to the matchmaker. While the Western individualistic approach to marriage is eroding other systems, much of the world still arranges marriages, often without the consent of the bride or groom. In some studies the stability of such marriages outperforms marriage based on personal choice.

Society in the time of Paul did not regard personal preference as any basis for the marriage covenant. Therefore, the matchmaker had to study carefully the family trees and the financial and social status of the prospective bride and groom. Above all, he had a protective role toward the bride. She must come to her husband a virgin, free from any moral taint.

The pastor in Paul saw the church at Corinth as a prospective bride for Christ. He wanted to bring her to Christ and present her pure and chaste, as a matchmaker might.

Having someone worthy of presentation to God captures the need for holiness and purity. The power of the Spirit will present living sacrifices to God, the very least that can be asked of the Christian (Rom. 12:1).

While Paul had concern for individual members, he wanted whole congregations to witness to the power of Christ. He taught that Christ will not only present us to the Father person by person, but as communities of faith.

Christ's sacrifice creates a holy community of people who once were enemies of God, showing their alienation by wicked works (Col. 1:21, 22). This community, its true membership known only to Him, Christ presents to God holy and without blame.

Does the community then hide the individual from responsibility? Not at all. What we do within and for the church affects its influence and witness.

Christ watches over us, forgiving, protecting, empowering. In His love He can, at last, bring the object of His supreme regard, faultless into the presence of the Father.

The church "is the case which contains His jewels, the fold which encloses His flock, and He longs to see it without spot or blemish" (Testimonies, *vol. 6, p. 261*).

ELECTION—THE ROAD TO FAITH

A voice came out of the cloud, saying, "This is My Son, My Chosen One; listen to Him!" Luke 9:35, NASB.

"Why me?" "Why us?" "Why were we chosen?"

You can hear these unspoken questions behind some of the most profound writing of the New Testament. God has elected this person to salvation, but that person has not found it. He has helped me see my need of grace, but another has sensed no need. Is faith the result of human temperament or mood?

The inspired writers reached the conclusion that God had a plan. It included a people chosen by Him. He would preserve them for His glory. He made this plan before the world was formed. Therefore it lies completely outside human action. His election of a people cannot be turned aside, but a person may turn aside from God.

Election is not selection. God does not pick on a random basis. He has no code that tags one and not another. In the early 1970s the date on which a person was born could determine his being drafted by the American Selective Service. If the gospel commission to all the world means what it says, then God wants all included among His elect people.

The voice from heaven on the Mount of Transfiguration said of Jesus, "This is my beloved Son." Luke used a different word than Matthew or Mark. Instead of "beloved" he used a word often translated "chosen." Here begins the act of God that culminates in the election of His people.

Jesus lived totally in His Father's will. He did not assert Himself, as well He might. At the cross the rulers mocked Him. They asked, "Can a person be chosen of God, and not help himself?" Jesus gave the answer through His silence and submission.

Because Jesus did not do His own will but the will of the Father, we see something of the nature of God. God can be seen only when the vehicle of His revelation sets self aside and lets God's nature and plan be seen through him.

The church fulfills a similar role in the world. In Christ, God has elected His church as a way of showing Himself to the world. He chooses you and me for the same reason. God's chosen will let Him be seen in them.

"The world will be convinced not so much by what the pulpit teaches as by what the church lives" (Testimonies, *vol. 6, p. 260*).

PERSUASION: THE PREACHING OF THE GOSPEL

Then Agrippa said to Paul, "Do you think that in such a short time you can persuade me to be a Christian?" Acts 26:28, NIV.

Paul called preaching the power of God. He had seen it work in the market places of the pagan world. Jews locked to synagogue worship had broken away to the freedom of Christ through preaching. On Mars Hill the preaching of the gospel had countered the great philosophies of Greece.

Paul did not regard it as a personal achievement. The power did not come from him, but from the Christ he exalted. Therefore, even Agrippa could feel its power. In the short hour of opportunity Paul called this Jewish ruler to decision. He turned Paul aside.

What went on in Agrippa's mind? We sense a little of the conflict by the words he chose. Paul had been in front of him only a few minutes, and now asked him to rule on the truth about Jesus. What did he expect? Did Paul want him to play the part of a Christian? Agrippa plucked from his vocabulary the technical words used by an actor. The persuasion was powerful, he had come close to choosing a new role, but he stopped short.

Paul had put Agrippa in a dilemma. If he denied the prophets (Acts 26:27), he could no longer claim orthodoxy, very important to him as ruler of the fractious Jews. If he said he believed, then he must agree publicly with Paul. He escaped the dilemma by putting off any decision.

In a world full of technical wizardry, of audiovisual extravaganzas, of the videocassette and home movie, where lies the power of preaching? To learn of its power, talk to a preacher. To know what it has done, talk to his congregation.

But Paul would not let Agrippa escape his dilemma easily. The persuasion that leads to faith had spoken that day. It was a time to remember. Perhaps the time was too short; but short time or long time, Paul left the decision to nag at the consciences that the Spirit had troubled. He would now pray that all there might believe in Christ.

The power of the preacher's persuasion begins and ends with its purpose. It uses the word of God to show Christ and His saving love. The Spirit enters and makes more of the event than mere words and man ever could. And so we hear not just God's man, but the word from God.

"Men will believe, not what the minister preaches, but what the church lives" (Testimonies, *vol. 9, p. 21*).

FAITHFULNESS: THE QUALITY OF GOD'S LOVE

Know therefore that the Lord thy God, he is God, the faithful God, which keepeth covenant and mercy with them that love him and keep his commandments to a thousand generations. Deut. 7:9.

Miners searching for precious minerals will often find them in small quantities. A pocket of gold here, a sampling of silver there, but the quantity may be so small and the quality so defective that they simply go elsewhere in their quest.

But when a sample proves more promising, shafts driven into the surrounding strata reveal the value of the find. The great gold mines of the world extend over large distances and invite development that may last for scores of years.

Because Bible writers span almost 2,000 years, their opinions stand the test of time. Moses mined his experience to tell his people about God. The shaft he drove into time declared Him faithful. Many hundreds of years later Jeremiah tested the gold of God's love and declared, "Great is thy faithfulness" (Lam. 3:23).

At times Israel's prophets found it surprising that God still loved and cared for His people. They had done more than enough to have Him turn elsewhere. But He continued to rescue and redeem them. He offered them the blessings of His covenant with a faithful love that went far beyond any human equivalent.

Moses gave reasons for God continuing to care for Israel. He found two:

1. "Because the Lord loved you" (Deut. 7:8).
2. "Because he would keep the oath which he had sworn" (verse 8).

For these reasons alone the Lord chose His people. He set them apart as holy to Him. Out of His choosing He sought to make a people that would show Him to the world through obedience to His will. If Israel would direct its will continually to fulfilling His commands, then the faithful God would not only preserve them but make them a blessing to all nations.

Hundreds more years on from Jeremiah, the prophet again tested the seam of God's love. He found it had the same quality as ever: "For he is faithful that promised" (Heb. 10:23). Wherever the people of God put Him to the test they will find this true.

"Nothing more quickly inspires faith than the exercise of faith" (Prophets and Kings, *p. 351).*

FAITH: LOOKING FOR GOD

I will wait upon the Lord, that hideth his face from the house of Jacob, and I will look for him. Isa. 8:17.

Israel learned lessons about faith through many experiences. God asked Moses to lead Israel out of Egypt. He quibbled. Would the people believe him when he told them of God's plan? God said that true belief does not separate God's message from the God who gave it. His plan is as strong as the One who gave it.

Jesus came with a message. But the real test lay elsewhere. Would the people not only believe Him but also believe in Him? The wasted years of Israel's wanderings showed how their faith wavered. At one time they would not believe the promise of Canaan. At another time they wanted other leaders. They could not hold together belief in God and belief in His purposes.

To have faith means both to believe what God does, and to believe in Him.

In his conflict with Ahaz, Isaiah was brutally blunt: "If ye will not believe, surely ye shall not be established" (Isa. 7:9). Only firm and constant trust in God would save the nation. If they would survive they had to build a new basis for the kingdom. Through faith they might lay a new cornerstone in Zion: "He that believeth shall not make haste" (Isa. 28:16). Flight would not help. Scurrying here and there would not save. Only belief in God and His plans would bring Israel through.

Isaiah saw the coming catastrophe. He saw the political shifts, the power alliances, the military preparations on which the king was relying. But where was the firm trust in God that would build Israel's future? The nation must learn the constancy of God and practice the same unfailing belief.

Through all uncertainties Isaiah himself showed his personal faith. Not for him the haste of human solutions; he would wait on the Lord. At that moment the prophet could not see His face. He did not know precisely how God would solve Israel's crisis. But if the nation waited and believed, God would soon show Himself.

Isaiah taught the essential lesson of hope. "I will look for him." In the future He waits to save and bless. I will remain constant and fix my hope in Him.

"Faith is the gift of God, but the power to exercise it is ours" (Patriarchs and Prophets, p. 431).

FAITH: WHERE RIGHTEOUSNESS BEGINS

Behold his soul which is lifted up is not upright in him: but the just shall live by his faith. Hab. 2:4.

That morning we did not take the tram to our high school. Instead, we went downtown to the university. In a huge and draughty enclosure of echoes and shuffling feet, we met our fate. In the best of British traditions, our teachers could only prepare us for university entrance examinations. Other persons gave them and then marked the papers.

Only one who has been through that experience can understand the fears and uncertainties. All depended on what was done during the three hours of examination on each subject. The questions stared out from strangely shaped pieces of paper, and one must write, write, write, and also, get it right!

Habakkuk's vision listed a divine examination at the end of time. God wanted His system of examination clearly understood. The prophet must write it plainly so that all could understand. No one would escape judgment. Who would pass the scrutiny of the Lord?

No wonder our text became critical to the thinking of the new covenant. It contrasts two responses to life and to God. The arrogant, lifted up, person fails the test. All that he writes about himself has no truth to it. His heart is wrong. He trusts in himself and has no righteousness.

Those whom God will declare just have approached their lives and God differently. They have kept their hold on God no matter what. They have trusted in Him. Therefore they are just, and are declared righteous.

Abraham showed this very characteristic and so became father of the faithful. When put to the test, he did not falter but maintained trust in God. Like Habakkuk, Abraham had a vision. The vision pointed to the future. God made specific promises about the future. There would be a land for Abraham and his seed. God would make of him a great nation. "He believed in the Lord; and he counted it to him for righteousness" (Gen. 15:6).

Abraham's response had the very quality that God was looking for in the covenant people. As we fellowship with God we sense His claim on us. He asks for trust and belief. In such attitudes He freely justifies. In them righteousness by faith begins.

"Faith is the hand by which the soul takes hold upon the divine offers of grace and mercy" (Patriarchs and Prophets, p. 431).

BREAKING THROUGH TO LIFE

To him that overcometh will I give to eat of the tree of life, which is in the midst of the paradise of God. Rev. 2:7.

He wears his decoration proudly. While some have researched the horror of the bridge over the River Kwai, this warrant officer in the Australian Medical Army Corps lived it. A skilled author may come close to showing the distress and fear of a death camp, but for him it hovers always on the verge of consciousness.

He was sent by the Japanese from Changi prisoner-of-war camp in Singapore to serve the Allied prisoners building the Burma railway. He kept ailing men alive by smuggling drugs from the medical stores into the barracks. Both Allied and Japanese military personnel owed their lives to his skill and care.

How did he manage to survive? He looked beyond the dying and the suffering to the life he would one day have with his sweetheart in far-off Australia. Hope for the future kept him alive when others died.

Perhaps that is why the Bible paints such vivid pictures of the paradise of God. Paul declares that we are saved by hope. Hope fixes on a future better than the present. With such a future in view, hope does not stumble or give up, no matter what may bar its way.

The church at Ephesus had fallen into a sorry state. Love for God, so secure and strong in the first heady days of faith, had slipped away. Now it must surmount the barrier of indifference to recapture its first love.

We know the feeling only too well: the first enthusiasm, faith that will not give up; then the gradual fading. Finally, the sudden start as we become aware of the barriers self has built against renewal.

Look, hope says, the tree of life still grows. It waits you in the paradise of God. Get up. Go on. Tough it out. You have a reward waiting for you that will make today's misery seem little more than a bad dream.

Story after story can be told of amazing human resilience to harsh and impossible conditions. We cannot know the full list of such heroes. Faith also has its heroes. Job we know, and Joseph, and John. But only heaven has counted the doubt overcome by abiding hope, and the despair turned to joy as faith looks at its future with God.

"The very trials that task our faith most severely and make it seem that God has forsaken us are to lead us closer to Christ" (Patriarchs and Prophets, *p. 129*).

GLORY IN HOW GOD CHANGES LIVES

Great is my boldness of speech toward you, great is my glorying of you: I am filled with comfort, I am exceeding joyful in all our tribulation. 2 Cor. 7:4.

Corinth had a reputation as sour as that of Sodom and Gomorrah. The Greeks even turned the name of the city into a verb. To live in lust and debauchery was "to Corinthianize." This port city had many claims to fame. It grew to great wealth. A system of rollers eased ships across the isthmus from the Adriatic Sea to the gulf of Corinth. Merchants paid big prices to avoid the long sea voyage around the stormy Aegean peninsula.

Once leveled by the Romans for participating in a rebellion, the city quickly recovered its former position. Temple prostitutes plied their trade among the seamen and religious devotees. Life was fast, loose, and uninhibited.

Into this unlikely place Paul brought the gospel. Here, for what may have been the first time, he built a congregation with little support from converted Jews or Gentile adherents to Judaism. He tested the power of Jesus' name to break through the barrier of paganism. Lives changed dramatically. What glorious victories the gospel won in the homes of Corinth!

His preaching of the cross others counted foolishness, a scandal, a stumbling block. But the saved called it the power of God.

Person by person, block by block, Paul built up the household of faith in Corinth. Perhaps nothing that had happened since the Damascus road so convinced him of the power of the risen Son of God. Christ was building the church in Corinth, sin city of Greece!

Paul might have given up when the Jews opposed him and blasphemed. But the promise of God drew him on into the future. How could he give up when the lure of "much people" spurred his evangelism?

Winning someone to Jesus isn't always easy, but it is never impossible. Therefore, like Paul, our witness and our prayers go on. When in doubt about whether the gospel will win, we look around at how other lives have changed. Perhaps, like Paul, we should remember our own transformation. The glory of the changed life never lets us forget what the Spirit may yet achieve.

"One soul won to Christ will flash heaven's light all around him, penetrating the moral darkness and saving other souls" (Testimonies, *vol. 6, p. 22).*

HOW WE WITNESS TO THE FUTURE

Call unto me, and I will answer thee, and shew thee great and mighty things, which thou knowest not. Jer. 33:3.

Zedekiah, Judah's last king, really was a sorry creature. He flirted with the Babylonians and then sought the hand of the Egyptians. Not that they were of use to him. Nothing could withstand the armed might of Nebuchadnezzar of Babylon. Egypt had troubles enough within its own borders and did little more than offer a few tut-tuts to the inroads of its northern rivals.

Jeremiah knew for sure what would happen. Jerusalem would fall. The king and the princes would go in chains to Babylon. The Temple would lie desolate. The land would appear like an uninhabited wasteland. He knew all that. But he knew something else as well. God planned a complete reversal of Israel's misfortune.

No matter what Jeremiah said, the king and the court regarded him as a prophet of doom. Zedekiah locked him up. The armies of Babylonians surrounded the city. How could the prophet show his hope in the future?

He did the most practical of things. He bought land. Probably it was going at bargain prices, under the circumstances. But still he bought that piece of land and had the documents notarized and stored safely away. Thus he witnessed to the future in which the fortunes of God's people would prosper.

They did come back out of captivity. Did any of Jeremiah's heirs claim the land he had bought? We do not know. We know only of his hope expressed in such a practical way.

What do you believe about the future? Do you see it bright with the fulfilled promises of God? I know a somewhat crotchety old man who has more than enough money. What does he do with it? He supports students studying for the ministry. He sends thousands of dollars off to help this project and that.

For some, Jeremiah has the label "prophet of doom" because he saw too clearly the results of the course taken by Israel's leaders. To others he was the prophet of hope. He saw just as clearly that God would reverse the present negative situation.

The future asks what you will do for it. How will you show your faith in it?

"Talk faith. Keep on God's side of the line" (Testimonies, *vol. 5, p. 514*).

PROBLEMS WITH SELF-WORTH

This man went down to his house justified rather than the other: for every one that exalteth himself shall be abased; and he that humbleth himself shall be exalted. Luke 18:14.

The cancer of wrong self-worth pervaded the life of Judaism. Nodules of self-righteousness infested the ruling Sadducees and the proud Pharisees. Among the ordinary people, a leukemia of despair weakened any resolve to live for God.

The Great Physician came to change the prognosis. "In him was life; and the life was the light of men." But the cure for both the bloated self-worth of the rulers and the deflated self-worth of the poor and despised did not come easy.

Not that things have changed all that much today. It never has been easy to believe in both the fallen nature sin imposes and the forgiven status God gives in Jesus Christ.

Jesus gave people a true sense of self-worth. Think of Zacchaeus. He had traded religious respectability for great wealth. The exaltation of wealth satisfied him, at least until Jesus appeared. Yet he longed for acceptance among his people. Materialism had boosted self to the point of pride and callousness. In Jesus he could accept himself as he truly was, a sinner in great need. The worth Jesus ascribed to him freed him from the bonds of materialism.

The Pharisee had it wrong. He parleyed the comparison game into a false self-worth that set him high on any human scale of worth. But he had no esteem for others. He only wanted to feel superior.

The tax gatherer had his own false views of self-worth. His sin confused him. How could he ever achieve a state where God would have him as His child?

Unless we know who we truly are in the sight of God, we will fall into either the Pharisee or the publican trap: convinced that outward appearances are what really matters, or that our sin has cut us off from any possible self-worth.

The Lord justified the tax gatherer, not because he was a great sinner but because he saw the Lord as his only source of worth. With the mercy of God given him, he could break through from the hell-hole of sin to the heights of a Heaven-sent righteousness.

Jesus "reached the hearts of the people by going among them as one who desired their good" (The Desire of Ages, *p. 151).*

GOD GOES INTO ACTION TO SAVE

He said unto him, Son, thou art ever with me, and all that I have is thine. Luke 15:31.

Poles apart, the two sons troubled the father. One so open and fun-loving, the other withdrawn and scheming. How could he help them find values that counted? What would make the younger care about others? How could the older see himself as totally self-centered and calculating?

The younger came stumbling up the path in rags. The father had thought this moment through, but this went beyond his worst dreams. Where had the gaiety of youth gone? Who had put fear in those eyes? His heart cried out for this sorry boy, back from a bitter lesson about life. "Run to him, then. Have compassion. Hold him to you."

Later he would chuckle over the son who did not know how to connive and scheme, yet came with what he thought a cunning plan. Fool his father by asking to be a servant? The father read him before he ever uttered the words. He didn't need a job; he needed love and restoring.

He had no plan at hand to deal with the older boy. How could he have predicted the haughty, furious response? How could that scheming mind go so far as to reject brotherhood? Did he not see that if he had no brother, he also had no father?

Before the angry youth lowered his accusing finger, the father did all that he knew. He entreated him, reminding him of who he was, what he had in store for him. "Son, you don't need a kid. You never were one for a party and friends. What you need is my love. Surely that should be enough."

When the barriers go up, what can God do? He can see the need. He knows the devious thoughts. He reads the sorry defenses. Schemes of repayment, or service to pacify the urgent sense of guilt, He brushes aside. He has the answer to them. Let Me give, He says. Don't you try to give just yet. Let Me be the giver.

For those who will have nothing of the celebration of God's love, the task grows harder. The Father entreats, and goes on entreating. "All that I have is yours," He says. "I am no poorer because I gave to your brother. I grow rich by giving My love. Won't you take your share?"

"The gift of Christ reveals the Father's heart. . . . He will spare nothing, however dear, which is necessary to the completion of His work" (Testimonies, vol. 9, p. 254).

SAVED BEYOND DOUBT

Wherefore he is able also to save them to the uttermost that come unto God by him, seeing he ever liveth to make intercession for them. Heb. 7:25.

Joe came into my life because I was the youngest and newest on the evangelistic team in Melbourne, Australia. Each of us had a portion of the metropolis to cover. We had more than enough interested people to visit. The address the card gave appeared to be in nobody's territory. After all, who would assign the city rubbish dump to someone?

There I found Joe. He based his scrap and salvage operation in a shack made of sheets of roofing iron. An endless choice of furniture arrived each day. He had chosen the least likely to collapse. The stench of trash fires and rotting garbage permeated everything.

Joe taught me a lesson that still stays clear and fresh. A person never knows what he can become until surrender permits God to do His best. With a fellow minister I spent most of one afternoon cleaning Joe up. The Dorcas Society provided him with fresh clothes for his baptism. Will I ever forget the scrubbed pink face beaming with joy as he came up out of the water?

Turn the clock forward 20 years; back in Melbourne, I visited the camp meeting. He came running after me. "Do you remember . . . ?" Of course, Joe. I'll never forget you. "I'm the deacon in the local church now." He shone with joy.

It's one thing to reach out and snatch a person from alcohol and disease but another thing to find the barriers to faith permanently dismantled and the life of the saved still on course.

Our High Priest saves beyond expectation because He goes on living. What He began in us, He will see to the very end. While our lives flick past in an endless procession of hope and need, His goes on and on.

Our choices, life's impositions, others' demands, fill the life with beginnings and endings. A friendship starts, another finishes. A habit dies, another begins. A victory cheers, a defeat dampens. But He goes on, the eternal constant in the equations of life.

For Joe the path could only be up. For you? For this reason look ahead with hope: Jesus lives forever to mediate for your benefit.

"It is those who by faith follow Jesus in the great work of the atonement who receive the benefits of His mediation in their behalf" (The Great Controversy, p. 430).

MISSION POSSIBLE

And he said unto them, Go ye into all the world, and preach the gospel to every creature. Mark 16:15.

Beware of the peddler of statistics. His figures and charts may be a two-edged sword.

Tidings of joy from the counting house of the faith confirm that the Adventist mission is succeeding. Membership is growing far faster than the world's population. More sobering figures warn that the world population grows, in just one month, more than the total membership of the church.

If you take a broader view and ask the question about the Christian church as a whole, the sums are more reassuring. But even then— Roman Catholics, Protestants, Orthodox, Mormons; add up all the accessions to Christianity in any one year—in most of the world, Christianity does little more than hold its own.

Mark records the most demanding of all Jesus' commissions to the disciples. "Preach the gospel to every creature," Jesus said. Who will make this possible? The Spirit working through human agencies. He will do it in the swelling witness of the loud cry.

In Tonga stands the Ha'amonga. About A.D. 1200 the king of Tonga ordered a stone archway erected. Tongan traditions tell of the cutting of the stones on a distant island, the transportation in huge canoes hollowed from the giant trunks of trees, the erection of the archway by thousands of willing subjects.

As an engineering feat this trilithon rivals Stonehenge and the giant heads of Easter Island. Two huge pillars, weighing at least 40 tons each, stand upright. A third monster fits into mortises cut in the two uprights. Why go to this bother? The present king of Tonga has conducted research that suggests that, like Stonehenge, the stones make a celestial calendar.

Sometimes when I visit an institution the church has created, or preach to a large gathering of church members, my mind goes to the pyramids, to Stonehenge, and to the Ha'amonga. Such things happen as God's people face their mission.

Therefore we gather resources: the people, the tithes, the offerings, the skills, together with the Spirit, make this good thing happen. In such ways the work will be done.

"Everyone who heareth is to say: Come. Not only the ministers, but the people. All are to join in the invitation" (Testimonies, *vol. 5, p. 207).*

SHARING THE TABLE

When they saw it, they all murmured, saying, That he was gone to be guest with a man that is a sinner. Luke 19:7.

Adventist travelers frequently return from international voyages bubbling over with the hospitality of the big family to which they belong. Though Africans and Pacific Islanders may never have heard of the expression *potluck*, they know how to organize one. A place will always open for a wayfaring brother or sister.

The banana leaves of Tonga, with their spread of watermelon, cassava, yam, and papaya, have the same "elastic" quality as the schoolroom-spread of Sligo church in the Washington, D.C., area.

Join a Ghanaian "bring and share" and you'll feel as much at home as you would if you had yourself organized a New Guinea "bung" supper.

In the time of Jesus, hospitality to strangers was a duty and a privilege, but it carried certain important overtones. When Jesus "ate with sinners," He wasn't only accepting their generosity—He was showing His willingness to accept them into His kingdom.

"Sinners" were not only those who transgressed the law. In Jesus' day, they formed a distinct grouping. The "righteous" thought them incapable of qualifying for salvation. Not only that, but the Pharisees argued that their continual uncleanness hindered God in His desire to set Israel free. These people Jesus called to Him. He went out of His way to fellowship with them.

Eating with Jesus were tax collectors, doctors, leatherworkers, shepherds, women, donkey drivers, money changers. All were suspect for a variety of ceremonial reasons, and hence, excluded from the fellowship of the Pharisees.

Jesus lived out a parable. It teaches us that God sees all men as candidates for His love. He calls all to the banquet of His love. None of us has the right to question the call of God to any other person to share the table with Him and us.

One outcast is not much different from another. That is what we all were until Jesus found us. The Host welcomes all, regardless; He calls all to rejoicing and to brotherhood.

"Love is the living principle of brotherhood. Not one nook or corner of the soul is to be a hiding place for selfishness" (Testimonies, *vol. 8, pp. 139, 140*).

FELLOWSHIP WITH GOD

That which we have seen and heard declare we unto you, that ye also may have fellowship with us: and truly our fellowship is with the Father, and with his Son Jesus Christ. 1 John 1:3.

John's Epistle poses the question "You say you have knowledge of God; what will that knowledge do for you?" If we enter the covenant relationship with the Father through Jesus Christ, how will it change our lives?

The early church had people who pretended to have the presence of the Spirit. Like Simon Magus, they wanted Christ and the Spirit because they envied the power He brought the church and its leaders. The gifts of the Spirit represented a kind of magic, they believed, that would give them power and wealth.

Nothing offered a greater threat to the early church than a false use of the name of Christ. If Christ's followers did not have a true knowledge, they would lead others to despair, not joy. The world was full of those who lusted for power to deceive others. Simon Magus, Elymas, and the seven sons of Sceva show the hold that magic and the occult had on people.

In the community to which John wrote his Epistle, church members claimed that fellowship with God meant a mystical mastery over God. To know or have fellowship with God benefited the Christian to the disadvantage of others. John attacked this belief.

Saving fellowship with Jesus Christ cleanses from sin. Knowledge of God and fellowship with the Son put us into right relationship with the Godhead. Our humanity remains subject to Him. He is the source of the obedient life and creates love for others.

Jesus came to bring light to a dark world. Joy flows from those who receive the light. The light that brings this great joy illuminates man's need and floodlights the cross. In Jesus the way to victory and joy appears. We see our need. We see the cross and go to Him to receive new hearts and share His love with others.

The fellowship of joy that the Father offers shares with us His love, His presence, His cleansing. To rejoice in the light is to share the gift of life from Jesus Christ.

"Jesus cares for each one as though there were not another individual on the face of the earth" (Testimonies, *vol. 5, p. 346).*

FELLOWSHIP OF THE LIVING

For to him that is joined to all the living there is hope: for a living dog is better than a dead lion. Eccl. 9:4.

Every day brings new evidence of how human action affects the environment. As I write this, scientists in the Soviet Union are spraying chemicals into cloud masses over the shut-down nuclear plant at Chernobyl. By limiting rainfall they hope to hold back the spread of radioactivity into surrounding farms and rivers.

In an ecology-conscious climate, considerable gains are possible. From being little more than an open sewer, the River Thames now boasts more than 100 species of fish.

The battle against man-made pollution goes on. New fronts continually open. In Sweden, acid rain has devoided lakes of life. Elsewhere, lakes polluted by factory wastes choke with algae. How bitter the lesson can be that no man is an island!

Solomon has something of the kind in mind, but says it of saving faith. In the community of faith hope may come to us. Israel had a strong sense of community. Salvation came from God through the nation. But a community of evil also exists. An Achan in the camp would cause defeat at the city of Ai.

In the New Testament the idea of community and fellowship goes over into the church. The fellowship in which we find life and joy includes our brothers and sisters who also believe. But it goes beyond that. The Holy Spirit fellowships with us. The Father and the Son are one with us. An ecology of salvation encloses us in an environment where we expect the Sun of righteousness to shine, the latter rain to fall, the Christ vine to flourish.

Paul pictures grace as a sphere of heavenly influence within which the Christian stands (Rom. 5:2).

The wise man wants us to look out into the community of faith and see it as an expression of hope in God. Death closes off hope and joy. If we have not found them in this life, then no second opportunity comes.

The one who spurns the place where God comes to fellowship with His people may appear like a lion, but he has death as his destiny. The lowliest of people have brighter prospects in God than the mightiest have in self.

"Our only safety is in standing constantly in the light of God's countenance" (Evangelism, *p. 121*).

"I'M COMING TOO, LORD"

Immediately he received his sight, and followed him, glorifying God: and all the people, when they saw it, gave praise unto God. Luke 18:43.

A beggar probably made a fairly good living at the Jordan River approach to Jericho. Caravans from the north and east crossed the river here. Bartimaeus had chosen this spot carefully.

The approaching tumult did not sound like a caravan or a group of pilgrims headed for the feast in Jerusalem. The answer to his questions filled his life with hope. "Jesus of Nazareth is passing by," people said. The fellowship of the blind and crippled had spread the word about the Healer from Galilee.

But Bartimaeus had his theology in better order than the crowd. Yes, Jesus was from Nazareth, but He was far more. Intimations of the kingdom of heaven had reached the blind man. Jesus was creating a community of faith, hope, and joy in which love reigned.

While they said, "Jesus of Nazareth," he said, "Son of David." He could see nothing special about Nazareth that would help him, but if the King of Israel was passing, that was a different story.

The first shout of Bartimaeus did not meet a response. Those with Jesus tried to hush him. The Greek tells us that his shout turned to a frenzied, desperate yell. This was his moment. He did not want to be left out.

Once he was healed, the procession moved on into Jericho. It had a new leader. Right behind Jesus came Bartimaeus, glancing this way and that but returning always to look at Jesus. The songs and rejoicing that finally brought Jesus to Jerusalem included the exultation of the man who would not be left out.

Time has created its procession toward the New Jerusalem. Jesus passes by this moment and that. He surprises us by appearing at moments when we least expect it. The cavalcade of life may suddenly split to show us Jesus gathering His people.

In that fellowship the joy extends out to us. Praise and thankfulness fill the air. The desperate cry of Bartimaeus speaks for all who truly know their need. "Heal me, Lord; I'm coming too."

"Union with Christ and with one another is our only safety in these last days" (Testimonies, *vol. 8, p. 240*).

"WHAT A FELLOWSHIP! WHAT A JOY DIVINE!"

Rather seek ye the kingdom of God; and all these things shall be added unto you. Luke 12:31.

What are "all these things" that the kingdom will add to us?

Jesus' discourse springs from an incident in the crowd. A man decides that Jesus, with His obvious wisdom, ought to be able to sort out a dispute between him and his brother. He points across the crowd, "Master, speak to my brother, that he divide the inheritance with me" (Luke 12:13).

Jesus moves immediately to talk about materialism and how it affects spiritual values. He tells of the man whose farm had prospered and who needed bigger barns to store the produce.

"I'm going to retire early," this man tells himself. "Then I'm going to give parties, go to parties, and have a good time."

It didn't work. That night he met the Judge.

Luke features the sharing of joy through food and fellowship. However, Jesus also gave warnings about wrong sharing of joy. God shares in our joy, yes, but joy as an end in itself has no future.

At least three characters, all unique to Luke's Gospel, teach this lesson. The prodigal returns from riotous living impoverished and forlorn. The rich man suffers in hell after a life of selfish living. And the man with the big plans drops dead.

Jesus therefore says, Put joy into the right perspective. I'm not against joy, per se. You know better than that. I am the One who goes to eat with sinners and tax gatherers. But if you want true joy to break through in your life, seek the kingdom first.

For Jesus, the prime emotion of the kingdom of heaven is joy. It breaks out wherever the kingdom breaks through. But joy can never live in isolation. It has to have company. The rich fool knew that; so did the prodigal son.

The community of the kingdom shares the joy Jesus brings. It opens itself to love and hope. It initiates joy in others.

"What a fellowship! What a joy divine!"

"The bright and cheerful side of our religion will be represented by all who are daily consecrated to God" (Testimonies, *vol. 6, p. 365*).

THE BIGGEST PARTY OF ALL

The lord said unto the servant, Go out into the highways and hedges, and compel them to come in, that my house may be filled. Luke 14:23.

The community at Bazega, in Upper Volta, decided that a banquet should mark the official opening of the church-run agricultural school south of the capital, Ouagadougou. Church members and locals joined in the preparations.

When we arrived, the tables groaned with food. Several goats provided by Muslim villagers turned slowly on spits over glowing coals. Vegetables and salads from the school garden abounded.

The crowds came, the wealthy farmers and the destitute. The year had been difficult and crops poor. The food melted away. Passing between rooms, I glanced across at the roasting animals just in time to see two men lift a whole carcass off the spit and run off into the dark with it! School officials soon had it back for sharing.

If you could create a worldwide party and invite all the undernourished and starving, what a mountain of food would be needed!

The parable gives God as the One who prepares the party. When the special guests offer all kinds of excuses declining the invitation, the banquet still goes ahead.

First Jesus and then the church carry out the will of God by searching for people to fill the seats and consume the good things provided. Jesus spoke in another place of the Father's house with its many mansions. Here He says that God wants His house filled.

If you have ideas about whom you want next to you at God's banquet, the celebration is not for you. If you have put material interests first, you won't even respond. If relationships mean more than the joy God is sharing, someone else will take your place.

The idea that the church is a banquet, a celebration, perhaps even a party, has God's endorsement.

When things do not go too well, we tend to put off the joy until the kingdom of God comes. But the parable has a present application also. The invitations are out. The celebration is already beginning.

"There are many from whom hope has departed. Bring back the sunshine to them. . . . Speak to them words of cheer. . . . Pray for these souls, bring them to Jesus" (Christ's Object Lessons, *p. 418*).

JOY IN THE DEEDS OF JESUS

When he had said these things, all his adversaries were ashamed: and all the people rejoiced for the glorious things that were done by him. Luke 13:17.

We can better understand the effect of Jesus' deeds on the people of Israel if we think of the way a city or even a nation responds to a great sporting triumph. When Jesus came, the people jammed the streets. They knew He would do something good and glorious; just what, they did not know, but they knew Him to be God's winner.

In succession He defeated illness, discomforted the haughty rulers, told of the grace of God. He went from strength to strength.

More than once Luke lends the tone of the great controversy to the struggle between Jesus and His opponents. Jesus shames His adversaries, as He will do in the judgment. His glorious and righteous deeds bring acclaim from the watchers, as they also will at the last day.

Even the incident that caused the people to share joy with Jesus carried with it the overtones of last events. Jesus described the woman as bound by Satan. He sets her free. In just such a way He will come to set all His people free from the chains of sin and death.

The Sabbath joy that flowed out through the city caused Jesus to comment in two parables. Joy brought through the gracious works of the Son of man carries the essential nature of the kingdom of God. Such joy produces the great kingdom tree that fills the earth. Lodged in the world of the Satan-bound, it lightens everything as leaven.

Joy breaks out on the Sabbath. Jesus took the Sabbath away from restriction and checklist mentality to joyous celebration of the delivering, sanctifying power of God.

In such events we better understand the purpose of worship and fellowship. As the crowds buzzed with the words of Jesus and all that He did, so should our worship services come alive as we hear the gospel and tell of what our Lord does for us.

The glorious things that the world sees in the church erupt into saving joy. Jesus again shows His power.

"Like the disciples, give what you have. Christ will multiply the gift. He will reward honest, simple reliance upon Him" (The Ministry of Healing, *pp. 49, 50).*

FAITH: THE UNLIMITED POSSIBILITIES OF LIFE

The apostles said unto the Lord, Increase our faith. Luke 17:5.

When the apostles said this, they had just heard one of Jesus' "hard" sayings. He had told them that even if a brother offend you seven times in one day and says he is sorry, you must forgive him.

Jesus repeatedly calls for faith. He responds to faith. Faith in Him saves and heals. What does He mean by faith? Jesus wanted to open the mind to the boundless possibilities of a life lived in a trusting relationship with God.

God will not content Himself with us as we are. He wants to bring us new ways of sharing with Him, and of relating to others. The Sermon on the Mount is about this kind of faith. It shows what the person of faith might yet become. Jesus saw how sin had choked us off from the full life we might live in God. What we have is small but it might be great.

Faith, as Jesus taught about it and expected it to appear in the life, contained at least the following elements:

1. Trust. To have faith in Jesus means to trust Him, trust His promises, trust His power. Trust Him, because He is the able one.

2. Knowledge. To have faith in Jesus means to know His will, to know what God expects of you. It also means to know about God. Blind Bartimaeus found healing in a confession that showed superior knowledge about Jesus. He knew Him as the covenant-keeping Son of David, not just as Jesus of Nazareth.

3. Decision. Faith in Jesus calls us to a continuing decision in favor of Him. To decide for Jesus means to decide in favor of life and of people. We choose in ways that affect others positively.

4. Obedience. Knowledge, decision, and obedience follow each other. Faith in Jesus acts in harmony with decisions based on true knowledge. The lifestyle of the Sermon on the Mount starts here.

5. Self-direction. Faith in Jesus gives self-worth, makes life something that lies within control. Through faith in Him we may choose and advance in areas once denied us.

"Lord, increase our faith."

"Every duty performed, every sacrifice made in the name of Jesus, brings an exceeding great reward. In the very act of duty, God speaks and gives His blessing" (Testimonies, *vol. 4, p. 145).*

FELLOWSHIP: BEING TOGETHER IN CHRIST

The cup of blessing which we bless, is it not the communion of the blood of Christ? The bread which we break, is it not the communion of the body of Christ? 1 Cor. 10:16.

When we come together for the Lord's Supper, we reach the pinnacle of sharing in Christ. The fellowship enlarges beyond the numbers of people present and the elements on the table. It includes, in a unique way, Jesus and the Spirit. The communion expands because we prepare for it, because we come expecting a blessing, and because we accept the promise of the Presence.

But that does not tell the whole story. What we do in remembrance of Jesus re-creates the sacrifice of Jesus, that which in essence binds Christians together. While the bread and wine remain symbols, as we eat and drink them we show Christ's death until He comes. Through them Christ's death comes to us anew as a saving event. We show our participation in the sufferings of Jesus.

But fellowship does not only occur at Communion time. Fellowship need number no more than two or three, and Christ joins in. His presence takes a gathering past a crowd, beyond an audience, to something better than a congregation. We enter fellowship in Christ.

The sacred Presence assembles with us and ministers to us in a way that a simple gathering never could. Fellowship in Christ restores and heals. When we are together in Him, He blesses and encourages us.

I remember teenage brothers in their Sabbath best plucking a buttonhole flower from their mother's garden and arriving early for church. Even for me, at that age, the special quality of Christian fellowship brought quietness, devotion, restoration. Another age? Perhaps, but the Spirit does shed the love of Christ abroad in our hearts as we fellowship in Him.

Today, at the end of a hectic week, with hundreds of decisions behind me, I go to meet the Spirit in the pulpit of a fellowship. Does it exhaust, burn yet more energies as I preach? No. I go from the encounter refreshed, renewed, as years ago.

Paul speaks of Communion as God's mystery. We do not understand why it accomplishes what it does. But the blessings themselves are no mystery. They are the heart of the human experience of God.

"It is at these, His own appointments, that Christ meets His people, and energizes them by His presence" (The Desire of Ages, p. 656).

VICTORY: CHRIST'S GIFT TO THE FAITHFUL

But call to remembrance the former days, in which, after ye were illuminated, ye endured a great fight of afflictions. Heb. 10:32.

In one of the paradoxes of the New Testament, Christian writers utilize the language of contest. Politicians and generals had no part in writing the gospel. The church's purposes differ totally from those of conflict. Jesus said that His servants did not fight. But the figures of fighting, wars, triumphs, sporting contests, and battle armor pervade the Epistles and the Revelation.

Christians fight against cosmic principalities and powers. Forces of satanic origin harass the church. The individual lands his punches squarely, not beating the air. He runs to reach the finishing line. A crown of victory waits him at the end of the contest.

Soldiers and athletes we are, but in a spiritual war, the Olympics of salvation. The contest has long since been decided but has not yet finished. Jesus has claimed the victory for all who have faith in Him. Armored with faith and the Spirit, holding the weapons of truth and love before us, we protect the victory.

Too many earthly conflicts have turned from victory to sour defeat. Those who won failed to ensure that the fruits of victory were theirs. The spiritual victory, which is Christ's gift to the faithful, also may fade to defeat unless we endure to the end.

Paul valued the hope of shared victory. The maturing Christian shares in the other's struggle, just as the other shares in his. Paul identified with the contest in every life. Through prayer and encouragement he sought victory for each.

The good fight of faith should not isolate us in an inner torment against demon forces. Christ has already won that battle. Instead, the Christian intercedes for another and makes that cause his own.

While we have an individual battle to win, the struggle is on behalf of Christ's body, that is, the church. Jesus remains always the hidden victor. He gives us victory while we wait for the universal acknowledgment of His victory. Because all receive the victory from Him, we share in the triumph of the church.

"The great Captain of our salvation has conquered in our behalf, that through Him we might conquer, if we would, in our own behalf" (Testimonies, *vol. 3, p. 457*).

FORGIVENESS: MERCY FULFILLS ITS NATURE

Help us, O God of our salvation, for the glory of thy name: and deliver us, and purge away our sins, for thy name's sake. Ps. 79:9.

The grubby, sticky fingers of sin wiped themselves on David's heart. Befouled! Contaminated! Soiled! Where would he find soap to foam him clean, or brush to scour away the filth? Out of the heart that cries for forgiveness and cleansing, he called to God. Mercy met the plea and answered in God's name.

From Eden itself the loss of innocence echoes through history with a haunting appeal for a new beginning. The gulf between God and mankind splits ever wider as the end approaches. Each day we call for the mercy that closes the chasm and bridges us back to the Father.

Our self-seeking hostility to God springs from Eden itself. We have learned too well the mocking chant "Hath God said?" To meet this need David begged for a clean heart, the new start every sinner craves. He could not bear the separation, nor the fear and the guilt. If only God could turn his thoughts and wishes always toward Him.

But his sinful nature had grieved God and wronged others. He had broken God's Ten Words of righteousness. He had failed the covenant relationship. He had sought his own pleasure rather than the welfare of his neighbor. This specific wrong, this identifiable sin, defiled God's name. It left him guilty beyond his own repair.

He found solace in God's mercy. His very words reveal what God does. To cry for a clean heart indicates that God can give it. To ask for purging from sin means God can forgive. To ask as David asked is to receive. To seek as David sought is to find.

God's mercy proclaimed is heartsease. Yet it has a wider purpose. Israel as a nation knew that purpose: for the glory of God's name the nation called for deliverance. For the sake of His name it yearned for cleansing.

A restored person, a restored people; God's plan provides for both. At the end of days He shall stand in defense of His people. They shall be His and no one will deny Him.

God's people "had obtained the victory, and it called forth from them the deepest gratitude and holy, sacred joy" (Early Writings, *p. 271).*

FORGIVENESS: JESUS AT WORK FOR US

And they that sat at meat with him began to say within themselves, Who is this that forgiveth sins also? Luke 7:49.

The supreme purpose of Jesus' ministry was to bring forgiveness to the people. He came to reconcile mankind to its God. Dealing with sin, giving forgiveness, bringing man close to God again, express all that He did.

The rabbis and rulers knew about forgiveness. On the Day of Atonement the high priest would bring sacrifices for the repentant. God in His grace could forgive sin. A person could acquire divine favor through obedience and pious works and so counterbalance sin.

Jesus brought a new view of how God would deal with sin. As the Messiah He brought forgiveness and power over sin. He could say to the woman found in adultery, "Go and sin no more." He told Mary, "Go in peace." Later Paul would remember these actions of Jesus and declare that sin no longer reigns in the heart of the justified.

Our text today gives the reactions of those who watched the interplay between Simon, Mary, and Jesus. They heard Jesus assure Mary that her many sins were forgiven. They caught the implication that Simon also had sin that needed forgiveness, but which he refused to recognize.

In His words they found hope. If Jesus could forgive, then what about them? Would He not also give them the reconciliation they desired? If Christ is forgiving, then the long-foretold Messiah has come. The new age has opened in which the people will turn their hearts to God.

Christ gave new status to those He saved. The prodigal has on the father's robe, Mary goes in peace. There is now no condemnation against the adulteress. All has changed, all is new for those whom the Saviour welcomes.

What Jesus does for us is not only the remission of past sins. He does remove them from us, and sink them in the depths of the ocean. But He also gives deliverance. He is God's freedom-giver. The power of sin can claim no final judgment against us. We have fellowship with God. We are His people and He leads us on.

"Holiness is not rapture; it is the result of surrendering all to God; it is doing the will of our heavenly Father" (Thoughts From the Mount of Blessing, *p. 149*).

JESUS: DOOR TO THE FOLD

I am the door: by me if any man enter in, he shall be saved, and shall go in and out, and find pasture. John 10:9.

In the days before the trailer trains of the Australian outback, drovers moved huge mobs of sheep across the arid heart of the Australian outback. If you were to take any long trip, you would have encountered at least one of these throngs crowding road and shoulders, with stockmen trying to urge the sheep along. On occasion even today you might find such a mob, with drover, dogs, and horses watching over the bleating mass, and the acrid smell of sheep mingling with dust and heat.

This is a far cry from Jesus' Palestine, where shepherd and sheep formed an alliance based on food and protection. No one shepherd ever cared for more than 300 sheep; usually the flock was far smaller. The flock of a hundred in the parables would be above average. In the personal care the shepherd gave, and the total dependency of sheep on shepherd, Jesus found an analogy for the human-divine relationship.

Twice Jesus says "I am the door," each time with different intent. "I am the gate," Jesus says in John 10:7 (NIV). Through Him the genuine shepherd approaches the sheep. False shepherds climb the wall to the fold, stealing, raiding. By the time John wrote, false shepherds were raiding the flock, distorting the truth. John remembered and recorded Jesus' emphasis. Good shepherds come only through Jesus, the Door.

But He is the door in another sense. Day by day the shepherd would lead the sheep out of the fold in the search for pasture. In Jesus' analogy the finding of pasture means salvation, just as it meant life to the sheep. The fold also represents the security of God's saving grace. Jesus secures the fold. Jesus provides the pasture.

Jesus excluded anything that did not come from God. He gathers to Himself all possible applications of the sheep and shepherd motif. He is door, He is shepherd, He is fold. Whatever image the picture suggests, it has its application in Jesus.

The image is rural, unfamiliar to many. However, the message it gives is specific and very appropriate. Jesus, our all, provides all. Look daily to Him; He will nourish, He will protect.

"As an earthly shepherd knows his sheep, so does the divine Shepherd know His flock that are scattered throughout the world" (The Desire of Ages, *p. 479*).

JESUS: THE TRUE VINE FOR ALL

I am the vine, ye are the branches: He that abideth in me, and I in him, the same bringeth forth much fruit: for without me ye can do nothing. John 15:5.

During the 1700s, gardeners planted a vine at Hampton Court Palace, up the River Thames from London. The vine still lives. Now called the Great Vine, it flourished while the American colonies still acknowledged the English monarch as sovereign, and before Governor Philip brought his mixed bag of settlers and convicts to Australia. Given the care it enjoys, experts say it may live another two centuries.

The vine itself occupies a large glasshouse, which protects it from winter cold. A two-acre field feeds the rambling monster. The area also hosts a spring spectacular of bluebells.

Jesus took pains to describe Himself as the true vine, just as He called Himself the good shepherd. No one can substitute for the life-giving Vine. Only branches from the divine Stock will bear fruit.

What did Jesus mean by abiding in Him? Life that begins in God cannot continue if it severs itself from God. Christ, the True Vine, feeds His branches so that they flourish and bear fruit.

Like the Good Shepherd analogy, and the discourse on the water of life, the parable-like figure of the vine urges the Christian to consider his alternatives. Self cannot feed self; a severed branch dies with the pruning. False vines put on a show but do not produce fruit.

But that is not all. When the vinedresser prunes a vine, he cuts the branches back close to the stock: only one or two growing shoots remain for the spring growth. These shoots burst into life and produce the fruit. The pruned cuttings have no future. They may harbor disease, and a wise farmer burns them.

Stay close to Christ, the parable urges. Don't separate yourself from Him. What this means is very clear. "If ye abide in me, and my words abide in you, ye shall ask what ye will, and it shall be done unto you" (John 15:7). The source of life is the True Vine; the fruit He looks for is obedience to His commandments.

Or as Jesus also put it: "As the Father hath loved me, so have I loved you: continue ye in my love" (verse 9).

"So long as the soul is united to Christ, there is no danger that it will wither or decay" (The Desire of Ages, *p. 676).*

THE WHEELCHAIR OPTIMIST

Let hope keep you joyful; in trouble stand firm; persist in prayer. Rom. 12:12, NEB.

Outside the little mission office, we waited for the director to come. A glance around showed that this Angolan outpost of Adventist missionary endeavor still had a long way to go. Yet activity and purpose filled the compound. A church was under construction down the road. Another construction crew was adding to the classroom block.

The clatter of a two-cycle motor drowned our conversation. A wheelchair darted around the corner of the building and pulled up alongside us in a flurry of dust and exhaust smoke.

Thus I met Jose de Sa, pioneer missionary in Angola, school and mission director, and, above all, builder for the future.

Some years before, he had been working on a scaffold, building the classrooms for his mission station. The scaffolding collapsed, injuring his spine and paralyzing him. With gritty determination he recovered his health. His wheelchair became his legs, and he returned to run the station.

Hope filled his conversation. "We will finish the church next year." "We plan to improve the clinic." "We are going to start some outposts to the south."

When we hope, we look to the brightest of any alternatives in the future. Let that hope lead us on. We sometimes speak of "foolish hope," of being "deceived by hopes," of "false hopes."

The quality of hope in Christ differs from the quality of secular hope. The latter may delude us and return to mock us. But not the hope God gives. Of course He does not guarantee that our secular and material hopes will come true. That isn't what Paul is talking about. The hope that maintains a constant flow of joy is a hope fixed in Christ.

Jose de Sa could hope with God and in God because he knew himself to be God's child doing God's work. Such a hope sustains in trouble and keeps us praying to the God of hope. Such a hope outrides the foolish and broken hopes of our material and secular world. It survives the bitter and the sweet. It has a different focus, a different support system, and thus becomes for the Christian, the root of joy.

"Soon the warfare will be over and the victory won, and if you are faithful you will come off more than conquerors through Him that has loved you" (Testimonies, *vol. 5, p. 309*).

MAKING STRAIGHT PATHS

The voice of one crying in the wilderness, Prepare ye the way of the Lord, make his paths straight. Luke 3:4.

When we came to Madura Pass, we were three days into our crossing of the great Nullarbor (No Tree) Plain. The only trees we had sighted lived precarious lives around the isolated homesteads. Elsewhere, the desert wilderness produced only low shrubs and tough grasses.

My father walked the pass first, to check it out. Later, we walked while he drove. Messages scrawled on wayside boulders told of past disasters. "Broke a spring. Held up 11 days." "Holed the radiator. Four days waiting." And so on.

In the 1930s Australia had no transcontinental highway. What passed for a road up the cliff turned out to be a sorting of boulders so that the really large ones were shoved to the edge and only the small ones threatened chassis and tires.

Remembering the despairing graffiti on those rocks called to mind another description: "At this I raised my eyes, and saw a straight and narrow path, cast up high above the world. On this path the Advent people were traveling to the city, which was at the farther end of the path. . . . If they kept their eyes fixed on Jesus, who was just before them, leading them to the city, they were safe" (*Early Writings*, p. 14).

In Ellen White's vision, we may think of the path as representing doctrine. Jesus leads the church safely along a difficult path of truth toward the heavenly kingdom. She tells how some fell off the path. Others kept their eyes fixed on Jesus and remained safe.

Sometimes we wonder whether doctrines really do matter. Isn't simple belief in Jesus enough? But simple belief itself has a basis of doctrine. To know the truth brings true freedom, Jesus said; He is the truth. Therefore to study doctrine is to study about Jesus Christ. In the thought world of the Bible, Jesus sends the Spirit, who guides us into truth.

Adventists hope to avoid the broken wrecks and sad messages from the history of various movements and denominations that have lost their way.

"Then Jesus would encourage them by raising His glorious right arm, and from His arm came a light which waved over the Adventist band, and they shouted, 'Alleluia!' " (Early Writings, *pp. 14, 15*).

KEEPING THE DOOR OPEN

While they went to buy, the bridegroom came; and they that were ready went in with him to the marriage: and the door was shut. Matt. 25:10.

The mistake was a simple one. My airplane ticket read 17:30, and I read it as 7:30. I arrived to see the plane standing on the apron with engines running. Was it coming or going? A mad rush to the check-in counter gave the answer I did not want. The plane was leaving, and the door was shut. One such mistake in 30 years of constant travel in church work is not too bad a record. But there is another door and another shutting.

The story of Peter and Rhoda helps us understand about shut doors in the ancient Middle East. Frequently a courtyard separated the living quarters from the gate. Security demanded a strict check on those entering. Each house had its wall and its door, and like a city with its gates shut at sunset, the inhabitants would refuse entry to any unknown arrival.

In the parable of the virgins, all the pleading availed nothing. The householder would not risk the security of his home. "There shall be weeping and gnashing of teeth" (Matt. 25:30).

Jesus' parables about the end-time carry a message of urgency and crisis. They are time-ridden. A day approaches, they say, when choices will have passed, the kingdom will have gone on by. "He hath appointed a day, in the which he will judge the world" (Acts 17:31).

The door has a simple interpretation. The narrow gate leads to life, the broad way to destruction. Jesus said, I am the Door. To go through the door means to believe in the Lord Jesus for salvation. A shut door means that we no longer have that choice. It can happen through our death, or through the coming of the end. Not, let me hasten to add, through God cutting anyone off before the appointed time. The unpardonable sin is the sin we do not confess and forsake, not some specific act that turns God's face away from us.

Life is a continuing process, not a game in which we wait our turn with the dice to see where the next jump will take us. In skipping preparation, the foolish virgins lost out. In staying prepared, the wise found the door open. The door is never shut on the life that trusts continually in God's power and saving grace.

"Christ has made every provision that His church shall be a transformed body, illumined with the Light of the world, possessing the glory of Emmanuel" (Christ's Object Lessons, *p. 419*).

GO THOU THY WAY

But go thou thy way till the end be: for thou shalt rest, and stand in thy lot at the end of the days. Dan. 12:13.

God gives a downpayment on all His promises for the future. The promise for Daniel carries two parts. First, God would give him rest, or peace of mind. Then God would give him a place in His kingdom.

If you look back to Daniel 8:14 you will read of the "days" that caused much distress to Daniel. So much so that at the end of that vision he fainted and was ill for several days. He understood more about those days when Gabriel explained the details about Israel and how the prophecy affected them.

Our text for today gives an assurance for all those who wonder about how they will fare in the final events. As with Daniel, God has allotted a place for them. The judgment will not exclude any of the saints mentioned in Daniel 7 and 8.

A few hundred years after Daniel's vision, the Son of man, whom Daniel had seen in a previous vision, gave His own promise: "Come unto me, all ye that labour and are heavy laden, and I will give you rest. Take my yoke upon you, and learn of me; for I am meek and lowly in heart: and ye shall find rest unto your souls. For my yoke is easy, and my burden is light" (Matt. 11:28-30).

These promises assure us that we need not wait till death or the new earth to experience the sublime rest that God gives. This rest removes from us the dominion and guilt of sin. As His sanctifying grace works in us, we learn from Him to be quiet and meek in spirit.

God told Daniel that He had no more information or visions to impart to him. He could now record what would occur between his time and the end. With that knowledge he should now rest comfortably in God's care, knowing that God would note him and prepare for him.

The visions Daniel had must have overwhelmed him—so much for one human to absorb and adapt to. Such feelings often sweep over the Christian as he or she considers the broadness of eternal issues. Where am I in these cosmic dramas? Who will remember me? As we face the end, it's good to know that the God who had Daniel in view also has each of His children accounted for.

"He cares for each one as if there were not another on the face of the earth" (The Desire of Ages, *p. 480).*

THE DEW OF LIGHT

But thy dead live, their bodies will rise again. They that sleep in the earth will awake and shout for joy; for thy dew is a dew of sparkling light, and the earth will bring those long dead to birth again. Isa. 26:19, NEB.

About 700 years after Isaiah wrote this prophecy, the early Christians wrote a hymn that caught its spirit. Paul records part of it. "Awake thou that sleepest, and arise from the dead, and Christ shall give thee light" (Eph. 5:14). From the ancient past comes this clear promise of the resurrection day. Something to sing about indeed!

The earth that holds the sleeping saints has the dew as its mantle. In the morning light the dew sparkles with life, just as God's power covers His children with the light of His love. Their future sparkles with the light of God's promises.

You can track this prediction through the writings of the Old Testament. Daniel knew about it. He links light and the stars to the raising of the dead in Daniel 12:2, 3. Those who arise to eternal life will shine with the glory of heaven itself.

But Paul's hymn has another view of this prophecy. Those locked into sin live in darkness. Light can come through Jesus. Christ will shine on the reborn. The new birth has the quality of the resurrection. In it God fulfills His promise to lift us from the certainty of the second death to the assurance of eternal life.

We groped our way by flashlight into the depths of the Carlsbad Caverns. The path meandered through dripping water and slippery rocks. One could only call the scenery ugly and uninviting. We rounded a corner, passed through a narrow entrance, and paused. The guide threw a switch on the wall. We gasped. Our eyes lifted from the slimy rocks and damp corners. Now we could see, and we knew beauty.

Death has its finality and its ugliness. But when Christ gives light, we see the glory of the resurrection. The old man of sin knows only too well the wretched misery of lust and greed. He has groped through pride and lies all his life. But then Christ gives light. Immediately we see purity, nobility, and truth in their beauty. And we cry out for the rebirth that will raise us from sin to life and light.

"Through His grace men may possess Christlikeness of character, and may rejoice in the assurance of His great love" (The Desire of Ages, p. 826).

CHOSEN FROM THE BEGINNING

God hath from the beginning chosen you to salvation through sanctification of the Spirit and belief of the truth. 2 Thess. 2:13.

In a typical direct mail sales pitch, the accompanying letter begins, "You have been selected . . ." But by the time you have read your way through the cards and glossy brochures, you know the price that you will have to pay if you want the benefit of that "selection."

A sergeant may line up his company and call for volunteers to carry out a certain detail. Then to shorten the process he simply declares, "You, you, and you will do!"

There is a kind of choosing that has a willy-nilly air to it. It swoops and grabs whomever it can. You get selected because you have your name on somebody's list. You have no control over the list. You cannot put yourself on it or take yourself off it. The only choice you have is to accept or reject another's choosing of you.

Another kind of choosing gives you no choice at all. Someone else counts you in and that is that.

God neither puts us on a list of those who get the chance to accept His salvation nor selects us to lose out on the honor of sharing in His redeeming grace.

Grace reaches out to provide for all, but it becomes active in those who respond. God has chosen salvation for all, but all do not choose salvation.

Paul wrote the words in our text for today as he finished his "little apocalypse," in which he describes the working of the mystery of iniquity. He contrasted those whom the Spirit was sanctifying and who believed the truth with those who would not receive the love of the truth but took part in unrighteousness.

The basic choosing lies with us. But once faith says yes to Jesus, God chooses to set the Spirit to work in our lives. He rules our lives, driving out sin. He guides us into all truth.

As the end-time approaches, the sanctifying power of the Spirit gathers significance. Jesus will come to find a people keeping the commandments and maintaining their faith in Him. They will remain faithful because their salvation has both the yes of the Spirit's continuing presence and the yes of constancy in believing the truth.

"The love of truth and righteousness must reign in the soul, and a character will appear which heaven can approve" (Testimonies, vol. 5, p. 43).

CHRIST SETS UP HIS HOUSE

But Christ as a son over his own house; whose house are we, if we hold fast the confidence and the rejoicing of the hope firm unto the end. Heb. 3:6.

Hebrews continually urges us to keep on with our faith and hope to the end. Perhaps the community of Christians to whom the Epistle first went had a pattern of starting out but not staying the distance. For us, Jesus is the author and finisher of the race set before us. He is the same yesterday, today, and forever. Therefore, do not cast away your confidence. Rather, hold it fast.

Recently our family joined the craze of searching out roots. We have discovered the documents that made my great-grandfather, who came from Denmark, a British subject. It happened a long time ago in Tasmania, Australia's island state. His papers indicate that Niels Peter Nielsen was a blacksmith. It appears that another great-grandfather was the son of a convict sent from England on smuggling charges! One thing is certain, we can learn about our ancestral house, but we cannot choose it.

In the rich imagery of Hebrews, Paul creates a picture contrasting stewardship and sonship. Moses served God faithfully. God trusted him with His house, Israel, and he did well with that trust.

On the other hand, God authorized Christ to build His own house. Christ has built a house on the faithfulness of those who hold on to the full assurance of salvation.

Hebrews uses the figure of the house to talk about the glory of Christ. The very presence of faithful, patient Christians shows that Christ has done the task appointed Him. His house, made up of the saints, will continue to the end. Only as we keep our confidence and hope can we continue as part of that house.

The roots of every Christian have just one generation. The born-again Christian has no grandfather, just a Father. He has a Brother, and brothers and sisters. Together they make up the ever-growing house of Christ. In this house human ancestry has no significance. What counts is the blessed assurance Christ gives, and the hope that we hold fast.

"I heard shouts of triumph from the angels and from the redeemed saints, which sounded like ten thousand musical instruments" (Early Writings, p. 290).

GATHERED IN JESUS' NAME

Where two or three are gathered together in my name, there am I in the midst of them. Matt. 18:20.

As Peter and John walked toward the Temple they may have remembered Jesus' promise. What did it mean to have Jesus in their midst? Here they were, just two. At Pentecost, 120 had received the rain of fire and felt the wind blow. The congregation had gone into the streets fulfilling the mission Jesus had given them.

Now, just two, the very smallest congregation possible, they saw the cripple sitting by the gate Beautiful. For more than three years they had watched the power of Jesus reach past their helplessness to save and heal. They could no longer look over their shoulders expecting Jesus to act. What would the Spirit do through these two who now called on the Name to heal the cripple?

Peter is one; John is one. But the Spirit is not a third character in the story. Unlike Jesus, the Spirit had no hands with which to reach past Peter and lift up the cripple. The hands of Peter and John lifted him up.

The Spirit never can be the additional Person, standing with us and doing for us. Rather, He adds to the sum of witness. The smallest congregation has power to share with the world because the Spirit forms the plus sign between the *ones* of the church and between the *us* of the church and the world.

Jesus described it this way: "If I do not go away, the Comforter will not come unto you." The absence of the real person of Christ gives room for the real presence of the Spirit, not to make three out of the Peter-and-John twosome, nor add one more to the assembly at Pentecost. Rather, God the Spirit gives our togetherness the power of the Name in which we gather.

Nor does the Spirit seek credit for what happens. Peter and John did not claim the Wind of Pentecost as the reason for the healing, but simply the name of Jesus. The cripple responded to the power of that Name, even as the world may today.

"We are carrying the last message to a perishing world, and God calls upon us to bring freshness and power into our work. We can do this only by the aid of the Holy Spirit" (Testimonies to Ministers, p. 313).

OUT OF HUMILIATION THE SEEDS OF FAITH GROW

And at midnight Paul and Silas prayed, and sang praises unto God: and the prisoners heard them. Acts 16:25.

In the days before hens were locked in henhouses to lay their lives away, a favorite way to keep them productive was to house them over deep litter. With up to two feet of shavings to scratch away in, and with adequate food and water, the eggs kept rolling into the crates.

When we arrived in New Zealand to take up an appointment at the Longburn Adventist College, we found a shed that had once housed hens the deep-litter way. Now, two years later, the farm manager needed the shed cleaned out. We took the litter and rotary-hoed it into our home garden.

I decided to plant squash and pumpkins.

By late summer the vines had woven a green cloak for the garage and festooned it with orange and green balls. Balloons of golden orange decorated shrubs and trees. The fence between us and the church staggered with giant green squash.

Humiliation and *humility* have the same root as *humus*. The humiliated may feel like the rubbish of the earth. Paul called all his accomplishments dung. Down into the soil and the straw and the refuse of the humus pile the seeds of faith fall and bring forth a harvest.

How badly people treated Paul and Silas that day in Philippi! They stripped away their clothes and flogged the two men, and threw them into the prison with common criminals. The two missionaries had no defenses there. They had come to the end of their tether. No signpost pointed the way ahead. At that point the Spirit entered to make their humiliation a glory to the name of Jesus.

When our defenses are down, when pride falls to the earth, when we have nowhere to turn, the Holy Spirit comes to us in renewal. For the church to feel humbled is far better than for it to pat itself on the back.

When Jesus looked for faith, He found it among the ones whom society rejected and scoffed at. The "rubbish" of the earth grew the mustard tree of the kingdom.

Out of the church that knows it is truly Laodicea, the seeds of faith may yet grow and fill the whole earth.

"Not for one moment does God lose sight of [humble, contrite workers]. . . . In the heavenly courts, when the redeemed are gathered home, they will stand nearest the Son of God" (Testimonies, *vol. 7, p. 26*).

NO ROOM SERVICE IN THE HOUSE CHRIST BUILT

If I then, your Lord and Master, have washed your feet; ye also ought to wash one another's feet. John 13:14.

Judas paid a premium for the upper room where Jesus and his fellow disciples gathered to celebrate the Passover. According to old manuscripts, landlords charged oversized rents at the times of the great feasts in Jerusalem. The 13 probably felt grateful that they had such a large and convenient room. Later it would hold 120 as they waited for the Spirit.

But the landlord did not provide room service. Not that he offered no amenities. Inside the door he had placed a large pitcher full of water, a basin, and a towel. With no servants waiting on them, the twelve overlooked the niceties of the moment and simply made no use of the water.

Did they remember Mary who had washed Jesus' feet with her tears? Apparently not. No better than Simon the Pharisee, they did not think of doing a servant's work.

Within hours Jesus would promise them the Comforter. If they would ever become the salt of the earth and the light of the world, they would have to serve one another as the Spirit would soon serve them.

As Jesus moved water and towel from disciple to disciple He drew them into His humility. In the church, the house that Christ has built, He offers no room service. Brothers go on errands for each other. They serve one another, for the glory of the Servant of servants.

Sometimes we talk as if the Spirit will do the work for us. We pray, "Send Your Spirit before us." The prayer has good in it as long as we do not expect the Spirit to gird Himself and do the work of the servant of Christ. Jesus left that role for us.

Rather than go before, or stand and urge, the Spirit draws the diverse parts of the church into a witnessing oneness. We wash one another's feet, not alone to show how humble we are, but to affirm that the life of service and witness represents the presence of the Comforter among us.

Because we bend before each other and do the servant's task, the world may also stretch out its feet to us for cleansing. The servants of the Lord are the world's servants.

"Those who have communed with Christ in the upper chamber will go forth to minister as He did" (The Desire of Ages, *p. 651).*

FOR ONE ANOTHER

I beseech you therefore, brethren, by the mercies of God, that ye present your bodies a living sacrifice, holy, acceptable unto God, which is your reasonable service. Rom. 12:1.

In its state symbolism, the Roman Empire emphasized the need for unity. One symbol showed a bundle of sticks tied together and an axhead attached at one end. Each stick by itself would snap. No one stick could carry the weight of an axhead. But tied together by common cause they could control the world.

By the time of Christ, many wrong ideas had taken over in Judaism. In one common error, the believing Jew trusted in the community to find his salvation. He expected God's acceptance through Temple and Torah. His very Jewishness gave him an unbeatable lead in the race for God's favor.

Jesus turned around the thinking of His compatriots. For the Jews, the person of faith looked inward to the community to find life. For the church, faith looked out to the world to bring to it hope in Christ.

When Paul says, "Christ in you, the hope of glory," he uses *you* plural, not singular. Not you the person, but you the church, display Christ, the hope of glory.

In our promise, Paul does not see a host of single sacrifices to God, one for each person in the community of faith. Rather, one corporate sacrifice of our bodies represents our reasonable service. The Bible will not let us escape from the togetherness through which the Spirit can create Christ's presence in the church and through it in the world.

In 1 Corinthians 6:19 Paul actually says "your [plural] body [singular] is the temple of the Holy Ghost." He does the same with "your body" in verse 20.

We must not overlook the great passages such as Romans 7:7-25, where the individual is in focus. However, in Christ we are for one another. The two or three or more that gather together express best the power of Christ.

When one is alone with self, the facts of sin and self weigh heavily. Through the presence of Christ the church comes alive to God. To be for Christ is to be for one another. Not just in the sense of the community of faith, but because in our togetherness we share God's favor.

"The grace and love of our Lord Jesus Christ and His tender relationship to His church on earth are to be revealed by the growth of His work" (Selected Messages, book 1, p. 113).

MAKE WAY FOR THE BURDEN BEARERS

Bear ye one another's burdens, and so fulfil the law of Christ. Gal. 6:2.

Airline stewardesses give out little notices reminding passengers of the effect of high altitudes. At the baggage pickup area, signs warn travelers not to be tempted to carry their own bags. La Paz airport rides high in the Andes. At 14,000 feet, lowlanders find even a briefcase a burden, and a gentle walk a breathtaking experience.

What really sets the newcomer back, though, is the Indian women. As in so many societies, Bolivian women carry large loads. As the visitor is struggling up a mild slope toward the market, one of the local women will slip past him at a steady jog, bowler hat jauntily atop her head, loaded with vegetables, and humming a tune. On market day the women will give a low warning whistle as they trot upward. It says, Make way for the burden bearers.

In nonmechanical societies, people routinely carry large loads. The peasant with his buckets swinging from either end of a balance pole may be found in a thousand cities and villages. In Jesus' day a Roman soldier could demand that a Jew carry his pack for a mile. Jesus suggested making that mile two, to show growth in the kingdom of heaven.

Perhaps Paul thought of that as he spoke of Christ's law. The principle behind "love thy neighbour" puts the Christian on the alert to sense the need of the other. One who loves always acts for the welfare of the other person. Therefore the disciple will bear another's burden.

But Paul did not have cabbages or sacks of corn in mind. He knew how easily we turn inward: our own burden is magnified out of proportion, but the load another carries is under our reducing glass. The sin that bedevils one person may never tempt another. Or the habit that throttles one life may never snake its coils around another.

So Paul asks for tolerance of each other. The strong is to look at the weak and say, I understand, let me help. The follower of Jesus continually positions himself to take the heavy end of the load. He knows that is where Jesus is lifting too, sharing the load.

In the society of faith, the helper and the helped go together toward the kingdom, sharing and bearing, as their Lord also does.

"Christianity is the revealing of the tenderest affection for one another" (Selected Messages, *book 1, p. 114).*

HOW PRAYER FOR ANOTHER HELPS

Confess your faults one to another, and pray one for another, that ye may be healed. The effectual fervent prayer of a righteous man availeth much. James 5:16.

The crowd pressed so tightly that people stood on each other's feet. How could she ever get through to Him? There is a way when the crowd is moving slowly. Make yourself an obstacle and force the crowd to part around you; but did she have the strength for that? Perhaps she uttered a thousand "Excuse me"s. Or did she go down on hands and knees and crawl through the open spaces, as a child will?

When she was close enough she said nothing; she simply reached out and touched Jesus. He knew only too well the touch of faith. One day soon He would mediate the prayers of a million of His children; should He not know the flick of faith then and there?

She went from that encounter saved and healed. In the New Testament, to be healed means to be saved. Not always so, however. Remember the 10 lepers? Jesus healed them all, but only one expressed faith.

What did James have in mind when He urged confession of faults one to another? Certainly not a maudlin outpouring of guilt and shame. He saw very clearly how much we need each other on the narrow way. If intercessory prayer would do its work for the wayfarers, then they must tell each other in what ways they need prayer.

James was urging specific prayers. Not just "Bless the missionaries and the colporteurs," but "Heal this man" or "Save this woman." In specific prayer for the other's need, God joins our quest for an answer.

He does not ask us to list the other person's faults. How easy that would be! And how often it is our way of approaching difficult relationships! Each of us has the initiative in what we will confess. The faults we identify may find healing through another's concern and prayer.

The righteous praying for each other holds immense power for good. They can help each other in ways that no one else would ever imagine. In their prayers the Spirit enters and makes one with them. He adds the one and the other together so that they possess more than if they remained alone without each other and without Him.

"True conversion is a change from selfishness to sanctified affection for God and one another" (Selected Messages, *book 1, p. 115*).

TOGETHER TOWARD THE KINGDOM

They brought to him a man sick of the palsy, lying on a bed: and Jesus seeing their faith said unto the sick of the palsy; Son, be of good cheer; thy sins be forgiven thee. Matt. 9:2.

In a memorable sermon in Washington, D.C.'s Sligo church, Dr. William Loveless described his view of the church. He said something like this:

"We are the walking wounded. We go together toward the kingdom, leaning on each other, helping each other. All of us need help. God wants us to find ways of sharing and caring for each other. We lean on Him, we sustain each other, and so we go onward, not expecting too much. But yet expecting everything, for the promise says that in Him and with Him we shall arrive together in His kingdom."

The essence of the caring church extends to us from a story about Jesus told by Matthew, Mark, and Luke. Luke must have told it with a twinkle in his eye. Four men, with a fifth on a litter. A crowd blocking the way. Through the doors? Impossible. Through the windows? Choked with people. Where, then? Ah, the roof.

"Now up you go. Steady a moment while we lift the tiles. Lower him gently. There's space in front of Jesus."

Four friends to help him to Jesus! How fortunate a man! Think a moment and name friends who would help you in a time of deep distress. What a joy to have good friends!

In such care, in such togetherness, grace gladly meets faith and gives the yes of salvation. Those five went together to Jesus, and who received the greatest blessing? The man on the bed? The four who helped him?

When a community of faith numbering only five men brought themselves to Jesus in their great need, all had their faith answered. But where did faith focus? On the specific need of one of that community.

Who needs help? You. Me. All need help. Shared faith creates the litter that carries need to the feet of Jesus. We encourage and strengthen each other. Which of those men alone could have struggled with their friend to the rooftop and safely lowered the bed?

In the togetherness of our faith, the compassion and care that our Saviour showed flourishes. And in that togetherness faith finds the healing it craves.

"God will work through a consecrated, self-denying church, and He will reveal His Spirit in a visible and glorious manner" (Selected Messages, *book 1, p. 117).*

PRAYER REMOVES SADNESS

Then Eli answered and said, Go in peace: and the God of Israel grant thee thy petition that thou hast asked of him. 1 Sam. 1:17.

A Hindu couple will visit temple after temple, make sacrifices to gods, and go on long pilgrimages in their yearning for a child. In Africa, women seek the advice of pagan priests or Muslim holy men in order to bear their husbands a child.

When procreation tops the marriage priorities, a sense of shame and inadequacy clouds a childless relationship. Lacking any sophisticated medical help, the woman is blamed for infertility.

In ancient Israel the cultural pressure went one step further. Without a son the name of a particular family line would die out. Even in Christ's day a father would reply to a question about his children with the number of sons he had. Only as an afterthought would he add the daughters!

Under such pressures Elkanah and Hannah came to the tabernacle. The simple assurance that Elkanah loved her would be enough for many modern-day Hannahs. But not back then.

Her hope lay in God. Only in Him could she find self-worth. The answer she sought would do more than give an heir; it would restore her personal dignity and establish her worth in the community.

We must see the granting of Hannah's prayer as more than a simple answer to her plea. God is very near to us. He sees the greater need. Through answering her prayer He could restore her to wholeness. No longer would she walk her village disgraced, inadequate. Her prayer speaks for all who carry the shame of guilt or failure.

Undoubtedly, God could have brought her to find consolation and pride in her husband's love. That also would have answered her prayer. He may even have brought her to understand that her relationship with Him provided more than any human tie.

In all His answers to our prayers God has a purpose. Before Hannah could know she had conceived, God had given her hope. The simple words of Eli reassured her. God spoke peace to her heart. "The woman went her way, . . . and her countenance was no more sad" (1 Sam. 1:18).

"Prayer is the opening of the heart to God as to a friend. . . . Prayer does not bring God down to us, but brings us up to Him" (Steps to Christ, *p. 93).*

"FEAR NOT: BELIEVE ONLY"

When Jesus heard it, he answered him, saying, Fear not: believe only, and she shall be made whole. Luke 8:50.

Without doubt, Jesus, and Luke, who recorded the incident, wanted more read into it than a resurrection miracle. Jesus' words of comfort answer all who come to Him for wholeness.

The story has a special feature that may easily escape us. To the Jew of that age, the birth of a daughter hardly sent him to the store for a box of congratulatory candy to share with his friends! He would accept what God had given and hope for a son next time.

The concern of Jairus for his daughter develops a theme prominent in Luke's writings. Jesus did not hesitate to give women a status equal to men. A father who so loved his daughter would mean much to the Saviour.

In the flow of Luke's narrative a woman in need delayed Jesus on His way to help the girl. Luke shows how Jesus encouraged a society in which discrimination had no rightful part.

In assessing what Jairus' request meant, we have to remember that children and adults were dying all around Jesus. The special quality of this healing lay in the father's persistence. When Jesus stopped to heal the woman who touched the hem of His garment, Jairus did not give up. Rather, he saw in this a reason for his own hope.

When servants brought news that all was past hope, Jairus accepted Jesus' assurance and walked with Him in faith toward his home.

Another cause for reflection lies in the reaction of those who waited at the house. When Jesus said that the girl lay asleep, they mocked Him. They knew that she had passed beyond hope.

The miracle brought joy to Jairus and his daughter. It left the people wondering at the power that Jesus possessed. We can share both these reactions with them and yet fail to assess the story correctly.

The story points to the present, where the impossible confronts us. Prayer helps us understand all the possibilities that God may have for us. Prayer brings wholeness, and in this way provides its own answer, whatever happens. Through the story we also look to the future, where even death suffers defeat through the prayer that fixes hope in Jesus.

"If we come to God, feeling helpless and dependent, as we really are, . . . He can and will attend to our cry, and will let light shine into our hearts" (Steps to Christ, *p. 97*).

THE CORN OF HEAVEN

The people asked, and he brought quails, and satisfied them with the bread of heaven. Ps. 105:40.

> Guide me, O Thou great Jehovah,
> Pilgrim through this barren land;
> I am weak, but Thou art mighty;
> Hold me with Thy powerful hand;
> Bread of heaven, Bread of heaven,
> Feed me till I want no more.

The male choirs of Wales sing this hymn as no others can. Their unison praise rises from the heart of the Welsh nation. And when you hear their voices lift to the tune Cwm Rhondda, an electric spark tingles your spine and you feel, for a moment, that you too must be Welsh!

Not that Wales is barren; far from it. But the principality has known many wars and much harshness. Out of the coalpits and the slag-sided valleys pour the songs of Wesley's reformation. They affirm faith in the One who leads through disaster and poverty and still rains on His people the Bread of heaven.

In the story of Israel, manna, the corn of heaven, came to represent the way God provides beyond our best hopes. If God could daily bring corn from the skies, could He not sustain Israel in all its needs?

The formula has a simplicity to it: "The people asked, and he . . ." The request produces the answer—as simple as that. God stays very close to us; He has an ear cocked to the cry of need. God does not forget that He has called us out and has responsibility for us.

In Jesus, the Manna of God came down from heaven. He is the Corn of heaven, the Bread of life. Day by day He sustains us. We go to gather what He gives, and it always satisfies. He has called us from the Egypt of discontent and oppression to the Canaan of plenty and freedom. He has responsibility for us, "pilgrims through this barren land."

In the great Welsh revivals the joy that hope gives rose from chapel after chapel. "He brought forth his people with joy, and his chosen with gladness" (Ps. 105:43).

"You must pray as though the efficiency and praise were all due to God, and labor as though duty were all your own" (Testimonies, *vol. 4, p. 538).*

PRAYER IS FOR ORDINARY THINGS

Give us this day our daily bread. Matt. 6:11.

The model prayer sandwiches the mundane between the sublime. Our longing for the kingdom of heaven shows as we plead for its coming. Submission to God's purposes stands on record both in heaven and on earth. God answers prayers that have to do with eternal realities.

From such high and heavenly thoughts, Jesus' sample prayer turns sharply to earthly realities. Pray too for daily bread. While we may, if we wish, lift this also to the plane of the spiritual, Jesus intended it literally. We need the Manna sent from heaven, but we also need the manna of daily physical sustenance. Ask God for it, Jesus said.

Therefore, teach children to pray for simple things. Ask for them yourself. Don't load your prayers totally with spiritual wants; spend time on your knees talking to God about practical things.

A caution might be worthwhile at this point. Adult Christians know that God may answer by helping them live with things the way they are. We teach young Christians best by helping them understand that God answers by giving us hope in Him whether or not our specific requests have their yes.

Many of the most satisfying prayers simply talk things over with God. They tell God about life the way it appears. How things seem to be going wrong. How desperate some needs are. The school of prayer teaches that God answers in the praying.

In the fascinating sequence of requests that flow in the Lord's Prayer, we go from the kingdom to bread to forgiveness. As the penitent speaks of ordinary needs, a realization dawns of spiritual needs. The model suggests that unless we can give our mundane daily existence to God's care, we will find it difficult to address the inner and spiritual lack. Only those who can humbly ask God for daily bread see that He also may give the Bread of life.

The sequence goes further. Ask Him for cleansing. Then you will see how relationships have fractured, where God can help between you and others. If you cannot let God have your common everyday life, how can you expect Him to help in that essential spiritual existence?

"When we realize His great love we should be willing to trust everything to the hand that was nailed to the cross for us" (Steps to Christ, *p. 104*).

ASK, SEEK, KNOCK

Ask, and it shall be given you; seek, and ye shall find; knock, and it shall be opened unto you. Matt. 7:7.

The New Testament repeatedly makes the point that God hears the requests made of Him. It takes the "might" out of prayer. But what does that mean in practice? Not every prayer has a recognizable answer. While there is truth in the maxim that God has three answers—yes, no, and wait—it hardly explains the New Testament thrust toward certainty.

Only certainty can keep prayer alive. If doubt weakens or lessens certainty, prayer will die. The certainty of God's involvement with the requests of His people operates as a spiritual law. So much depends on it that faith cannot survive without it, just as physical life depends on the operation of physical laws.

Jesus assures us that our Father delights to give. He is good and loving. Just as a father will give to a son who asks, so the heavenly Father gives to His children.

The command to seek and knock helps us understand further. When the Bible talks of seeking, it often has God as the one sought. Our seeking has God in view. Our asking is in keeping with the nature of God. True prayer asks that which is well pleasing to God. It seeks and asks according to the will of God.

When the son comes to his earthly father, he asks for "good" gifts (Matt. 7:11). When we go to the Father, He responds with good gifts. In another place Jesus said that the right and good gift to ask for is the Holy Spirit (Luke 11:13).

This means that we dare not come in doubt to God. Remember always that He is the living one, the almighty, with whom nothing is impossible. In Him the request made in faith has the certainty of being heard. In that certainty our faith remains secure, for we know that our Father hears and acts with benevolence and love.

The prayer of certain faith has a sure reaction. Because we know that to ask is to receive, to search is to find, and to knock is to have it opened to us, the answer comes with the praying. In such prayer, hope turns continually to joy.

"He is as willing to listen to the prayer of faith as when He walked visibly among men. The natural cooperates with the supernatural" (The Great Controversy, p. 525).

DOWN ON YOUR KNEES

When Simon Peter saw it, he fell down at Jesus' knees, saying,
Depart from me; for I am a sinful man, O Lord. Luke 5:8.

In Bible times, whether one prayed standing, kneeling, or prostrate
carried its own message. During the reign of David, Israel bowed with
head touching the ground. Shadrach, Meshach, and Abednego stood
like trees in a field of waving grain as they refused to bow down at
Nebuchadnezzar's command.

By the time of Jesus, kneeling or bowing down before God showed
humility and awe before Him.

One of the common expressions for prayer is to "bow the knees." In
this way the praying Christian recognizes the might and sovereignty of
God. In going down on one's knees where no idol exists, the Christian
shows that all his adoration and worship go to the invisible God. In this
way too we acknowledge God as the supreme judge, and Jesus Christ
as Lord of all.

For Peter it had even deeper meaning. He had questioned Jesus'
authority. What could Jesus know about fishing? Who was He to offer
advice to an expert? If the toil of Peter and his friends brought
nothing, what could a carpenter tell them? While Peter obeyed, did he
do it as a servant obeying the supreme Lord, or out of respect?

At the marvelous catch of fish, Peter changed direction. He fell at
Jesus' knees to show repentance. He had not trusted enough. He had
not earned such a gift. Now he had the attitude of one who had
received Christ's abundant grace. The gift came without any of his
expertise.

The story does not teach that we must first try everything we can,
then turn to God. Quite the opposite is the case. We go to God and He
provides. But all too often we do not know how well He can provide
until we have first tried everything we know.

Jesus used the total lack of success of these fishermen to turn them
in His direction. They gained nothing from their own efforts, but by
obeying the command of Jesus, all they sought was theirs.

Peter teaches us that man's extremity is God's opportunity. When
we have tried and failed we may turn to Him and receive. How much
better if we fall on our knees sooner rather than later.

"Every morning take time to begin your work with prayer. . . .
By this means success and spiritual victory will be brought in"
(Testimonies, *vol. 7, p. 194*).

SPEAKING TO GOD

Hear me, O Lord, hear me, that this people may know that thou art the Lord God, and that thou hast turned their heart back again. 1 Kings 18:37.

The test presented Israel with what has become a familiar choice. Formal religion would meet heart religion, and God would decide.

Israel had grown accustomed to the prayer techniques of Baal's priests. Colorful ceremony, the repetitive formula of words, the dance of ecstasy—all very impressive, and perhaps even persuasive. Jezebel's countrymen had command in Israel. Should not the liturgy of Baal produce more than just respect?

All day the chant went on—"O Baal, hear us; O Baal, hear us." Like the mantras of Eastern religion, it produced excitement but no practical result. The story asks the question What purpose prayer if at the end of it all nothing happens?

Elijah approached God in an entirely different way. He stepped aside from formulas and techniques and spoke to God as a personal being. After all, Jehovah was no dumb deity, but the living Lord.

Perhaps more than anything else, the awareness of God as a person distinguishes true prayer from ritual mumbo jumbo. One does not insult a personal God with repetitious words, slogans, and routines.

Once I sat in a plane for five hours with a devout Catholic beside me. All the way her lips were moving as she fingered her rosary.

Elijah looked into the past and recalled how God had appeared to the patriarchs. Though Jehovah ruled the nations, He also accepted Abraham, Isaac, and Jacob as His subjects. He would therefore know Elijah's name. He would have seen the senseless fanaticism of Baal's priests.

The Bible has much to say about the interaction between God and specific individuals. Elijah and Israel had their answer that day.

"One petition offered up to God in faith has more power than a wealth of human intellect" (Testimonies, *vol. 2, p. 279).*

JOY AFTER SORROW

These things I have spoken unto you, that in me ye might have peace. In the world ye shall have tribulation: but be of good cheer; I have overcome the world. John 16:33.

The moment was a poignant one. The final days of Jesus' ministry brought Him deep concern over the "little flock," the 12 apostles. Could they bear the sorrow and parting so soon to come on them?

When the one you love most must leave you, how you hang on words and gestures! The disciples finally began to understand a little of Jesus' fate. They said to Him, "Now you are speaking plainly, and are not using a figure of speech" (John 16:29, NASB).

But they had heard only part of what He said. He had spoken of going to the Father, of leaving them. He had also said that He came from the Father. That part they had heard, but not the other.

How easily we hear what we want to hear, and block out what we do not wish to know! The mind defends itself against the unpleasant. Chaplains and physicians report that relatives of terminally ill patients often fail completely to accept what has been said, and fasten instead on some detail that encourages.

But later the disciples would remember. After the cross, after Pentecost, after the quick surge of evangelistic success, they recalled what Jesus had said. There, out in the world, they faced tribulation. The world proved unfriendly to reformers. Not too many wanted to get ready for the return of Jesus. Few enough answered their call to holy living.

When the current of popular opinion turns against you, when friends scoff at your attempts to overcome the world, when relatives want no word from the Lord, be of good cheer. Jesus has overcome, and in Him you also overcome. The world brings tribulation, but Jesus gives peace.

A few hours after He gave this promise, the disciples hid. He went to the cross without benefit of their support. But that did not end the story. Within days He had risen, taught them, sent the Holy Spirit. In the continuing presence of Jesus they found peace and courage. If He could restore their optimism after the shame of the cross, what could they not do for Him?

"There is but one power that can break the hold of evil from the hearts of men, and that is the power of God in Jesus Christ" (Testimonies, *vol. 8, p. 291*).

THE FULLNESS OF JOY

Hitherto have ye asked nothing in my name: ask, and ye shall receive, that your joy may be full. John 16:24.

Jengre Hospital serves a large area of northern Nigeria. To it come the poor and the needy from the Muslim and pagan tribespeople. When sickness strikes, it represents their only hope.

When the state government decided to take over the hospital, some thought it good, but most regarded it as unfortunate. The church did its best to turn it over in good condition. The government, in an unusual move, paid the church compensation for the plant.

What should the church do with the money? "Put it in the bank," we counseled. "Most likely, the government will find it hard to maintain services at the hospital and will want to return it to us."

More than once we eyed that million dollars, imagining what we could do with it. But caution said, "Wait a little longer."

Meanwhile, the church in Nigeria began to pray that God would restore our witness in this mainly non-Christian area. He answered our prayers. The government said, "Please, you can do this better than we. Let us have the money back and you can have the hospital."

Today Jengre Hospital centers a network of clinics and aid posts. It has become far more than we ever hoped. Thus prayer answered hope and gave joy in place of disappointment and loss.

What should we ask in Jesus' name? Ask for relief from sadness and sorrow. He is the Lord of all true joy. Ask for comfort; He comforts those who mourn. Ask for friendship; He is the friend of sinners.

He says, Ask in My name. Jesus' name gives authority to our requests. He is the Christian's business card. We represent Him on earth. As bearers of His delegated authority we can look around, size up our world, and ask Him to answer its needs.

Hope is the bud, joy the full flower. In the flowering of hope, joy appears to gladden and scent the life.

Experience will teach us that fullness of joy has its roots in the practice of prayer life. What a judgment against the apostles! "Up to this point, you have not used My name in your prayers." Jesus' power had exploded around them many times. Did they think that His promise of power would die with Him?

"Faith is the hand by which the soul takes hold upon the divine offers of grace and mercy" (Patriarchs and Prophets, *p. 431).*

JESUS GIVES BIRTH TO JOY

Verily, verily, I say unto you, That ye shall weep and lament, but the world shall rejoice: and ye shall be sorrowful, but your sorrow shall be turned into joy. John 16:20.

In the book of Revelation the great red dragon waits for the birth of the Man-child, ready to devour Him at the moment of birth. God catches the Child up to heaven. The woman flees into the wilderness. A terrible struggle wages between Michael (another name for Jesus, the man-child) and the devil. The armies of heaven defeat the devil and hurl him out of heaven. He continues the struggle against God on earth.

In John's Gospel, Jesus spoke of His death and departure to the Father as an approaching time of great sorrow. But His disciples must keep it in proper perspective. The birth of a child matches this kind of sorrow. After labor and childbirth, joy breaks out at the new life cradled in the mother's arms.

Both the apocalyptic vision of the Revelation and Jesus' words have a similar purpose. Jesus died and rose again. God has won the victory of victories. Satan wages his campaign from a diminishing enclave. The salvos of salvation pound away, the final triumph approaches, and shouts of joy and victory ascend.

The cosmic conflict is one thing; what about the individual battle waged in each life? Events pressed against the disciples' faith. Beyond the fate that Jesus said awaited Him, they struggled to see any hope.

Jesus had come as the man of joy. Now He would go. Such a parting, they believed, could never bring joy.

But how little they understood. What they feared most would result in the final defeat of Satan. A greater joy would replace the joy of His ministry. The Holy Spirit would give Him to them forever.

They didn't find it easy to understand all that Jesus said to them. He taught new truths, established new criteria of faith. They faltered as they tried so hard to match their expectations with Jesus' predictions. Later they would understand.

Sooner or later every life needs to learn the lesson of joy. You have sorrow now. You do not understand. Hope flickers, faith falters. But that is foolish. Jesus is joy, and He is yours.

"Faith looks beyond the difficulties, and lays hold of the unseen, even Omnipotence, therefore it cannot be baffled" (Gospel Workers, p. 262).

THE PRACTICE OF JOY

When he had brought them into his house, he set meat before them, and rejoiced, believing in God with all his house. Acts 16:34.

"Pastor, I'm going to kill myself."

The words came from a friend of years past. We had attended church together as teenagers. Then life had pushed us apart.

The call came on Friday evening. A life of sin and occasional crime had caught up with Wayne. The prison authorities allowed him one phone call. I was the one he called.

I remember the midnight dash through the night-quiet streets of Sydney, the prison doors opening, the waiting room, and then Wayne. What I cannot remember too clearly is what he said and what I said. He was no Paul or Silas with an earthquake soon to happen. Life had no future for him.

"Well, I didn't kill myself," the voice chuckled at me over the phone. "I'm out now. Things are better. That pastor you put on to me really helped straighten me out."

Later I talked with the pastor to whom I had given Wayne's name. The therapy of service had turned Wayne away from self. Now he was reaching out, helping others. The prospects looked good. In fact, the pastor baptized Wayne. His former life of debauchery caught up with him a few years later. He died, however, with joy, and with a host of friends whom he had helped.

In the story of the Philippian jailer who also almost killed himself, he turned from himself to others the moment he found salvation. The hands that had shackled Paul and Silas found refreshing. The jailer found far more. His work for others restored him. It gave him joy.

To bring joy to the life, nothing works quite like helping others. To accept Jesus immediately poses the question What can I do for others? One way of testing for a true Christian experience is to ask yourself, What am I doing for others?

The jailer carried out orders in putting Paul and Silas in the stocks. When he believed on Jesus Christ he accepted new orders. The way he treated Paul and Silas set a model for the practice of joy that every converted life might follow.

"Those who are in Christ's service must watch every outpost. Our object is to save perishing souls from ruin" (Testimonies, *vol. 9, p. 220).*

THE GARMENT OF PRAISE

To appoint unto them that mourn in Zion, to give unto them beauty for ashes, the oil of joy for mourning, the garment of praise for the spirit of heaviness. Isa. 61:3.

The Western world places a gloss over death. It hides in the embalming chambers of the mortician, and comes from his hands in the semblance of sleep. Tears wash the face at the graveside. Arms of comfort briefly embrace the mourner. Then sorrow withdraws into a personal capsule that only time can release.

Not every culture has dealt with death that way. Weeping, wailing, processions of mourners, hired bands to play dirges—all are part of the litany of death. In Fiji I shared sorrow with a Hindu family who stood silent and weeping around the funeral pyre. In Malaysia I walked behind a decorated bier while hired mourners wept their purchased sorrow.

Israel publicized death. The wealthy would rent a funeral band to perform as the procession moved through the street. They would throw dust into the air, beat their chests, and lament loudly. Relatives would cover themselves with ashes and wear coarse cloth.

Neither the hiding away of death nor its public display shows how the Christian should relate to it. The resurrection of Jesus has written the axiom from which Christian attitudes extend. Jesus has conquered death.

Death, however, is no friend. He is the last enemy, and joins the devil in the lake of fiery destruction at the end of sin. Death opposes the will of God. God created mankind for life, not death. For this reason Jesus came saying, "I am the resurrection, and the life."

Anyone could pick out the mourners of Jesus' day. Their ashen heads, and clothes made of sacking, marked them apart. Death affronted Jesus. With the gospel came joy. That joy washed away the ashes of death and poured scented oil in its place. Joy took off sackcloth and put on the embroidered and ornamented garments of the wedding feast.

It is said that Jesus had to be specific when He commanded, "Lazarus, come forth." Otherwise, the whole cemetery would have come to life! At the last day Jesus will redeem the purchase of His blood. Myriads will rise to life. What a day of rejoicing that will be!

"Hope bears our spirits up. . . . The Life-giver is coming. . . . He bursts the bands of death, breaks the fetters of the tomb" (Selected Messages, *book 2, p. 260).

JOY THAT NO PERSON CAN STEAL AWAY

Peace I leave with you, my peace I give unto you: not as the world giveth, give I unto you. Let not your heart be troubled, neither let it be afraid. John 14:27.

How do the gifts of God differ from the gifts of this world? Jesus says that He gives peace, but that the gift has a different quality from those things the world gives.

Jesus continually taught eternal values. The world represents transition and change. His gifts last through eternity. Those who accept gifts from Him will not let the world divert or discourage them.

Like so many others, the young man appeared at the edge of the crowd around Jesus. He listened. Jesus' teaching troubled him. He sensed in Jesus something that would change him for all time.

At last he found the moment to put the question. "Good Master, what shall I do to inherit eternal life?" He wanted a guarantee that he would inherit the promises given to Israel.

Jesus offered him the usual answers of the day. In obedience the faithful Israelite would find life. But the ruler was not satisfied. There must be more to it than that. Was there not some added action that would swing the balance in his favor?

The ruler let the world steal away his prospects of joy. The Spirit troubled him, brought him to know his need. What a moment to decide! He troubled himself, the world troubled him, and the Spirit troubled him, but he refused the peace of the everlasting covenant.

Ten years later, did he even remember his time of opportunity? Did the world still trouble him? Did he still feel his lack? Perhaps he no longer asked such questions. He had inherited wealth; must he also strive for eternal life?

Yes, the gifts of this world can deaden the goads of the Spirit. A quiet conscience is not necessarily a good conscience. The gifts of Jesus have permanence. In Him the troubled become the joyful.

The rich young ruler came with sorrow in his heart. He measured the price of joy and rejected it. For him, sad story, it could never be joy after sorrow, but would forever be sorrow after sorrow.

"He who uses his entrusted gifts as God designs becomes a coworker with the Saviour" (The Desire of Ages, p. 523).

JOY AND GLADNESS, GIFTS OF GOD

The Jews had light, and gladness, and joy, and honour. Esther 8:16.

In Jewish homes as the Sabbath begins on Friday evening, candles twinkle in the dusk. They mark the delivering power of God. After the darkness of oppression or evil, God gave light through His salvation.

The writer of Esther tried his very best to convey the sense of relief and release that flooded over the Jewish people when Ahasuerus answered the plea of Esther and gave freedom to the people. While the book has no specific reference to God, it does not need it. God takes over the story and makes it a parable of His delivering power.

How many times have God's people languished under threat! As I write this, our church in Burundi has been closed and disbanded. What this means for the future seems far from clear. Stories of hardship and dismay show us that the way of truth is not always simple or easy.

We know, however, that such setbacks can have remarkable turnarounds. In Nigeria, some years after government takeover of hospitals, the church is under pressure to take theirs back. The turnaround in Uganda from a banned church to an Adventist as prime minister was an "Esther" experience. His chief claim to distinction within the Adventist Church was his role as Sabbath school teacher.

After the threats of Haman, the Jews watched for signs of their fate. They would know it when Mordecai came from the king's presence. Listen to the exultant note: "Mordecai went out from the presence of the king in royal apparel of blue and white, and with a great crown of gold, and with a garment of fine linen and purple: and the city of Shushan rejoiced and was glad" (Esther 8:15).

Now words tumble over each other to describe the reaction among the Jews. They had light, gladness, joy, and honor.

The story of Esther is a parable of how the faithful wait their fate while the forces of Satan plot and maneuver. Finally the king declares in favor of God's people. Joy breaks out. God will do it again at the end. But He also fulfills it for you. Jesus rules at the right hand of glory. Therefore, His people have light and joy and honor.

"Today, as in the days of Esther and Mordecai, the Lord will vindicate His truth and His people" (Prophets and Kings, p. 606).

COATS OF THE LORD'S MAKING

Unto Adam also and to his wife did the Lord God make coats of skins, and clothed them. Gen. 3:21.

The story of mankind's fall builds around four points. At some unknown period after Creation, Adam and Eve separated, perhaps to attend to the chores of the garden, perhaps to be alone. Eve went in the direction of the two God-planted trees at the heart of the garden.

From the tree of knowledge the serpent hissed his subtle question, "Yea, hath God said, Ye shall not eat of every tree of the garden?" Eve eyed the beautiful beast curled around the branches of the tree. When her fingers stretched upward, the serpent's body pressed a branch toward her hand until the fruit nestled in it.

Later that day, distraught and dismayed, the couple made clothes of fig leaves. When God came to talk with them they hid in the forest. But who can hide from the Lord? And who can remain silent when the Lord asks the question "Where art thou?"

Not the fear, not the hiding place, plucked at the heart of God. "Who told thee that thou wast naked?" No longer could the brightness God gave them merge naturally with His glory. Darkness had settled on Planet Earth.

God saw the tragedy and the consequences. "What is this that thou has done?" He asked. They had spoiled the hopes of God for them.

The four points describe the despair of humanity:

1. Tempted by evil, innocence gone.
2. Lost and forlorn, afraid of God.
3. Exposed and wretched, seeking human solutions.
4. Guilty and self-centered, blaming others.

Genesis gives no quick relief within the sorry story. Reading it, one wishes that it might be rewritten, wound back and rerecorded as a tape might be. But no human skill can unwind Eden and its disaster.

Yet even there, when all appeared lost, God gave hope. Clothed in the skins of animals, Adam and Eve could see both their own guilt and the hope from God. He could provide garments in Eden. He would one day restore both the garment of light and Eden itself.

"The atonement of Christ alone could span the abyss and make possible the communication of blessing or salvation from heaven to earth" (Patriarchs and Prophets, *p. 67*).

LOVE'S GARMENT BRINGS DESPAIR

Israel loved Joseph more than all his children, because he was the son of his old age: and he made him a coat of many colours. Gen. 37:3.

What a price Jacob paid for his act of favoritism! But why the fuss over one coat?

In Jesus' parable of the wedding feast, the head of the house provided an outer garment for his guests. In the story of the prodigal the father called for "the best robe." A landowner kept a cloak worn only on special occasions. When visiting dignitaries arrived, he would wear it as a sign of respect. On more important occasions he would offer it to the most distinguished guest.

None of the sons of the family could wear this special coat. It signified the status of the father. After his death, the oldest brother could claim the coat or have one made for himself.

In Joseph's coat, the 10 brothers saw their rejection. They suspected that Jacob would seek to give the chief role to Joseph. Jacob would play on them the same kind of trick he had played on their uncle Esau.

To Reuben's credit, the one most threatened by the coat, he turned aside the plan to kill Joseph. But he helped dip the coat in goat's blood. He tried to ensure the birthright for himself.

In the story of Joseph the nation of Israel could read its own fate. God chose them and loved them. He gave them His Torah, clothing them with a righteousness no other nation possessed. But jealous nations saw Israel's unique blessings as an affront. Enemies overran Canaan. Many times they bloodied and defiled the chosen of God. Many times Israel herself shucked off the coat of holiness.

As He had done with Joseph, God brought them out of the pit. Even when they were oppressed He remembered them and made a great nation of them. But at the end, the God of Jacob had to turn from them and choose elsewhere.

It isn't always easy to wear the cloak of the Lord's making. Joseph's brothers would not even speak a civil word to him. When hope wears the bright colors of purity, holiness, and victory, the world around may feel rebuked or cheated. Israel lost God's choosing because it came to fear and despise His robe of righteousness.

Please, not us, Lord!

"The merits of Jesus blot out transgressions, and clothe us with the robe of righteousness woven in the loom of heaven" (Evangelism, *p. 186).*

HOPE WEARS ITS BRIGHT CLOTHES

Aaron shall bear the judgment of the children of Israel upon his heart before the Lord continually. Ex. 28:30.

The procession wound through St. Paul's Cathedral. Bright robes, scarlet, gold, and blue predominating, paraded against the somber stonework of Christopher Wren's masterpiece. London, always good at pageantry, excelled itself. The prince of Wales was meeting his beloved Diana at the marriage altar. Gold coaches, liveried horsemen, color piled on color, climaxing in the gorgeous display in the old church.

Ancient Israel had its own pageantry. God instructed Moses to call on the best workmen to make garments for Aaron. "They shall take gold, and blue, and purple, and scarlet, and fine linen" (Ex. 28:5).

God had the garments made "for glory and for beauty" (verse 2). The ephod carried two onyx stones, on which craftsmen engraved the names of the 12 tribes of Israel. Surrounded by intricate embroidery of different colors and set in gold, they gleamed in dark beauty as Aaron moved through the camp to the sanctuary.

The breastplate boasted 12 precious stones, each engraved with the name of one of the tribes. Blue cord attached the breastplate to the ephod. Here in the breastplate shone the Urim and the Thummim. Through these God would respond to questions about the welfare of Israel. Aaron literally bore the destiny of the nation next to his heart.

In the garments of Aaron the whole story of God's saving grace was typified. He went to the sanctuary to cleanse the nation and atone for its sins. The glorious garments bedecked him, not in honor of a prince or princess, but in honor of the Holy Lord Himself.

Jesus gathers into Himself all the hopes that both garments and high priest represented. Jesus wears the bright robes of the Great High Priest before the judgment seat of God. He holds in His hands destiny and hope. Grace and mercy shine from His robes. He holds your name close to His heart. He is the eternal yes of divine forgiveness and love.

"Christ, the great High Priest, pleading His blood before the Father in the sinner's behalf, bears upon His heart the name of every repentant, believing soul" (Patriarchs and Prophets, *p. 351).*

MIGHTY TO SAVE

Who is this that cometh from Edom, with dyed garments from Bozrah? this that is glorious in his apparel . . . ? I that speak in righteousness, mighty to save. Isa. 63:1.

The Lord advances as a solitary warrior, a divine Samson, bent on the destruction of His enemies. He has dyed His garments blood-red, like the cliffs of Petra, Edom's ancient capital. He sweeps out of the east, bent on justice and judgment.

No 7,000, Elijah's faithful remnant, spring to His aid. He treads the winepress alone. No Gideon's 300 marshal alongside Him. He looks around and finds none to help, not even an armorbearer such as Jonathan had. Alone, unaided by any of Israel's mighty, the Lord treads down His enemies and with His arm brings salvation.

In the past it had been that way. Egypt's armies drowned in the Red Sea. The walls of Jericho toppled. The Assyrians set to fighting themselves, Israel watching and rejoicing.

Who can stand before such a Warrior? Call for the rocks to fall on you, the prophet advised. Better that than the anger of the Lord. Never forget His righteous indignation. In judgment He is terrible. But also never forget His love. He is mighty to save.

"I will mention the lovingkindness of the Lord," sings Isaiah (Isa. 63:7). The prophet contrasts the wrath that will fall on the unrepentant with the steadfast love of God for those who look for salvation. The garments dyed in blood speak both of judgment and of saving love.

Israel's rebellion had placed them among the enemies of God. They had climbed into the winepress. God may trample them also as He judged the nations. Could there yet be hope for them?

Isaiah pleads to God as Father. "Doubtless thou art our father, though Abraham be ignorant of us," Isaiah cries (verse 16). Abraham? What does Abraham have to do with this?

Ah, yes. God made His promises to Abraham. If we are truly his seed . . .

"He will withhold from man no needed aid that he may take the cup of salvation, and become an heir of God, joint heir with Christ" (Selected Messages, *book 1, p. 323).*

VISION OF JUDGMENT

The Ancient of days did sit, whose garment was white as snow, and the hair of his head like the pure wool: his throne was like the fiery flame, and his wheels as burning fire. Dan. 7:9.

In this vision God the Holy One sits in judgment on the world. A time for consideration and investigation has arrived. Now He will open the books and examine the record.

Out of the ocean, four animals have emerged to claim sovereignty. From the fourth a voice has challenged God. Time goes on. The voice blares out its bombast and blasphemy. It singles out the people of God, God's law, and God's very nature. Who will answer for God?

Then God takes the initiative. He establishes His court. He calls the myriads of heaven together. He opens the books. The apostate powers of evil suffer divine wrath. The judgment destroys them.

Who will rule God's world? To whom must all give allegiance? As the judgment singles out apostasy for punishment, it also examines the lives of God's people. Is the little horn right? Does he have the power to wear them into nothingness?

Before the white robe of God's absolute holiness the Son of man appears. To man's Representative God gives dominion and a kingdom. Through suffering and a sinless life, He offers His own holiness and purity. The Ancient of days accepts and gives Him right to establish a kingdom made up of His sanctified ones, or "saints."

In the judgment God's holiness meets Christ's holiness. The holy God may rule in favor of the Son's people because they belong to the kingdom of the Son of man. Of such, the word from the judgment is "he that is holy, let him be holy still."

When we give our stained and ragged lives to Jesus, He accepts us, makes us one of His citizens, clothes us in His white robe of holiness. Through His power our lives are sanctified, made holy. Thus God has a holy people fit for the kingdom of heaven.

"Those who live nearest to Jesus discern most clearly the frailty and sinfulness of humanity, and their only hope is in the merit of a crucified and risen Saviour" (The Great Controversy, *p. 471).*

THE WAYWARD NATION RETURNS

They set a fair mitre upon his head, and clothed him with garments. And the angel of the Lord stood by. Zech. 3:5.

Israel, God's son, His delight, took the promises of God, saddled the ass of his own righteousness, and departed with them to a far country. He wasted God's precious gift in idolatry and riotous living. God had set up a bank where He lodged the treasure that came from His fatherhood. But Israel drew and drew on the goodwill of heaven until the Father could no longer keep him from the results of his wastrel life.

By the pigpen of Babylon he remembered Zion. He came to his senses and wept for how he had failed his Father. How could God ever call him "son" again? The prophets held out the promise of renewal and restoration.

Joshua, the high priest, represented his people. He had come fresh from the journey back to the Holy City. The gorgeous robes of the high priest had long since filled a pillager's sack. He came unsanctified, impure, clothed in dirty rags.

Satan, once older brother to all created beings, barred the way to Joshua. By what right could God accept this ragged, unclean refugee as His son and heir to His promises?

Hear God's answer: "The Lord rebuke thee, O Satan; even the Lord that hath chosen Jerusalem rebuke thee: is not this a brand plucked out of the fire?" (Zech. 3:2).

Swiftly God reversed the sorry state of Joshua. Put a miter on his head. Put clean garments on him. Stand beside him to sustain and protect him. Let him walk in My courts. God gave to His people far beyond anything their hope might create.

A prodigal people, a forgiving and restoring God—how much we need Him today. Like Israel we waste away in Babylons, some of which we have chosen for ourselves. Will we remember the Father and His kingdom? Will we yearn for it enough to make the journey back?

For the wretched, the blind, the miserable, and the naked, God holds out the garment of Christ's righteousness. Will Laodicea accept such a gift?

"Man, all undeserving, stands before the Lord cleansed from all unrighteousness, and clothed with the imputed righteousness of Christ. Oh, what a change of raiment is this!" (The SDA Bible Commentary, *Ellen G. White Comments, vol. 4, p. 1178).*

CHRIST'S RIGHTEOUSNESS—COVERING OR CHANGE?

Awake, awake; put on thy strength, O Zion; put on thy beautiful garments, O Jerusalem, the holy city. Isa. 52:1.

The robe of Christ's righteousness is no more a mask for wrong behavior than right behavior may substitute for Christ's righteousness.

Isaiah's call to Zion evokes the ceremony of Temple and royal palace. On feast days and holy days the city came alive with the pageantry of Levites, singers, the royal family, the priests, and above all, the high priest. Everyone's closet secreted a garment for such days.

Once while visiting a village in India, I watched the people emerge for the Sabbath service. Packed mud and earthen floors provided tiny dwellings for each family. I expected the members to come to church in the workaday clothes of yesterday.

But each little house was a cocoon. Like butterflies emerging, the women of the village stepped through their doorways in brilliant saris, the men in the whitest of shirts and slacks.

When the love of God calls us from the grubby cocoon of sin, we emerge in the robe of Christ's righteousness. He puts on us His beautiful garments, our only strength.

But that only begins what God intends. He wants us pure within as well as without. Our lives must suit the garment of righteousness He gives us to wear.

Beneath the covering, change occurs. No Christian dons the robe of righteousness and then lives a life of disobedience to God's will. In the prophecy of Isaiah God calls for clean lives, those that represent the beautiful garments of salvation.

Our lives will always need the covering robe of righteousness. They will never represent that robe correctly unless change comes with it. The robe of righteousness is not simply a cloak to hide our guilt, a covering for an unlovely life; it is also a character lived in harmony with God's will.

"It is in this life that we are to put on the robe of Christ's righteousness. This is our only opportunity to form characters for the home which Christ has made ready for those who obey His commandments" (Christ's Object Lessons, *p. 319*).

THE HOPE OF GLORY

God would make known what is the riches of the glory of this mystery among the Gentiles; which is Christ in you, the hope of glory. Col. 1:27.

On Inauguration Day, in Washington, D.C., the nation gives honor to its newly elected president. Parade and ceremony mark the event.

For an even more splendid display, nothing quite rivals the British monarchy. Gilded coaches, liveried coachmen, platoons of horse guards dazzle the streets of London.

The Tower of London opens its jewel box to show the crown jewels. Settled on their velvet cushions, they glitter and gleam with the glory of a lost, but not forgotten, empire.

Soon the God of glory will outshine any earthly ruler or monarch as He claims this world as His own. But, as the text says, He is not without His glory now.

In the Gospel of John, Jesus prayed that He might have the glory He shared in heaven with the Father. That glory flashed out in full splendor only once. On the Mount of Transfiguration, Peter, James, and John fell awestruck at the glory of the Son.

Where, then, is God's glory today? Paul identified it in those whom God has rescued from the domain of Satan. The riches of God's glory mount as He shows what He is doing with people through Jesus Christ.

We must tread carefully at this point. Glory belongs to God, not to us. If we add to His glory, then we do so because God has willed it so in Jesus Christ. "Christ in you" does not call us to become "little christs," but to acknowledge the saving grace of God in Christ.

A life yielded to Jesus brings glory to God. But that is not all. Such a life prophesies about the future. The prospects of greater glory to God increase.

The hope of a glory to come begins and ends with Christ. The success of His mission lengthens the triumphal procession. To join in the victory parade and so add to God's glory is the supreme contribution of the saved.

"Every sinful tendency, every imperfection, that afflicts them here has been removed by the blood of Christ, and the excellence and brightness of His glory . . . is imparted to them" (Steps to Christ, *p. 126*).

HONORED WITH GOD'S PRESENCE

The cloud of the Lord was upon the tabernacle by day, and fire was on it by night, in the sight of all the house of Israel, throughout all their journeys. Ex. 40:38.

In forgotten times Polynesian explorers found almost all the island gems of the South Pacific. Using wind and current and keen observation, they wandered and searched in their huge canoes.

Three signs of land lured them onward. Birds ranging far from island homes might indicate an island. Land could be located by following a trail of debris against the current. As they came closer a stationary cloud would hover in the blue sky. Beneath it they would find land. New Zealand, "The Land of the Long White Cloud" in Maori language, gained its first migrants, and its original name, through these techniques.

Israel moved about the wilderness for more than 40 years with the cloudy pillar of fire leading them. Its brilliant whiteness marked their movements by day, and its soft luminescence filled the nights. It belonged to the Lord, His gift to the people He had chosen.

What did God intend by this miracle? He placed His glory upon the people to show His choosing of them. The nations must know that He had made them His special treasure, a chosen nation. The glory of the Lord hovered over the ark of the testimony, between the cherubs. It showed Israel His pure and holy nature. It marked the gulf between man and God that the sanctuary service bridged.

God is glorious because of His character. Glory floods out from the throne of God because He is pure, holy, just, and merciful. The glory of the Lord calls mankind to purity, holiness, justice, and mercy. Because God went with them, Israel must differ from the other nations, or they would not show His glory.

Pagans plated wooden statues with gold, adorned them with gems, lacquered them with brilliant colors to make them glorious. In the literal sense they gave glory to their gods. Israel had no control over the glory of God. It resided with Him and went with them at His will. They did not give glory to God with gold, silver, and gems. Rather, God called them to holy living. In their lives they might give Him glory.

"So the followers of Christ are to shed light into the darkness of the world. . . . The light of [God's] glory—His character—is to shine forth in His followers" (Christ's Object Lessons, *p. 414).*

TALKING FACE-TO-FACE WITH GOD

It shall come to pass, while my glory passeth by, that I will put thee in a clift of the rock, and will cover thee with my hand while I pass by. Ex. 33:22.

When Jesus went to the Mount of Transfiguration, two men came from the glory of heaven to meet Him there. Peter wanted to make the event even more glorious by making booths for Jesus, Moses, and Elijah.

What was so special about these two men? The Old Testament has a similar story about each of them. After the rebellion of the golden calf, God threatened to abandon Israel. Moses pleaded for the nation. God talked with him as with a friend.

Moses wanted to see the face of God. There in the sanctuary, protected by the cloudy pillar of fire, he heard God's voice but saw no person. Was it not possible for God to show His face to His friend?

God took Moses and put him in a crack in one of the cliff faces of Mount Horeb. Then the Lord passed by, lifting His hand at the last moment so that Moses saw the departing form.

Centuries later a similar event focused on Elijah. Israel had followed Baal. There on Mount Carmel God had shown His power, and the people had responded. But a few days later Elijah was hiding in a cave at Mount Horeb. Elijah heard the still small voice of God.

God took both Moses and Elijah to be with Him. They had known Him so well, had stood for Him against overwhelming apostasy, that God honored them with eternal life.

They showed, by their actions, that they understood the essential holiness of God and the depravity of humanity. They sought to build a bridge between sinful man and God by offering their lives. They set themselves against all that defamed and dishonored God.

In the last days God is preparing a people to meet Him face-to-face at the Second Coming. Apostasy abounds. Sin has taken control. The golden calf of materialism attracts even those who claim God's name. Horeb and Carmel loom above us, calling us to meet our God and show our faithfulness to Him. What Moses and Elijah saw and heard of God, our hearts may also see and hear.

"We are to continue to learn of Christ until we come into the full noontide of a perfect gospel faith" (Testimonies, *vol. 8, p. 318).*

FROM GLORY TO GLORY

We all, with open face beholding as in a glass the glory of the Lord, are changed into the same image from glory to glory even as by the Spirit of the Lord. 2 Cor. 3:18.

You might call it looking-glass religion. The Spirit, God's mirror, provides a view of Jesus Christ. The Spirit pulls back the veil. Nothing prevents us from beholding the glory of Christ.

Israel had its own vision of God. Moses came from the mount, face aglow from his encounter. But he had a veil over his face. Not even the reflected glory of God shone fully on the people. But now, through the Spirit, all Christians behold the glory of the Lord.

True, we still live in America, or Europe, or Australia. We can no more shift from New York to the New Jerusalem than Moses could opt out of Horeb into heaven itself. Yet through the Spirit, God is moving His people on from this world to the next.

The Spirit is beginning in us now the change that will climax at the Second Coming. In a sense, the new heaven and the new earth come from the future into our lives to begin the transformation now.

As the people of God's future, living in the present, we see Christ, and in seeing Him the transformation begins. Here Paul does not want us to think of ourselves as reflecting Christ so that others can see Him through us. While this is also true, in this passage we behold Christ so that change may occur in our lives.

Moses saw God. Isaiah saw Him high and lifted up. The Spirit grants the same gift to the Christian. Like Moses we see God. The metal mirrors of Paul's day had many small imperfections. They seldom reached the high quality of a glass mirror. Our view of the Lord may not be that of the final transformation. Nonetheless, we see Him with a clarity that matches the vision of the prophet.

As we behold Jesus a change takes place. Those who look at Him are changing to what they see. They acquire and share in the glory of the Lord. Not that the Christian initiates the change. All that is of Christ is by the Spirit. He clears our view so that the change may begin.

"The Lord Jesus is making experiments on human hearts through the exhibition of His mercy and abundant grace" (Testimonies to Ministers, *p. 18*).

THE GLORY AND JOY OF THE WITNESSES

For what is our hope, or joy, or crown of rejoicing? Are not even ye in the presence of our Lord Jesus Christ at his coming? For ye are our glory and joy. 1 Thess. 2:19, 20.

It did not begin badly for Paul in Thessalonica. For three Sabbath days he reasoned with the Jews in their synagogue. As a visiting Pharisee, a rabbi, and a student of the great Gamaliel, he was welcomed gladly by the rulers of the assembly.

Great success accompanied his preaching, especially among the God-fearing adherents to Judaism. A great number of the Greeks believed and attached themselves to Paul and Silas.

Then things went wrong. A mob of Jews, jealous of Paul's success among the Greeks, raided Jason's house. Had they found him, they would have lynched him. As it was, they dragged Jason before the city rulers and accused him of harboring Paul and Silas. They alleged that these two led a conspiracy intended to place another king, one Jesus, on the throne of the empire.

So in a matter of less than a month the visit ended. But what an impression it made! Thessalonian Christians accepted the soon return of Jesus. They worked to prepare for that day. Paul looked on them as one of the great triumphs of his missionary journeys.

Because the congregation did not have many true pagans, Paul filled his Epistle with allusions to the Old Testament. Just as God rejoiced in His people, so Paul rejoiced in the Thessalonians. Through the prophet Isaiah the Lord called Israel a crown of glory. Paul thought of the church in the same way.

God regards His redeemed as jewels in His crown. He speaks of those who turn many to righteousness as shining forever like the stars. The glory of the gospel witness shines in converted lives. God wants His glory beaming out into a dark world. Adding to the number of the redeemed adds to the light of the world.

Hope, glory, and joy blaze in a world of darkness through the lives of God's children. Turn up the light today.

"The unstudied, unconscious influence of a holy life is the most convincing sermon that can be given in favor of Christianity" (The Acts of the Apostles, *p. 511).*

THE SUN ON THE HUSKS OF LIFE

Unto you that fear my name shall the Sun of righteousness arise with healing in his wings. Mal. 4:2.

I know a place where the road winds toward the evening sun. It leads up through the pinks and ochers of the eucalyptus tree trunks. It leaves behind the tree ferns. At the very point where farm takes over from forest, the sun creates a miracle.

On both sides of the road a blaze of pink materializes, and then vanishes as you look for it in the rearview mirror.

Step out of your car into the early spring air, bend and examine the source of beauty, and you will find the husks of last summer's grass. The afternoon sun shines through empty, seedless shells and gives them a glory they could never have on their own.

How Israel needed healing! Malachi lists her faults, one sorry failure after another. A time to weep, he said. A time for sackcloth and ashes. A time to reform the life. A time to give God His due. The list grows as he considers his nation's plight.

The people should shine as polished jewels with the light of God's glory. But they had so covered themselves with evil that no glory showed.

Yet hope called them to the Source of brightness. Into the spent force of Judah God would bring the healing Sun of righteousness. He would shine on them and restore them.

When self has orbited us into the dark side of sin and we drift powerless, the Sun will rise upon us. What a promise! In the vision of the Laodicean church all seems lost. What hope is there for a lukewarm, loveless, wealthy crowd of self-boosters? Malachi asks the same question.

What we lack, the Lord will provide. Jesus the living Sun gives glory to His people, as the sun gives life to the world.

Do you see your life as nothing but a husk of what might have been? Have purpose and meaning slipped away and left you with nothing but the shell of conformity? The Sun has the answer.

If you take my road downhill away from the sun, all you will see is dead grass, soon forgotten in the regrowth of spring. The Sun that shines *through* to bring beauty also shines *upon* to reveal what we are without the Light of the world.

"In order to live in the light, you must come where the light shines" (Testimonies, *vol. 4, p. 106*).

SUNSHINE IN MY LIFE

For God, who commanded the light to shine out of darkness, hath shined in our hearts, to give the light of the knowledge of the glory of God in the face of Jesus Christ. 2 Cor. 4:6.

As he wrote this, did Paul remember the journey to Damascus? The light from heaven flared around him more brilliantly than the sun at noon. Blinded, grovelling, he had asked, "Who are you, Lord?" The Divine One branded onto his consciousness, "I am Jesus."

As it did before Moses on Mount Horeb and Peter, James, and John on the mountain, the light flamed from a Person. Paul was seeing the glory of the risen Christ. The road he had been taking seemed light enough. He was defending the law, the Temple, and Israel. But now he knew he was going, not just in darkness, but with darkness itself. If he succeeded in stamping out Chrisitanity he would extinguish the light of the world.

Into that abominable darkness, Jesus shined. Paul came to know Jesus as perhaps no other man would know Him—risen, glorious, powerful, and, above all, compassionate and caring. The years passed. Jesus came again and again to him, advising, directing, comforting. Moses had asked to see God face-to-face but had been denied. Paul had asked nothing but had seen the face of the glorified Christ.

Sustained and steeled by these encounters, Paul had gone out preaching Christ Jesus the Lord. Even the Pharisees, who had helped to bring Paul to trial before the high priest, accepted that Paul had seen "a spirit or an angel" (Acts 23:9). For many he was totally convincing. Who can deny the overwhelming experience of another, especially when it has with it the logic of Scripture?

My experience was not just for me, says Paul, but for you as well. The light shines also in "our hearts." In the looking glass of the Spirit we see the face of Jesus Christ.

Paul does not ask us to become mystics, seeking by trance and meditation to achieve what Christ revealed to him on the Damascus road. He wants for us the conviction, the certainty, that will turn us around. Through His grace we may rightly expect to know more and more of God, to obey Him more completely, to be changed from glory to glory.

"Live in the sunshine of the Saviour's love. Then your influence will bless the world" (Testimonies, *vol. 7, p. 50).*

THE LORD HID THEM

It may be they will present their supplication before the Lord, and will return every one from his evil way. Jer. 36:7.

The word came through, loud and clear, "Jeremiah, you must take a book and write down everything I have told you. Don't miss out anything, whether it tells the sins of Israel and Judah, or predicts the fall of the heathen nations. Write it all down. That way, the people might repent when they read and hear what I am saying about them."

Shut up in prison, Jeremiah did what the Lord commanded, with Baruch's help. Jeremiah then commissioned his scribe to read to the people what he had written. Eventually, the princes of Judah asked to hear it as well.

In the story, the princes seem somewhat sympathetic. They ask, "Did the prophet really speak all these words?"

"Yes, indeed," Baruch answers. "He dictated, and I wrote."

"Then," said the princes, "you and Jeremiah [who apparently had been released from prison by this time] had better hide yourselves. The king isn't going to be happy with either of you."

Not only the two servants of God were hidden. In a *Ministry* magazine article, Larry Herr reports on the finding of clay seals that bear the names of key characters in this story. One seal carries Baruch's name. Two bear the identities of members of the posse that the king sent after the fugitive duo. Jerahmeel and Seraiah didn't succeed, because the Lord hid the prophet and his helper.

These seals, some 2,500 years old, bring the Bible story alive. The hands of living men, the men of the Bible story, actually pressed their seals into wet clay. And we have those very seals today!

The end of the story doesn't quite match the drama of its beginning. Though the courageous Baruch read the prophet's scroll, and though the Lord hid His servants, neither the king nor the people repented. All too soon the warnings came true and the scramble began to hide legal documents and personal wealth from the invading armies. Probably the vast store of seals that has been discovered represents a last desperate attempt by a court official to fulfill his function.

Only these seals remain to give us details of the ancient city's court system and its prophet. They, and the Word of the Lord, which brings its message, are as relevant as ever today. God continues in hope that those who hear the word may repent and turn to Him.

"The long-suffering of God is wonderful. Long does justice wait while mercy pleads with the sinner" (Christ's Object Lessons, p. 177).

FACING AN UNCERTAIN FUTURE

And she called the name of the Lord that spake unto her, Thou God seest me: for she said, Have I also here looked after him that seeth me? Gen. 16:13.

"How can I go back there? After all she has done to me, I could not stand that place again."

The culture of the day made her the chattel of her mistress. She found no comfort in being a pawn of Abraham and Sarah in their desperate quest for a son.

Hagar was paying the price of jealousy. Forced from the camp, pregnant with her master's child, she fled to a spring in the desert. What future was there for her, an Egyptian servant, in the tents of these Semites?

But the angel had a message for the distraught woman. God had seen and noted her plight. Her child would father a great nation. She must go back to the results of her deeds and those of her masters. As in so many cases, Hagar carried her own share of responsibility for what had happened. She had usurped Sarah's place as Abraham's wife with too little thought about possible reactions.

Her flight had taken her from the place of security. But her panic had given God opportunity. He put up the stop sign, turned her around, and sent her back to the little settlement.

What did Hagar think of the angel and the voice by the water springs? How much of Abraham's faith had rubbed off on her? The recorders of Israel's history did not forget that an Egyptian woman could know God and hear His voice. She may not have had the knowledge of Hebrew to give God the name Abraham would have, but she knew Him just the same.

When this incident was written up as history, the well of "Him-that-liveth-and-seeth-me" still flowed at the spot between Kadesh and Bered. You could go there and remember Hagar and the unborn Ishmael. You could measure your perplexity and fear against hers and remind yourself that the same Lord was looking after you. Your life too may have such places where God's intervention has created wells of hope in the land of uncertainty.

"As a perpetual reminder of His mercy, she was bidden to call her child Ishmael, 'God shall hear'" (Patriarchs and Prophets, p. 146).

ON GOD'S ERRAND

And he said unto me, The Lord before whom I walk, will send his angel with thee, and prosper thy way. Gen. 24:40.

As Abraham wandered his way from Ur to Canaan, he picked up a mixture of servants. Hagar, Sarah's maidservant, came from Egypt. Abraham had found Eliezer, a Syrian from Damascus, to manage his interests. Both Hagar and Eliezer played important roles in the unfolding of God's plan for Abraham.

While Sarah offered Hagar to Abraham as a way of providing an heir, Abraham had seen Eliezer as the one most likely to inherit his wealth (Gen. 15:2). The tension between the true action of faith and human manipulation permeates the ancient story.

Eliezer, like Hagar, had to learn what God could accomplish. Lessons of witness were flowing out from the chosen of God.

Abraham had encountered God, but Eliezer had not. How could the latter go confidently to find a bride for Isaac? Abraham had to encourage him. Eliezer went timidly, wondering if it would work out. When he finally came to Nahor, he still lacked confidence. He set his own test for God.

God chose this occasion to build Eliezer's faith in Him. The incident at the well unraveled precisely as Eliezer asked that it should.

Later generations of Israelites would have dubbed both Eliezer and Hagar as Gentiles and excluded them from God's promises. But Eliezer showed by his simplistic approach to his errand the kind of faith that Israel later lacked. Because Abraham hoped in God, his servant also hoped.

In the story of Abraham, faith begets faith. He was father of the faithful long before he had progeny to call him father. His witness to God's leading affected person after person. His whole camp followed the Lord, no matter what their origins.

A sense of being caught up in God's plans pervades the history of the patriarchs. What can such a faith do for us? Eliezer watched at the well, knowing that he was on God's errand. He did not know just how God would guide him, but he was sure that He would. He had learned such lessons of faith by remembering Abraham's past. History has its lessons of faith and hope for all who do God's will.

"He whose heart has responded to the divine touch will be seeking for that which will increase his knowledge of God, and will refine and elevate the character" (The Desire of Ages, p. 468).

POSSESSING THE KINGDOM

Caleb stilled the people before Moses, and said, Let us go up at once, and possess it; for we are well able to overcome it. Num. 13:30.

For the best part of this century the area of The Rocks gradually ran down. No one wanted the tiny rooms, the steep staircases, and the picture-frame windows. Deadbeats lived there, lounging in the doorways of seedy bars, panhandling their way through life. The streets took on the air of a ruin in process of happening.

The Sydney City Council set up a committee to discuss the future of The Rocks. Of no use to anyone, counseled the majority. A small minority dreamed of a restored area of specialty shops, of derelict warehouses turned to craft workshops, of the rows of houses refurbished and rented to young business people. The debate went on. Finally the minority won and restoration began.

One person has vision and drives forward to complete it. Another sees only obstacles and gives up. Caleb shared a similar characteristic with Martin Luther King, Jr., and John F. Kennedy. He could dream of the bright prospects of the Promised Land and could hardly wait to begin the conquest.

Where do you see promise waiting to be fulfilled? Through that question the world changes. Patient Caleb waited 40 years for his dream to come true. When the land was divided, under Joshua's eye, Caleb had his share and a little extra for courage.

In 1888, leaders of the Seventh-day Adventist Church met in Minneapolis. God laid out before them the bright promises of righteousness by faith. Some would go over at once and possess that land of hope. Others dithered away the opportunity, afraid of the changes that might come, arguing from entrenched doctrinal positions.

When Ellen G. White called for the church to follow on to victory, not all would go. Those who spy out the future do not always bring the Lord's report. For Israel we can only ask, What if . . . ? For the contemporary church we might also ask, What if . . . ?

Do you see a promise of God that you cherish above all others? Each of them is yes, in Jesus Christ. Possess the promise. God wants no epitaphs about you, "What if . . . ?"

"I see heights and depths that we may reach, accepting every ray of light and going forward to a greater light" (Selected Messages, *book 1, p. 362*).

BALK OR BLESSING

I shall see him, but not now: I shall behold him, but not nigh: there shall come a Star out of Jacob, and a Sceptre shall rise out of Israel. Num. 24:17.

Balaam would rather balk than bless. Time and God led him around, like a reluctant horse faced with a water crossing, or a pole-vaulter looking up at the bar set at a new level. He went this way and that. He even got into an argument with his donkey! Like a cowardly lion afraid to attack its prey, Balaam shifted and paused, and shifted yet again.

Balak of Moab thought Balaam was his man, but the Lord had His hand over the prophet's lips. King Balak knew the power of prophecy. Whatever Balaam said would happen. God knew that belief, and wanted no self-fulfilling prophecies. If Balaam cursed Israel the nation would hear of it, and fear would give His people quaking knees.

What should we believe about Balaam? Did God take him over and force words from his reluctant tongue? No, the problem lay with Balaam; he would not say what he knew to be true and right. He did not want God to place Jacob in the ascendancy and give the kingship to Israel. Nevertheless, ultimate salvation lay with God's people, not with the schemings of Balak.

Balaam became a parable to the children of Israel. God wanted them to bless His name, witness to His cause. He led them again and again to the stream of fulfillment, but they turned back and would not cross. Only with the coming of the Star of hope, the birth of the King of kings, could the promise meet its destiny. Even then, the Lord had to go outside Israel to see His name glorified and hear His salvation proclaimed.

To balk or to obey, the choices mount before us constantly. Out in the world of everyday life, to turn aside seems easier than to act. The Sabbath affirmation of faith and fellowship frays into the secular week, and we balk. But God also lives. He brings us again and yet again to confess the true and the right.

"One cherished sin will, little by little, debase the character, bringing all its nobler powers into subjection to the evil desire" (Patriarchs and Prophets, *p. 452*).

TOWARD THE FINAL DELIVERANCE

So let all thine enemies perish, O Lord: but let them that love him be as the sun when he goeth forth in his might. Judges 5:31.

Some of the details of stories of deliverance hardly make for pleasant reading. The story of Ehud, who plunged his dagger into Eglon, has its moments of horror. Eglon was obese, and must have died a sickening death. When Jael hammered a nail through Sisera's head she helped deliver Israel, but the captain of the Canaanites died in agony.

Even the New Testament does not flinch from such stories. The final moments of Judas have their share of gore. And when Herod boasted against God he met a hideous fate.

But the writers of the Bible know only too well that the detail of such bloody vengeance is not the heart of the event. When Deborah sang her song of victory she mentioned the deed of Jael but moved quickly to the real point. God had delivered Israel yet again, and so hope still filled the future.

It would not be hard to list similar situations in modern times. From being almost social outcasts, Adventists in Spain have moved to a respected and even envied role in society. Changes in the government of Colombia have turned back a tide of persecution.

In such events one reads the delivering power of God. Not that the individual acts had His prompting, but that His overarching purpose has met fulfillment.

The New Testament does not search for salvation within politics and statecraft. Deliverance does not wait within this system or that, but with the Lord. The saving acts of God occur on a person-by-person basis. We can discern and count what God is doing for us as individuals.

Deborah knew that fresh enemies would arise. That hard-won victory would not end the assaults. A Jael might trick Sisera this time, but new Siseras were coming. Would deliverance come also?

In every future, whether for a person or the church, the Lord will look for those that love Him. For them He will provide the nail of truth and the hammer of conviction. Thus we will go toward the final deliverance, triumphing afresh in the might of the Lord who saves.

"All heaven awaits our demand upon its wisdom and strength" (Patriarchs and Prophets, p. 554).

UNDER HIS WINGS

The Lord recompense thy work, and a full reward be given thee of the Lord God of Israel, under whose wings thou art come to trust. Ruth 2:12.

When Ruth came out of the Gentile world into the community of Israel, she left more than her country. Each people had its national god. He protected and fought for his devotees. As a daughter of Moab she would have worshiped Chemosh. However, she began to know Jehovah through the influence of her husband, Mahlon, and more especially from Naomi.

Famine had gripped the countries of the eastern Mediterranean, but now Israel had bread. But this was not what really attracted Ruth to Israel. She cherished the godly character of Naomi. She would worship with her mother-in-law rather than go back to Chemosh.

Worship in Israel focused in Shiloh, where the tabernacle rested. But the influence of God spread throughout the nation. Wherever the faithful Israelites lived, their manner of life set them apart. The Book of the Law set standards far higher than that of any of the surrounding peoples.

The story behind today's text revolves around the levirate, the responsibility of a kinsman to raise up children to preserve the name of his relative. First Naomi and then Boaz regarded this command seriously. Even a foreigner should have its benefit.

All these practical aspects of the law made up the "wings of the Lord." The levirate provided Ruth a husband. A family glad to obey their God made that possible.

Ruth has an important point to make. God loved His children; that she had seen from afar. But what was perhaps even more impressive, His children took the divine covenant and applied it to each other. Just as God acted for their welfare, so they acted for each other's welfare. To love their neighbor, as the law commanded, meant to always act for the best welfare of the other person.

Not the easiest of demands for the selfish human soul. The new covenant confirmed by the Son of David, one of Boaz' descendants, places responsibility on all within it. The wings of the Lord are His people taking seriously His will about loving their neighbors.

 "If we would humble ourselves before God, and be kind and courteous and tenderhearted and pitiful, there would be one hundred conversions to the truth where now there is only one" (Testimonies, *vol. 9, p. 189*).

THE JOY GOES ON

Rejoice in the Lord alway; and again I say, Rejoice. Phil. 4:4.

Watch this tall, distinguished man enter the crowded room. See his eyes scan the faces, searching. Then he smiles and moves purposefully forward. You follow his gaze. A woman across the room is smiling at him. You know the look. They are husband and wife.

We all know the joy that blossoms from such close relationships. All too often we share too little of the joy that they bring. But we know that certain people brighten visibly in the presence of certain others. Immediately when they get together, smiles pass and an easy, relaxed chat begins. Before long, they are trading everything from news and opinions to the most intimate of secrets.

How good a relationship is that lets you lower your guard, that says welcome at the end of a hectic day, that offers repose from tension, that enfolds and sustains you, and never turns you away!

What makes joy jump like a spark between two people? Trust, loyalty, frankness, gentleness, forgiveness, sympathy, contribute. Time spent together strengthens friendship. The feeling of security and predictability that another gives makes his or her presence a sheer joy.

When Fanny Crosby wrote "Safe in the Arms of Jesus," she had this very idea in mind. The sinner may lie safe and secure in the love and friendship of the Lord Jesus. Here the soul may sweetly rest. Therefore, we may rejoice always. The security that Jesus gives makes joy flourish in His presence.

The joy our text speaks of builds from steady, constant trust; it doesn't spring up spontaneously. As we trust our Lord, we learn to trust Him more. Only as we constantly communicate with Him can we understand what it means to trust Him with everything. As He answers our needs we learn to ask for more. Thus, the joy of forgiveness that explodes around us at the moment of conversion transfers into the abiding joy that the constant presence of Christ's power alone brings.

Joy never grows in a vacuum. Being together with our Lord makes the flowers of joy grow. We need Him constantly. We never let ourselves be far from His side.

"Prayer is the key in the hand of faith to unlock heaven's storehouse, where are treasured the boundless resources of Omnipotence" (Steps to Christ, *pp. 94, 95).*

TO SEE HIS FACE

They shall see his face; and his name shall be in their foreheads.
Rev. 22:4.

John's finger played lightly over my face. He touched my lips, my nose, my eyes, my hairline.

"Is that a mole you have there? Those bumps on your forehead feel like you are going to grow horns! You've got thin lips and a wide nose. Frown for me. H'mmm. I don't like that. Smile, then. That's better. I like that.

"Thank you for letting me see you," he concluded. "It couldn't be as good as sight, but it helps."

John the revelator loved the Lord Jesus. He remembered only too well His features: the way a smile would break out, His looks of compassion, the sorrow and anguish of Calvary. He had seen more than the other apostles. He had watched all the torment of the cross and had accepted the charge to care for Jesus' mother, Mary.

Like the other New Testament writers, he made no attempt to describe the physical appearance of Jesus. Instead, he let the fingers of his words play over the nature and character of Jesus.

With Jesus on the throne, compassion and mercy would continue for all. The tree of life would offer eternal health to the thousands around the throne. The One who multiplied the loaves and fishes would provide all the physical needs of the new-earth people.

At Jesus' command, devils fled. He had seen Satan fall from heaven. Nothing of the curse of sin would remain in His new world. The blind saw, the lame leaped, the dumb spoke, as John's Lord healed and saved. Thus it was with surprise to John that he was shown that the redeemed would enjoy continued well-being, absence of sorrow, and joy everlasting in His presence.

John saw Jesus as the Word that lights all who come into the world. Therefore, the New Jerusalem had no need of sun or moon. Night could not enter the dwelling of the Light of the world.

The fingers of faith, like those of the blind, touch and learn a little of the Saviour. Because of what is written and what we experience, we list His characteristics. We know Him, and yet we do not know enough of Him. But soon we shall know Him even as He knows us. Best of all, in the joy that goes on forever in the paradise of God, we shall see His face.

"Faith is the spiritual hand that touches infinity" (Testimonies, *vol. 6, p. 467*).

"WE MAKE NO SECONDS"

Unto him that is able to keep you from falling, and to present you faultless before the presence of his glory with exceeding joy. Jude 24.

Recently owners of huge mineral deposits in the north of Australia made an unusual discovery. Bores testing for gold-bearing quartz came across a seam of china clay. After months of tracking its course the operators announced their find to the mining world. Immediately their share prices soared. The high quality of the clay made it extremely valuable as a coating for paper.

But high grade china clay has another use. It makes the finest of porcelain. A visitor to the Royal Doulton factory in the Midlands of England can see the whole process. Artisans prepare the pure white clay for stamping and shaping. Craftsmen apply the transfers or painstakingly brush on color after color. Gold, silver, or platinum stripes and edgings are added as the porecelain spins slowly on a wheel. The kiln fires the china almost to diamond hardness.

In another part of the factory stands a brick-lined bay. The sound of breaking china rings and clatters. Figurines, plates, porcelain, bone china, it matters not.

A sign reads, "Quality control!"

Other companies stock the reject-china shops, or offer two grades of "perfection," or sell seconds cheaply in a factory outlet shop.

God makes no seconds. Consider the scrutiny of the presence of His glory. Could a faulty life survive the X-ray of such holiness? Whatever God offers in the way of salvation must be complete. It cannot be left to the clumsy hands of human righteousness.

Not that God throws those who do not pass His scrutiny against the wall of righteousness. Jude assures us that Jesus can keep us from falling. In His hands the clay comes from the kiln faultless.

The mirror of reality will tell you this could never be. The splotches of sin and the crazing of self mar all. But, thank God, He is able to bring us faultless into God's presence. From such splendid deeds excess of joy rings through heaven and earth.

"Through faith in Christ, every deficiency of character may be supplied, every defilement cleansed, every fault corrected, every excellence developed" (Education, *p. 257).*

WALKING IN TRUTH

I rejoiced greatly that I found of thy children walking in truth, as we have received a commandment from the Father. 2 John 4.

When the samurai curtain lifted from New Guinea toward the end of World War II, missionaries probed into the former strongholds of the Adventist mission work. What would they find? The entire population of the islands of Mussau and Emirau had turned to the Lord. Had they remained faithful? In the Solomon Islands, the Morovo Lagoon had flourished for God. Had the past few years rooted out the plants of faith?

Then stories began to filter out from the advance parties. Adventist nationals had organized teams that rescued Allied fliers and passed them along the Kokoda Trail to safety. These "fuzzy-wuzzy angels" had refused to work for the Japanese Army on Sabbath. Even when angry army officers held pistols to their heads they had said no.

In one famous incident, the native crew of a small ship had dismantled the engine, coated the parts with grease, and buried them, to await the return of the missionary. To the astonishment of all, the reassembled engine started up almost immediately.

A new generation of national missionaries waited on Mussau and Emirau as well as in Morovo to evangelize the highlands of New Guinea. Schools had continued, though books had literally worn away.

The crisis to the truth in the South Pacific during World War II was an external crisis. The crisis that affected the Christian community to which John wrote was an internal threat to the truth. He wrote "for the truth's sake" (2 John 2). He mentions truth five times in the first four verses. A faulty view of Christ and His nature energized the crisis. An antichrist had risen, teaching that Jesus had not come in the flesh.

Apparently this imposter had attracted many. At times John appears to be an outsider, striving manfully to defeat the error that has almost completely taken over the community. However, he found great joy in this church, where many children walked in the truth.

Crises of various kinds continue to afflict the church. Some have to do with doctrine. At times, leaders will apostatize. Attitudes will drive some people this way, some that. In such circumstances the courageous and clear-visioned walk on in truth.

To John's joy, some had remembered the commandment of the Father and had loved it. Truth seen, loved, and obeyed, holds out joy.

"Through the application of divine truth the perfect image of God will be reproduced, and in heaven it will be said: 'Ye are complete in Him'" (Testimonies, *vol. 6, p. 167).*

JOY THAT SURVIVES TRIALS

My brethren, count it all joy when ye fall into divers temptations. James 1:2.

Did James know Job? Did he think about Job when he wrote these words? Did he really think that a person drowning in trials would surface long enough to remember his optimism? Yet, he is right; people do remember the Lord, and even in the very hardest of circumstances manage a smile and a joyful heart.

The pastor pointed out an elderly couple in the congregation. They sat quietly, listening, enjoying the service.

In 1984, fighting had broken out in New Caledonia. Eugene and Irma Guerin lived in the isolated north of the country. Looking for an outlet for their frustration and anger, Kanak activists descended on the Guerin farm. Their grandson resisted and was shot, though not fatally. The attackers cornered the Guerin couple and beat them with fists and sticks, and left them for dead. They rounded up 200 cattle, burned the motor vehicles, set fire to the house, and fled, driving the cattle with them.

When police found the Guerins, they were lying, bruised and bleeding, in one of the farm buildings. Later the gendarmes asked if the family wished to press charges. "No," they said, "they are our people. We remember them as friends. We do not think they meant it personally."

In my limited French I asked them about it. One phrase I remember: "*Notre joie*" ("Our joy").

If you read on in James you find that he has a faith-building system to offer. Trial leads to patience, patience leads to the perfecting of faith, and so the faithful one lacks nothing. Therefore, he says, we should count trials as joy.

Job had his troubles, and Jacob his, but troubles and trials did not end with those men. Many a modern Job sits in the pew with you on the Sabbath day.

What is there about faith in Christ that produces the paradox of joy in the midst of trial? Two things. First, the Christian knows what Jesus endured to give us the joy of eternal life. Second, the prize of eternal life waits at the end. For these two reasons the joy goes on.

"All trials that are received as educators will produce joy. . . . He desires every soul to triumph in the keeping power of the Redeemer" (Testimonies, *vol. 6, pp. 365, 366).*

AFTERWARD

Now no chastening for the present seemeth to be joyous, but grievous: nevertheless afterward it yieldeth the peaceable fruit of righteousness unto them which are exercised thereby. Heb. 12:11.

What does the author of Hebrews mean by chastening? Is he thinking of the ordinary troubles that come in life? Does he have a concept of God laying His hand on us in order to correct our ways?

He wants us to look chiefly at the testing of our faith. Hebrews 10 challenges us to have a faith in Christ that will take us into the very presence of God.

Some, he says, even give up their faith. The way ahead stretches too far. The waiting has gone on too long. They cast away their confidence. Time tests us. Will we have the patience to hold fast to our faith in the Great High Priest?

In Hebrews 11, one by one the examples of faith march before us. The point behind this parade of the great is not hard to find. God made promises to Abel, Abraham, Jacob, Joseph, and Moses. What made them stand out from their contemporaries was their absolute trust that God would fulfill those promises. Time did not defeat them. In the end, they did not lay aside their faith simply because of rough going.

Our text today continues to make the point about what time means to the Christian. For the present, waiting grieves us. To discern the finish line when the future fogs over with uncertainty is not easy. Only as we look to Jesus the Finisher of our faith will we ever arrive.

However, the present will yield to the afterward. In the afterward grows the fruit of righteousness. But is that aftertime beyond the Second Coming only? Not if you look at the examples given. Jesus found joy in providing salvation. Moses found joy in leading Israel toward Canaan. Joy comes in believing the promises of God and trusting God while we await their fulfilling.

God will always fill the future with His promises. He will always call us forward to meet His answer. Until the Lord comes we will never escape the chastising, or the joy that follows afterward.

"The time spent here is the Christian's winter.... When Christ comes, sorrow and sighing will be forever ended. Then will be the Christian's summer" (SDA Bible Commentary, *Ellen G. White Comments, vol. 7, p. 988).*

BENEFIT FROM THE BROTHERS

I do wish, brother, that I may have some benefit from you in the Lord; refresh my heart in Christ. Philemon 20, NIV.

The King James Version says, "Let me have joy of thee." The joy or benefit Paul wants from Philemon will reconcile two estranged brothers. Modern society could deal with the matter very simply. No one has a right to keep anyone in slavery. Philemon is in the wrong. He should receive Onesimus as a brother. He should also emancipate him.

But hold on a moment. Take the issue into parallel situations. Onesimus is not just a brother, he is an asset. Philemon's net worth included his slaves, Onesimus among them. This slave had robbed Philemon by taking himself out of the property register of Philemon.

What touches the pocket touches the heart. Could Philemon forgive Onesimus? The slave had no hope of repaying his master for lost services. A parallel today would be a fellow Christian whose business fails, or who does not or cannot honor a contract or debt.

"You owe me, Philemon. Remember what I did for you?" Paul presses. "Now, pay me back by receiving Onesimus as a brother should, with forgiveness and acceptance."

Like the prodigal, this slave has taken from his master and wasted the master's assets in a far country. Now he is coming back. Will the master accept him as the father welcomed the repentant child? Will Philemon have the forgiving heart that accepts, or the crippling spirit of the elder brother, which accuses and measures to the last penny?

In the community of faith, tensions between members arise over big and small matters. A mediator may step in, seeking reconciliation. But goodwill and brotherly kindness cannot be imposed. However penitent the erring brother may be, no reconciliation will come without positive attitudes on both sides.

Some regard Philemon as more than a story. They read into it an allegory of Christ's mediatorial ministry. To others it speaks of the church as mediator in a sinful world.

Primarily it speaks to the great need of reconciliation. God has reconciled us to Himself in Christ. Will we also provide the joy of reconciliation through the power of Christ?

"God wants us to love one another as brethren. He wants us to be pitiful and courteous. . . . Love begets love" (Testimonies, *vol. 9, p. 193*).

THE TIME DRAWS NEAR

And as ye go, preach, saying, The kingdom of heaven is at hand.
Matt. 10:7.

The kingdom is standing just over there where one can touch it with the hand. The kingdom moves toward us. The Greek original has both these ideas. Time has brought the kingdom to us, but the kingdom also looms always nearer.

When Cape Canaveral prepares for a rocket launch, the countdown begins many hours before. Around the world, technicians in tracking stations watch. But the world itself goes on uncaring, ignorant, self-involved. In the first days of wonder at orbiting astronauts and moon walks, the whole world hung on news of space shots. I remember urging my companions into Shillong, in Assam, India, so that I could buy a newspaper to read of the first moonwalk.

The kingdom of God is not waiting for ignition and lift-off. That took place in the ministry of Jesus Christ. Since then, the kingdom has followed the divine trajectory. It has moved with man through the ages, but approaches ever nearer for the moment of touchdown.

As the kingdom draws near there is both promise and preparation. The promise stands sure. But what of the preparation? Those who track the signs of the times warn and prepare. The kingdom may pass many by, unseen and unrecognized but for the witness of the preparers.

Back to the Greek for a moment. A double truth hides behind the coming near of the kingdom. It is drawing near and has drawn near. The ministry of Jesus not only marks the beginning of the kingdom message, but also proves that the kingdom is among us. In the fruits of faith and the action of the Spirit the kingdom comes.

The all-embracing, world-changing kingdom of God has not yet appeared in its glory. The kingdom among us has the same nature, but not the new earth and heaven it promises. To know that we have the kingdom at touching distance gives hope and courage for today. To know that the kingdom of glory orbits toward us on a converging trajectory makes preparation the key function of belief.

"Those who have been overcoming by the blood of the Lamb and the word of their testimony will be found with the loyal and true, without spot or stain of sin" (Selected Messages, *book 2, p. 380).*

PROTOCOL FOR THE KINGDOM

Many that are first shall be last; and the last first. Mark 10:31.

At times protocol has caught up with me. On two occasions recently independent South Pacific island nations asked me to represent the church at services in Westminster Abbey. It did nothing for my ego when protocol put me last on the list.

Jesus' proverb had the meaning, "How quickly the fortunes of a person can change." He applied it to rewards in the last day. In the society of that day, the nobles, the kings, and the rulers came first. At the bottom of the list came slaves and outcasts. Jesus predicted that the kingdom will reverse the order. Those who enter before the doors close will include many from among the poor and despised.

The kingdom turns topsy-turvy the order of precedence that the world prescribes. God takes to Himself those whom the world regards as the lowest and unlikeliest. In the procession toward Jerusalem, blind Bartimaeus, lonely and outcast, follows after Jesus. The young ruler, rich and powerful, walks past the tail of the line into oblivion.

This word from the Lord also asks that we begin to practice it now. In the church, human pride will make some people want to establish orders of rank. What would Christ have us do? His own disciples quarreled over position. Jesus said, "If any man desire to be first, the same shall be last of all, and servant of all" (Mark 9:35).

What does that mean in practical terms? Those to whom the church gives responsibility are to serve.

Whoever you are, the model remains the same. Every Christian follows Jesus. Service to others represents the highest expression of the change of life that Jesus brings.

Paul wanted to correct the religious fanaticism sweeping the church at Corinth. He paraded the apostles as a spectacle: a group without rank or title but still the bearers of the divine commission. The ambassadors of Christ may come last in line, but not for ever. The kingdom turns on its head human evaluation.

"The one who in the homelife represents the character of Christ . . . may in the sight of God be more precious than even the world-renowned missionary or martyr" (Christ's Object Lessons, p. 403).

AT THE LAST DAY

Who verily was foreordained before the foundation of the world, but was manifest in these last times for you. 1 Peter 1:20.

Peter's line of thinking expressed in this text begins several verses earlier. He knows how easily the Christian can forget the calling to pure and holy living and fall victim to temptation. Yet the One who is Himself holy calls His people to maintain a holy lifestyle. Don't let the word *holy* move your thoughts in the wrong direction. Peter is talking about commandment-breaking and the common sins that affront the holy nature of God.

The sharp memory of what we were, compared with what we now are in Christ, should keep us from falling. After all, the price paid for us is not measured in silver or gold but with the precious blood of Christ. God added up the price and prepared to pay it before He made man.

In these last times, salvation takes over and replaces despair with faith and hope. The last day draws us, magnet-like, to the final glory of Christ's appearing. God has given today as the time to get ready. Being ready for Jesus to come has our top priority.

The last times advance toward a climax. Time is not standing still while men repent, but moves forward. God has had other days; they are past. The last day has come and its hours are passing too.

When Paul wanted to emphasize the urgency of the message of salvation he proposed two representatives of the human race: the first Adam and the Last Adam. The first Adam represents lost mankind, powerless, doomed, alienated from God. The Last Adam represents the new humanity created in Christ's image.

The Last Adam is the Adam for the last day. God raised Him from the dead and established salvation through Him. Those who live in the *eschaton*, the last day of the New Testament, put their trust in Jesus, the *eschaton* Adam.

Holy living characterizes the remnant of the last day. Raised to newness of life in Christ Jesus, they practice holiness. Pray that Christ may give you a new life fit for the last day.

"Let those who wish for something new seek for that newness of life resulting from the new birth" (Selected Messages, *book 1,* p. 173).

GRACE: GOD'S CONSTANT FAVOR

I thank my God always on your behalf, for the grace of God which is given you by Jesus Christ. 1 Cor. 1:4.

In the geometry of the circle, every equation contains the constant pi. Whether computing radius, diameter, circumference, or area, the figure 3.14 must enter the calculations.

In the equations of salvation God's love inserts the constant, grace. Without grace one cannot even talk of salvation. With it sin never presents an insoluble problem.

Grace operates always and only because of Jesus Christ. Faith represents the constant turning of the life toward God; grace, the face of God turned always toward the sinner.

When Jesus began His ministry He pronounced it the year of the Lord's favor. In Jesus, a new time began in which God provided a new vocabulary of salvation. Not that the Old Testament knows nothing of grace. Far from it. But by Jesus' day the rabbis had placed it on the other side of the successful doing of works and meeting of obligation.

In the contrasts of the kingdom, grace, righteousness by faith, the gospel, and hope stand opposite works of the law, a person's own righteousness, worldly wisdom, and futility. Through the great gift of Jesus Christ the sinner receives acquittal. In Him justice may grant pardon.

Some key ideas about grace include:

1. Through grace the Divine Judge pardons; He reckons the righteousness of Christ to the repentant sinner.

2. Sin did not originate grace. It comes from God as an essential part of His character, made effective through Jesus.

3. In Christ grace accepts the sinner into its dominion. It removes the tyranny of sin and death from man.

4. In any saving action by God, grace excludes works righteousness.

Today there will be situations in life in which you will need God's presence to provide and protect. Remember, He gives grace freely because of who He is. His grace is yours and is available in every situation and all the time.

"Through the grace of Christ every provision has been made for the perfecting of Christlike characters" (Counsels to Parents and Teachers, *p. 58).*

GRACE: ENDOWMENT FOR SERVICE

By the grace of God I am what I am: and his grace which was bestowed on me was not in vain; but I laboured more abundantly than they all: yet not I, but the grace of God which was with me. 1 Cor. 15:10.

Perhaps you have wondered why so many prisoners return to crime immediately after their release. Can't they see the results of crime? Haven't they learned their lesson? Those who work with parolees and newly released convicts know the importance of relatives, acquaintances, a support system, and new opportunities.

Grace has a role beyond the justification of the sinner. All that happens after justification has the support of grace. The grace of God makes the new man what he is. It works in the midst of human weakness. What a person cannot overcome because of the hold of sin, he overcomes through the flowing power of God's grace.

But grace does more. Grace endows for service. We call this charisma. Charisma in its original, spiritual sense is not what we perceive in an attractive personality. Charisma is grace bestowing on the Christian that which serves the community and the world. To have grace is to have the Spirit, to have the Spirit is to have spiritual gifts.

In the true sense of the word, every Christian is a charismatic person: the gifts of grace are his. Paul saw grace as a special world of power and privilege. There, God provides what is needed for the church to flourish. When the grace of God takes hold of your life, you do not shut yourself off in contemplation of God's character or the mysteries of the cross. Grace pardons from sin and then provides for service.

You can see Paul's thought clearly expressed in the text for today. Grace had pardoned and justified him. All that he was came from grace. If grace had stopped short at that point it would have been futile. But through his charisma, or gifts, he worked and witnessed. His gifts represented the grace of God working through him.

For these reasons every day is a day of grace. If you ever needed grace, you need it today. Not just for victory over sin, but so you may serve and witness for Christ.

"His Spirit, working through His servants, imparts to sin-sick, suffering human beings a mighty healing power that is efficacious for the body and soul" (Testimonies, *vol. 6, p. 227*).

ABUNDANT PROVISION FROM CHRIST

Therefore they gathered them together, and filled twelve baskets with the fragments of the five barley loaves, which remained over and above unto them that had eaten. John 6:13.

All the accounts of the miracle of the loaves and fishes tell of huge quantities of leftover food. The superabundance of food typifies the measureless grace God provides. There is bread, yes, but there is far more. Jesus gives life "more abundantly" (John 10:10).

John Newton taught us to sing, "Amazing grace! how sweet the sound, that saved a wretch like me!" As much as God's grace amazes us, it also abounds in an overflowing fullness that cannot be exhausted or diminished. The prodigal son reflected that his father's servants had more than enough to eat. God holds out His abundant grace to the lost. You can receive it day after day. At the end of each day the baskets of dusk will weigh more than the loaves of dawn.

The fail-safe grace of God overrides the condemnation of law and eclipses the splendor of the past. If sin abounds, then grace overflows ever more fully. And we may be thankful for that grace, because no one can ever rely on mere obedience to bring salvation. All is of Christ. All is of grace.

The self cannot provide security from judgment. God will see through the whitewash of hypocrisy and uncover its patched and crumbling wall of works. Whatever a person piles together to satisfy selfishness or boost human weakness will collapse like a balloon touched by a flame. Riches, in the widest sense, will not help. Nor does it help to argue our way through God's commands. Doctrinal interpretation or networks of texts and quotations offer no more security than the casuistry of the scribes.

If grace abounds then obedience will also abound. Even the righteousness of God will not be out of reach. Christ's followers are to be perfect as the Father in heaven is perfect.

The demand that abounding grace places on us is obedience. Just as Christ makes the impossibility of salvation a reality, so faith may claim grace to live totally for God. If grace flows over to save and heal, then faith may claim that grace to trust and obey.

"God has an abundance of grace and power awaiting our demand. But the reason we do not feel our great need of it is because we look to ourselves and not to Jesus" (Testimonies, *vol. 5, p. 167*).

GOOD NEWS ABOUT JUDGMENT

O the depth of the riches both of the wisdom and knowledge of God! How unsearchable are his judgments, and his ways past finding out! Rom. 11:33.

It seems so long ago now, but on this date in 1844 our spiritual ancestors waited and watched for the Judge of the universe to intervene. Time has removed the hurt and disappointment from personal feeling. We cannot feel with the disappointed saints, but we can follow them as they rethought the meaning of the words "Unto two thousand and three hundred days; then shall the sanctuary be cleansed" (Dan. 8:14).

The morning after, those who dared venture the abuse and scoffings of neighbors, asked each other what it meant. Before long, a handful had studied and shared the belief that the investigative judgment is now in session. Soon it will end and the Lord Jesus will return.

They wrote their faith and belief across the pages of religious history. They created a worldwide movement that today continues to call for preparation for present and future judgment. The good news about the judgment is Christ's presence in the inner apartment of the heavenly sanctuary. From there the benefits of the atonement now flow to aid the sinner in the testing times of the last days.

That distant group of believers, however much they understood the sanctuary and its cleansing, never lost sight of Jesus Christ. They put total trust in Jesus Christ.

The good news about the judgment centers in Jesus Christ. He is declaring before the Father the names of all His own. Not one of them will be lost. The judgment is as much *for* the believer as it is *against* the unbeliever.

Judgment brings the world to crisis, to climax, to the winding up. To say that we meet judgment in Jesus Christ every day is true enough, but it fogs the real issue. Through the judgment sin will end, the transgression will finish, and everlasting righteousness will come in.

These last few phrases come from Daniel 9:24. What the judgment will give to the redeemed, Christ has already achieved for them.

"Let none, then, regard their defects as incurable. God will give faith and grace to overcome them" (The Great Controversy, p. 489).

WHEN YOU KNOW PERFECTLY WELL

You know perfectly well that the Day of the Lord comes like a thief in the night. 1 Thess. 5:2, NEB.

Martin Van Buren, governor of New York in 1829, made one of the most quotable comments of that decade when he wrote, "Dear Mr. President: The canal system of this country is being threatened by a new form of transportation known as 'railroads.' . . . As you may well know, Mr. President, 'railroad' carriages are pulled at the enormous speed of 15 miles per hour by 'engines' which, in addition to endangering life and limb of passengers, roar and snort their way through the countryside, setting fire to crops, scaring the livestock, and frightening women and children. The Almighty certainly never intended that people should travel at such breakneck speed."

Let us also list the names of those who said that powered aircraft would never fly, men would never reach the moon, and ova could not be fertilized outside of the womb, "because God would not permit it."

Those who "know perfectly well" what God will or will not tolerate are likely to have their claims revised a few years or generations down the road. God will not stop surprising us. While we may know a lot about dates and times (see 1 Thess 5:1) we also have the warning about the freedom with which God moves into human affairs.

It takes an Adventist eye to look out at the world and count off the signs of Christ's soon return. We see them leering at us from the newsstands, proclaiming themselves over television and radio, encircling us in technological marvels.

Yet, the same Word of God warns that those who number off the days and interpret the times may be the very ones caught napping when Jesus returns. The clock of God's time will lock the door against them.

Paul says, they "sleep like the rest" (verse 6, NEB). The common wisdom of the world dominates their thinking; the pressures of social expectations overrule their biblical hopes; the lures of sin trap them.

Such will agree with other Christians about the state of the world. They will nod their heads sagely at preachers who tell forth the signs of the times. But they will say, it isn't quite the time yet for God to act. And in that thinking lie the seeds of their damnation.

"I am bidden to say to you that you know not how soon the crisis may come. It is stealing gradually upon us, as a thief" (Fundamentals of Christian Education, *p. 354*).

FINDING A REFUGE

In the Lord I have found my refuge; why do you say to me, "Flee to the mountains like a bird"? Ps. 11:1, NEB.

In one of those ironies of history, the eruption of Mount St. Helens came just one day short of the anniversary of the Dark Day of May 19, 1780. In case you're short on Adventist history, that day became one of the major factors that convinced William Miller's followers that Jesus would soon return. Adventist evangelists and scholars still see it as an event of great importance.

The 1980 event spread darkness for more than 150 miles, but in 1780 much of the Eastern seaboard of North America found daytime turned to night.

In Washington State in 1980 the possibility of an eruption first bubbled through in the warnings of scientists. But others pooh-poohed the idea. "Not likely," said Donald Mullineaux of the U.S. Ecological Survey. "Not just yet," prophesied the agency's chief ecologist.

Lulled into false security and gambling on their chances, some who lived in the shadow of the mountain refused to budge as loudspeakers roared, "Get out!"

How many times has history taught us that people die simply because they refuse to listen to warnings? Some quirk of human nature drives us to take risks, ignoring the experts and the evidence.

One such example comes from the Bible. Jeremiah offered Moab, a traditional enemy of Israel, its final chance: "Flee, flee for your lives like a sand-grouse in the wilderness" (Jer. 48:6, NEB). Within a matter of weeks Nebuchadnezzar destroyed their culture and garnered his usual harvest of captives and slaves. Moab vanished from history.

David puts before us the alternatives of creating our own security or trusting in the Lord. For him the decision may well have arisen in the face of physical threats. For us a sudden disaster may as easily come from the temptation to trust ourselves rather than our God.

Being ready for Jesus' return means seeing Him as the ruler and the goal of history, and making His sacrifice and His provisions our refuge. The formula for latter day salvation might well be written this way: "Trust in the Lord, and keep your eyes open."

"No power can take out of His hands the souls that go to Him for pardon" (Patriarchs and Prophets, *p. 516).*

THE BLESSED HOPE

Looking for that blessed hope, and the glorious appearing of the great God and our Saviour Jesus Christ. Titus 2:13.

Hope in the soon return of Jesus brightened every aspect of the early Christian's life. Jesus had gone away to be with the Father. He would come again. The early church went through many different experiences. In the first days after Pentecost, the Second Coming meant judgment and redemption. All in Jerusalem, Judea, and Samaria must repent, accept Jesus as Messiah, and wait for His return.

The hope of the returning Son of God made Christianity entirely different from the pagan religions that abounded at that time.

Because hope looks to the future for its fulfillment, it represents one way in which mankind relates to time. The mind looks over the pattern of events in the life thus far. It sees options that may occur as time continues. Those that would create positive results it accepts as hopes.

Related to the life of a Christian, the pattern of the past includes the moment when the assurance of Christ's salvation first reached out and found acceptance. Christ has come and entered the life and changed all for the good. The present teaches us over and over that Christ continually comes to save and bless. These refreshings from the Lord carry with them the essential blessing that will reach its fullest expression at Christ's coming.

Because we know Christ today, because the Spirit brings us face to face with Him, we look for His coming with joy. Paul called it the blessed hope because it would bring Jesus Christ among His people once more. The fellowship we have in the Spirit with Christ, will translate into the fellowship of His face.

For early Adventists the words *blessed hope* provided a catch cry. It filled their sermons, they wrote it into their hymns, they even signed their letters "yours in the blessed hope." Any person who believes the message of the Bible never lives far from the blessed hope.

Such a hope has that special quality that radically changes the present. Owners of the blessed hope live under its instruction. What will it teach you this day?

"Work in a way that will cause hope to spring up in the place of despair" (Testimonies, *vol. 7, p. 272*).

CONTRASTS FROM THE FUTURE

I would not have you to be ignorant, brethren, concerning them which are asleep, that ye sorrow not, even as others which have no hope. 1 Thess. 4:13.

Perhaps no one has perceived the contrasts between life now and the life to come better than Annie R. Smith. The sister of Uriah Smith, she wrote many poems. Three of them appear in *The Seventh-day Adventist Hymnal.* Her longing for the transformation of the Second Coming fills her poetry. She wrote,

> Toil on a little longer here,
> For thy reward awaits above,
> Nor droop in sadness or in fear
> Beneath the rod that's sent in love;
> The deeper wound our spirits feel,
> The sweeter heaven's balm to heal.

Afflicted with poor eyesight, she had to give up teaching. Her poem "Fear Not Little Flock" led to James White employing her as an assistant in editing the *Review and Herald.* Tuberculosis gave her only 27 years. She saw clearly that the temporary suffering of this world would change very shortly.

In 1852 she captured the spirit of early Adventism with her poem "The Blessed Hope."

Annie Smith possessed the essence of Christian hope. She could see beyond her personal plight and the hardship others endured, to the bright promise of the new creation of God. Christian pilgrims see farther than those without the blessed hope. They possess joy and peace while others flounder in despair and turmoil.

If you tread a path "bedewed with tears," think of the blessed hope. If you feel "weary, sad, and torn," remember the coming joy. If you have "trials deep and conflicts sore," the blessed hope will bring "a smile of joy."

> O! what can buoy the spirits up?
> 'Tis this alone—the blessed hope.

"We are to minister to the despairing, and to inspire hope in the hopeless" (The Ministry of Healing, *p. 106).*

LIGHT FROM HEAVEN

*Made manifest by the 'appearing of our Saviour Jesus Christ,
who hath abolished death, and hath brought life and immortality
to light through the gospel. 2 Tim. 1:10.*

Metal detector in hand, a father and son swept a small field close to
their village in Ireland. When the detector clicked they scooped away
sod and soil. They unearthed a silver chalice, richly ornamented and
with what looked like jewels embedded in it.

A flurry of excitement twirled through the dusty corridors of
Ireland's national museum. The two farmers had brought to light a
sixth-century communion cup. The museum offered the pair £25,000
for their find. They refused to part with it. Eight years later a court
ruled that they might keep the cup; since then it has been valued at
£10 million to £12 million!

Life and immortality, those most precious gifts, have always existed,
waiting the moment when Christ would show them to the world.

What makes us long for immortality? The fullness of life that Jesus
gives in the gospel. No one would want an endless future of emptiness
or suffering. The life that Jesus gives has that abundance that makes
it infinitely desirable. One half hour spent with Christ is enough to
make us long for immortality.

To one person, life offers only "a tale told by an idiot, full of sound
and fury, signifying nothing." Another struggles for power or enters
the contest to acquire as much as possible. Yet another looks on life as
a nightmare from which no awakening will come.

A loving heavenly Father waits to welcome all into the mansions of
His house. Today all may have fellowship with Him. Purpose and
activity fill the life of the one who communes with God. Immortality
enhances and continues that fellowship.

Treasure in an Irish field—what a prospect! If only the thousands
who had walked over it during 1,400 years had known! But there is
something we do know. Jesus has plowed the field of the Father's love
and brought to light life and immortality. They are not for sale, but
they are yours for the asking.

*"If we receive no light from the Sun of Righteousness, we have
no connection with the Source of all light; . . . we can never be
saved"* (Selected Messages, *book 1, p. 299*).

WITH SALVATION IN VIEW

So Christ was once offered to bear the sins of many; and unto them that look for him shall he appear the second time without sin unto salvation. Heb. 9:28.

From time to time there are reports of plans to rebuild the Temple in Jerusalem and to begin the sacrificial system again. Some believe that this will have to happen before God sets up His kingdom on earth! They have even calculated the sheep, cattle, and goats needed for the services!

Golgotha and its cross replaced goats and sheep. The temple of faith has its location in heaven, where the sinner now receives forgiveness and refuge. While the sacrifice of Christ has traveled with the needy race through two millennia, Jesus' death occurred historically in A.D. 31.

Hebrews makes much of the "onceness" of Christ's sacrifice. God has no intention of repeating Calvary. Nor will He ever again set up a round of animal sacrifices. At the cross Jesus "put away" sin. Sin can no longer contend for the life of the one who trusts in Christ. Just as the sins of Israel were confessed and put away from Israel, so Christ puts them away from us "by the sacrifice of himself" (Heb. 9:26). But Christ also has a "secondness," which no one dare overlook.

The first great deed of Christ was the putting away of sin; the second great act saves those "that look for him" at the judgment. Man has the "onceness" of death, which he cannot escape. He also has the "secondness" of the judgment, which he cannot escape. Because Christ has put away sin we need not fear death. Because He will appear in the judgment we look for salvation.

Christ comes to judgment bearing salvation. Today, if you are listening, the Spirit will speak to you of your failings. He will show you again how pure and spotless the Lamb of God is. He will bring you to the cross to claim its benefits. And He will speak to you of salvation, not just in the present sense of forgiven sin, but in the eternal sense of a life with God, without sin.

"The work for you must be done here. This earth is the fitting-up place. You have not one moment to lose" (Testimonies, *vol. 1, p. 706*).

THIS SAME JESUS

This same Jesus, which is taken up from you into heaven, shall so come in like manner as ye have seen him go into heaven. Acts 1:11.

Do you ever feel that someone whom you have known well, and even loved, has changed? Counselors report this as one of the chief reasons for tensions within marriage. The human personality does not, and cannot, remain static. Environment, heredity, and health shape the clay of development. Time has us constantly on the potter's wheel. Age stiffens and brittles the clay, but still change goes on.

The angels' words locked into place the Jesus the disciples knew. As Hebrews puts it, He is the same yesterday, today, and forever. Perhaps it would be good to think about what this does *not* mean. It does not mean that He is unbending, unaware, old-fashioned, or out-of-touch. We might say that He is changeless in the way He changes, or even that He is changeless in the way He deals with our changing.

The word about the "same Jesus" not only encouraged the disciples to leap over time to the Second Coming, it encouraged them in the present crisis they faced. God will not change the rules, now that Jesus has gone to heaven. Quite the reverse. He will come again, the same Person He was while on earth.

One only has to read the Gospels to see what this meant. The caring, compassionate Lord has gone to heaven. His care and compassion now govern heaven in its relations with humanity. When He comes back He will still be that caring, compassionate One.

He offered forgiveness and acceptance to all who would put faith in Him. These control His mediation in heaven and His actions at His coming. He gave joy and grace to the sinner. He continues to create joy and victory.

We are right to emphasize that Jesus carries His humanity with Him in heaven and will return as truly the Son of man. Yet that may not be the main point behind the comforting words of long ago. We know only too well how the same human form can house wildly fluctuating emotions and reactions. The truly significant sameness of Jesus includes His undying love, His unchanging compassion, His unending search for sinners, His unquenchable grace.

"Reflections of Calvary will awaken tender, sacred, and lively emotions in the Christian's heart" (Testimonies, *vol. 2, p. 212*).

CONFUSED SIGNALS

As the Lord liveth, there shall not one hair of his head fall to the ground; for he hath wrought with God this day. So the people rescued Jonathan, that he died not. 1 Sam. 14:45.

This was a bad time for Israel. The Philistines dominated the region. How could the people of God defend themselves when the Philistines had a monopoly on the forging of iron? The only smithy's tool the Israelites had was a file. Even for the reshaping of plows at the beginning of the planting season they had to trek off to Philistia.

Into this sorry servitude came Jonathan, Saul's son. With his armorbearer he scaled the cliffs of Bozez and Seneh and routed the Philistines. Saul sent the army after the enemy, anxious to waste no daylight.

He made a foolish vow: anyone found eating before nightfall would die. With such a vow he sought assurance of divine guidance.

Then Saul wanted God's word on the next step to take. God did not answer. What had gone wrong? The king looked for external reasons for God's silence, rather than into his own experience. He blamed the people for eating meat from the spoil. He tried to atone for that by making the people slay their own cattle.

In the investigation that followed it turned out that Jonathan, not knowing about his father's order against eating, had dipped the end of his spear into a beehive and sucked off the honey. Thinking this had made the Lord angry, Saul vowed to execute his son. But the people stepped in. They protected the younger man.

What are we supposed to learn from this story? Jonathan's valor attracts us. He inflicted the first major defeat on Israel's enemies, which led some years later to the great peace of the reigns of David and Solomon.

Jonathan might have died that day and Saul would still have had no word from the Lord. Yet if Saul had listened to the prophet and his message he would have had God's guidance. In trying to force the Lord he risked not only his son's life but the future of God's cause. The people knew better. They were content with the day's victory and saw in it proof of God's presence among them. In that victory they read the future God planned.

"Put your trust in God. Pray much, and believe" (Testimonies, *vol. 7, p. 245*).

NABAL THE CHURL

David said to Abigail, Blessed be the Lord God of Israel, which sent thee this day to meet me: and blessed be thy advice, and blessed be thou. 1 Sam. 25:32, 33.

The Bible says of the couple, "Abigail . . . was a woman of good understanding, and of a beautiful countenance: but the man [Nabal] was churlish and evil in his doings" (1 Sam. 25:3).

After the death of Samuel, David and his followers went into the wilderness of Paran. He sent his men to ask the wealthy Nabal for supplies. He had reason to ask because David had protected Nabal's interests during the struggle with Saul. But Nabal gave a churlish answer: "Who is David? and who is the son of Jesse? there be many servants now a days that break away every man from his master" (verse 10).

It might have led to a raid by David. In fact, he had already set out to take what he needed by force when Abigail met him. She came with food and good counsel, both of which David sorely needed. If Nabal was churlish, Abigail was generous. She took the blame for Nabal's attitude; she asked David to forgive her for Nabal's actions! Of Nabal she said, "Nabal ["fool"] is his name, and folly is with him" (verse 25).

But Abigail had even greater insight. She did not see David as a servant escaped into the wilderness, but as God saw him. She prophesied of David's future. She saw him secure, his soul "bound in the bundle of life with the Lord" (verse 29). On the other hand, she said, the Lord would throw out David's enemies like a stone from a slingshot.

In the last days the Lord will call for great sacrifices from His people. Perhaps we are hearing His voice today. The cause of God advances toward its climax. The needs mount up. When the message of need comes from the forefront of advance, what will we say?

God deliver us from the churls and the fools like Nabal. He needs Abigails, not mean-spirited, nasty-minded, narrow thinkers like Nabal. From the Abigails of the church comes healing. Reconciliation flowed from her sweet spirit and noble nature. Through her what might have led to disaster became a road to progress and peace.

With such spiritual gifts God builds toward the day when the Son of David will finally take the kingdom.

"The world needs to see worked out before it the miracle that binds the hearts of God's people together in Christian love" (Testimonies, *vol. 9, p. 188*).

TEMPLE OR TABERNACLE

Heaven is my throne, and earth is my footstool: what house will ye build me? saith the Lord: or what is the place of my rest? Acts 7:49.

What will you build for the Lord—a temple or a tabernacle? Stephen saw little merit in the Temple. As did the prophets, he pointed to the wilderness and the tabernacle as the ideal representation of God's relationship with His people.

There came a time in the life of David when the kingdom had peace. He considered his responsibility to God. He had his own palace, but God had no temple. With wealth flowing, this was the time to honor God, the one who had made all this possible.

But the Lord said no. In that refusal Stephen saw the true nature of God. Those who try to house Him in building or system will not contain Him. He dwells everywhere; why seek to enshrine Him here or there? In Stephen's day Judaism confined God in three ways: He dwelt only in the Temple, He spoke only through the law, He acted only through Israel.

More than a thousand years before, the Lord had seen this danger. When had He requested a temple, He asked David. A few years later Solomon built a temple, and the Lord graced it with His presence. But it no more represented the sole dwelling place of God than any other location. God accommodated Israel's national aspirations in two ways: He permitted a king, and He let Solomon build the Temple.

The hope that wins for God sees God differently. He moves ever with His people. He cannot be contained by system or building. He retains the freedom to go before His people wherever time and circumstance lead them. He is the luminous cloud and fiery pillar of the wilderness. God's people can pick up their faith, as Israel picked up the tabernacle, and go with Him wherever He leads.

Many Christians like to confine God within thought systems that they believe are unassailable. However correct such systems may be, they are not the arbiters of God's actions. He will not deny truth, but He will show where we should go in the future.

In the wilderness of the last days God establishes His faithful remnant. They are the ones who follow the Lamb wherever He goes.

"God never leads His children otherwise than they would choose to be led, if they could . . . discern the glory of the purpose which they are fulfilling as coworkers with Him" (The Ministry of Healing, *p. 479).*

THE PASSING OF THE GIANTS

For by thee I have run through a troop: by my God have I leaped over a wall. 2 Sam. 22:30.

Goliath had three relatives, each of them of huge stature, each of them bent on revenge. One of them, Ishbi-benob, went to battle intent on killing David. He carried a huge spear and new sword. But he failed. After the conclusion of this personal vendetta David created a psalm from which the words of our text for today come.

The rich imagery of battle and deliverance fill his song. The Lord is rock and fortress, shield, horn, high tower, and refuge. Sorrows have engulfed David, death has threatened him, ungodly men have flooded him with dangers, but from them all God has delivered. His memory overflowed with the wonders of God's saving might. He poured out praise for what God had done.

All too often as the years pass we add together those things that have gone wrong, rather than count up the good things of life. If David has any word of advice drawn from his psalms, it would be to say thank you to God.

Not that his life was without overwhelming trial. Son after son disappointed him; one even tried to take his throne. People played nasty tricks on him. Those he trusted turned against him.

Also, the giants grew and growled from the ranks of the Philistines. Ishbi-benob struck right and left and came within a few feet of taking revenge for Goliath's death. David fainted at the stress of battle. Abishai, companion of his wilderness adventures, took care of Ishbi-benob.

As the end came closer, David looked back over life. All that had been threat and danger seemed like a troop of warriors set to slay him. But with God's help he had run through them all unscathed. Like a camera following a high-speed chase through city streets, his memory flashed them by. He had dodged here, barged ahead here. And here? Why, he had jumped the wall of death; how else could he have escaped?

"He drew me out of many waters; he delivered me from my strong enemy. . . . The Lord was my stay. He brought me forth also into a large place."

"Let us be hopeful and courageous. Despondency in God's service is sinful and unreasonable" (The Ministry of Healing, p. 481).

WILL GOD TREAT US BETTER THAN MAN?

I am in a great strait: let us fall now into the hand of the Lord; for his mercies are great: and let me not fall into the hand of man. 2 Sam. 24:14.

It was one of those times when self and pride brought downfall to David. Overweening pride in Israel's prosperity made him wonder how extensive and numerous his realm was. He ordered a census made of Israel.

A perfectly innocent event, we would think. After all, the church keeps the reports rolling in for projects such as Harvest 90. What was wrong with David's action? The result of his census puts the problem before us: the only statistic the Bible lists is that there were 1.3 million fighting men.

How far David had gone from God's promise "I will fight for you"! The king saw Israel's future in terms of armed might rather than God's providence. He had turned from hope that leaned on God to hope that leaned on man.

After all that God had done, how could he be so foolish? And yet his sin attracts every life. All too often we add up our assets or count our achievements rather than look to God.

Judgment waited for David. Whom would he have as the executor of that judgment? The anger of God could devastate and destroy the nation in a matter of moments. On the other hand, the armies of Israel had outfought all their enemies. Could they not fight their way out of any human punishment?

David did not hesitate. The nations around would have no mercy. They had a lot to avenge against the all-conquering David.

The plague killed 70,000 men in a matter of hours. In anguish David asked God to punish him, not the people. Then God showed David a way to turn aside the disaster, and the pestilence abated.

It would be nice to think that Israel learned its lesson once and for all. But, no, they did not. Never has any person learned it easily or completely. The presumptuous heart rises up continually against God. The price of such folly meets its judgment—unless the sinner repents and the God of mercy answers his hope.

"Our heavenly Father has a thousand ways to provide for us of which we know nothing" (The Ministry of Healing, *p. 481*).

"WASH, AND BE CLEAN"

My father, if the prophet had bid thee do some great thing, wouldest thou not have done it? how much rather then, when he saith to thee, Wash, and be clean? 2 Kings 5:13.

With his strange mixture of faith and pride, it is surprising that Naaman was ever healed. In the manner of the desperately ill he clutched at every morsel of hope. He took the gossip of a servant maid seriously and sent a letter to Jehoram, king of Israel, together with a small fortune in silver and gold. The letter asked him to make Naaman well.

Naaman made his first mistake there. The maid had talked of a prophet; Naaman wrote to the king. The Syrian thought Jehovah, like his own god, to be very much under the control of the people of power. King Jehoram knew the God of Israel well enough to know that he, of all people, had no influence with Jehovah. His prayers and interests were elsewhere.

Neither the king nor Elisha saw Naaman in person. Elisha's message to him left him angry and confused. He almost lost his hope of being healed. Jordan, notorious for muddy water, and nearly dry in the summer, had no attraction to this man from the better-watered hills and plains of Syria.

Mistake number two for Naaman. But he had the good sense to listen to his own servant. Naaman took servants quite seriously! He went and did as Elisha had commanded. He was to make one final mistake. He tried to pay for God's gift of life, but Elisha would not let him. Gehazi, the third servant in the story, after the manner of Simon Magus hundreds of years later, squeezed what he could out of Naaman. Elisha showed God's anger against those who try to cash in on His mercy. Gehazi, like Simon Magus, suffered for his greed and insolence.

Naaman's story shows how carefully God marks the way to His blessings. God could not help Naaman while he knocked at the door of one of Israel's most wicked kings. He could not heal him while his pride kept him from obedience.

The story tells of Naaman wanting some mighty deed to do for God. If God would not accept his money, would He take his valor? The hope that wins for God follows God's appointed way, obedient and humble.

"He is able and willing to bestow upon His servants all the help they need" (The Ministry of Healing, *p. 482*).

OPEN MY EYES

Elisha said, Lord, open the eyes of these men, that they may see. And the Lord opened their eyes, and they saw; and, behold, they were in the midst of Samaria. 2 Kings 6:20.

Israel was hardly the place where God might be thought to perform miracle after miracle. Ahab's son Jehoram had a somewhat better relationship with God than did his father. He put away the idol Baal that his father had made. Yet he did not make the radical correction necessary. Israel still worshiped Jehovah at the shrines Jeroboam had built, rather than at Jerusalem and the Temple.

Perhaps because of the modest reforms Jehoram made, God delivered Israel on more than one occasion. More likely, the presence of Elisha, the man of faith, gave God opportunity to work among His people.

Chapter 6 begins with the miracle of the axhead. Then follows a test of faith for Elisha's companions. Elisha kept telling Jehoram where the marauding bands of Syrians were camping. The Syrians sent a large group of soldiers to capture Elisha, then living in Dothan. Chariots and soldiers ringed the city.

Elisha's servant feared for the future. All hope seemed gone. How could they escape? But the Lord gave the servant the eyes of faith. He saw the chariots of the Lord ready to fight, not for Dothan, nor for Israel, but for Elisha.

But his servant was not the only one to have his eyes opened. God blinded the Syrian detachment. Elisha made himself their guide, promising to bring them to the man they sought. He led them into Samaria, the Israelite capital.

Again Elisha prayed that God would open eyes. Jehoram would have executed them. Elisha told the king to give them food and send them back to Syria. Could these soldiers ever forget the kindness and deliverance given that day?

The eyes of faith see two things about God. He protects, and He is gracious. Elisha's servant needed to know that God had not forgotten. How often we overlook the involvement of God with our situation! In the time of "what shall I do," remember God.

"We have nothing to fear for the future, except as we shall forget the way the Lord has led us, and His teaching in our past history" (Life Sketches, p. 196).

JOY TO THE WORLD

Let the floods clap their hands: let the hills be joyful together before the Lord: for he cometh to judge the earth. Ps. 98:8, 9.

The freshets and flash floods of spring and early autumn tumbled down the gullies and gulches of David's mountain hideaways. Stones and boulders drummed against each other. Water hissed and rumbled. David drew together the sounds of nature and the music of men to create an orchestra of praise to God. Harp, trumpet, cornet, ocean, mountain stream, and hill sounded out the righteousness and power of God.

Isaac Watts captured the essence of this psalm in his hymn "Joy to the World." But when will this joy break out? The compilers of *The Church Hymnal* placed this hymn in the middle of its section on the Second Coming. "Joy to the world, the Lord *will* come!" its first verse exults. The more recent *Seventh-day Adventist Hymnal* gives it a central place in the section on the first advent. "Joy to the world, the Lord *is* come!" it triumphs.

According to researchers, Isaac Watts pointed the hymn toward the birth of Jesus. But even before his death a version had appeared that changed one word and directed it at the Second Advent.

No one who reads Luke's record of the birth of Jesus can doubt that it came with the joyful shout of angels and the praises of devout men and women. The message from heaven called for joy to begin.

Yet to see in Psalm 98 a clear pointer to the future kingdom of righteousness gives a Second Coming flavor to the hymn. This is the Lord, whose right hand and holy arm have given Him victory (verse 1). He is the one who will judge the world with righteousness, and His people with equity (verse 9). The first advent and Second Advent form part of the one divine event.

As the judgment dismisses sin from the universe, praise to the righteous God ascends. The re-formed and re-created natural world again joins its harmony with the songs of the redeemed. The Seed of Joy that Love planted in the world at Bethlehem has produced the Victorious Branch. The Water of Life flows through the pastures of heaven. The Hill of Zion bears the many mansions of the redeemed. God and His creation are in harmony.

"All the works of God are speaking to our senses, magnifying His power, exalting His wisdom" (Testimonies, *vol. 3, p. 377).*

CITY OF LIGHT

*The nations of them which are saved shall walk in the light of it:
and the kings of the earth do bring their glory and honour into it.
Rev. 21:24.*

Almost every great city has its vantage point. If nature hasn't
provided a mountain, then man has set a tower to the sky. From the
Empire State building on a clear day, you can see forever, or at least
as far as the upper end of Long Island! At night from this vantage
point, New York dances its myriad lights in a man-made mirroring of
the stars above.

As one drifts down toward the international airport in Los Angeles
on a rare smogless night, one sees the city twinkle like a carpet of
jewels. Centrepoint Tower in Sydney spreads a palette with the
midnight blue of ocean, harbor, and inlet mixed with a lacery of street
lights.

Yet to go down into those cities is to find beauty turned into squalor
and crime. The streetlamp that lights a drug dealer or a drunken party
on its way home sours the charm of the view from above.

Cities came first from the mind of man. God put Adam and Eve in
a garden, but Cain built a city and called it Enoch (Gen. 4:17). Man's
sin has corrupted every city he has built. Some cities in the world are
so full of sleaze, crime, poverty, and disease that the only apparent
solution would be to destroy them and start all over again.

Yet God takes the concept of the city and makes it the focus of the
Christian vision of the new earth. If man has his cities, God has the
ideal city. If man fills his cities with crime and greed, God fills His with
love and righteousness.

In the ancient world, as in ours, cities accumulated wealth. There
kings might display their conquests, priests build temples to their
gods, the wealthy build their mansions. The New Jerusalem attracts
whole nations to praise God.

John had written that Jesus lights every person who comes into the
world. Jesus is the light of the world. So too are we, the saved. In the
earth made new the Light of the world joins with the light of the world
to create the great city of light. This city knows no sin, sickness, death,
and despair, but promises joy, health, and endless life.

*"The rapture of that hour when the infinite Father, looking
upon the ransomed, shall behold His image, . . . and the human
once more in harmony with the divine!"* (The Great Controversy,
p. 646).

BRIDE TO THE LAMB

There came unto me one of the seven angels which had the seven vials full of the seven last plagues, and talked with me, saying, Come hither, I will shew thee the bride, the Lamb's wife. Rev. 21:9.

John's description of the Holy Jerusalem boggles the mind. Was he seeing a literal city? Is this symbolic? The answer must be: both.

The Chinese seem intent on turning Hong Kong into one vast jewel box. The hotel shopping plazas dazzle the senses with wall-to-wall jewel shops. One can only marvel at the imagery of John that turns the city of God into one massive crown set with myriad jewels.

Beauty and abundance are one goal of the prophet's vision. But we are to see more. In the Old Testament, Israel is God's crown, the redeemed people His jewels. The New Jerusalem shines with the success of God's mission. A city of jewels, a city of the redeemed: the image answers the reality of the new earth.

The great metropolitan complexes of the world such as London, New York, São Paulo, and Tokyo fill endless hills and valleys. The vision says, Put them all together and lose them in the spreading wonder of God's megalopolis. Dig up old Babylon, Nineveh, and Machu Picchu; incorporate them with Brasilia, New Delhi, and Washington, and they are squalid villages in comparison.

You could plant all the cities the world has ever known, with all the people that have ever lived in them, within the confines of the New Jerusalem and still have room to spare. Its vastness responds to the numberless multitudes around the throne of God.

God's people, the bride to the Lamb, the overcomers, will fill the city foursquare. Years before John's vision he had heard his Lord speak of the "many mansions" of the Father's house. Now his vision encompasses that reality. In those years gone by he might have numbered one through twelve as he assigned one house to each of the Twelve. He possibly even had visions of occupying the dwelling next to the tabernacle of God!

How small it all seemed after Patmos! A multitude that no man could number, the nations of the saved, the enormous city . . .

"Christ is the truth of all that we find in the Father. The definition of heaven is the presence of Christ" (The SDA Bible Commentary, *Ellen G. White Comments, vol. 7, p. 989*).

IN THE BANQUETING HOUSE OF GOD'S LOVE

He brought me to the banqueting house, and his banner over me was love. S. of Sol. 2:4.

The day is coming when the Lord will set table with the exotic fruits of heaven.

In Madagascar, the November stalls groaned with sprays of strawberry-pink litchis. Who could resist their sweet and succulent berries? In Davao City the church members introduced me to the delights of durian, "a fruit with hard rind and pulp of foul smell but fine flavor." I liked it the first time I tasted it. In Singapore you can taste the mangosteen, with rose-colored flesh of exquisite texture. New Zealand has given the world kiwi fruit; Washington State exports its Bing cherries to the world. What will God bring to His banqueting house?

Should we take the marriage supper of the Lamb literally? Yes, of course. The fellowship of food has provided Christianity with one of its most potent symbols. In the bread and the wine we look to the day when the Lord will break bread with us in the kingdom. At the very center of God's new earth He will plant the tree of life.

Why would Jesus want to eat with us? You will remember that in His resurrected form He called for food and even prepared a meal for the disciples. He has taken humanity to heaven. In the earth made new He will be among us as Son of man.

But to concentrate on the literal, however attractive, overlooks the essential truth behind the coming wedding feast. To eat with Christ means to share fellowship with Him. He accepts us, and we accept Him. The Pharisees repeatedly condemned Jesus for eating with "sinners." Why? Because to eat with a person was to show him or her acceptable. Therefore, the first event in the new world of God's creation is a feast.

By faith we share fellowship with Christ and with each other here and now. Day by day He brings us to the banqueting house and spreads the fruit of the Spirit before us. Day by day the riches of His love provide and protect. He places over us the banner of love, and who can ever want within that shelter?

"After the entrance of sin, the heavenly Husbandman transplanted the tree of life to the Paradise above; but its branches hang over the wall to the lower world" (The SDA Bible Commentary, *Ellen G. White Comments, vol. 7, p. 989).*

THE TECHNOLOGY OF THE NEW EARTH

They shall build houses, and inhabit them; and they shall plant vineyards, and eat the fruit of them. Isa. 65:21.

Consider the technology of the new earth. Ask the building contractor in your church what he would need to build a house over there. Or inquire of a farmer at the next camp or district meeting about how he would go about planting crops.

Now, I'm not suggesting that the roar of front-end loader or the busy rumble of combine harvester will shatter the pristine air of a perfected world. But one would hardly expect houses to spring up or vineyards to grow simply by the exercise of mental power.

Or consider modes of transport. That Sabbath-by-Sabbath assembly at the throne will bring some people 12,000 miles. The journey they must take to reach the Temple may not be a sunny stroll down a street of gold, but a major trip. Jet lag and travel blues will not droop heads in the throne room, but technology will have to care for travel.

Fascinating thoughts, aren't they? Looking at the new earth as a real place in which we shall live real lives helps us understand about life today. The world of the mind with its concepts of divine love, grace, faith, and hope has its satisfactions. But they have to meet the test of automobiles, computers, and rapid transit systems.

There are as many lessons about sanctification in driving your car through the city as in a day of meditation. If you want to know what it means to love your neighbor, spend a day as a clerk at the checkout counter of a supermarket!

While heaven is no dream world, dreams of that world can so fill the mind that a Christian becomes of no earthly use. One cook used to say, "Put a little grace into the gravy." If you have ever tried to make gravy starting with flour and butter, you will know what she meant!

Technology has solved so many problems and tensions that we may forget they ever existed. But not even the most dreamy-eyed of us escapes the tensions that new technology brings. So while you are sparing a thought for what heaven will be like, think longer and harder about how you can make home and workplace a little more heavenlike.

"If we only realized that the glory of God is round about us, that heaven is nearer earth than we suppose, we should have a heaven in our homes while preparing for the heaven above" (The SDA Bible Commentary, *Ellen G. White Comments, vol. 7, p. 961*).

THINGS THAT MUST SHORTLY BE DONE

These sayings are faithful and true: and the Lord God of the holy prophets sent his angel to shew unto his servants the things which must shortly be done. Rev. 22:6.

These words immediately follow John's vision of the new earth. By the time of Patmos he had learned both how well things could go and how wrong they could go. He had seen the splendid beginning of the gospel in Jerusalem. Then he had felt the iron claws of Rome crush the life out of churches and believers. Domitian sought the annihilation of the Christians, whom he considered troublemakers.

From within the church new menaces to faith assailed the true gospel. Captivity on Patmos brought visions that took the trauma and discouragements of his day and projected them into the cosmic arena. What his churches were suffering, time would bring upon the whole church.

Yet the same visions brought hope and joy. The multitudes around the throne, the victor songs on the sea of glass, the Lamb on Mount Zion, showed him how temporary were the present trouble and crisis. God would lead through to final victory and would share His triumph.

John learned that the final destiny of the world did not hinge on his own plight or that of the churches he loved. However, he learned also that the persecuted, the apostate, and the faithful, all are projected onto the screen of the future. Persecution, as in Pergamos, is the lot of the church through all time. Apostasy, seen so clearly in Thyatira, had taken on cosmic dimensions. Faithfulness like Philadelphia's would bring a people through to the kingdom.

He knew how precious the fellowship he and others had shared with Jesus. The visions of the New Jerusalem took this close and sweet communion and made it the governance of the new earth. Death and sickness had fled from the Son of God. It would flee from the earth forever.

Were John to live today, he might be surprised that we still wait for the things that must shortly be done. But he would not be surprised at the joy that fills our hearts as we think ahead to God's future for us. He would remember fellowship with Jesus. He would remember the vision of the future. And he would urge us in the prayer "Even so, come, Lord Jesus."

"Morning and evening the heavenly universe behold every household that prays, and the angel with the incense, representing the blood of the atonement, finds access to God" (The SDA Bible Commentary, *Ellen G. White Comments, vol. 7, p. 971).*

SEVEN-DAY ROAD

And it shall come to pass, that from one new moon to another, and from one sabbath to another, shall all flesh come to worship before me, saith the Lord. Isa. 66:23.

You may find the road in the southwest corner of Australia. It cuts across country between two small towns, a useful link with an interesting history. When the Seventh-day Adventist message penetrated this part of the island continent, population was sparse, roads few and primitive.

In order to fellowship with other Sabbathkeepers, one family took ax and saw and carved a way through the forest so that they could get to church each week. Clearing a track through the superhard jarrah and karri stands took several months. Finally a horse and wagon made the 30-mile journey. It took three days to make the round trip.

Today the hardtop road takes only a few minutes to negotiate, but the memory of persevering faith lingers.

There is something about seeing people arriving for church on Sabbath morning that sends a thrill up the spine: mothers, fathers, little children, youth, the elderly, all dressed neatly, crossing the street, driving into the parking lot, walking up the steps to the church. What a day it will be when the saints walk the streets of the New Jerusalem to the tabernacle of the testimony!

Sabbathkeeping had become a problem in Isaiah's time. He called the people to true observance of God's holy day. You are going to keep it in the new earth, why not here? he said.

God set it in place in Eden. He will call His people to its fellowship in the new creation. In this in-between time He also commands us to keep it.

Not that obedience comes easily. The forests of pleasure, business, and secular involvement frequently stand between us and God's day. But the axes of commitment and the saws of determination can build a road to the Sabbath rest and worship.

The joy that Sabbath observance brings to our personal world gives us a taste of the future. It was, is, and will be the weekly road to God's presence and the unique blessing it provides.

"Daily it will be their prayer that the sanctification of the Sabbath may rest upon them" (Testimonies, *vol. 6, p. 353*).

YOU CAN HEAR GOD'S VOICE

Other sheep I have, which are not of this fold: them also I must bring, and they shall hear my voice; and there shall be one fold, and one shepherd. John 10:16.

George Whitefield, a companion of Methodist founder John Wesley, spoke so clearly and with such power that 40,000 people could hear him in the open air. Ellen White had similar powers of projection and clarity. In the highlands of New Guinea, tribespeople communicate verbally every day across the ridges and up the valleys. Certain individuals selected in childhood develop exceptional vocal force.

Technology takes the human voice and broadcasts it to millions at a time. The voice that cries in the wildnerness of these latter days encircles the globe seven times while your heart beats once.

So much for the voice; what about the ears? Will they hear? In the Bible, to hear means to obey. If you have not obeyed, then you have not heard. The sheep do not hear the voice of the shepherd and then follow their own whimsy or follow a false shepherd. They know the voice of the Good Shepherd and follow Him.

God imprinted ancient Israel with Himself by speaking to them personally at Mount Sinai. The nation never has forgotten the Ten Words of God or the experience of hearing God speak to them.

The Christian hears the voice of Jesus. God the Son talked and taught. He was here with us. He has imprinted us with His person through the words He spoke.

Our faith unites around Jesus to form the church. He lifts Himself above all earthly systems and human powers, and draws the world to Himself.

Stephen called those who would not hear the truth about Jesus, "uncircumcised in heart and ears." To listen, to know the words spoken, and harden your heart against them is to close off the message.

The last warning message goes with a loud voice to all people. It calls all to gather around the Lamb on Mount Zion. Behind the symbols of Lamb, mountain, and remnant people lies the eternal truth about the voice of the Lord. Those who truly hear the voice obey its message.

"The eyes, the ears, and the heart will become unimpressible if men and women refuse to give heed to the divine counsel" (Testimonies to Ministers, *p. 402*).

WHAT IT MEANS TO BE HOLY

She said unto her husband, Behold now, I perceive that this is an holy man of God, which passeth by us continually. 2 Kings 4:9.

What a perceptive woman! From casual contact, the Shunamite formed a correct opinion of Elisha. A few meals with the prophet, and she knew both God and His prophet.

The Old Testament describes rituals that made objects holy, and others that set people apart as holy. However, holiness of character cannot be passed from one to another like a contagion. True holiness appears when God enters a human life and changes its character.

The Old Testament can speak of holy ground, holy bread, holy place, holy Temple. The New Testament instructs us to look to how the Spirit shows itself in the life. Then it gathers those who show this holiness into the holy and royal priesthood of the believers.

The Lord's Prayer recites, "Hallowed be thy name." This does not mean just to reverence and honor God. The Christian hallows God by obedience to His commands, which prepares the way for His kingdom.

When a ruler ascends to authority and power, his people give him homage. The life that obeys the King of kings bows before Him and shows His rule and holiness. Though we speak of a holy people, what is at stake is the holy character of God. As the Spirit governs the life, its actions match those of God. It declares His glory and holiness.

The holy life of Elisha was an unlikely thing in a wicked world. It pointed past him to the God he served, who required and provided such holiness. The sanctified life declares God holy in the eyes of the world. He sanctifies us so that He might be sanctified. Through our lives we may say, "Holy, holy, holy! Lord God Almighty."

Glory and holiness go together. That which is truly glorious is holy. That which is truly holy is glorious. God shows His saving grace by declaring us justified through the power of Christ. He shows Himself holy by sanctifying us through the Spirit—holy lives that give glory to Him in a sinful world.

"Holiness is agreement with God. . . . It is the work of the Christian in this life to represent Christ to the world" (Testimonies, *vol. 5, p. 743*).

GREAT CHANGES ARE POSSIBLE

Such were some of you: but ye are washed, but ye are sanctified, but ye are justified in the name of the Lord Jesus, and by the Spirit of our God. 1 Cor. 6:11.

Corinth's population contained all the dregs of any modern city. Sexual immorality and perversion, swindlers, down-and-outs, black-mailers—Paul could have named them if he had wished. In the name of Jesus Christ these crooks and rogues were washed, sanctified, justified. The Spirit turned a rogue's gallery into a parade of the saints.

Sanctification, which is both the condition of holiness and the process of becoming like the One who sanctifies us, speaks to us of a relationship with God. In this relationship the Spirit leads us in holiness. He does this throughout our lives until at last, at Christ's coming, He leads into the inheritance of God's people.

The psalmist speaks of the One who leads in the paths of righteousness. The Holy Spirit can lead us in no other path than the path of holiness. Only right living responds correctly to the sanctifying grace of God.

But we have it wrong if we think that what the Spirit wants is simply nice and worthy people. The world has many of those. Any of the great religious systems can produce moral and upright people.

To understand sanctification, think in a circle. God saves us in Jesus Christ. He acquits us, calls us His holy people. Therefore we live the way He says we are. Our lives show the character of the One who makes us holy. But this is only because God saves us in Christ; it has no saving value in itself. The essential elements of saving faith are not "niceness" or "worthiness," but Jesus Christ, who saves through His sacrifice, and the Spirit, who leads through life.

Peter gives very practical and blunt advice: "As obedient children, not fashioning yourselves according to the former lusts in your ignorance: but as he which hath called you is holy, so be ye holy in all manner of conversation" (1 Peter 1:14).

The good words from God talk both about what He does for us and what the Spirit does through us. He builds the spiritual house of God, the holy priesthood that shows God's character to the world.

"The unstudied, unconscious influence of a holy life is the most convincing sermon that can be given in favor of Christianity" (The Acts of the Apostles, *p. 511).*

THE NOW AND FUTURE KINGDOM

If we live in the Spirit, let us also walk in the Spirit. Gal. 5:25.

From time to time a hermit used to visit me in my office. He arrived in business suit, shirt, and tie. In fact, he looked most unhermitlike. But when he was not masquerading as a normal citizen you could find him living alone in a disused cellar in an ancient building. From this forest hideaway he would emerge to buy supplies and contact friends.

He willingly confessed what he was and spoke glowingly of the hermit existence. Why do it? "That way I find I come closer to God." From the third century on, men and, on occasions, women, have chosen the exclusion of the world in order to enjoy the benefits of the kingdom better. Out of this thinking the great orders of monks and nuns flourished in the Middle Ages.

In the Bible view of life, one does not turn one's back on society. Caves and cloisters are not the dwelling places of the Christian. Life goes on in marketplace and house, school and street. Life in Christ, moreover, means that we no longer live for self but for God, Christ, and our neighbors. We have life *with* Christ and *for* others. The future kingdom enters life today and gives its eternal rewards.

We live in the Spirit. This means that the promise of eternal life has met us today. We have God's yes to the life to come. But we also walk in the Spirit. The patterns of life that will occur in the new creation are ours today. To obey God's commands, to bear the fruit of the Spirit, to live under the ministration of the Spirit—in these ways we walk in the Spirit.

No one who lives in the Spirit ever walks away from obedience. To do so would be to deny the very nature of the life God has given through Christ. We cannot escape the command to heavenly actions simply because we still have an earthly existence.

The guarantee of the life we now live in the Spirit and of the life we shall have in the future kingdom is profoundly simple. Because Jesus died and rose again, we may die to sin and live for Him, and hope also in the life that will be ours at His coming.

"Genuine sanctification ... is nothing less than a daily dying to self and daily conformity to the will of God" (Life Sketches, *p. 237*).

THE SEEDS OF ETERNITY

This is the will of him that sent me, that every one which seeth the Son, and believeth on him, may have everlasting life: and I will raise him up at the last day. John 6:40.

Every so often reports appear of the finding of seeds in archaeological digs. Some come from the second millennium before Christ. In some of the stories featured in the media, these seeds, once planted, spring to life.

While botanists might raise their eyebrows at such possibilities, seeds show remarkable ability to survive, especially in dry climates. In central Australia, where the desert may lie parched and waterless for decades, a sudden rain shower will bring a burst of plant life both beautiful and prolific. The nardoo, a tiny fernlike plant, has such a determined hold on life that when it rains, it will complete a life cycle in about 24 hours.

Belief in Jesus plants the seed of eternal life in the Christian. Christ has immortality. He holds eternal life for the benefit of humanity. Those who believe on Jesus will germinate out of this life with its death and grave into everlasting life.

How can we tell that Christ has sown these seeds of eternity in us? "We know that we have passed from death unto life, because we love the brethren. He that loveth not his brother abideth in death" (1 John 3:14). Those that have life obey the commandments, John says.

To believe on the Son whom God sent brings life. The Christian does not live in fear of judgment or death, certain as they may be. Rather, he waits to see the glory of God at the resurrection. To see that glory will complete salvation.

Jesus called us to "see" Him. What did He mean by that? It means that we acknowledge who He is, His purpose in coming to this earth, and what He is doing for those who believe in Him. Most will not "see" Him. They do not heed the invitation "Come and see" (John 1:46).

To see Christ is to know Christ. To know Him is to have eternity in our hearts. For this divine purpose God sent His only begotten Son. Through this purpose everlasting life comes to us.

"Every new victory gained over self will smooth the way for higher and nobler triumphs. Every victory is a seed sown to eternal life" (Testimonies, vol. 5, p. 120).

GOD LIGHTENS THE DARKNESS

Thou art my lamp, O Lord: and the Lord will lighten my darkness. 2 Sam. 22:29.

If you ever approach Kwailibesi at night, you will know the value of one small light. It shines only when a small ship is on the way in to the harbor. This mission station sits atop Malaita, one of the Solomon Island group. Corals have marshalled battalions of pikes and spears to protect the little jetty. On a dark night an approaching ship turns this way and that, but always in relationship to the glow at the end of the wharf.

While the glory of God may fill the heavens or flash from Sinai, He also comes as the small, personal lamp to the faltering feet of faith. Isaiah may see Him exalted in the bright white light of the throne, but David knew Him as the wilderness torch that flickered in mist and gloom as he struggled toward safety.

I stood with the captain of the *Davare*, a little 24-foot boat, as he guided it through the coral heads toward the pale glow in the distance. I could see nothing. What did he see? "I watch the prow of the boat in relation to the light. I can see the outline of the hills ahead. I've been here many times, and it's safe enough."

While life has cycles and patterns, we seldom come again to just the same place in the same way. We have changed, others have changed, and each change brings its risks. Sudden, major changes occur: sickness, accident, broken relationships, change of job—the channels of life run between the spikes of change and uncertainty.

How many lives has God guided through to His haven? Has He not seen your crisis, your weakness, your heartache before? His wisdom and knowledge ally themselves to us. We may see nothing ahead, but He sees and knows.

The One who is Light shines for you. He comes from outside to lighten the path. His Word illuminates the way. Because He is the Light of the world, He so brightens our lives that we may reflect Him. With that reflected light, we share Light with others. Because we travel safely with Him to light our way, others may also set their course by, and toward, Him.

"Humanity has in itself no light. Apart from Christ we are like an unkindled taper" (Thoughts From the Mount of Blessing, *p. 40).*

SEEING THE LIGHT

Giving thanks unto the Father, which hath made us meet to be partakers of the inheritance of the saints in light. Col. 1:12.

Words about light gleam repeatedly from the Scriptures. "God is light." His dwelling place dazzles with His glory. Truth sent from God is light. Jesus, the Light of the world, fills every corner of the globe with the potential of those who will come to the Light. God's people shine like lights set on a hill. They will be a light to the Gentiles. Those who come to a knowledge of God have seen the light.

When Jesus came to this earth, the star announced His coming and angels filled the heavens with light. When He died, a display of divine light pushed aside the darkness of that hour. When He comes again, He will be accompanied with light and with angels.

In the world of the New Testament some pagan religions had given light and darkness personal qualities. Zoroaster, a Persian mystic, had created the foundation for Mithraism with its conflict between divine light and Godlike darkness. In Qumran, the Jews listed under "light" all that was true and good, and under "darkness" all that was evil and false. These writers almost personified the two characteristics.

The Bible captures some of these ideas for God. Jesus carries the title of Light. Satan is the prince of darkness. Jesus rescues us from the domain of darkness and delivers us into the light of the saints' inheritance. We are children of light and not of darkness.

In Jesus' day, light and darkness carried with them an even greater weight of spiritual significance. In declaring Jesus the light that fills every man, John spoke against paganism and gnosticism. Paul rejected the claims of Mithraism and eastern enlightenment.

The quest for subjective light, enlightenment from within through meditation and trance, goes on ever more in recent times. The occult sucks into Christianity like an insidious parasite.

For all these reasons, the Word would point us away from self to the person of Christ. Christianity takes its light from an objective Source, not from within. We look to Jesus and the Word of God. To see the light must always and ever be to see Jesus.

"Humanity, united to the divine nature, must touch humanity. ... If Christ is dwelling in the heart, it is impossible to conceal the light of His presence" (Thoughts From the Mount of Blessing, pp. 40, 41).

JESUS

And, behold, thou shalt conceive in thy womb, and bring forth a son, and shalt call his name JESUS. Luke 1:31.

In such a simple statement begins the hope of the world. The commonplace, yet miraculous and marvelous, moment came to Mary as it comes to uncounted other women. But the divine record does not spend time on the how of Jesus' conception. It is enough to know that the Holy Spirit will care for it. Much more important is the who that is now going to be born.

Jesus means one who saves. In Anglo-Saxon culture no one calls a son "Jesus." We reserve the name for the holy Child of Bethlehem. Not so in Latin America. Many a parent chooses the precious name for a newly born son. But the world knows only one Jesus who is Saviour.

Jesus brings us to history. In this name we go again to Bethlehem and Palestine and join the crowds as they pressed around Him. Because He is Jesus, He is of us, ever with us, and ever for us.

Before we give Him any other title, we must call Him our Saviour. For this purpose He came, for this reason He lived; to this end He died.

Zacharias, the father of John the Baptist, called Him the "horn of salvation" (Luke 1:69), the One who would save and deliver the people from their enemies.

The angels announced Him as Saviour, the joy bringer, the creator of peace. Through Him God was opening grace and favor for all people. In Him the Father would now bring to His presence the nations of the saved.

Simeon went to his grave in peace because he had seen the salvation of God. In the Temple that day Simeon held salvation in his arms as he blessed God for the One now come to save. Can we not also hold Him out to God and say with this just and devout man, "This is my salvation"?

Jesus went into the world to seek and to save. He forgave sins. He broke down the jailhouse of sin. He bound up the wounds of weakness and despair. He had compassion on all. Even on the cross His forgiveness reached across the few inches between Him and the thief and saved a criminal.

Does the world need saving today? Foolish question! Do you need saving today? Yes, Lord, and every day.

"There is need of a decided, daily conversion to God" (The SDA Bible Commentary, *Ellen G. White Comments, vol. 6, p. 1115*).

SON OF DAVID

I Jesus have sent mine angel to testify unto you these things in the churches. I am the root and the offspring of David, and the bright and morning star. Rev. 22:16.

Though the New Testament refers many times to Jesus in terms of David, He was not often addressed as Son of David. As Jesus approached Jericho on His final visit to Jerusalem, Bartimaeus called from the roadside, "Jesus, thou son of David, have mercy on me."

But you meet David far sooner in the gospel story. Zacharias saw salvation coming from the house of David. Messiah would be one of David's descendants and would bring to Israel the benefits of the covenant God had made with David.

At a critical point in Jesus' ministry He challenged the scribes. How could Messiah be both David's son and David's Lord, as Psalm 110 indicated? Yet the answer lies in the question. Only a Messiah both from David's line and of divine origin could claim both titles.

That is the point behind the glorious paradox of Revelation. Jesus possesses the authority of David, but translated to a cosmic scale. Jesus gave to David the very covenant hope that He would later fulfill in Himself. "Root and Offspring" applies to the covenant the same paradoxes as "First and Last" and "Alpha and Omega."

The title captures two essential elements of salvation. To call Jesus "Son of David" asserts without qualification His human ancestry. Against this declaration the miracle and power of His resurrection shine out. God set His eternal approval on the human character of Jesus, the Son of David.

Second, the carefully traced descent of Jesus from David makes Him the object of the promises of the covenant given to David. It remained for Jesus to secure the covenant for Himself and His kingdom.

In a remarkable leap of thought, blind Bartimaeus saw what we all must see. To call the Messiah "Jesus of *Nazareth*" does nothing more than give Him a place in an address book. We must also accept Him as the only One who can fulfill God's best plans for us.

"Man gains everything by obeying the covenant-keeping God" (The SDA Bible Commentary, *Ellen G. White Comments, vol. 7, p. 932*).

SON OF MAN

That ye may know that the Son of man hath power upon earth to forgive sins, . . . I say unto thee, Arise, and take up thy couch, and go into thine house. Luke 5:24.

Jesus forgave sins. This startling and irrefutable fact provided the core of His earthly ministry. Startling, because no one had ever done that before. One could seek God's forgiveness. The prophets could give the basis of forgiveness and define sharply what needed forgiveness. The one who forgave with finality ranked higher than a prophet and was doing what only God Himself could do.

Irrefutable, because of the results of that forgiveness. When human thought ties sin and punishment together as cause and effect, the forgiveness of sin must remove the punishment. The palsied man suffered for his sins, it was believed. Jesus forgave his sins. And He also caused the palsy to leave the man. The Jews were right in saying that only God could do this.

Jesus called Himself Son of man. That troubled the Jews. As man's representative, the Son of man would receive the kingdom from God. They believed that from their study of Daniel 7. But nothing in all their study and surmising had led them to consider that the Son of man would walk among them while the Gentiles still ruled Israel. They failed totally to grasp the link between "Son of man" and "kingdom of heaven."

Jesus, under authority from the Ancient of days, was inaugurating the kingdom. Into that kingdom He was calling all who would seek and accept His forgiveness. Now, as the prophet Daniel had predicted, He was showing divine favor to those who sought it.

The same kind of thinking that the Jews had may cut us off from the blessings of the kingdom of grace. The Son of man operates within the kingdom of grace to forgive. That remains His prime function. Preparation for the kingdom begins and continues through the forgiving Son. The Jews measured human righteousness against the yardstick of obedience. Christ would have us measure it against His sinlessness.

The scribes were right in deciding that punishment results from sin. What they did not see was that all punishment is reversible through the powers of the Son of man. He heals the sinner today and for eternity.

"When we trust God fully, when we rely upon the merits of Jesus as a sin-pardoning Saviour, we shall receive all the help that we can desire" (Selected Messages, *book 1, p. 351).*

THE LORD'S CHRIST

It was revealed unto him . . . that he should not see death, before
he had seen the Lord's Christ. Luke 2:26.

God anointed Jesus as both priest and king. Because God authorized the anointing of both the high priest and the king, some Jews of
Jesus' day were looking for two messiahs who would fulfill different
roles in Israel. The New Testament presents Jesus as "Christ": both
the anointed High Priest and the anointed King.

The writings of the Apocrypha help us understand Jewish hopes for
the Messiah. By the time of Jesus he had evolved into an endtime
figure, an ideal national leader. He would not only free Israel from any
Gentile yoke but also rule over the nations.

Jewish hopes for this type of messiah continued after Christ. About
A.D. 132 the great Rabbi Akiba greeted one Simeon Bar Kokba as the
"Star out of Jacob." The collapse of his movement shook Jewish belief
in a political messiah, though Orthodox Jews still expect a messiah.

The New Testament does two things. It relates to such expectations
and shows how Jesus fulfilled them. The Messiah has come, not for a
political kingdom but to set up the kingdom of heaven. He qualifies
through His power, His sinless life, His great following among the
people. Second, it looks back at the prophecies of the Old Testament
and shows how Jesus' life fulfilled them.

For Simeon, his journey to the Temple brought great peace. He had
studied; he knew the promises. Now he saw for himself and was
content. The Holy Ghost confirmed to him that he had found the
Messiah. He made the journey of faith that turned knowledge into
trust and belief (see Luke 2:25-35).

Some of us may see the Lord's Christ before we die. Some may not.
But all may take the journey of faith—know what the Word says about
Jesus the Christ; know that He is not the messiah of Rabbi Akiba or
any other person, but that He is the Lord's Christ. The prophets spoke
of Him. He fulfills what they say of the Messiah. The journey of faith
begins where we are, but it takes us always to the Lord's Christ.

"Christ and His righteousness—let this be our platform, the very
life of our faith" (Evangelism, p. 190).

LORD AND CHRIST

Therefore let all the house of Israel know assuredly, that God hath made that same Jesus, whom ye have crucified, both Lord and Christ. Acts 2:36.

It began as a polite form of address and ended with Jesus the Lord, God the Son. Anyone of significance could be called lord, much as we might call someone "sir." The gospels show how quickly the meaning shifted to the One whom men might obey and worship.

But there are "lords many." The writings of Buddhism refer to the founder as "Lord Buddha." Contemporary gurus acquire the title deliberately or through the devotion of their followers. Even Confucius, whose religion has a strongly secular base, can have the title "lord." How does Jesus differ?

Our promise picks up at least three of the many reasons. He is the crucified Lord. From the day His ministry began, He had His death as a sacrifice in view. The cross gives Him lordship, because He died without sin and because God accepted that sacrifice. He wears the crown of thorns as a coronation diadem. Through the cross He bought back this world, and He may therefore claim it and its people as His. Jesus won the world for God, and it is His.

He now lives as the resurrected Lord. Death could not keep the sinless One from His inheritance. In the Resurrection the world knows His power. He came from the grave to rule among His people. As victor over death He stands unchallenged, truly Lord of lords.

But as the ascended Lord, He spreads hope through the habitations of despair. He might have remained on earth, building a temporal empire, defeating Rome, and conquering the world. But God has no place for theocracy in the present world of sin. The kingdom He desires has a people who gladly acknowledge Jesus as Lord. The ascended Lord governs His kingdom and assures its success through the work of the Holy Spirit and His own intercession at the right hand of God.

We call Him Lord for His death, His resurrection, and for His ascension; Lord because we serve Him, obey Him, love Him.

"The humble, self-denying life of our divine Lord we are to keep constantly in view" (Testimonies, *vol. 2, p. 358).*

MY BELOVED SON

The Holy Ghost descended in a bodily shape like a dove upon him, and a voice came from heaven, which said, Thou art my beloved Son; in thee I am well pleased. Luke 3:22.

Because God made us, He calls us each "child." We are the sons and daughters of God, obedient and disobedient. No one escapes being a child of the heavenly Father, though many deny the relationship. But to call Jesus the Son of God means something entirely different.

On that far-off day, as Jesus prayed following His baptism, the voice singled Jesus out. No one else received the dove of the Spirit. The voice spoke of Him alone—"my beloved Son." What this meant took some time to register in the early church. In fact, Christians still grapple with the meanings of "Son of God" and "Son of man." In what ways, we ask, is He God the Son? In what ways Son of man?

By the time John wrote, the Spirit had made it very clear. Jesus had existed before with the Father. He came to express the will of God for this sinful race. Paul gave the Son a position of equal authority with God, not as a competitor or even as an alternative, but as One who knew, shared, and enacted the purposes of God as God.

But we talk this way of Jesus not only in order to express our belief in His deity. In the sonship of Christ we find an identity. We are the sons and daughters of God, and we shall be like Him.

He is Elder Brother. Like Him, we share in the family of God. Like Him, we receive its rights and privileges. Not that God shares His deity with us—not at all. But He loved the Son, and He loves us, His children. Through Jesus, Son of God, He brings many sons to glory.

Paul speaks of our adoption into the family of God. It could happen only because the Son of God came and died for us. We see Him as laying aside His divinity and stepping into this earth.

But the relationship between the Father and the Son, once assumed, cannot be severed. Within the family of God we look across to Him. We see how He lived, and we follow His example; we see how He suffered, and we remain content with our humanity. We see how God glorified Him, and we wait patiently for that glory.

"The Lord Jesus came to our world, not to reveal what a God could do, but what a man could do, through faith in God's power to help in every emergency" (The SDA Bible Commentary, *Ellen G. White Comments, vol. 7, p. 929*).

MY SERVANT

Behold, my servant shall deal prudently, he shall be exalted and extolled, and be very high. Isa. 52:13.

The distant past provides one of the most impressive visions of Jesus. To Isaiah, God revealed the suffering and the rewards of God's plan to redeem man. He watched as the Suffering Servant went through immeasurable agony to pay the price for the fallen race's sin.

You feel Isaiah groping for words to describe the torment. Jesus' visage was marred more than any man. He had no beauty to make Him desirable. Despised, rejected, sorrowful, grieving—the words bore in on the price of sin.

That tells us how it affected Jesus to die for sin. But what did He do for us? Again, words seem hardly able to express the total. Bearer of griefs, carrier of sorrow, smitten of God, afflicted, wounded for our transgression, bruised for our iniquity, chastised for our peace. And all for us! This He did as servant.

In looking to Jesus as servant we learn both the price paid and the role accepted. Hebrews tells us that Jesus accepted the body made for Him. Philippians reminds us that He took on Him the form of a servant.

When the early church began to take Isaiah's prophecy and apply it to the Messiah, it startled many. Not so much because suffering was to have been His lot, but that the suffering of Jesus became the goal and glory of His messiahship.

Perhaps the greatest lesson Jesus has given humanity He teaches in His suffering. God can throw Satan and his cohorts out of heaven, but His Son has to die to remove the evil dominion from earth.

Because the cross is glory, we learn that suffering is God's road to the glory of deliverance. Our own suffering pales to a faint shadow compared with what the will of God asked of the Son.

Do we want a suffering Lord? If we do, then we will learn submission as He did. If we do, then we will pour out Gethsemane tears for the grace to say, "Thy will be done."

If God could not spare His Servant, how can we ask any more than the strength to bear what life brings to us, and to do the will of God?

"The contemplation of the matchless depths of a Saviour's love should fill the mind, touch and melt the soul, . . . and completely transform the whole character" (Testimonies, *vol. 2, p. 213*).

THEY WROTE "KING" ABOVE HIM

A superscription also was written over him in letters of Greek, and Latin, and Hebrew, THIS IS THE KING OF THE JEWS. Luke 23:38.

What His tormentors meant as mockery, the gospel uses to give glory to Christ. Like the cross itself, the cheap joke told the truth about Jesus. In this way God turns scorn into praise, and mockery into homage.

I live in a country that has Queen Elizabeth II as its monarch. Though others may think of her as queen of England, Australia has also declared her queen of this country. Just how that works and what it means in practice would take more than this page to tell. More than figurehead, but far less than chief executive, would approximate the present position.

However, if you wish to understand how most Australians feel about the queen, keep up with the media coverage. She and her family can grab the headlines with the smallest of incidents.

A queen out of sight in another country is one thing, a King who left His people nearly 2,000 years ago, another. Yet in the spiritual realm of the kingdom of heaven He truly rules. We call Him King of kings because His kingdom claims allegiance from citizens of every country. He reigns over Zulus and Lapps, Ethiopians and Laotians.

The hidden kingdom of God began its existence through Jesus' ministry. He went everywhere announcing the kingdom. The theme of the kingdom permeates the New Testament. Scholars say that everything written in the New Testament deals with the kingdom.

One might call it a figure of speech, but that would ignore its true nature. As any kingdom might, it has its laws, its tribute, its ceremony, its citizens. The kingdom rule of love makes this world a better place. Our citizenship shows.

But if you want the best news of all, the King is coming. Soldiers could not keep Him on the cross. He was called King, and as King He rose from death to reign at the right hand of God. When He comes, He will reign over the redeemed and their world in love and justice. Love will have its day. Justice will triumph. An eternal kingdom will secure the world against hate and wrong.

"All who shall inherit these blessings must be partakers of the self-denial and self-sacrifice of Christ for the good of others" (Testimonies, *vol. 5, p. 732*).

LOOKING BEHIND GOD'S LOVE

Because the Lord loved you, and because he would keep the oath which he had sworn unto your fathers, hath the Lord brought you out with a mighty hand. Deut. 7:8.

From the distant past comes this word about God's love. Even with Israel it stood outside anything the nation did or might do. It continued apart from the oath made to Abraham. That oath had its authority in a love that existed before it.

Love forms the key foundation stone on which God builds the human future. It could not be any other way. Take a look at the depraved nature we share. Could that ever be acceptable to the holy God? Consider our puny efforts to set the world straight. Can the pure and righteous God make anything of such efforts?

Therefore the only basis on which God can provide deliverance is His love. Love undergirds and stays all that God does for us.

God's love gives deliverance. For 430 years Israel had suffered in Egypt, closed off from the promised inheritance in Canaan. The slave people could never have fought their way clear of Pharaoh's hosts. A few bricklayers' trowels and shepherds' rods could never beat off chariots and armored horsemen.

Despair! Yet God's love provided a way. They checked in their trowels with the Egyptian slave bosses, picked up their rods, got their families together, and walked out of Egypt. God did the impossible. He saved Israel without help from them. All they did was trust God and go with Him.

In this way we should understand God's love. It has that constant, steadfast quality that does not waver or deflect when it meets hard hearts or appalling disobedience. At the root of God's concern is the truth that God is for us, not against us.

Even His justice, which abhors sin and evil and plans their final destruction, stems from His love. In Jesus, love meets justice and provides the divine solution to the human dilemma. Because of Christ, the King of love may maintain both His love and His justice. Because the Lord loves you, He will save you through Jesus Christ.

"He knows our every necessity. He has all power. . . . His infinite love and compassion never weary" (Testimonies, *vol. 8, pp. 38, 39*).

THE KING OF LOVE

Surely goodness and mercy shall follow me all the days of my life: and I will dwell in the house of the Lord for ever. Ps. 23:6.

> "The King of love my Shepherd is,
> Whose goodness faileth never;
> I nothing lack if I am His,
> And He is mine forever."
>
> —H. W. Baker

They had good reason to nail the inscription above Jesus on the cross. A little thought would have told them how appropriate it was. In the realm of concern, mercy, compassion, and love Jesus ruled.

Behind the mockery a serious charge had developed. Not by what He said, but by the way He acted, Jesus asserted His kingship. He made Himself the subject of His teachings about the kingdom of God. By the end of His ministry the King and the kingdom intertwined so much that they could not be separated.

In the psalmist's song, goodness and mercy follow and protect the sheep. They cannot escape from these two who gently shepherd them into the fold of God. At first glance, goodness and mercy might seem poor aids for the Shepherd. Should we not talk of might and power, of Sinai's thunder and Carmel's fire? God would have it otherwise. Christ did not coerce people into the kingdom. His goodness and mercy directed them to the house of the Lord.

The Jews, and with them the Romans, feared that goodness and mercy might prove more powerful than Temple and empire. If the Good Shepherd could lead great crowds toward Jerusalem simply because He loved them and cherished them, might not these forces overthrow established religion?

Those who follow "gentle Jesus, meek and mild," will meet the same opposition Jesus met. The King who leads on to the better land with goodness and mercy as His standard-bearers has an authority that overrides other claims.

The King of love set up His kingdom during His stay on earth. Some saw it as a threat to their position. To give it a political value was wrong, but to deny its power was foolish. To crucify the King of love could not end the kingdom. Rather, it released its force.

"Talk of His love: tell of His power to save" (The Ministry of Healing, *p. 144*).

344

THE SERVANT KING

After that he poureth water into a bason, and began to wash the disciples' feet, and to wipe them with the towel wherewith he was girded. John 13:5.

Genesis records at least four occasions when the host provided water to wash the guest's feet. The guest may have washed his own feet, or one of the servants may have done it for him. But no biblical record exists of a host washing the guest's feet until the story of the upper room and the Lord's Supper.

The Christian church has had difficulty with taking this practice literally. With most Christians, it carries no greater significance than a story about humility and service for the church to admire.

The custom did have a foothold in English Christianity. Records show that as early as the seventh century the senior clergy were washing the feet of the poor and the lower clergy on Maundy Thursday each year. One cleric—Oswald, archbishop of York—actually died while washing the feet of the poor. In Westminster Abbey one can see the copper eyes into which the abbot would hook his kneeling carpet while performing the ceremony.

About A.D. 1320, Edward II adopted the ceremony and washed the feet of 50 poor men. Later monarchs gave money instead of kneeling to wash feet. A tradition once set up seems to keep on. Every year Elizabeth II gives Maundy money to poor people, but she washes no feet! Her noble predecessor Elizabeth I did better. A miniature painting shows her, white apron over blue gown, preparing to wash the feet of the poor.

Adventists take the Lord's command seriously. The practice of foot washing speaks to us both about our own need for humility and service, and about the present work of Jesus. He continues as servant king. From the throne of God He serves us through the ministry of the Holy Spirit. He intercedes for us; He is our advocate, ever available, ever ready to help.

As servants of the servant king, our ministry reaches out. The giving of money, along with washing the feet, shows unity and gives practical help. We are one before our King, with no distinctions in our spiritual needs. But differences in resources exist. We serve each other best by sharing in brotherhood and love, just as Jesus both washed the disciples' feet and sent gifts to them.

"It is the work of the Holy Spirit from age to age to impart love to human hearts, for love is the living principle of brotherhood" (Testimonies, *vol. 8, p. 139*).

TO MAKE HIM KING

When Jesus therefore perceived that they would come and take him by force, to make him a king, he departed again into a mountain himself alone. John 6:15.

To be popular, or to be alone with God—Jesus chose the latter. They had every reason to make Him king. He had fed them by performing a great miracle. God had sent manna at the request of Moses. Jesus had multiplied a boy's lunch to satisfy 5,000 people. He had also awakened the hope that God had sent the Messiah prophet.

A thousand years before, their ancestors had looked across the crowd and seen Saul. They made him king by popular acclaim. The same route lay open to Jesus. But He turned from it to talk with His Father.

What kind of king would you like Jesus to be? The Jews wanted a king who provided for material needs, who had power in his right arm, who could change the status quo. Now, that kind of king would be useful; perhaps, for some, essential. What if we had a president who could sort out all problems and wipe out poverty and disease?

In caring for human need, Jesus showed that God does concern Himself with practical matters. However, He has not made Jesus to be a king in order to set up a privileged class or to defend an enclave of plenty and good health.

Jesus rejected political involvement. Not for Him the dagger men who terrorized Jews who fraternized with Romans. Not for Him the call to arms that false messiahs sent from their wilderness hideouts. His servants would not fight, because He ruled a different kingdom.

The people crowded around Him the day after the miracle. They were there, He said, because of the food, not because of the message. They wanted more of the same, rather than wanting to know about the God who was providing the Bread of Life.

As the church grows and prospers, each of us must keep it in perspective. Jesus is not the king of numbers or of buildings. He rules a people. If we acclaim Him only because we see Him bringing what we call success, we are making Him a king after our own hearts. He cannot rule on that basis today any more than He could in Galilee.

"From a worldly point of view, money is power; but from the Christian standpoint, love is power" (Testimonies, *vol. 4, p. 138).*

JESUS SHARES HIS THRONE

*And hath made us kings and priests unto God and his Father;
to him be glory and dominion for ever and ever. Amen. Rev. 1:6.*

If you have English blood, you are just 14 generations away from
royalty. Somewhere lurking in your past, an ancestor had a close blood
link with the English royal family. Of course, if you follow your family
tree in other directions, you might be tempted to reach for the axe to
cut off one or two branches.

But faith opens another kind of royalty for us to share. The idea that
God's people share in kingship goes back to Israel's wilderness
experience. The Lord said, "Ye shall be unto me a kingdom of priests"
(Ex. 19:6). Thus God explained the governance of Israel's theocracy.
God was king. The people acted under Him as ministers of His will. As
priests, they received their role from Him and governed for God.

The New Testament takes this idea and applies it to Christians. The
Israelites turned aside from their kingly role when they rejected God
in favor of Saul and David. Christ brings it back to us.

If Christ is prophet, priest, and king, then His people may also take
these roles to themselves. To witness to Christ represents the heart of
prophecy.

If Christ is high priest, then His people come to Him as priests. They
may approach God in His name. The priesthood of the believer is not
about altars and robes but about how the believer may gain the benefit
of Christ's atonement.

The reign of the believers is the rule of righteousness that governs
the life of faith. The kingship of the believer results in the law of love
and godly living. The kings of the Apocalypse are those who keep the
commandments of God. They share the throne with God.

In ancient Israel the kings should have lived in righteousness as
God's representatives. Repeatedly they failed. As we live in righteousness we display the kingly attributes of just and right acts. Not
because we do them of ourselves, but because the Spirit guides and
empowers. Thus we show the deeds and compassion of the King of
love.

*"No truth does the Bible more clearly teach than that what we do
is the result of what we are"* (Education, *p. 146).*

THE THRONE OF HIS GLORY

When the Son of man shall come in his glory, and all the holy angels with him, then shall he sit upon the throne of his glory. Matt. 25:31.

In that medieval masterpiece that is Westminster Hall, you may see the great wooden throne where the monarchs of England are crowned. Look under it and you will observe a large stone. This is the Stone of Scone. On this stone the ancient kings of Scotland sat to exercise their authority. In recent years Scots and English have argued over this piece of granite. Some Scots are pressing for more political autonomy, and the Stone of Scone has assumed a symbolic role in that struggle.

In the same way, the throne of Christ's glory symbolizes authority and power. Jesus has borrowed the imagery direct from Daniel 7. In his judgment visions, Daniel saw myriads of angels about the throne of God. When Jesus comes as judge, He will carry full divine authority. He will descend with the glory of God's ministering angels.

By His death, Jesus bought the right to judge. The cross judges the world. Some reject it, driven away from salvation. Others accept it, drawn to accept God's grace. Every day the cross lifts above each of us, calling attention to our weakness and humanity, and drawing us to seek the Saviour. In this sense, Christ has a continuing work of judgment.

But Jesus did not leave the matter there. A day approaches when the Judge will call all to the throne. By the authority of His sacrifice, the King of love will judge the nations. They will go from the throne in two streams: one with eternal life, the other into final destruction.

Thus love has its way. Only One who has paid the price for all sin has the authority to decide whom He has bought back. While Jesus came to seek and to save, His universal gift has not been universally accepted. Only faith that claims its rewards will receive them.

At the final judgment Jesus confirms the eternal provisions of His sacrifice. He died that we might inherit the kingdom. Before ever sin entered, God set His kingdom in place. At the judgment the gates will open and the redeemed will enter.

Love provides the future kingdom. Love assures it to the faithful. Love says, Enter.

"He identifies Himself with every child of humanity. That we might become members of the heavenly family, He became a member of the earthly family" (The Desire of Ages, p. 638).

TIME AND CHANCE

The race is not to the swift, nor the battle to the strong . . . ; but time and chance happeneth to them all. Eccl. 9:11.

When you read this, do you feel that perhaps you've walked into the mind of a cynic? It seems to say, "Listen, it isn't worth trying. After all, you don't have control over your own destiny. Your powers will finally fail before two of man's great enemies: the passing of time or the vagaries of chance."

Yet what at first appears cynical may, after thought, be seen simply as fact. A sudden happening may snatch success or even life itself from us. And if we escape the unexpected, time will care for us in any case. If not cynicism, is the wise man suggesting a shrug-of-the-shoulders fatalism? "I'll be taken care of ultimately; time or chance will end it for me, so what's the purpose of life?"

Not even that captures the mood of the ancient philosopher. He believes in God. He tells young and old to fear God and keep His commands. What he suggests is that we must live with the end in view.

Being swift or strong should not satisfy as goals in themselves.

When I was a teenager, my friend Harold interested me in muscle building. How I sweated over those springs and weights! Nothing attracted me more than the short-term goal of sculpted biceps. It didn't happen, as anyone who knows me can testify. The program failed the ultimate test of usefulness.

"Look beyond," Solomon says. "What will all those efforts mean? You can't escape your humanity. Who will remember you a hundred years from now?"

What survives, according to the Bible, comes only from God. Our status before the judgment seat of Christ means an eternal name for us. This gives the present its real significance. Whatever else we do with our lives, we must get one thing right—our relationship with God. When that is right, the race is won, the war is over.

Today's moment, lived for God, puts love into our contacts with our neighbors. It adds worth to every hour. One thing outrides time and outguesses chance: the gift of life through Jesus. Through this gift the accidents of chance fail to hinder God's purpose, and time itself comes under God's rule.

"God grants men the gift of time for the purpose of promoting His glory. When this time is used in selfish pleasure, the hours thus spent are lost for all eternity" (Counsels to Parents and Teachers, p. 354).

HIGH TIME

Knowing the time, that now it is high time to awake out of sleep: for now is our salvation nearer than when we believed. Rom. 13:11.

The ancient world awoke to God's two alarm clocks—the breaking of dawn and the crowing of cocks. To know the time meant to be aware of the environment. What was happening in nature told the time of day.

Paul studied the evidences of the return of Jesus. He had a strong sense of time. He knew that Jesus had arrived according to God's timetable (Gal. 4:4). The Spirit had shown him what would intervene during the waiting for Christ's return (2 Thess. 2).

God gave him no more knowledge than any of the other apostles. Like them, he looked around and decided that time was short. But that was not the only aspect that demanded urgency.

To awake out of sleep means to know one's true condition and take advantage of the saving grace God is now offering. Now the time has come to declare Christ's righteousness that justifies the sinner (Rom. 3:26). Christ died according to the timing established by God (Rom. 5:6).

Paul sees the age of the new covenant as a time for hope. His hope reaches in two directions. First, hope fixed in Jesus will justify the sinner. The God of hope will take over and fill lives with joy and peace. Second, the blessed hope of the Second Coming leads on into the future, where Christ will surely appear.

Be aware of the condition of the world. Be aware of your spiritual needs. Paul could hardly talk of "minutes to midnight," in a world without clocks. But he had his own figure of speech: "The night is far spent, the day is at hand." Listen, the cocks are crowing. Look, first light is breaking.

What should we do by the dawn's early light? Use it to examine ourselves. Put away those things that belong to the dark area where Jesus does not rule. Reach for the light from God, which protects as armor against the forays of the evil one.

We might think it high time that Jesus returned. After all, the condition of the world demands radical change. But the Word says that it is high time for us to awake to life. Time is passing, and this is our best opportunity to accept God's offer.

"It is now that we are to form characters for the future, immortal life" (Christ's Object Lessons, *p. 342*).

TIME NO LONGER

To the woman were given two wings of a great eagle, that she might fly into the wilderness, into her place, where she is nourished for a time, and times, and half a time. Rev. 12:14.

In this vision, prophecy has a rendezvous with history. Scripture's most-mentioned time prophecy brackets a church in trouble. Arrogant powers of politics and apostasy have driven true faith into the wilderness.

The 1260-day prophecy plants its first marker in A.D. 538. According to the year-for-a-day principle of prophetic interpretation, the second marker reaches to A.D. 1798. Both these dates represent critical turning points.

The first marks the sudden decline of the secular powers in Rome, which led to the pope gaining political ascendancy. The second marks the era of the American and French revolutions, which set a climate of liberty. In such a climate, truth might be sought and accepted. Apostasy might be driven back, and a people called to obedience to God's Word.

What might be expected, happened. A movement arose in 1844, at God's will, to continue and conclude the journey to truth.

A period in which there is "time no longer" moves us on to the hour of Christ's return, which no man knows. When there is time no longer, urgency rules the life. When there is time no longer, we have entered the last of the last days.

In the vision of the last days John saw the church almost overwhelmed. The faithful remnant retreat from the flood of error and seek the higher ground at the side of the Lamb. But just as the surging tide of apostasy threatens to sweep the church away to destruction, a bastion of liberty arises to protect and cherish the small remnant.

We come then to the time of hope. As the evil lord isolates and assails the rearguard of faith, God intervenes to ensure their safety. He points to them as the faithful few to which all might look for an example in constancy and endurance.

In the last days they do not gather around a time marker. But they are not left unguided or uncertain. A time, no; but a Man, yes. Look no more to calendars and dates, but look to the Lamb.

"God's people are called upon to rally without delay under the bloodstained banner of Christ Jesus. . . . Triumph always follows decided effort" (Testimonies, *vol. 7, p. 30).*

THIS TIME OF TROUBLE

The salvation of the righteous is of the Lord: he is their strength in the time of trouble. Ps. 37:39.

About 500 years after David wrote, Daniel changed forever the way God's people think of "the time of trouble."

David spoke from experience. He had known many times of trouble. God had strengthened him in countless tight spots and disasters. In a matter of weeks things went from crisis to disaster. Absalom rebelled. His rebellion seemed certain to succeed. Shimei even flaunted the revolt to David's face, while the Israelite army watched and wondered if the aging king had lost his grip. Forced to flee, David crossed the Jordan, determined on making a last stand. In all this, David's heart was breaking for Absalom, his beloved son.

In the end David won. The branch of a tree caught in Absalom's hair, and he was killed by David's men. The story records the deep sorrow of David, not at the rebellion, but at the loss of his son.

David knew only too well that not every story has a happy ending. The solving of one problem leaves others without solution. Reconciliation with one person may leave one at odds with another. Many problems just do not go away, they go on.

What David says has the force of realism. What we really need is strength, for the time of trouble may not soon end.

Later Daniel took personal experience and projected it into the cosmic realm. Like David, he knew trouble enough. Some of his trials never went away. Did he ever satisfy those who carped at his prayer life? Could he hide the stigma of his Jewish origins?

His vision of Daniel 12 took the deliverance of the lions' den and made it speak to the last days. He saw the threat to God's people. The lion's roar was sounding in his ear. But he remembered the sudden quiet in the den, the angel presence, his sleep with the king of beasts.

Yes, that was what the vision was saying. God would stand by all His people as He had once delivered Daniel. The ultimate time of trouble would deliver the saints not just into safety but into the kingdom of God.

"In this hour of trial the saints were calm and composed, trusting in God and leaning on His promise" (Early Writings, p. 283).

A TIME FOR SINGING

The flowers appear in the country-side; the time is coming when the birds will sing, and the turtle-dove's cooing will be heard in our land. S. of Sol. 2:12, NEB.

In Cornwall the narrow lanes turn into flower gardens as spring urges its children. You drive between banks of pink, blue, and scarlet and wish you could turn every city street into such a flower-lined extravaganza.

Once on an evening in May, my wife and I walked from the train station to the sanitarium at Skodsborg, Denmark. For long minutes we stood and listened while the song of the nightingale spilled over us. In our Southern Hemisphere ignorance we did not know that this was the northernmost limits for the nightingale, or that it sings for only about six weeks. But we still marvel at the incomparable beauty of its song.

Such is spring, reminding us of the time when God will make all things new. Through the rhythms of Solomon's ancient love song, God pleads with us: "Arise, my love, my fair one, and come away" (S. of Sol. 2:13).

More than any other season, the spring turns the mind to the new creation of God. A drive out of town threads us through patterns of crops straining toward the sun. Lambs and calves assure us that the cycle of renewal continues. In parks and gardens cherry blossoms, dogwoods, and crab apples splash their colors against winter's lawns and leafless tree branches.

In winter, remember spring. When the birds have fled and nature falls silent, remember spring. When trees strain mist and fog through nets of twigs and branches, remember spring.

What spring is to winter, hope is to doubt. A promise from God's Word sings to you with all the sweetness of a nightingale. The drab streets of loneliness and monotony come alive with the flowers of God's love. Hope sets the heart to singing when logic demands weeping.

Jesus calls us to the eternal spring of His love. Hope fills the countryside of the future with flowers that flourish at the touch of one of God's promises. Hope lowers the needle of faith onto the track of joy.

Can't you hear Him? "Arise, my love, my fair one, and come away."

"Words cannot describe the peace and joy possessed by him who takes God at His word" (Messages to Young People, *p. 98).*

TIME TO SEEK THE LORD

Sow to yourselves in righteousness, reap in mercy; break up your fallow ground: for it is time to seek the Lord, till he come and rain righteousness upon you. Hosea 10:12.

Hosea had a long memory. He called Israel back to the events at Gibeah and the beginning of the rift between the 10 northern and the two southern tribes. By any standards, the story of that era smells. Gangrape, bloodthirsty revenge, genocide, kidnapping, and treachery fill the last two chapters of Judges. From that time on, suspicion and hate would break out between the tribes at the slightest of excuses.

In that far-off event the prophet sorted out the great sin of Israel. "Thou didst trust in thy way, in the multitude of thy mighty men" (Hosea 12:13). Pride and self-sufficiency had fastened on to the nation. They felt no need for help from God.

Could God make a time for hope for the people? Hosea picks on a common enough event to show what might happen. Let Judah and Jacob farm together. Yoke them to the plow and the harrow, and let them turn over the soil, preparing it for sowing.

Both North and South had sinned. Both must break up the fallow ground and repent. How could they produce righteousness if they never let the Sower scatter His seeds? God would rain righteousness on the seeds of repentance and produce a harvest of righteousness.

In the farming lands that border the arid interior of Australia, great stretches of country lie fallow. The farmer waits, tractor ready, seeds at hand. When rain falls, he will plow and sow without a break, day and night. The time to seek a harvest has come, and nothing must delay him. But then he must wait again and hope for rain.

God has already set the clouds in place. The rain of righteousness will surely fall on the one who repents. Do we see ourselves as He does, fallow ground, unsown? Are we content with the straggly grass and scant pasture of a land without rain?

The latter rain falls where repentance and reformation have prepared the soil for the harvest of righteousness.

"Do not rest satisfied that in the ordinary course of the season, rain will fall. Ask for it. . . . God alone can ripen the harvest" (Testimonies to Ministers, *p. 508*).

JACOB'S TROUBLE

Alas! for that day is great, so that none is like it: it is even the time of Jacob's trouble; but he shall be saved out of it. Jer. 30:7.

When circumstances corner you and no escape route opens, what do you do? Jacob faced death for himself and his family. Esau came at him, intent on slaughter and revenge. Flight? Impossible with the mothers and children. Fight? Hopeless; he had no bodyguards, let alone an army. He did what any prudent man might—he sued for peace and tried to protect the innocent.

But the trouble did not end there. As he slept, alone, distant from his family, an attacker came out of the night. In desperation Jacob fought him off and finally gained the advantage. He did not know with whom he wrestled. But he held on until he knew.

> In vain Thou strugglest to get free;
> I never will unloose my hold;
> Art Thou the Man that died for me?
> The secret of Thy love unfold;
> Clinging, I will not let Thee go,
> Till I Thy name, Thy nature, know.
> —Charles Wesley

It was that way for Israel in Jeremiah's day. They were cornered in Jerusalem, the Babylonians were pressing their siege, and no one could escape.

In the days ahead danger will surround God's people. Revelation pictures them beset by the dragon, the beast, and the false prophet. The threat will be real and physical.

In the final days the faithful go through the anguish of Jacob. Jacob did not trust his puny efforts to protect himself. Yet if he could keep hold of the mighty Wrestler, such a Warrior might deliver him.

The time of Jacob's trouble does not leave us without God but calls us to lay hold of Him as never before. When nothing but the promise remains, cling to the promise. When nothing but grace remains, cling to grace. Do not let go of the Lord.

Even now, every day, individuals wrestle to hold on to faith. Perhaps today you will need to learn Jacob's lesson.

The greatest victories "are gained in the audience chamber with God, when earnest, agonizing faith lays hold upon the mighty arm of power" (Patriarchs and Prophets, *p. 203).*

HOW THE ARK CAME TO JERUSALEM

So David and all the house of Israel brought up the ark of the Lord with shouting, and with the sound of the trumpet. 2 Sam. 6:15.

A modern motorcade spread-eagles the normal traffic patterns of a city. Security procedures make things even more complicated. When Prince Andrew married Sarah Ferguson, hundreds of police stood with their backs to the parade, watching the crowd. Sharpshooters covered the scene from rooftops. Plainclothesmen mingled with the people.

But if the possibility of danger comes from the procession itself, how can one provide security?

Incident after incident occurred when David tried to bring the ark of God from Kirjath-jearim to Jerusalem. The king handpicked 30,000 men, the elite of Israel's army. No Philistine guerrillas would get near it!

The ark had resided in the house of Adinadab for some time. David had it mounted on a new cart. Ahio and Uzzah, sons of Adinadab, drove the cart. Joy broke out. David led the royal orchestra with his own playing. But cautious eyes turned always toward the ark of God.

When he reached out to steady the ark, Uzzah died at the hand of the Lord. Now what could David do? He did not want more of his people at risk. He decided to leave the ark at the house of Obed-edom.

That family prospered. Taking this as a good sign, David again set the procession in motion. This time he played and danced before the Lord, offering sacrifices all along the way. He "brought up the ark of the Lord with shouting." What a day!

Every so often the Bible reminds us that God is particular. This story shows how important obedience is. To tamper with the holy has a high risk rate!

But the real point of the story is joy at God's presence. But not all rejoiced. The shriveled soul of Michal looked out at the celebration and despised David's joy.

What should we do when some would question the joy that faith brings? David had an answer for us: "I will celebrate before the Lord" (2 Sam. 6:21, NIV). The presence of God is always reason enough for joy!

"Where the church is walking in the light, there will ever be cheerful, hearty responses and words of joyful praise" (Testimonies, *vol. 5, p. 318*).

WHEN THE KING OF GLORY ENTERS

Lift up your heads, O ye gates; and be ye lift up, ye everlasting doors; and the King of glory shall come in. Ps. 24:7.

Scholars suggest differing reasons for the writing of this psalm. David may have written it when he brought the ark to Jerusalem. Or he wrote it as part of the annual Day of Atonement ceremonies to celebrate the Shekinah glory. Christian interpreters have long regarded it as a song about the return of Christ to the welcome of the heavenly hosts.

David must have known many occasions when Jerusalem prepared itself for his return from battle or from a visit among the tribes. The great doors of the city wall did not swing on hinges but were hauled up, much like a modern-day garage door. He watched as the gates lifted up their heads. He saw the joy, joined in the music, shared with satisfaction the celebration.

But if God did not dwell in His city, of what use was such joy? The psalm called to the people to look beyond their ruler to the King of glory, who must always reign in Jerusalem.

Because a holy city demands a holy people, the psalm asks questions about those who may dwell there. "Who shall ascend into the hill of the Lord? or who shall stand in his holy place?" Those with clean hands and pure hearts will receive blessing and righteousness.

Out of such poetry as this, John gathered images to describe the Holy City of God. Those who have washed their robes may enter. The gates open to all the tribes of earth. God and the Lamb have their glorious throne at the center of the heavenly metropolis.

Countless times I have waited while immigration officers check through their fat books to see if this person is counted among the undesirables! What if my name was on that list! I can imagine the quiet words, the firm grip, the locked door, the speedy departure.

David had a different view. Those who enter God's kingdom prepare ahead. The joy of entry begins now, not later. The Holy City encloses the faithful now. In faith we walk the streets of gold, sing the song of deliverance, go to meet the King of glory.

"Open to me the gates of righteousness: I will go into them, and I will praise the Lord" (Ps. 118:19).

"He died that He might wash away our sins, clothe us with His righteousness, and fit us for the society of heaven, where we may dwell in light forever" (Testimonies, *vol. 5, p. 317).*

THE WHOSOEVER PROMISES

Whosoever shall call on the name of the Lord shall be delivered: for in mount Zion and in Jerusalem shall be deliverance, as the Lord hath said, and in the remnant whom the Lord shall call. Joel 2:32.

In this text begin the great "whosoever" promises of the New Testament. Joel looked far ahead and saw the end of time. Then God would pour out His Spirit, nature would herald the new age, and God would tear down any restrictions to salvation. No Old Testament passage did more to provide a launching pad for the mission to the Gentiles.

Jesus began the formidable task of demolishing Jewish privilege by declaring the universal call to salvation. Nicodemus heard it and knew it included him. He marveled as it also plotted the circle of divine love around all people, in all times. "Whosoever believeth in him should not perish, but have everlasting life" (John 3:16).

Peter borrowed from Joel this great promise and made it the basis of his appeal at Pentecost. The Spirit had entered the mission of love. Through Him the followers of Jesus were boldly saying, "Whosoever shall call on the name of the Lord shall be saved" (Acts 2:21). The Lord who saved had given the church a worldwide, nondiscriminatory mission.

Paul picked up the "whosoever" chorus and let it sound in his great tract on faith. "Whosoever shall call upon the name of the Lord shall be saved" (Rom. 10:13). He wrote it as he reflected on the way the gospel was spreading out to all the world; he asked for decision and commitment.

John turned it to advantage as he wrestled with burgeoning heresy at the close of the first century. Only the Jesus he knew, a Man of flesh and blood, who now reigned with God, could answer the broad sweep of God's whosoever. "Whosoever believeth that Jesus is the Christ is born of God," he exults (1 John 5:1).

By the time the visions of the Apocalypse have closed, "whosoever" has become the catchcry of Christian mission. It lends authority to the angel that flies to every nation. It results in the great multitude at the throne of God.

We need say no more, and the time of joy begins. "Whosoever will, let him take the water of life freely" (Rev. 22:17).

"It is His purpose that every Christian shall be surrounded with a spiritual atmosphere of light and peace. He desires that we shall reveal His own joy in our lives" (Prophets and Kings, p. 720).

THE PROMISE DRAWS NEAR

When the time of the promise drew nigh, which God had sworn to Abraham, the people grew and multiplied in Egypt. Acts 7:17.

In the most unlikely places and at the most unfriendly times, God fulfills His promise. He did it for Israel in Egypt. Stephen carefully makes a point of this. The Jews of his day wanted to confine God's saving action to Jerusalem and the Temple. Stephen used example after example to show that God knew no such boundaries. He could bless and multiply Israel in Egypt as easily as in Canaan.

When the bamboo curtain cut off the church's view of China, many wondered if this might be the end of the Advent mission there. Reports made it difficult to believe otherwise. Denominational hospitals were taken over, offices occupied, churches turned to other uses, church leaders imprisoned; a night of retreat and loss had begun.

But it was not the end. House communions took the place of churches. Instead of books and magazines, the members talked quietly to their friends. The message survived and flourished.

History records many sad losses to the Christian faith. Islam drove almost all traces of Christianity out of its territories. The witness begun in China soon after Pentecost, faded and died. In other places the church drew its skirts so tightly together that it shrank and lost its mission. According to tradition, Thomas claimed India for Christ, but the spiritual descendants made their faith an enclave for the wealthy and the privileged.

But circumstances cannot chain faith forever. If not one way, then another, Stephen urges. If, because of famine, the people of God cannot multiply in Canaan, God can measure their number against the stars and the sand even while they are in Egypt.

In God's calendar there never is a time for doubt. He does not plant His witness in any place where He does not watch and nourish it.

Egypt stands for any place or time where circumstances go against the kingdom. Egypts abound here, there. But God makes every day a time when the promise draws near.

"That which God purposes, man is powerless to disannul. Even amid the working of evil, God's purposes have been moving steadily forward to their accomplishment" (Prophets and Kings, p. 720).

TAKING TIME FOR JOY

Redeeming the time, because the days are evil. Wherefore be ye not unwise, but understanding what the will of the Lord is. Eph. 5:16, 17.

Business lecturers make much of time management. Experienced teachers charge high fees to explain to executives how they can manage their time. I wonder how well they would fare in cultures where the event has priority over the timing.

I had to learn that lesson, and like it, too, when I first visited West Africa. While I could start my meetings on time, that may not have started the event the right way. The Western mind fumes and frets at passing minutes. But those with another view of life will fret and fume if the event does not include all who should or might share in it.

In the Pauline world, where no one argued the merits of analog versus digital clocks and watches, Paul still thought it good to "redeem" the time. The word means just the same as "Christ hath redeemed us from the curse" (Gal. 3:13). In what sense can we "buy back" time?

Paul saw time as short. If not managed correctly it would not preserve the believer blameless until the time of Christ's coming. If the Ephesians did not guard their time, they would be like the foolish virgins. The time for the door of salvation would close, and they still would not have done the will of the Lord.

Taking time for the Lord and His will isn't easy in this busy world. Who schedules into his appointments that daily hour of meditation on the closing scenes of Christ's life? Who fixes times for joy and worship each day? They would be the wise, not the foolish.

In Christian time management, any moment may go to God. The formal times of prayer and the family worship appointments have their importance. The Christian values the events of faith more than their timing. If prayer happens, if the Word is read, if fellowship occurs, if faith is practiced, that means more than when these occur.

To redeem time means to buy it back from the world and give it to God. The particular hour doesn't matter, but the event within that time can make all the difference to joyful faith.

"Those who shall finally inherit the heavenly kingdom" "must be pure in heart and life and possess symmetrical characters" (Testimonies, *vol. 5, p. 350).*

A TIME TO REAP

Thrust in thy sickle, and reap: for the time is come for thee to reap; for the harvest of the earth is ripe. Rev. 14:15.

In the parables of the harvest, the time of reaping is the time of judgment. John's vision of the reaping Son of man carries on the theme of the judgment-hour message of verse 7. The sequence goes like this: the time of judgment has come; the gospel therefore has a new urgency; the world has had its warning; the issues have been made clear; now carry out the judgment.

One of the parables teaches us to relax about the final fate of individuals. God will let tares grow along with the wheat.

By the time Matthew wrote, the Christian community he served held obviously good members as well as dubious members. The pressure was growing to deal with those who besmirched the name of Jesus. Matthew remembered the story Jesus told. He included it to put the brakes on any haste to judge. In the final judgment, God will be God. Our evaluation will count naught. Therefore, to judge ahead, to gather people into bundles with our labels attached, presumes to do God's work.

In another picture of the harvest, the grain develops and multiplies. The Reaper has His eye on a bountiful harvest and measures according to results. The sowing belongs to Christ's followers, the assessment of results to Christ, the reaper—a fitting reminder that we should look first to sowing.

In the equations that parables create, harvest equals maturity. It also equals the end-time. Does maturity mean the completion of the mission of the church, or the completion of a work within the waiting Christian? While the emphasis goes to a completed mission, each of Christ's followers must look to personal holiness.

If you join with the Spirit in examining your life, you may find growth; but you will also find immaturity. The fruit of the Spirit still ripens toward the perfection of Christ's righteousness.

In the time of joy that gathers the saints into the heavenly barn, those who trust Him will have Christ's righteousness. They will lack nothing.

"The object of the Christian life is fruit bearing—the reproduction of Christ's character in the believer, that it may be reproduced in others" (Christ's Object Lessons, p. 67).

THOSE THAT THE FATHER SEEKS

The hour cometh, and now is, when the true worshipers shall worship the Father in spirit and in truth: for the Father seeketh such to worship him. John 4:23.

In Hyderabad we stopped for a procession. In the ever-changing panorama of India, one never knows quite what to expect. For example, the time I saw a huge elephant, held by little more than a string, trotting along behind a man on a bicycle. But this was different. A garlanded bull, attended by brightly dressed handlers, stepped sedately along the sidewalk. Crowds followed, chanting and whistling.

We joined the end of the procession. A temple loomed ahead, the bull turned in at the gate, so did the crowd; I stopped. I still have no idea what it all meant.

Almost everyone everywhere has an attachment to some religion. But what does it mean to worship God in spirit and in truth? God has sent the Son to fulfill the ancient prophecies. He will give everlasting life to those who will accept it from Him.

To worship in spirit means to accept what God is giving in Christ. To worship in truth means to obey His will. At the end of the story of the woman at the well, a great crowd approaches from the Samaritan city. The disciples must forget the soil from which this harvest has grown, and accept it as a God-given response to Jesus' message.

To the Jews, the Samaritan brand of their ancient faith was totally flawed. They avoided sleeping in a Samaritan house or eating at a Samaritan table. But in the time of joy such considerations meant nothing. The Indian cult that brings a bull to its god stands so far from me that the thought processes escape me. Yet there too the true worshipers wait for the message that will bring them in spirit and in truth to the Lord of harvest.

But the impact of the story does not end there. Those who follow Jesus must respond to Him. In Nazareth they spurned the Son of God. Samaria had more true worship than Jesus' hometown. In the crowd from that Samaritan town Jesus saw the response that God wanted.

In many a heart joy trembles on the threshold. The hour for it to take over has arrived, but will the heart know that its time of joy has come?

"Upon many is a soul sickness which no earthly balm can reach nor physician heal. Pray for these souls. Bring them to Jesus" (Prophets and Kings, p. 719).

BIBLES FOR BRIDES

Thy word is very pure: therefore thy servant loveth it. Ps. 119:140.

In the Western world an expensive ring adorns most prospective brides. In India a gold chain around the neck or golden bangles on the wrists will do. But in Ghana nothing quite matches the occasion so much as a Bible bound in white leather.

When I was visiting Ghana, more than one young Ghanaian asked me for a Bible. At first I thrilled at their love for God's Word. Then I discovered the reason—without the Bible, the lady of their choice just might say "No."

For many years the economic situation in Ghana has been difficult, to say the least. White Bibles have soared in price to well over $100. For such reasons men run after the Word of God!

People put in glass cases Bibles that have come through trying circumstances, such as those that survived the Nazi extermination camps or that stopped bullets.

Yet when the psalmist spoke of the word he probably wasn't thinking of the written Scriptures. The Bible as we know it didn't exist. A copy of the Torah or law of Moses rested securely in the Temple, but most people never actually saw the Sacred Writings, let alone read them.

Hence the words about God's revelation have a different ring to them. "Thy word have I hid in mine heart," meaning "I've learned it till I know it letter perfect." In an oral society, knowing the word of God meant mostly listening and remembering. The one who loves the Word because he finds it "very pure" has savored its words, seen its meaning, and applied it to his life. He has hidden it, not in the ark of the covenant but in his heart. He can recall great sections of it. It comes readily to mind as a way of testing the rightness of his actions.

I sometimes envy those societies that demand feats of memory. Ellen White tells us that before the end we will be relying on our memories for the Word of God. For decades this prediction motivated church members to memorize parts of the Bible.

Whatever the reason for knowing God's Word, we are the better for it. To know it *and* love it is best of all.

"Several times each day precious, golden moments should be consecrated to prayer and the study of the Scriptures, if it is only to commit a text to memory, that spiritual life may exist in the soul" (Testimonies, *vol. 4, p. 459*).

FROM THE BEGINNING WERE EYEWITNESSES

Even as they delivered them unto us, which from the beginning were eyewitnesses, and ministers of the word. Luke 1:2.

A causeway links Lindisfarne, or Holy Island, with the far northeast coast of England. From here, more than 1,300 years ago, a Christian witness converted Northumbria. It did not start out too well. King Oswald sent to Iona, a missionary center off the west coast of Scotland, for an evangelist. Corman answered the call, but he found the people "uncivilized, of obstinate and barbarous temperament." He gave up.

A year later, in A.D. 635, Aidan arrived from Iona. He chose Lindisfarne for his headquarters. A tireless preacher, he converted large numbers of heathen. According to some records he introduced the seventh-day Sabbath. Before a century had passed, the island had produced the Lindisfarne Gospels, which now reside in the British Museum. Their beautifully decorated pages record the richness of Celtic culture.

But more than 600 years before that, Luke was putting together a connected narrative of Jesus' life. This was no copying job, such as the devout on Holy Island practiced. Instead, Luke tells us that he had to research and record, until he shaped the story of Jesus in a way that suited his evangelistic purposes.

Luke is something special. He anchors our faith in history, giving the names of emperors and governors. He found and wrote stories about Jesus that no one else has given us. He loved people. His physician's craft made him very aware of how weak and vulnerable human flesh is. He told stories of the poor and how Jesus helped them. He pushed back the barriers of discrimination and class hatred.

But we love him most for his stories of Jesus' birth. Only Luke tells us of Zacharias in the Temple, and of Elisabeth, his wife. Luke gives us shepherds and the manger. He found out about the visits of Simeon and Anna to the infant Jesus. He records the great songs and psalms of those early years.

We would not call Luke an eyewitness, but he was a heartwitness. He loved his Lord and delighted to tell of Him. Wherever hearts yield to Christ, witness burgeons.

"The heart of him who receives the grace of God overflows with love for God and for those for whom Christ died" (Christ's Object Lessons, *pp. 101, 102).*

HIDDEN IN A FIELD

The kingdom of heaven is like unto treasure hid in a field; the which when a man hath found, he hideth, and for joy thereof goeth and selleth all that he hath, and buyeth that field. Matt. 13:44.

"They came like stinging hornets, like ravening wolves, they made raids on all sides, slaying not only cattle but priests and monks. They came to the church at Lindisfarne, and laid all waste, trampled the holy places with polluted feet, dug down the altars, and bore away the treasure of the church." Thus Simeon of Durham recorded the raiding parties that came from the United Kingdom of Norway, Sweden, and Denmark. They pillaged Lindisfarne in A.D. 793.

But they did not pocket the Lindisfarne Gospels. About a hundred years later, in another flight from the Vikings, monks hid them. They surfaced 300 years later in Durham. After being lost for another 400 years, they reappeared at Westminster in London during the seventeenth century.

One wonders how many other treasures await discovery, buried in fields, stuffed into coffins, poked into attics, lost in libraries.

How very fortunate we are to have the Word of God. The Dark Ages might have swallowed it up. The plundering Greeks might have sailed away with all the Old Testament copies. Domitian's persecutions might have burned manuscripts along with their owners. At critical stages there may have been only one copy of the original manuscripts. Was the copy Hilkiah found in the Temple the only copy of the Pentateuch existing at his time? It seems likely.

Through perilous years the Lord preserved and guarded His Word. He even put a copy of some of the precious documents in the caves of the Dead Sea for protection!

The Bible does not seem at much risk today. As the world's all time best-seller, it can be found almost anywhere. In our age of version after version and of disposable paperback Bibles, could the Word of God ever be at risk again?

But the Word of God is a field in which waits the treasure of the gospel. To preserve the word is one thing, to find the gospel and possess it another.

"Search, O search the precious Bible with hungry hearts. Explore God's Word as the miner explores the earth to find veins of gold" (Christ's Object Lessons, *p. 111*).

STAR OF WONDER

Where is he that is born King of the Jews? for we have seen his
star in the east, and are come to worship him. Matt. 2:2.

> O star of wonder, star of night,
> Star with royal beauty bright,
> Westward leading, still proceeding,
> Guide us to thy perfect light.
> —John H. Hopkins

Matthew heralds the wonder of Jesus' birth. Out of the east came Wise Men, students of the scrolls of Israel, searching for the Promised One. Did they read Daniel and calculate the time? Did they study Micah, and Isaiah, and the Psalms?

When Herod challenged the chief priests and the scribes, they knew where to look for the prophecy of the coming Messiah. They even mapped the little village where He would be born. The Wise Men probably had similar sources.

The Bible plainly announces the coming Messiah. Those who wanted to could know of His coming. It was left to three men from distant lands to alert the religious leaders of the coming event. Thus even those who should know ignore the most obvious signs. The analogy in today's world would be for pastors and church departmental leaders to fail to see that the return of Christ is near, and so not warn the people.

But the words of the Wise Men look ahead. They echo the words of the inscription tacked above the crucified form of Jesus. Matthew wants us to know that even at the birth of Jesus, God has another event in view. Jesus' birth began the earthly route to Calvary. To sing of His birth is to sing of Golgotha, for the two are one sublime happening.

It was Balaam who first spoke of the Star arising out of Jacob. Jesus, the bright and morning star, stands above the world, leading its truly wise to find the King of Love. He is light, He is compass. Like sailors lost at sea, we look to the Star by which all may chart their path. The darkness that obscures the future has been forever pierced. He is our future, He is our star, He is our hope.

> Glorious now behold Him arise,
> King and God and sacrifice;
> Alleluia, Alleluia!
> Sounds through the earth and skies.

GOOD CHRISTIANS, NOW REJOICE

The time is fulfilled, and the kingdom of God is at hand: repent ye, and believe the gospel. Mark 1:15.

> Good Christians, now rejoice,
> With heart, and soul, and voice;
> Now ye hear of endless bliss:
> Jesus Christ was born for this!
> He hath ope'd the heav'nly door,
> And we are blessed for evermore.
> Christ was born for this!
>
> —Tr. John M. Neale

Mark says nothing of the birth of Jesus. We learn only later of His mother and brothers. While Luke wants us to see the work of the Spirit at the time of Jesus' birth and Matthew wants us to accept Jesus as King, Mark goes straight to the heart of the gospel. He begins with the preaching of John the Baptist, which prepares the way for Jesus.

When Jesus enters the story, He is calling for repentance, because the kingdom of God has arrived. He immediately gathers to Himself a core of helpers and proceeds to teach and perform miracles.

None of the Gospels make mention of the years between Jesus' infancy and His ministry, except for the incident with the doctors of law in the Temple. The fanciful theories that have arisen about Jesus' teen years and early adulthood have no basis in recorded fact.

What we know of origins tells us that miracle and prophecy came along with His birth. Already, those whom the Spirit inspires are telling the gospel story. Jesus is Saviour. He is God with us. He has come to deliver and bring salvation. Hope has found its fulfillment. Joy should fill hearts and touch lips.

> Good Christians, now rejoice,
> With heart, and soul, and voice;
> Now ye need not fear the grave:
> Jesus Christ was born to save!
> Calls you one and calls you all
> To gain His everlasting hall.
> Christ was born to save!

THAT GLORIOUS SONG OF OLD

The shepherds returned, glorifying and praising God for all the things that they had heard and seen, as it was told unto them. Luke 2:20.

> It came upon the midnight clear,
> That glorious song of old,
> From angels bending near the earth
> To touch their harps of gold:
> "Peace on the earth, good will to men,
> From heaven's all-gracious King";
> The world in solemn stillness lay,
> To hear the angels sing.
> —Edmund H. Sears

Luke, right at the beginning of his Gospel, sums up the right response to the gospel. Accept and witness, the twin appeals which he makes, will change completely the life that hears and sees the Saviour King.

Hidden behind the amazing scene at Bethlehem are several points that Luke makes. While Matthew tells of the Wise Men who came to worship Jesus, Luke records the visit by the shepherds. Because they handled animals day after day and because they were believed to rob their masters, the Pharisees and scribes regarded shepherds as "sinners." Therefore ritual uncleanness was their lot, and the ritually clean should avoid them.

From the very beginning Luke stresses Jesus' involvement with the poor and outcast. He wants the world to see Jesus as the Saviour of the world. No one must feel left out, least of all those whom the powerful leave out.

Jesus saves to the uttermost. He seeks out sinners. He lifts burdens. He is the man on our side, the helper, the one who loves and redeems the lost, the bringer of hope and joy.

> And ye, beneath life's crushing load,
> Whose forms are bending low,
> Who toil along the climbing way
> With painful steps and slow—
> Look now! for glad and golden hours
> Come swiftly on the wing;
> O rest beside the weary road,
> And hear the angels sing.

THE WISDOM FROM ON HIGH

*No man hath seen God at any time; the only begotten Son, which
is in the bosom of the Father, he hath declared him. John 1:18.*

O come, Thou Wisdom from on high,
And order all things, far and nigh;
To us the path of knowledge show,
And cause us in her ways to go.
—Henry S. Coffin

Like Mark, John gives no details of the birth of Jesus. But he adds
a glorious aspect. He tells us that Jesus lives from eternity. He has
always been with God. We know God from knowing Jesus.

From the time of Abraham the Jews had speculated about the
person and form of God. They did it within strict bounds, never
attempting to translate their thoughts into idol or sacred painting.
They also pondered His character.

Jesus wanted the world to know the true nature of His Father. He
rejected notions of special privilege and racial pride. He presented
God as especially interested in relationships and motivations. His
people would love Him, their neighbors, and even their enemies.

He presented faith, not legalism, as the key to forgiveness and
wholeness. He offered His own sacrifice as an example of love. He said
that such a sacrifice would draw the world to faith and trust in God.

In John's special vision Jesus comes to men as the Lamb of God,
collecting into Himself all the hopes of purity and power that the
ceremonial system sought. If the people of the world would come and
see Jesus, then they would go away changed, for they would have seen
God. But to see is to believe and trust. Jesus lighted all the world with
the knowledge of the true God. In Him we may know and be saved.

O come, Desire of nations, bind
All peoples in one heart and mind;
Bid envy, strife, and quarrels cease;
Fill the whole world with heaven's peace.
Rejoice! Rejoice! Immanuel
Shall come to thee, O Israel!

369

THE PRICE LOVE PAID

[He] made himself of no reputation, and took upon him the form of a servant, and was made in the likeness of men: and being found in fashion as a man, he humbled himself, and became obedient unto death, even the death of the cross. Phil. 2:7, 8.

> Shepherds, in the field abiding,
> Watching o'er your flocks by night,
> God with man is now residing;
> Yonder shines the Infant Light;
> Come and worship, come and worship,
> Worship Christ, the newborn King.
> —James Montgomery

What can we say about the loss to Jesus of heaven and the Father's presence? I suppose if one multiplies a thousandfold a family's grieving at the final farewell of a loved son, he might begin to taste the sadness and loss. What computer could program for us the feelings of angels and unfallen beings? We have no wordsmiths able to hammer out the phrases or forge the syntax.

Jesus gave His reputation back to God; He who knew no sin was made sin for us. He worked as a carpenter, fulfilling the orders of others. He accepted the role of the Suffering Servant. He stooped to wash the soiled feet of His followers. He who had commanded the ministering spirits of God became Servant to all.

The One who was truly God became truly Man. There resides a mystery that denies final analysis. He made Himself one of us, that we might become one with Him.

The will of the Godhead brought Him to earth as babe. That silent and holy night gave us Heaven itself. He came, knowing the ultimate price He would pay. When you think of Bethlehem, remember Gethsemane. When you consider the humility of the manger, remember the shame of the cross. For love He came. For love He lived. For love He died.

> Saints, before the altar bending,
> Watching long in hope and fear,
> Suddenly the Lord, descending,
> In His Temple shall appear;
> Come and worship, come and worship,
> Worship Christ, the newborn King.

REJOICE FOREVER

Rejoice evermore. 1 Thess. 5:16.

Paul spills out the instructions one after the other, as if they were the summing up of all good advice:

> Rejoice evermore.
> Pray without ceasing.
> In every thing give thanks. . . .
> Quench not the Spirit.
> Despise not prophesyings.
> Prove all things;
> Hold fast that which is good.
> Abstain from all appearance of evil.
> — 1 Thessalonians 5:16-22

Have you ever asked someone to forgive you and felt from them a grudging, superior kind of forgiveness? "You don't really deserve my compassion, but since you ask for it and God tells me I ought to forgive, then I forgive you." That's how some people forgive. In fact, their whole experience of Christ has an air of discipline and forced submission.

Have you ever met a person who bubbles over with Christian faith? Who cheers just by being with you? Who has met many heartaches and still has a smile and a chuckle? That's the person who prays without ceasing, who gives thanks in everything.

Look at attitudes, the apostle says. How are you relating to life? How are you using the ways God has given you of feeling good about being one of His children? If someone gives a cheerful hello, if the Spirit speaks in the life and testimony of someone else, be glad about it. If the preacher has a good word from God or even a word of counsel or rebuke, don't turn away from it; approach it positively.

A positive approach pumps more gas, sells more brushes, wins more friends, makes better Christians, brings more people to Christ. Activate the positive and eliminate the negative.

Not that life always puts you on the freeway to paradise. Curves, chuckholes, roadblocks, and diversions abound. However, the narrow path has a sure destination, and the views of the future are glorious.

Besides this, the future also has a Roadmaker who opens the way, removes obstacles, points us on. "Faithful is he that calleth you, who also will do it" (verse 24).

"Those who travel in the narrow way are talking of the joy and happiness they will have at the end of the journey" (Testimonies, *vol. 1, p. 127).*

THE HEART GROWS FONDER

Having many things to write unto you, I would not write with paper and ink: but I trust to come unto you, and speak face to face, that our joy may be full. 2 John 12.

Many a missionary goes without comforts and keeps the family budget at the stretch in order to stay in contact with family and friends. For more than a decade the direct-dial international phone system sustained our family while we were serving 12,000 miles from them.

A network of radio transmitters still holds together the scattering of mission stations through the islands of the South Pacific. In Nigeria it took large sums of money and a benevolent government to permit the church to link together its mission headquarters with radiotelephone.

Audio and videotapes, letters and telexes, all provide links for those who wish to stay in touch. How the heart longs for communication! What extraordinary steps people will take to communicate. From smoke signals to satellite, from Babylonian to BASIC, the ancient and the modern have spanned distance and talked to each other.

Because absence makes the heart grow fonder, the longer the parting and the greater the distance, the more pressing the urge. But what, after all that communication technology offers, can ever take the place of face-to-face talk? The English love to chat, the Australians love to "chin wag," the Americans "just have to talk" to each other.

John knew how much personal contact meant to Christians. He concluded both his Second and Third Epistles with the promise of face-to-face contact.

The first few verses of the First Epistle tell us how much John valued his memories of Jesus. He presses the point that he has seen Jesus face to face, touched Him, fellowshipped with Him.

Prayer lets us talk to God. Hymns let us praise God. A sermon lets us hear God. The Bible opens God to us.

Soon the distance barrier will collapse; soon time zones will merge into eternity; soon the Lord will reverse Babel and give us all the speech of heaven; soon we shall see Him face to face.

"Even here we are by faith to enter into the Saviour's joy. Like Moses, we are to endure as seeing the Invisible" (The Ministry of Healing, *p. 504*).

HOPE IN ISRAEL

We have trespassed against our God, and have taken strange wives of the people of the land: yet now there is hope in Israel concerning this thing. Ezra 10:2.

Signs warn the tourist and the unwary. "KING WAVES KILL," they shout. Yet every year the waves terrorize and kill people. The southern coast of Western Australia skirts an ocean trough. Oceanographers theorize that the freak waves are created by the effect that this gash in the sea bottom has on ocean currents and the masses of ice that have broken off the Antarctic shelf.

Fishermen trolling lines from secure perches 60 feet above the normal wave break have had to run for their lives as immense waves have suddenly loomed above them. Some have not escaped. Off the Cape of Good Hope more than one supertanker has had its back broken as a huge wave has stressed the steel and rivets too far.

Writing to his beloved but troublesome Corinthians, Paul said, "If you feel sure that you are standing firm, beware! You may fall" (1 Cor. 10:12, NEB).

In Ezra's time, ignorance of the law left many in sin. Now the law had been read. What should the people do about it? Ezra prayed and confessed the sins of Israel, "weeping and casting himself down before the house of God." The people "wept very sore" (Ezra 10:1).

Nowhere else in the Old Testament does the Word paint such a picture of repentance. The hard road of obedience waited before them. It meant new patterns of life. The Bible records no defensiveness, no excuses on their part. They had sinned. What could they do except repent and make it right with God? Not easy for any of them, but totally necessary if Israel would obey as the covenant asked.

Because there was hope in Israel, they dared to expect God's acceptance. And He did hear and come near to His people.

When spiritual disaster threatens, when the king waves of doubt and disobedience threaten to engulf and destroy, the Hope of Israel will deliver. Nothing lies beyond His power and competence. Out of repentance and weeping come forgiveness and joy.

"Blessed, humble, grateful confidence will be an abiding principle in the soul. Unbelieving fear will be swept away before living faith" (Testimonies to Ministers, *p. 226).*

THE GREEN PASTURES OF JOY

In a great trial of affliction the abundance of their joy and their deep poverty abounded unto the riches of their liberality. 2 Cor. 8:2.

Have you ever felt that someone else has life easier than you? Looking across the valleys of life, peering through the trees of time, you see green pastures, and you say, "I wish it were like that for me!"

Lest the Corinthians should feel sorry for themselves and start looking inward too much, Paul told them about the churches in Macedonia. They were scraping splinters off the bottom of the barrel. But in their desperate poverty they gave with joy and liberality. Their mites made scarcely a tinkle in the collection pot, but they sounded loud and clear in God's record.

The fires of affliction had refined the ore of circumstance and the precious metals of joy and generosity had flowed. When writing to the church at Thessalonica, Paul had remarked on how they received the word with the joy of the Holy Spirit, even in the midst of great trials.

What did Macedonia look like from a Corinthian perspective? The church there did not have to meet the depraved immorality of Corinth or the excesses of enthusiasts. Some in Corinth may have thought that things might actually be easier in rural Macedonia, away from the glitter and evil of Corinth.

Of course, it never is quite like that. Each has his own trial to bear. If joy breaks out, then that has come from the Spirit at work in lives, not from the goodness of the circumstances around that joy.

Green crowns surround the watering holes of the desert. If the water spills around a little, shrubs and trees appear. A little more water, and an oasis flourishes. It isn't the desert that creates the oasis, it is the water that wells from below.

Joy welled up in Macedonia in a desert of poverty and persecution. From afar it looked inviting, and so it was. How fortunate to be a Christian there! or anywhere! The oasis of joy from the Spirit can flower and fruit, no matter where. The wells are full, the pump works, the faucets are open—let the water of life flow.

"Thousands have drawn water from these wells of life, yet there is no diminishing of the supply" (Christ's Object Lessons, *p. 133*).

JOY THAT FAILS

They, which in an honest and good heart, having heard the word, keep it, and bring forth fruit with patience. Luke 8:15.

Two families emerge from the mists of memory. For the Thrale family, the message of the kingdom filled them with joy. They wanted more and yet more again. In the local church their candle of faith flared higher and higher. The day they joined the church, everyone rejoiced.

Three months later Mr. and Mrs. Thrale asked me to visit them. What a list of grievances they had! I do not think I have ever had such a negative conversation.

At the same time, the Tring family were studying with me. They too heard with joy. Their enthusiasm delighted the church members. It was a great day when the Trings joined the Thrales in baptism.

Thirty years later the Trings have a son in the ministry and a daughter whose scholarly work does credit to the teaching profession. The family continues in joy.

What goes wrong and what goes right in such cases? Perhaps the biggest lesson I learned from these two families comes from their attitude to the Word. The Thrales relied on feeling. They felt good about the message. The Trings also felt good about it, but they wanted everything they believed to be founded securely on the Word.

Jesus' parable of the sower tells of the "joy" of those who hear the word and receive it, but have no root. The first trial shrivels the joy, and the plant of faith dies.

Abiding joy, Jesus says, comes from "an honest heart." Our Lord was not suggesting that some people turn more naturally to the Word than others. What He calls an honest heart is the one who hears the Word, keeps it, and applies patience to belief. Such a life brings forth fruit, "some an hundredfold, some sixtyfold, some thirtyfold" (Matt. 13:8).

The way Luke tells the parable, it has a special little twist. Jesus, on the occasion Luke records, spoke only of an hundredfold (Luke 8:8). That harvest comes is what really matters.

A joy that flames and then flickers away has no root in the Word. The joy that endures keeps its faith in Jesus and continues in the will of the Lord.

"The only channel through which the Spirit operates is that of the truth. . . . Our faith and hope are founded, not in feeling, but in God" (Selected Messages, *book 2, p. 49*).

TASTE AND SEE!

O fear the Lord, ye his saints: for there is no want to them that fear him. . . . They that seek the Lord shall not want any good thing. Ps. 34:9, 10.

What does it feel like to come to the end of another year? Do you think things have gone well for you? On a scale of one through ten, how would you rate this year? Can you look back and say that you have not lacked any good thing? Has God provided? Has He answered?

Let me share with you some of the great promises from this psalm of joy. If they have worked for you during this year, well and good. If you need them for the new year, here they are:

"I sought the Lord, and he heard me."

"This poor man cried, and the Lord heard him, and saved him out of all his troubles."

"The angel of the Lord encampeth round about them that fear him, and delivereth them."

"O taste and see that the Lord is good: blessed is the man that trusteth in him."

Frank Breaden arrived for our committee meeting with his face split wide with a grin. He was a man given to infectious smiles, in any case.

"Tell us, Frank." He never needed urging.

"Our little daughter, Heather, got at the promise box. She put one of the rolls of paper in her mouth. We dug it out of her mouth against her protests. The soggy scrap read, 'O taste and see that the Lord is good.' "

If we could only make the promises of God ours by eating them! They tell us what the Lord is providing. They give hope. They produce joy. To read them, to understand them, to recite them, helps. But only as they enter our experience and apply to real situations can they bring continuing joy.

His promises have the backing of infinite power. To taste the promise of God, to trust it, is to see how good God is. This year has been His in which to fulfill His promises. Next year is also His. In the days that await, all the promises of God are yes in Jesus Christ. Such bright hopes! Taste and see!

"What has been the record of the past year in your Christian life? . . . Make a different life history the coming year from that of the past. . . . As long as you look to Christ, you are safe" (Testimonies, *vol. 4, pp. 521, 522*).

SCRIPTURE INDEX

378